THE
CURRICULUM
STUDIES
READER

D1504102

THE CURRICULUM STUDIES READER

Second Edition

David J. Flinders

Stephen J. Thornton

Editors

RoutledgeFalmer

NEW YORK AND LONDON

Published in 2004 by
RoutledgeFalmer
270 Madison Avenue
New York, NY 10016
www.routledge-ny.com

Published in Great Britain by
RoutledgeFalmer
2 Park Square
Milton Park, Abington,
Oxon OX14 4RN U.K.
www.routledge.co.uk

Copyright © 2004 by Taylor & Francis Books, Inc.
RoutledgeFalmer is an imprint of the Taylor & Francis Group.

Printed in the United States of America on acid-free paper.

10 9 8 7 6 5 4 3 2 1

Library of Congress Cataloging-in-Publication Data

The Curriculum studies reader / edited by David J. Flinders and Stephen J. Thornton.—2nd ed.
     p.   cm.
  Includes bibliographical references and index.
  ISBN 0-415-94522-4 (hard : alk. paper) — ISBN 0-415-94523-2 (pbk. : alk. paper)   1. Education—United States—Curricula—Philosophy.   2. Curriculum planning—United States.   3. Curriculum change—United States.   I. Flinders, David J., 1955-II. Thornton, Stephen J.
  LB1570.C957   2004
  375'. 000973—dc22

Contents

Preface to the Second Edition

THIS IS THE SECOND EDITION OF *The Curriculum Studies Reader.* We have designed it as a basic sourcehook to be used in the study of curriculum theory, practice, and research. We have brought together in this collection some of the field's most influential writings. On one hand, the diversity of this work has allowed us to juxtapose different, often opposing points of view. On the other hand, enduring curriculum scholarship tends to be scholarship that helps us link the field's past and present. We hope that students using the second edition will take away a heightened appreciation for the ways in which the field's traditions and contemporary perspectives relate to one another. Specifically, we have designed the book as an opportunity to ask about the broad contours of the field. What are the hallmarks of curriculum scholarship? What are its central questions and recurrent themes? How do various lines of scholarship fit together? Where do they overlap? What distinguishes one line of inquiry from another?

We have found these questions useful in our own teaching about curriculum theory and practice. However, the second edition of the *Reader* does not attempt to survey the field "from above" or remove curriculum scholarship from the fray of national debates over education. The readings that follow are very much a part of the arguments that mark any serious examination of what children should learn. Curriculum studies is a complex, sometimes messy undertaking. Often it is a contentious undertaking as well.

Given the field's dynamic features, we have also approached this edition as an opportunity to make significant changes. From the first ediltion we have kept this book's chronological organization, adding only one, albeit an important piece by Jane Addams to Part I. We have also added excerpts from Ralph Tyler's classic *Basic Principles of Curriculum and Instruction* to Part II of the book. Otherwise, these first two parts will be quite familiar to those who have used the *Reader's* first edition. Parts III and IV, which focus on reconceptualism and contemporary scholarship respectively, are changed more radically. We have replaced about half of the original readings in Part III, and all but one of the original readings in Part IV. With these changes we have updated the book's contnet. We also hope our changes have strengthened this edition's representation of the field's conceptual foundations, thereby enhancing the book's utility across areas of educational study.

A final point is related to the broader context of curriculum scholarship. The first edition was published in 1997, and we are writing this preface to the second edition in 2004. That span of seven years prompts reflection not only on how the field of curriculum has changed, but on social and educational trends at large. We feel more at odds with today's trends than we recall feeling seven years ago. We worry in particular over the politics of teaching. Today, for example, we are told (especially by those outside the profession) that it is a matter of urgency, even a matter of national security, that classroom teachers had better hunker down and teach to the test. A rigorous allegiance to the textbook or program guide is touted as paramount. It seems almost unpatriotic to question the received content of the day, to ask what schools should teach and why they should teach it. While these trends are explored by very capable authors in Part Four, we want to acknowledge up front that for some it is already obvious what our schools need to improve. They need random drug testing, abstinence-only programs, more metal detectors, a longer school day, school vouchers, a national curriculum, more attention to character education, and so it goes.

This rapid proliferation of popular remedies has increasingly led the nation to expect complex and perennial problems to yield to simple and speedy solutions. But if history is any guide, tough questions about what schools should teach, how it should be taught, and how we evaluate the conduct and outcomes of the enterprise will always be with us. The curriculum is like weather conditions, we cannot take a snapshot and pronounce how we should dress for all time, or perhaps even for tomorrow. Forecasting the weather never ends as does pondering the curriculum. The best we can do, perhaps, is to bring to bear clear thinking and sensitivity to the lessons of experience on the pressing curriculum questions of the day. In this sense, it is apt that this volume "reads" curriculum rather than prescribes pat answers to "obvious" problems.

Introduction

WHAT DO SCHOOLS TEACH, WHAT SHOULD THEY TEACH, and who should decide? Is the primary aim of education to instill basic skills or foster critical thinking? Should education aim to mold future citizens, transmit national values, engender personal development, or inspire academic achievement? Must education have an aim? And what beliefs, values, or attitudes are learned from the way classrooms are? That is, what lessons are taught but not planned, acquired but taken for granted? These are some of the perennial questions around which curriculum scholars have organized theory, research, teaching, and program evaluation. Collectively, such efforts constitute the academic study of curriculum and the focus of this book.

Although stating the book's focus implies a clearly delineated topic, the field of curriculum studies is anything but narrow. On the contrary, our topic sprawls out like the seemingly endless suburbs of a modern megalopolis. Its wide reach overlaps with every subject area; with cultural, political, and economic trends; with philosophical concerns; and with social issues. In addition, contemporary models of curriculum theory and research draw on increasingly diverse disciplinary perspectives and increasingly diverse inquiry methods. While this diversity can bewilder those unfamiliar with the field's intellectual terrain, others see both the need and the room for still greater diversity. Even without further development, the current range of work makes it useful to adopt broad perspectives from which to identify the field's various regions and familiar landmarks. No one can accurately represent the field from a single perspective. Yet, the trade-offs of accommodation are involved here as well. The more inclusive one's perspective, the more challenging it is to represent the field in ways that clearly illustrate its contributions to educational policy and practice.

Our choice in responding to this challenge is to portray the field, its various regions and familiar landmarks, through the genre of a "reader"—a collection of informed and influential writings. All of the writings in this reader are previously published articles, book chapters, research reports, or excerpts from larger works that sample the past and present trends of curriculum scholarship. The primary advantage of this approach is not comprehensiveness but rather the opportunity it allows for getting close to the ideas and debates that have inspired such wide interest in curriculum studies to begin with. Like other curriculum textbooks, this reader seeks to cast a broad net by attending to the field at large rather than to a certain type of curriculum work or area of specialization. However, the views and perspectives introduced in this collection do not stand above the fray of academic disagreements, arguments, and strongly held convictions.

On the contrary, the reader is intentionally designed to capture some of the contentious discourse and outright disputes for which the curriculum field is known. This animation of ideas and values plays and important role because it has nurtured the field in unlikely settings and through otherwise lean times. Surprisingly to some, the study of curriculum has held its own, even flourished, when no national crisis demanded an immediate educational response, when no vast infusion of federal dollars poured into research and development, when no mobs of angry parents clamored at the schoolhouse door, and when no technological marvels promised new ways to build better curricular mouse traps. All of these factors have had their day, and many are likely to recur in the future. Yet, with or without any added impetus, the questions of curriculum theory and practice are questions that have captured the imagination of educators and lay people from one generation to the next.

This enduring interest is found in both specific and general curriculum issues, and the writings in this volume also vary with respect to scope. Some readings are broadly conceived around the purposes and politics of schooling in general. Others focus on particular topics such as national testing, the use of instructional objectives, or curriculum integration. Even the most narrowly focused of these readings, however, illustrate recurrent themes and historical antecedents. Curricular debates, in short, represent intellectual traditions. Furthermore, the issues raised in curriculum studies often cut across a variety of subject areas and levels of education. One could reasonably argue that basic curriculum issues, or at least some of those issues, extend well beyond schooling to include the concerns of anyone interested in how people come to acquire the knowledge, skills, and values that they do.

Be that as it may, our collection does focus mainly on the types of learning that are intended to take place in schools and classrooms. These institutional settings simply provide a window onto broader issues. Yet, our focus is still expansive, and as with any book of this kind, the difficult task has been to winnow down an extremely large body of material by selecting only a sample of that material. Having done so, we cannot claim to be representing the field in a comprehensive way. Our challenge reminds us of a common story told among cultural anthropologists. Seasoned ethnographers like to ask their fellow researchers just returning from fieldwork whether they have captured the entire culture of the particular group being studied. The question is asked tongue-in- cheek because all but the most naive know full well the impossibility of learning everything there is to know about other people. Like those returning anthropologists, we are unable to provide a complete or definitive account of all that is going on in the field-the norms, kinships, and relations of curriculum scholarship are simply too complex. This limitation of our work may sound harsh, but it can also be viewed together with another adage from ethnographic research—that we are not required to know everything in order to learn something.

To say that this book was created by sampling a much larger body of scholarship still leaves unanswered the questions of what criteria were used in selecting that sample. How did we choose some readings over others, and for what reasons? While this process was almost always more ambiguous than anticipated, three concerns stand out as having a prominent influence on our decisions. First, we sought to include work that is well recognized within the field. This criterion is not so much a matter of name recognition as it is a matter of a work's endurance or impact on how others think about curriculum issues. In a few cases, we have included authors (John Dewey or Paulo Freire, for example) who might not be considered curriculum scholars per se, but whose ideas have been so influential to curriculum studies that they can be considered part of the intellectual traditions on which others continue to build.

Writers who achieve this type of legacy also tend to be those who are grappling with ideas and problems that often surface in different areas of curriculum practice. In other words, certain issues and problems are recurrent or even thematic to the point of being recognized as common to the field. We looked for writings that possess this thematic quality because they lend continuity to the particulars of practice, and without that continuity it would be difficult to connect the otherwise broad range of topics on which curriculum scholarship is carried out.

A second consideration in deciding the book's content has been our desire to include pivotal work. This consideration has played out in an effort to identify writings that most clearly signal turning points in the development of the field, or that serve as prototypes for exploring issues previously taken for granted. Exactly what constitutes ground-breaking work is conceptually difficult to pin down. Nevertheless, our aim is to represent not only the continuity of the field but also its dynamic qualities. The field is constantly changing, if not always in its underlying philosophical concerns, then in the field's ways of responding to concerns as they take on new shades of emphasis. Topics come and go as well, and some specific developments of current interest such as AIDS education could not have been anticipated by earlier generations.

The first two considerations we have mentioned concern the conceptual foundations and development of the field. Our third consideration differs by emphasizing pedagogy. Because we teach curriculum courses at both the undergraduate and graduate levels, we often found our attention drawn to work that is accessible across a wide audience. In part, this means we have tried to select examples of scholarship that avoid the jargon of education and its associated disciplines. Much of the work in curriculum studies is and should be intellectually challenging, but some of that work (as in all fields) is challenging for reasons unnecessary to understanding its subject matter. We hope to have avoided the latter, sampling only from the most accessible work available.

The final issue we want to address concerns the organization of the book's content. Overall, the readings are divided chronologically into four parts. Part I, "Looking Back: A Prologue to Curriculum Studies," is centered on the work of four prominent figures: Franklin Bobbitt, John Dewey, Jane Addams, and George Counts. Their writings are brought together with a historical critique that introduces some of the early traditions of curriculum scholarship. Not only are all of these readings worth revisiting from time to time, but they also serve to provide enough historical information for beginning students of curriculum to start to appreciate the antecedents and changing social contexts in which the field's contemporary theories are rooted.

Part II, "Curriculum at Education's Center Stage," sets out to illustrate the optimism and contradictions of an era marked by unparalleled national support for curriculum reform. Whatever complacency Americans had about education seemed to vanish with the launch of Sputnik I in 1957. For almost two decades after that event, hardly anyone questioned the need and urgency for large-scale curriculum reforms. Yet, this same period is remembered for an increasing sense of uneasiness within the field. Debates grew over how curriculum work should be carried out, earlier traditions became the targets of some criticism, and greater scrutiny was given to the field's underlying purposes.

These undertones of discontent were not short-lived. On the contrary, in many ways they presaged the soon-to-blossom political and reconceptualist movements. Among other achievements, the reconceptualists, together with the open education movement, brought into focus the sociocultural and personal dimensions of curriculum with greater emphasis and clarity than had earlier generations. The efforts to achieve this are represented in Part III, "Pondering the Curriculum." This section, however, is not limited to political and reconceptualist thought, which in and of itself is quite diverse. While curriculum studies had taken a reflective turn that is today very much alive and well, the field's most conventional scholarship did not stop simply because other ways of understanding that scholarship were made more readily available. To put this another way, the field seemed to annex new territory rather than move its location.

This annexation of various topics, ideas, and perspectives is examined as a contemporary issue in Part IV, "After a Century of Curriculum Thought." Our aim in this section is to suggest the various ways in which current scholarship reflects both the change and continuity of the field. The readings we have selected to represent this theme may at first seem unbridled, which is exactly how some people have come to view curriculum studies. Topics range from postmodernism to the growing debate over national standards. We have selected these readings to illustrate in as concrete a way as possible the breadth of issues on which today's curriculum scholars work, and at the same time, how this work builds on previous traditions.

If we were pressed to summarize what this final set of readings has to say about the current state of the field and its future directions, we would have to fall back on the truism that "much changes while staying the same." But that comment is not at all meant to be glib. Changes in both the tenor and focus of contemporary work make a difference in what receives attention and what does not. In this way, such trends make a difference in discussions of educational policy and practice, and in the levels of sophistication at which these discussions are carried out. In current decision making at the levels of research, policy and practice, informed points of view are valued by those engaged in such work. If anything, the need for informed scholarship today seems by past standards to be increasingly urgent.

I

LOOKING BACK:
A PROLOGUE TO
CURRICULUM STUDIES

CURRICULUM THEORIZING AND DEVELOPMENT ARE AS old as educating institutions because any educational program must have a content. Although theorists and practitioners have (perhaps without conscious awareness) dealt with curriculum questions since at least the time of Plato's design for education in his ideal state, the notion of curriculum as a professional or scholarly field is recent. Historically, curriculum decisions were largely left to that small, usually elite, portion of the public most directly concerned with the operation of schools. In the United States, curriculum began to emerge as a field of scholarly inquiry and professional practice only toward the close of the 19th century, a time that roughly coincided with the rise of public schooling for the masses.

The burgeoning population of the public schools at the dawn of the 20th century was only one of a number of tumultuous and consequential developments in American life. One result of all this upheaval was the Progressive movement, a broad-based effort aimed at assuring the realization of American ideals in an increasingly urban-industrial and pluralistic nation (Cremin, 1964, pp. 8–10). Thus, the first self-conscious curriculum scholars saw their work as part of this broader reformation of American life. The responses of the Progressive educational reformers were to institutionalize many of the now characteristic features of school curriculum, including such practices as tracking, standardized testing, and civic education (Tyack, 1974).

Although early curriculum specialists frequently perceived themselves as "Progressives," these educational reformers, like their fellow Progressives in politics and other fields, worked with diverse, even contradictory, conceptions of what "Progressive" meant (see Curti, 1959;

Kliebard, 1995; Lagemann, 2000). Thus, from its earliest days, the curriculum field has been characterized by vigorous disagreements about its proper aims and practices. For example, the various meanings assigned by curriculum specialists to terms such as "learning" and "democracy" are not merely esoteric concerns without consequences for the world of practice. To the contrary, how one defines terms to a great extent determines the resulting character of education.

The first set of readings we introduce includes four of the seminal early formulations of the curriculum field: the work of Franklin Bobbitt, John Dewey, Jane Addams, and George S. Counts. Each of these formulations retains an important contemporary presence in curriculum scholarship (see Eisner, 2002). In this sense, conflicting conceptions of curriculum have never been an aberration in the field. On the contrary, differing views have been present since the very first generation of curriculum scholarship. Indeed, the work of the first two early curriculum scholars we will encounter, Franklin Bobbitt and John Dewey, exemplify how different archetypes of the meaning of "curriculum" result in radically different views of educational aims and practice.

When he wrote *The Curriculum* (1918), Bobbitt was a professor at the University of Chicago as well as a sought-after curriculum consultant to school districts across the nation. He is an apt starting point for tracing the development of professional curriculum scholarship and practice in the United States, as the essentials of his approach to curriculum have been dominant in practice ever since. Moreover, Bobbitt was a self-proclaimed pioneer of the field. He asserts in the excerpt reproduced in this volume to be writing the "first" curriculum textbook. Although it is not self-evident what constitutes the "first" curriculum textbook, Bobbitt's claim is often conceded. In any case, there is no doubt that Bobbitt's *The Curriculum* has had enduring influence, particularly in its insistence that curriculum developers begin with the identification of proper goals. "Pioneer" implies finding one's way in unfamiliar terrain, but Bobbitt seems to have had few doubts that he was headed in the right direction. He epitomized the "can-do" attitude of the new professional elites of the Progressive era, a time when professionals in a variety of fields were increasingly considered the preferred means by which a forward-looking society addressed its problems. Bobbitt was quite sure of what ailed curriculum making: For too long it had been in the hands of amateurs, and it was high time it became a professional undertaking.

Bobbitt was convinced that professional knowledge applicable to curriculum work could be found in the logic of "scientific management," which had been applied to raising worker productivity in industry (Callahan, 1962, pp. 79–94). In a nutshell, Bobbitt believed that curriculum work, like work in industry, should be managed in the interests of efficiency and the elimination of waste. These same interests, after all (it seemed obvious to Bobbitt and many of his contemporaries), in significant respects accounted for the world preeminence of United States manufacturing industry. Use of the same methods would bring the same world-class standards to the school curriculum.

Bobbitt's claim that curriculum work was out of date, having not kept pace with other advances in schooling, is almost poignant. *The Curriculum* was Bobbitt's solution to this unfortunate state of affairs. As he makes plain in the preface, he proposed to lay out how curriculum can be constructed in a manner that honors scientific procedures. For Bobbitt, "scientific" suggested a systematic series of procedures, carried out by curriculum professionals, prior to implementation in a school district (see Eisner, 1985).

The content of any given curriculum, according to Bobbitt, could be "discovered" by a process of surveying what successful adults know and can do (Bobbitt, this volume). In turn, the results of this process of discovery would be used to formulate educational objectives from which the curriculum scope and sequence (i.e., what is taught and in what order) would be derived to address where students fell short of successful adults. After instruction with this kind of curriculum, he believed, students would be prepared to lead successful lives in their adult years.

Efficiency, of course, suggests not only smooth operating procedures but minimization of "waste" as well. Thus, in addition to scientific curriculum making, Bobbitt wanted to minimize sources of wasted instructional time. He believed that diagnostic testing and other procedures proposed by behavioral psychologists such as Edward L. Thorndike would make possible prediction of the kind of errors students typically made. This would enable more efficient curriculum making as well as prevent unnecessary time being spent on the costly business of instruction, especially grade-level retention of students, which Bobbitt considered enormously wasteful. As in industrial enterprises, Bobbitt wanted to maximize output (i.e., student learning) at minimum cost (i.e., paying teachers).

This outlook also held significance for the content of the curriculum. Bobbitt believed that "the shortcomings of children and men" in subjects such as spelling and grammar were "obvious," and hence these fields needed to be included in the curriculum. It was less apparent to Bobbitt, however, what shortcomings were overcome by "social" subjects such as literature, history, and geography. He urged attention to identifying significant educational objectives to which these social subjects could contribute (Bobbitt, this volume).

Because Bobbitt's approach to curriculum work was based, he argued, on a dispassionate analysis of what youngsters needed to lead productive lives as adults, he dismissed arguments about the interests of children as irrelevant to the educational process. Moreover, Bobbitt did not question whether the existing social and economic order was just; he merely took that for granted. Hence, he saw the aim of schooling as matching individuals with the existing social and economic order (Lagemann, 2000, p. 107).

As the version of "My Pedagogic Creed", this volume shows Dewey's view of curriculum provides a vivid contrast with Bobbitt's. Although at different times both Dewey and Bobbitt served on the faculty of the University of Chicago, the contrasts between the two men are more revealing than their similarities. Bobbitt believed curriculum work was a practical task whose only need for theoretical justification had been "discovered" analyzing the behavior of successful adults. Although Dewey had founded and directed the Laboratory School at the University of Chicago, he spent most of his professional life as a philosophy professor at Columbia University. And while he was also involved with the more practice-oriented world of Columbia's Teachers College, Dewey's greatest interest in problem solving was in the world of ideas, not in the mechanics of consulting in school districts about curriculum development. This by no means suggests, however, that Dewey lacked concern about the consequences for education raised by the work of Bobbitt and other adherents of "scientific" Progressivism.

Dewey recognized only too well that, if one accepted Bobbitt's premises about relevant subject matter, meaningful learning, desirable social arrangements, and so forth, then Bobbitt's industrial metaphor for curriculum development followed in a disarmingly straightforward manner. Dewey, however, emphatically rejected Bobbitt's premises. Where Bobbitt argued that adult society is the mold for the school curriculum, Dewey (this volume) said such a view "results in subordinating the freedom of the individual to a pre-conceived social and political status." "True education," Dewey insisted, "comes through the stimulation of the child's powers by the demands of the social situations in which he finds himself." Similarly, Bobbitt's reliance on behaviorist methods to Dewey signified external imposition whose effects "cannot truly be called educative." Indeed, Dewey pointed out the worth of subject matter could only be determined by its educational uses. For example, along with Bobbitt, Dewey (this volume) questioned the value of history as a school subject if it was the customary "inert" study of "the distant past." But Dewey maintained history "becomes full of meaning" if "taken as the record of man's social life and progress . . . as the child is introduced . . . directly into social life."

The distinctions Dewey drew, although consequential, are frequently subtle. While Bobbitt spoke in familiar language, Dewey spoke the less-familiar language of reform, of education as a means of extending and reforming democratic, community life in the United States. The relative novelty of his language and views may help explain why Dewey's theory of curriculum has been often and widely misunderstood, even by those purporting to be his followers. In this regard, he wrote *Experience and Education* (1938) toward the end of his career because he believed, for example, his insistence on curriculum planning beginning with the experience of the child was being wrongly interpreted as disdain for the "progressive organization of subject-matter." Similarly, Dewey emphasized that starting with the experience of the child, far from producing laissez-faire classroom arrangements, increased rather than replaced the demands on judgment by the teacher in directing each pupil's learning toward worthwhile goals.

What would Dewey's ideal curriculum look like in practice? Although too lengthy a question to answer fully here, probably the most authentic answer can be obtained by examination of the Laboratory School Dewey established and oversaw during his years at the University of Chicago (see Mayhew and Edwards, 1966; Tanner, 1997). In broad terms, Dewey's curriculum broke down the barriers, customary in schools a century ago as well as today, between children's life experiences and their experiences in the classroom. Hence, the heart of the curriculum would be activities based on a simplification of "existing social life." In this scheme of things, boundaries between traditional school subjects would be traversed. Children might, for example, examine how the local community deals with its problems and, in this context, develop measuring skills ordinarily assigned to mathematics, drawing skills ordinarily assigned to art, map skills ordinarily assigned to geography, and so forth. The logical organization of school subjects, Dewey insisted, was the organizational schema of adults; children require the "psychological" organization of subject matter, moving gradually toward adult modes of understanding associated with formal school subjects.

In sum, the school, for Dewey, was an integral part of community life; it was also an instrument for social reform. Whereas Bobbitt saw the school as an agent of social reproduction, Dewey (this volume) portrayed "the school as the primary and most effective interest of social progress and reform." Just as there should be no strict boundary between the curriculum and community life, Dewey believed the curriculum held the potential for society to remake itself.

Jane Addams, friend and collaborator of Dewey, also saw no sharp boundary between the curriculum and democratic community life. In 1889 Addams and her longtime associate, Helen Gates Starr, established a social settlement, Hull House, in Chicago's West Side slums. While Dewey's curriculum thought was mainly directed at formal schooling, the primary site of Addams's work was Hull House and its adjacent community. As Richard Bernstein (1967) observed, while Dewey brought "the theory and methods of social philosophy to bear on the concrete facts," Hull House "provided him with the 'facts'" (p. 37). Moreover, as Ellen Condliffe Lagemann (1994) has noted, Addams's location outside of the academy "enabled her to develop and sustain an approach to social analysis that was broad, synthetic, and problem- as opposed to discipline- or profession-centered" (p. xiii).

Hull House reached out to immigrants, to laborers, to mothers and children, to all in an urban-industrial community who needed or wanted its educational and social programs. Celebrated almost from the beginning, Hull House aimed through its educational programs to address the range of problems and aspirations of ordinary and needy people in an era when public schools often appeared inadequate to the task. Although Addams wrote and spoke widely about education, she considered these activities no substitute for the direct caring she saw as necessary (Noddings, 2001, p. 184). As Addams wrote in her autobiographical *Twenty Years at Hull House*, first published in 1910, she believed she was filling educational needs that were otherwise either unrecognized or unmet:

> It sometimes seems that the men of substantial scholarship were content to leave to the charlatan the teaching of those things which deeply concern the welfare of mankind. . . . A settlement soon discovers that simple people are interested in large and vital subjects. . . . (Addams, 1961, p. 282)

Hull House strove to value both the traditions immigrants brought to the United States and necessary adjustments to their new environment. "The ignorant teacher," Addams (this volume) wrote, "cuts [immigrant children] off" from their parents and their parents' traditions, while "the cultivated teacher fastens them because his own mind is open to the charm and beauty of that old-country life." It is therefore not surprising that Addams understood that a one-size-fits-all curriculum to "Americanize" immigrants may not fit the needs of any individual. Coercion was not part of her stock in trade.

Rather, through provision of choice and individualization, the extraordinary breadth of Hull House curricular offerings aimed to both expand student horizons and connect to their aspirations and needs. But these ambitious goals were as far as possible harmonized with the community. Courses were offered in cooking, arithmetic, history, athletics, clay modeling, English for Italians, and many other subject matters. As well, classes were offered on writers such as Dante, Browning, and Shakespeare, and a Plato club and Dewey lecturing on social psychology were made available to "groups consisting largely of people from the immediate neighborhood" (Addams, this volume). Although fully supportive of the exceptional community member who was college-bound, more fundamentally Hull House aimed to "connect him with all sorts of people by his ability to understand them as well by his power to supplement their present surroundings with the historic background" (Addams, 1961, pp. 284–285).

Since at least Addams's time, great significance and considerable disagreement has been attached to the connection of cultural pluralism and the school curriculum. The educational program enacted at Hull House in this regard has always held the potential to inform discussion of this issue. Its curriculum modeled how to foster intergenerational and intercultural communication, open-minded and balanced debate, and the relationship of education to community betterment. As Nel Noddings (2001) writes:

> Life at Hull House was proof that people could cooperate, actually live together, despite differences of religion, nationality and economic status. There were no ideological tests at Hull House beyond the common commitment to improve the neighborhood, Chicago and, more generally, the lives of working people. (p. 185)

If building a more humane and democratic society was integral to Dewey's and Addams's theories of curriculum, it was almost the singular goal of George S. Counts. From the time of his earliest, major works in the 1920s, Counts was concerned with the injustices of democracy and capitalism in the United States, particularly as they played out in the context of schooling (see Kliebard, 1995, pp. 158–159). Like Dewey, Counts grew increasingly restive with "child-centered," Progressive educators who appeared to be ignoring the social context of education in the business-dominated atmosphere of the 1920s. For Counts, the seemingly dominant stream of Progressive education spoke to the "needs" of the child as though these had meaning outside of the society in which education unfolded.

The catastrophic economic slump of the 1930s ushered in a much more receptive environment for the disenchanted intellectual critics of the business civilization of the 1920s. American social thought became more polarized, and collectivist thought enjoyed possibly its most widespread popularity in the history of the United States (see Bowers, 1969). Counts (this volume) caught the spirit of the times when he remarked in *Dare the School Build a New Social Order?* (1932) that "the so-called 'practical' men of our generation—the politicians, the financiers, the industrialists"—had acted selfishly and bungled the well-being of Americans. Counts appealed for teachers to lead the schools and the public "for social regeneration." For Counts and his fellow social reconstructionists, several of the most prominent of whom such as Harold Rugg were Counts' colleagues at Teachers College, Columbia University, it seemed apparent that the age of collectivism had arrived.

Aspects of Counts' vision of a regulated and directed economy in order to serve more than society's elite were, of course, consistent with the more radical elements of the New Deal yet to come. Indeed, it is a sign of how Counts was in touch with the times that later some of his main ideas were to find their parallels in the words and policies of President Franklin D. Roosevelt during the early New Deal years. Nevertheless, given what he viewed as the failure of individualism in American life, Counts looked to school curriculum as a place to inculcate collectivist ideas. Counts maintained that all school programs already inculcated ideas, but those ideas had been ones that primarily served the interests of the ruling classes. As Counts (this volume) put it, "the real question is not whether imposition will take place, but rather from what source it will come."

Counts's theory of curriculum found a ready audience during the depths of the Great Depression in the early 1930s. For example, he and his colleague, the historian Charles A. Beard, were dominant forces in the Commission on the Social Studies, which had been established by the American Historical Association to make recommendations for the schools. The commission's reports, although stopping short of formulating an actual curriculum, nonetheless leaned heavily toward an activist-oriented social studies curriculum consonant with the tenets of social reconstructionism. Furthermore, beginning in the 1920s, Rugg oversaw the development of social studies curriculum materials that were based to some extent on social reconstructionist principles. In contrast to most available materials, their explicit focus was on the problems of American life (see Thornton, 2001). Rugg's materials became bestsellers and were widely adopted across the United States. This is all the more remarkable given the economic hard times faced by school districts during the 1930s.

Rugg's social studies materials probably mark the greatest success of the social reconstructionists in the implementation of their ideas in school programs. As the Great Depression and the New Deal waned, however, Rugg's textbooks came under growing fire from conservative groups. For this and other reasons, the series eventually fell out of favor. Almost the same fate befell social reconstructionism itself as the 1930s wore on and World War II approached. Conservative criticism and the changing climate of educational opinion increasingly shifted Counts and other social reconstructionists from at or near the center of educational debate to a more peripheral position (Kliebard, 1995, pp. 176–178). Nevertheless, the flame of social reconstructionism in educational thought was never entirely extinguished and was, as we shall see, visible again in the 1970s and after.

Before leaving Counts, however, it should be noted that his view of curriculum attracted criticism not only from educational and political traditionalists. No less a progressive figure than Dewey, while sympathizing with some of Counts's collectivist goals, found parts of Counts's curriculum thinking worrisome. For example, Dewey always championed teaching students to think for themselves. From this perspective, the preordained ends of Counts's "imposition" seemed hard to distinguish from indoctrination.

To round out this first section, we have included a well-known essay by curriculum historian Herbert M. Kliebard (1975) dealing with the early years of the curriculum field. Kliebard's focus is the influence of "scientific" curriculum making. Although we have already noted that the scientific strain of curriculum thought has tended to be dominant ever since the field's inception, Kliebard places it in historical context, pointing out how "scientific" approaches to curriculum and other educational matters have come to pervade educational thought and practice in the United States.

REFERENCES

Addams, J. (1961). *Twenty Years at Hull House.* New York: Signet Classic.

Bernstein, R.J. (1967). *John Dewey.* New York: Washington Square Press.

Bowers, C.A. (1969). *The Progressive Educator and the Depression.* New York: Random House.

Callahan, R.E. (1962). *Education and the Cult of Efficiency.* Chicago: University of Chicago Press.

Cremin, L.A. (1964). *The Transformation of the School.* New York: Vintage.

Curti, M. (1959). *The Social Ideas of American Educators, with a New Chapter on the Last Twenty-Five Years.* Totowa, NJ: Littlefield, Adams.

Dewey, J. (1938). *Experience and Education.* New York: Macmillan.

Eisner, E.W. (1985). "Franklin Bobbitt and the 'Science' of Curriculum Making." In E.W. Eisner (Ed.), *The Art of Educational Evaluation* (pp. 13–28). London: Falmer.

Eisner, E.W. (2002). *The Educational Imagination (Third Ed.).* Upper Saddle River, NJ: Merrill Prentice Hall.

Kliebard, H.M. (1995). *The Struggle for the American Curriculum, 1893–1958 (Second Ed.).* New York: Routledge.

Lagemann, E.C. (1994). "Introduction to the Transaction Edition: Why Read Jane Addams?" In Jane Addams, *On Education* (pp. vii–xvii). New Brunswick, NJ: Transaction Publishers.

Lagemann, E.C. (2000). *An Elusive Science: The Troubling History of Education Research.* Chicago: University of Chicago Press.

Mayhew, K.C., and Edwards, A.C. (1966). *The Dewey School.* New York: Atherton.

Noddings, N. (2001). "Jane Addams, 1860–1935." In J.A. Palmer (Ed.), *Fifty Major Thinkers on Education: From Confucius to Dewey* (pp.182–187). London: Routledge.

Tanner, L.M. (1997). *Dewey's Laboratory School.* New York: Teachers College Press.

Thornton, S.J. (2001). "Harold Rugg, 1886–1960." In J.A. Palmer (Ed.), *Fifty Modern Thinkers on Education: From Piaget to the Present* (pp. 10–15). London: Routledge.

Tyack, D.B. (1974). *The One Best System.* Cambridge, MA: Harvard University Press.

1

Scientific Method in Curriculum-making

Franklin Bobbitt

Since the opening of the twentieth century, the evolution of our social order has been proceeding with great and ever-accelerating rapidity. Simple conditions have been growing complex. Small institutions have been growing large. Increased specialization has been multiplying human interdependencies and the consequent need of coördinating effort. Democracy is increasing within the Nation; and growing throughout the world. All classes are aspiring to a full human opportunity. Never before have civilization and humanization advanced so swiftly.

As the world presses eagerly forward toward the accomplishment of new things, education also must advance no less swiftly. It must provide the intelligence and the aspirations necessary for the advance; and for stability and consistency in holding the gains. Education must take a pace set, not by itself, but by social progress.

The present program of public education was mainly formulated during the simpler conditions of the nineteenth century. In details it has been improved. In fundamentals it is not greatly different. A program never designed for the present day has been inherited.

Any inherited system, good for its time, when held to after its day, hampers social progress. It is not enough that the system, fundamentally unchanged in plan and purpose, be improved in details. In education this has been done in conspicuous degree. Our schools to-day are better than ever before. Teachers are better trained. Supervision is more adequate. Buildings and equipment are enormously improved. Effective methods are being introduced, and time is being economized. Improvements are visible on every hand. And yet to do the nineteenth-century task better than it was then done is not necessarily to do the twentieth-century task.

New duties lie before us. And these require new methods, new materials, new vision. The old education, except as it conferred the tools of knowledge, was mainly devoted to filling the memory with facts. The new age is more in need of facts than the old; and of

Public Domain, Preface and Chapter VI in Franklin Bobbitt, *The Curriculum*. Cambridge, MA: The Riverside Press, 1918.

more facts; and it must find more effective methods of teaching them. But there are now other functions. Education is now to develop a type of wisdom that can grow only out of participation in the living experiences of men, and never out of mere memorization of verbal statements of facts. It must, therefore, train thought and judgment in connection with actual life-situations, a task distinctly different from the cloistral activities of the past. It is also to develop the good-will, the spirit of service, the social valuations, sympathies, and attitudes of mind necessary for effective group-action where specialization has created endless interdependency. It has the function of training every citizen, man or woman, not for knowledge about citizenship, but for proficiency in citizenship; not for knowledge about hygiene, but for proficiency in maintaining robust health; not for a mere knowledge of abstract science, but for proficiency in the use of ideas in the control of practical situations. Most of these are new tasks. In connection with each, much is now being done in all progressive school systems; but most of them yet are but partially developed. We have been developing knowledge, not function; the power to reproduce facts, rather than the powers to think and feel and will and act in vital relation to the world's life. Now we must look to these latter things as well.

Our task in this volume is to point out some of the new duties. We are to show why education must now undertake tasks that until recently were not considered needful; why new methods, new materials, and new types of experience must be employed. We here try to develop a point of view that seems to be needed by practical school men and women as they make the educational adjustments now demanded by social conditions; and needed also by scientific workers who are seeking to define with accuracy the objectives of education. It is the feeling of the writer that in the social reconstructions of the post-war years that lie just ahead of us, education is to be called upon to bear a hitherto undreamed-of burden of responsibility; and to undertake unaccustomed labors. To present some of the theory needed for the curriculum labors of this new age has been the task herein attempted.

This is a first book in a field that until recently has been too little cultivated. For a long time, we have been developing the theory of educational method, both general and special; and we have required teachers and supervisors to be thoroughly cognizant of it. Recently, however, we have discerned that there is a theory of curriculum-formulation that is no less extensive and involved than that of method; and that it is just as much needed by teachers and supervisors. To know what to do is as important as to know how to do it. This volume, therefore, is designed for teacher-training institutions as an introductory textbook in the theory of the curriculum; and for reading circles in the training of teachers in service. It is hoped also that it may assist the general reader who is interested in noting recent educational tendencies.

The technique of curriculum-making along scientific lines has been but little developed. The controlling purposes of education have not been sufficiently particularized. We have aimed at a vague culture, an ill-defined discipline, a nebulous harmonious development of the individual, an indefinite moral character-building, an unparticularized social efficiency, or, often enough nothing more than escape from a life of work. Often there are no controlling purposes; the momentum of the educational machine keeps it running. So long as objectives are but vague guesses, or not even that, there can be no demand for anything but vague guesses as to means and procedure. But the era of contentment with large, undefined purposes is rapidly passing. An age of science is demanding exactness and particularity.

The technique of scientific method is at present being developed for every important aspect of education. Experimental laboratories and schools are discovering accurate methods of measuring and evaluating different types of educational processes. Bureaus of educational measurement are discovering scientific methods of analyzing results, of diagnosing specific situations, and of prescribing remedies. Scientific method is being applied to the fields of budget-making, child-accounting, systems of grading and promotion, etc.

The curriculum, however, is a primordial factor. If it is wrongly drawn up on the basis merely of guess and personal opinion, all of the science in the world applied to the factors above enumerated will not make the work efficient. The scientific task preceding all others is the determination of the curriculum. For this we need a scientific technique. At present this is being rapidly developed in connection with various fields of training.

The central theory is simple. Human life, however varied, consists in the performance of specific activities. Education that prepares for life is one that prepares definitely and adequately for these specific activities. However numerous and diverse they may be for any social class, they can be discovered. This requires only that one go out into the world of affairs and discover the particulars of which these affairs consist. These will show the abilities, attitudes, habits, appreciations, and forms of knowledge that men need. These will be the objectives of the curriculum. They will be numerous, definite, and particularized. The curriculum will then be that series of experiences which children and youth must have by way of attaining those objectives.

The word *curriculum* is Latin for a *race-course*, or the *race* itself—a place of deeds, or a series of deeds. As applied to education, it is that *series of things which children and youth must do and experience* by way of developing abilities to do the things well that make up the affairs of adult life; and to be in all respects what adults should be.

The developmental experiences exist upon two levels. On the one hand, there is the general experience of living the community life, without thought of the training values. In this way, through participation, one gets much of his education for participation in community life. In many things this provides most of the training; and in all essential things, much of it. But in all fields, this incidental or undirected developmental experience leaves the training imperfect. It is necessary, therefore, to supplement it with the conscious directed training of systematized education. The first level we shall call undirected training; and the second, directed training.

The curriculum may, therefore, be defined in two ways: (1) it is the entire range of experiences, both undirected and directed, concerned in unfolding the abilities of the individual; or (2) it is the series of consciously directed training experiences that the schools use for completing and perfecting the unfoldment. Our profession uses the term usually in the latter sense. But as education is coming more and more to be seen as a thing of experiences, and as the work- and play-experiences of the general community life are being more and more utilized, the line of demarcation between directed and undirected training experience is rapidly disappearing. Education must be concerned with both, even though it does not direct both.

When the curriculum is defined as including both directed and undirected experiences, then its objectives are the total range of human abilities, habits, systems of knowledge, etc., that one should possess. These will be discovered by analytic survey. The curriculum-discoverer will first be an analyst of human nature and of human affairs. His task at this point is not at all concerned with "the studies"—later he will draw up appropriate studies as *means*, but he will not analyze the tools to be used in a piece of work as a mode of discovering the objectives of that work. His first task rather, in ascertaining the education appropriate for any special class, is to discover the total range of habits, skills, abilities, forms of thought, valuations, ambitions, etc., that its members need for the effective performance of their vocational labors; likewise, the total range needed for their civic activities; their health activities; their recreations; their language; their parental, religious, and general social activities. The program of analysis will be no narrow one. It will be wide as life itself. As it thus finds all the things that make up the mosaic of full-formed human life, it discovers the full range of educational objectives.

Notwithstanding the fact that many of these objectives are attained without conscious effort, the curriculum-discoverer must have all of them before him for his labors. Even though the scholastic curriculum will not find it necessary to aim at all of them, it is the function of education to see that all of them are attained. Only as he looks to the entire series can he discover the ones that require conscious effort. He will be content to let as much as possible be taken care of through undirected experiences. Indeed he will strive for such conditions that a maximum amount of the training can be so taken care of.

The curriculum of the schools will aim at those objectives that are not sufficiently attained as a result of the general undirected experience. This is to recognize that the total range of specific educational objectives breaks up into two sets: one, those arrived at through one's general experiences without his taking thought as to the training; the other, those that are imperfectly or not at all attained through such general experience. The latter are revealed, and distinguished from the former, by the presence of imperfections, errors, shortcomings. Like the symptoms of disease, these point unerringly to those objectives that require the systematized labors of directed training. Deficiencies point to the ends of conscious education. As the specific objectives upon which education is to be focused are thus pointed out, we are shown where the curriculum of the directed training is to be developed.

Let us illustrate. One of the most important things in which one is to be trained is the effective use of the mother-tongue. It is possible to analyze one's language activities and find all of the things one must do in effectively and correctly using it. Each of these things then becomes an objective of the training. But it is not necessary consciously to train for each of them. Let an individual grow up in a cultivated language-atmosphere, and he will learn to do, and be sufficiently practiced in doing, most of them, without any directed training. Here and there he will make mistakes. *Each mistake is a call for directed training.*

The curriculum of the directed training is to be discovered in the shortcomings of individuals after they have had all that can be given by the undirected training. This principle is recognized in the recent work of many investigators as to the curriculum of grammar. One of the earliest studies was that of Professor Charters.[1] Under his direction, the teachers of Kansas City undertook to discover the errors made by pupils in their oral and written language. For the oral errors the teachers carried notebooks for five days of one week and jotted down every grammatical error which they heard made by any pupil at any time during the day. For the errors in writing they examined the written work of the pupils for a period of three weeks. They discovered twenty-one types of errors in the oral speech and twenty-seven types in the written. The oral errors in the order of their frequency were as follows:—

1.	Confusion of past tense and past participle	24
2.	Failure of verb to agree with its subject in number and person	14
3.	Wrong verb	12
4.	Double negative	11
5.	Syntactical redundance	10
6.	Wrong sentence form	5
7.	Confusion of adjectives and adverbs	4
8.	Subject of verb not in nominative case	4
9.	Confusion of demonstrative adjective with personal pronoun	3
10.	Predicate nominative not in nominative case	2
11.	First personal pronoun standing first in a series	2
12.	Wrong form of noun or pronoun	2
13.	Confusion of past and present tenses	2
14.	Object of verb or preposition not in the objective case	1
15.	Wrong part of speech due to a similarity of sound	1
16.	Incorrect comparison of adjectives	1
17.	Failure of the pronoun to agree with its antecedent	0.3
18.	Incorrect use of mood	0.3
19.	Misplaced modifier	0.3
20.	Confusion of preposition and conjunction	0.2
21.	Confusion of comparatives and superlatives	0.1

Each error discovered is a symptom of grammatical ignorance, wrong habit, imperfect valuation, or careless attitude toward one's language. The nature of the deficiency points to the abilities and dispositions that are to be developed in the child by way of bringing about the use of the correct forms. Each grammatical shortcoming discovered, therefore, points to a needed objective of education. It points to a development of knowledge or attitude which the general undirected language experience has not sufficiently accomplished; and which must therefore be consciously undertaken by the schools.

Scientific method must consider both levels of the grammar curriculum. One task is to provide at the school as much as possible of a cultivated language-atmosphere in which the children can live and receive unconscious training. This is really the task of major importance, and provides the type of experience that should accomplish an ever-increasing proportion of the training. The other task is to make children conscious of their errors, to teach the grammar needed for correction or prevention, and to bring the children to put their grammatical knowledge to work in eliminating the errors. In proportion as the other type of experience is increased, this conscious training will play a diminishing role.

In the spelling field, Ayres, Jones, Cook and O'Shea, and others have been tabulating the words that children and adults use in writing letters, reports, compositions, etc. In this way they have been discovering the particularized objectives of training in spelling. But words are of unequal difficulty. Most are learned in the course of the reading and writing experience of the children without much conscious attention to the spelling. But here and there are words that are not so learned. Investigations, therefore, lay special emphasis upon the words that are misspelled. Each misspelled word reveals a directed-curriculum task. Here, as in the grammar, error is the symptom of training need; and the complete error-list points unerringly to the curriculum of conscious training.

In the vocational field, and on the technical side only, Indianapolis has provided an excellent example of method of discovering the objectives of training. Investigators, without pre-suppositions as to content of vocational curriculum, set out to discover the major occupations of the city, the processes to be performed in each, and the knowledge, habits and skills needed for effective work. They talked with expert workmen; and observed the work-processes. In their report, for each occupation, they present: (1) a list of tools and machines with which a workman must be skillful; (2) a list of the materials used in the work with which workers need to be familiar; (3) a list of items of general knowledge needed concerning jobs and processes; (4) the kinds of mathematical operations actually employed in the work; (5) the items or portions of science needed for control of processes; (6) the elements of drawing and design actually used in the work; (7) the characteristics of the English needed where language is vitally involved in one's work, as in commercial occupations; (8) elements of hygiene needed for keeping one's self up to the physical standards demanded by the work; and (9) the needed facts of economics.

Many of the things listed in such a survey are learned through incidental experience. Others cannot be sufficiently learned in this way. It is by putting the workers to work, whether adolescent or adult, and by noting the kinds of shortcomings and mistakes that show themselves when training is absent or deficient, that we can discover the curriculum tasks for directed vocational education.

The objectives of education are not to be discovered within just any kind or quality of human affairs. Occupational, civic, sanitary, or other activity may be poorly performed and productive of only meager results. At the other end of the scale are types of activity that are as well performed as it is in human nature to perform them, and which are abundantly fruitful in good results. Education is established upon the presumption that human activities exist upon different levels of quality or efficiency; that performance of low character is not good; that it can be eliminated through training; and that only the best or at least the best attainable is good enough. Whether in agriculture, building-trades, housekeeping, commerce, civic regulation, sanitation, or any other, education presumes that the best that is practicable is what ought to be. Education is to keep its feet squarely upon the earth; but this does not require that it aim lower than the highest that is practicable.

Let us take a concrete illustration. The curriculum-discoverer wishes, for example, to draw up a course of training in agriculture. He will go out into the practical world of agriculture as the only place that can reveal the objectives of agricultural education. He will start out without prejudgment as to the specific objectives. All that he needs for the work is pencil, notebook, and a discerning intelligence. He will observe the work of farmers; he will talk with them about all aspects of their work; and he will read reliable accounts which give insight into their activities. From these sources he will discover the particular things that the farmers do in carrying on each piece of work; the specific knowledge which the farmers employ in planning and performing each specific task; the kinds of judgments at which they must arrive; the types of problems they must solve; the habits and skills demanded by the tasks; the attitudes of mind, appreciations, valuations, ambitions, and desires, which motivate and exercise general control.

Facts upon all of these matters can be obtained from a survey of any agricultural region, however primitive or backward. But primitive agriculture is the thing which exists without any education. It is the thing education is to eliminate. The curriculum-discoverer, therefore, will not investigate just any agricultural situation. He will go to the farms that are most productive and most successful from every legitimate point of view. These will often be experimental or demonstration farms which represent what is practicable for the community, but which may not be typical of actual practices in that community. Where such general practices are inferior, agricultural education is to aim not at what is but at what ought to be.

When the farming practices are already upon a high plane, education has but a single function: it is to hand over these practices unchanged to the members of the new generation.

Where the practices of a region are primitive or backward, education has a double function to perform. It is not only to hand over to the new generation a proficiency that is equal to that of their fathers, but it is also to lift the proficiency of the sons to a height much beyond that of their fathers. Within such a region, therefore, agricultural education has the additional function of serving as the fundamental social agency of agricultural progress.

What we have said concerning agriculture is generally applicable throughout the occupational world. For discovering the objectives for a training course in bricklaying one will analyze not the activities of bricklayers in general, but those where bricklaying has been carried to its highest practicable level of efficiency—as this efficiency is judged on the basis of all legitimate standards. Education will aim, not at average bricklayers, but at the best types of bricklayers.

When stated in broad outline, the general principle is obvious. In practical application, it presents difficulties. Men do not agree as to the characteristics of the most desirable types of work. The employers of the bricklayers will be inclined to use maximum productiveness as the criterion of superior work; and unquestioning obedience to orders and contentment with any kind of hours, wages, and working conditions as proper mental attitudes. The employees will judge otherwise as to some of the factors. The employers will invite the curriculum-discoverer to investigate situations where productiveness in proportion to costs is greatest; the employees, where the total welfare of the worker is considered alongside of the factor of productiveness. Both sides will agree that education should aim at the best and that scientific investigations as to objectives should seek to discover the characteristics of only the best. They disagree as to what is the best, and therefore where the investigations are to be made.

The general principle of finding the scholastic curriculum in the shortcomings of children and men is quite obvious and entirely familiar to teachers in its application to the curriculum of spelling, grammar, and other subjects that result in objective performance, such as pronunciation, drawing, music, computation, etc. It is not so clear in connection with the highly complex subjects of history, literature, geography, etc. What are the social shortcomings that are to be eliminated through a study of these social subjects? Our ideas are yet so vague, in most cases, that we can scarcely be said to have objectives. The first task of the scientific curriculum-maker is the discovery of those social deficiencies that result from a lack of historical, literary, and geographical experiences. Each deficiency found is a call for directed training; it points to an objective that is to be set up for the conscious training. The nature of the objectives will point to the curriculum materials to be selected for these subjects. A major obstacle is lack of agreement as to what constitutes social deficiency. There is however no justification for scholastic training of any kind except as a gap exists between the training of general experience and the training that ought to be accomplished.

Society agrees sufficiently well as to many social shortcomings. Education needs to assemble them in as accurate and particularized a form as possible. They can then be used as the social symptoms which point to the objectives of history, literature, geography, economics, and other social studies. Society will disagree as to many suggested deficiencies. A program can be scientific, however, without being complete. The thousand spelling words presented by Mr. Ayres is a good list notwithstanding the fact that it presents not more than a quarter of the words needed. It is a secure beginning that can be completed by further studies. In the same way in our social training, we shall do very well if we can set up a quarter of the desirable objectives. That would be a great advance over none at all, as at present; and would provide the nucleus, the technique, and the vision of possibilities, necessary for gradually rounding out the list.

The principle involves us in similar difficulties in its application to civic, moral, vocational, sanitational, recreational, and parental education. It is equally valid, however, in connection with each of these. Only as we agree upon *what ought to be* in each of these difficult fields, can we know at what the training should aim. Only as we list the errors and shortcomings of human performance in each of the fields can we know what to include and to emphasize in the directed curriculum of the schools.

NOTE

1. Charters, W. W., and Miller, Edith. A Course of Study in Grammar based upon the Grammatical Errors of School Children in Kansas City, Missouri. University of Missouri, Education Bulletin, no. 9.

2

My Pedagogic Creed

John Dewey

ARTICLE ONE: WHAT EDUCATION IS

I Believe that—all education proceeds by the participation of the individual in the social consciousness of the race. This process begins unconsciously almost at birth, and is continually shaping the individual's powers, saturating his consciousness, forming his habits, training his ideas, and arousing his feelings and emotions. Through this unconscious education the individual gradually comes to share in the intellectual and moral resources which humanity has succeeded in getting together. He becomes an inheritor of the funded capital of civilization. The most formal and technical education in the world cannot safely depart from this general process. It can only organize it or differentiate it in some particular direction.

- The only true education comes through the stimulation of the child's powers by the demands of the social situations in which he finds himself. Through these demands he is stimulated to act as a member of a unity, to emerge from his original narrowness of action and feeling, and to conceive of himself from the standpoint of the welfare of the group to which he belongs. Through the responses which others make to his own activities he comes to know what these mean in social terms. The value which they have is reflected back into them. For instance, through the response which is made to the child's instinctive babblings the child comes to know what those babblings mean; they are transformed into articulate language, and thus the child is introduced into the consolidated wealth of ideas and emotions which are now summed up in language.

- This educational process has two sides, one psychological and one sociological, and that neither can be subordinated to the other, or neglected, without evil results following. Of these two sides, the psychological is the basis. The child's own instincts and powers furnish the material and give the starting-point for all education. Save as the efforts of the educator connect with some activity which the child is carrying on of his own initiative independent of the educator, education becomes reduced to a pressure

From "My Pedagogic Creed," *Journal of the National Education Association*, Vol. 18, No. 9, pp. 291–295, December 1929. Reprinted by permission.

from without. It may, indeed, give certain external results, but cannot truly be called educative. Without insight into the psychological structure and activities of the individual, the educative process will, therefore, be haphazard and arbitrary. If it chances to coincide with the child's activity it will get a leverage; if it does not, it will result in friction, or disintegration, or arrest of the child nature.

- Knowledge of social conditions, of the present state of civilization, is necessary in order properly to interpret the child's powers. The child has his own instincts and tendencies, but we do not know what these mean until we can translate them into their social equivalents. We must be able to carry them back into a social past and see them as the inheritance of previous race activities. We must also be able to project them into the future to see what their outcome and end will be. In the illustration just used, it is the ability to see in the child's babblings the promise and potency of a future social intercourse and conversation which enables one to deal in the proper way with that instinct.

- The psychological and social sides are organically related, and that education cannot be regarded as a compromise between the two, or a superimposition of one upon the other. We are told that the psychological definition of education is barren and formal—that is gives us only the idea of a development of all the mental powers without giving us any idea of the use to which these powers are put. On the other hand, it is urged that the social definition of education, as getting adjusted to civilization, makes of it a forced and external process, and results in subordinating the freedom of the individual to a preconceived social and political status.

- Each of these objections is true when urged against one side isolated from the other. In order to know what a power really is we must know what its end, use, or function is, and this we cannot know save as we conceive of the individual as active in social relationships. But, on the other hand, the only possible adjustment which we can give to the child under existing conditions is that which arises through putting him in complete possession of all his powers. With the advent of democracy and modern industrial conditions, it is impossible to foretell definitely just what civilization will be twenty years from now. Hence it is impossible to prepare the child for any precise set of conditions. To prepare him for the future life means to give him command of himself; it means so to train him that he will have the full and ready use of all his capacities that his eye and ear and hand may be tools ready to command, that his judgment may be capable of grasping the conditions under which it has to work, and the executive forces be trained to act economically and efficiently. It is impossible to reach this sort of adjustment save as constant regard it had to the individual's own powers, tastes, and interests—that is, as education is continually converted into psychological terms.

In sum, I believe that the individual who is to be educated is a social individual, and that society is an organic union of individuals. If we eliminate the social factor from the child we are left only with an abstraction; if we eliminate the individual factor from society, we are left only with an inert and lifeless mass. Education, therefore, must begin with a psychological insight into the child's capacities, interests, and habits. It must be controlled at every point by reference to these same considerations. These powers, interests, and habits must be continually interpreted—we must know what they mean. They must be translated into terms of their social equivalents—into terms of what they are capable of in the way of social service.

ARTICLE TWO: WHAT THE SCHOOL IS

I Believe that—the school is primarily a social institution. Education being a social process, the school is simply that form of community life in which all those agencies are concentrated that will be most effective in bringing the child to share in the inherited resources of the race, and to use his own powers for social ends.

- Education, therefore, is a process of living and not a preparation for future living.
- The school must represent present life—life as real and vital to the child as that which he carries on in the home, in the neighborhood, or on the playground.
- That education which does not occur through forms of life, forms that are worth living for their own sake, is always a poor substitute for the genuine reality, and tends to cramp and to deaden.
- The school, as an institution, should simplify existing social life; should reduce it, as it were, to an embryonic form. Existing life is so complex that the child cannot be brought into contact with it without either confusion or distraction; he is either overwhelmed by the multiplicity of activities which are going on, so that he loses his own power of orderly reaction, or he is so stimulated by these various activities that his powers are prematurely called into play and he becomes either unduly specialized or else disintegrated.
- As such simplified social life, the school life should grow gradually out of the home life; that it should take up and continue the activities with which the child is already familiar in the home.
- It should exhibit these activities to the child, and reproduce them in such ways that the child will gradually learn the meaning of them, and be capable of playing his own part in relation to them.
- This is a psychological necessity, because it is the only way of securing continuity in the child's growth, the only way of giving a background of past experience to the new ideas given in school.
- It is also a social necessity because the home is the form of social life in which the child has been nurtured and in connection with which he has had his moral training. It is the business of the school to deepen and extend his sense of the values bound up in his home life.
- Much of present education fails because it neglects this fundamental principle of the school as a form of community life. It conceives the school as a place where certain information is to be given, where certain lessons are to be learned, or where certain habits are to be formed. The value of these is conceived as lying largely in the remote future; the child must do these things for the sake of something else he is to do; they are mere preparations. As a result they do not become a part of the life experience of the child and so are not truly educative.
- The moral education centers upon this conception of the school as a mode of social life, that the best and deepest moral training is precisely that which one gets through having to enter into proper relations with others in a unity of work and thought. The present educational systems, so far as they destroy or neglect this unity, render it difficult or impossible to get any genuine, regular moral training.
- The child should be stimulated and controlled in his work through the life of the community.
- Under existing conditions far too much of the stimulus and control proceeds from the teacher, because of neglect of the idea of the school as a form of social life.

- The teacher's place and work in the school is to be interpreted from this same basis. The teacher is not in the school to impose certain ideas or to form certain habits in the child, but is there as a member of the community to select the influences which shall affect the child and to assist him in properly responding to these influences.
- The discipline of the school should proceed from the life of the school as a whole and not directly from the teacher.
- The teacher's business is simply to determine, on the basis of larger experience and riper wisdom, how the discipline of life shall come to the child.
- All questions of the grading of the child and his promotion should be determined by reference to the same standard. Examinations are of use only so far as they test the child's fitness for social life and reveal the place in which he can be of the most service and where he can receive the most help.

ARTICLE THREE: THE SUBJECTMATTER OF EDUCATION

I Believe that—the social life of the child is the basis of concentration, or correlation, in all his training or growth. The social life gives the unconscious unity and the background of all his efforts and of all his attainments.

- The subjectmatter of the school curriculum should mark a gradual differentiation out of the primitive unconscious unity of social life.
- We violate the child's nature and render difficult the best ethical results by introducing the child too abruptly to a number of special studies, of reading, writing, geography, etc., out of relation to this social life.
- The true center of correlation on the school subjects is not science, nor literature, nor history, nor geography, but the child's own social activities.
- Education cannot be unified in the study of science, or so-called nature study, because apart from human activity, nature itself is not a unity; nature in itself is a number of diverse objects in space and time, and to attempt to make it the center of work by itself is to introduce a principle of radiation rather than one of concentration.
- Literature is the reflex expression and interpretation of social experience; that hence it must follow upon and not precede such experience. It, therefore, cannot be made the basis, although it may be made the summary of unification.
- Once more that history is of educative value in so far as it presents phases of social life and growth. It must be controlled by reference to social life. When taken simply as history it is thrown into the distant past and becomes dead and inert. Taken as the record of man's social life and progress it becomes full of meaning. I believe, however, that it cannot be so taken excepting as the child is also introduced directly into social life.
- The primary basis of education is in the child's powers at work along the same general constructive lines as those which have brought civilization into being.
- The only way to make the child conscious of his social heritage is to enable him to perform those fundamental types of activity which make civilization what it is.
- In the so-called expressive or constructive activities as the center of correlation.
- This gives the standard for the place of cooking, sewing, manual training, etc., in the school.
- They are not special studies which are to be introduced over and above a lot of others in the way of relaxation or relief, or as additional accomplishments. I believe rather

that they represent, as types, fundamental forms of social activity; and that it is possible and desirable that the child's introduction into the more formal subjects of the curriculum be through the medium of these constructive activities.

- The study of science is educational in so far as it brings out the materials and processes which make social life what it is.
- One of the greatest difficulties in the present teaching of science is that the material is presented in purely objective form, or is treated as a new peculiar kind of experience which the child can add to that which he has already had. In reality, science is of value because it gives the ability to interpret and control the experience already had. It should be introduced, not as so much new subjectmatter, but as showing the factors already involved in previous experience and as furnishing tools by which that experience can be more easily and effectively regulated.
- At present we lose much of the value of literature and language studies because of our elimination of the social element. Language is almost always treated in the books of pedagogy simply as the expression of thought. It is true that language is a logical instrument, but it is fundamentally and primarily a social instrument. Language is the device for communication; it is the tool through which one individual comes to share the ideas and feelings of others. When treated simply as a way of getting individual information, or as a means of showing off what one has learned, it loses its social motive and end.
- There is, therefore, no succession of studies in the ideal school curriculum. If education is life, all life has, from the outset, a scientific aspect, an aspect of art and culture, and an aspect of communication. It cannot, therefore, be true that the proper studies for one grade are mere reading and writing, and that at a later grade, reading, or literature, or science, may be introduced. The progress is not in the succession of studies, but in the development of new attitudes towards, and new interests in, experience.
- Education must be conceived as a continuing reconstruction of experience; that the process and the goal of education are one and the same thing.
- To set up any end outside of education, as furnishing its goal and standard, is to deprive the educational process of much of its meaning, and tends to make us rely upon false and external stimuli in dealing with the child.

ARTICLE FOUR: THE NATURE OF METHOD
I Believe that—the question of method is ultimately reducible to the question of the order of development of the child's powers and interests. The law for presenting and treating material is the law implicit within the child's own nature. Because this is so I believe the following statements are of supreme importance as determining the spirit in which education is carried on.

- The active side precedes the passive in the development of the child-nature; that expression comes before conscious impression; that the muscular development precedes the sensory; that movements come before conscious sensations; I believe that consciousness is essentially motor or impulsive; that conscious states tend to project themselves in action.
- The neglect of this principle is the cause of a large part of the waste of time and strength in school work. The child is thrown into a passive, receptive, or absorbing attitude. The conditions are such that he is not permitted to follow the law of his nature; the result is friction and waste.

- Ideas (intellectual and rational processes) also result from action and devolve for the sake of the better control of action. What we term reason is primarily the law of order or effective action. To attempt to develop the reasoning powers, the powers of judgment, without reference to the selection and arrangement of means in action, is the fundamental fallacy in our present methods of dealing with this matter. As a result we present the child with arbitrary symbols. Symbols are a necessity in mental development, but they have their place as tools for economizing effort; presented by themselves they are a mass of meaningless and arbitrary ideas imposed from without.
- The image is the great instrument of instruction. What a child gets out of any subject presented to him is simply the images which he himself forms with regard to it.
- If nine-tenths of the energy at present directed towards making the child learn certain things were spent in seeing to it that the child was forming proper images, the work of instruction would be indefinitely facilitated.
- Much of the time and attention now given to the preparation and presentation of lessons might be more wisely and profitably expended in training the child's power of imagery and in seeing to it that he was continually forming definite vivid, and growing images of the various subjects with which he comes in contact in his experience.
- Interests are the signs and symptoms of growing power. I believe that they represent dawning capacities. Accordingly the constant and careful observation of interests is of the utmost importance for the educator.
- These interests are to be observed as showing the state of development which the child has reached.
- They prophesy the stage upon which he is about to enter.
- Only through the continual and sympathetic observation of childhood's interests can the adult enter into the child's life and see what it is ready for, and upon what material it could work most readily and fruitfully.
- These interests are neither to be humored nor repressed. To repress interest is to substitute the adult for the child, and so to weaken intellectual curiosity and alertness, to suppress initiative, and to deaden interest. To humor the interests is to substitute the transient for the permanent. The interest is always the sign of some power below; the important thing is to discover this power. To humor the interest is to fail to penetrate below the surface, and its sure result is to substitute caprice and whim for genuine interest.
- The emotions are the reflex of actions.
- To endeavor to stimulate or arouse the emotions apart from their corresponding activities is to introduce an unhealthy and morbid state of mind.
- If we can only secure right habits of action and thought, with reference to the good, the true, and the beautiful, the emotions will for the most part take care of themselves.
- Next to deadness and dullness, formalism and routine, our education is threatened with no greater evil than sentimentalism.
- This sentimentalism is the necessary result of the attempt to divorce feeling from action.

ARTICLE FIVE: THE SCHOOL AND SOCIAL PROGRESS
I Believe that—education is the fundamental method of social progress and reform.

- All reforms which rest simply upon the enactment of law, or the threatening of certain penalties, or upon changes in mechanical or outward arrangements, are transitory and futile.

- Education is a regulation of the process of coming to share in the social consciousness; and that the adjustment of individual activity on the basis of this social consciousness is the only sure method of social reconstruction.
- This conception has due regard for both the individualistic and socialistic ideals. It is duly individual because it recognizes the formation of a certain character as the only genuine basis of right living. It is socialistic because it recognizes that this right character is not to be formed by merely individual precept, example, or exhortation, but rather by the influence of a certain form of institutional or community life upon the individual, and that the social organism through the school, as its organ, may determine ethical results.
- In the ideal school we have the reconciliation of the individualistic and the institutional ideals.
- The community's duty to education is, therefore, its paramount moral duty. By law and punishment, by social agitation and discussion, society can regulate and form itself in a more or less haphazard and chance way. But through education society can formulate its own purposes, can organize its own means and resources, and thus shape itself with definiteness and economy in the direction in which it wishes to move.
- When society once recognizes the possibilities in this direction, and the obligations which these possibilities impose, it is impossible to conceive of the resources of time, attention, and money which will be put at the disposal of the education.
- It is the business of everyone interested in education to insist upon the school as the primary and most effective interest of social progress and reform in order that society may be awakened to realize what the school stands for, and arouse to the necessity of endowing the educator with sufficient equipment properly to perform his task.
- Education thus conceived marks the most perfect and intimate union of science and art conceivable in human experience.
- The art of thus giving shape to human powers and adapting them to social service is the supreme art; one calling into its service the best of artists; that no insight, sympathy, tact, executive power, is too great for such service.
- With the growth of psychological service, giving added insight into individual structure and laws of growth; and with growth of social science, adding to our knowledge of the right organization of individuals, all scientific resources can be utilized for the purposes of education.
- When science and art thus join hands the most commanding motive for human action will be reached, the most genuine springs of human conduct aroused, and the best service that human nature is capable of guaranteed.
- The teacher is engaged, not simply in the training of individuals, but in the formation of the proper social life.
- Every teacher should realize the dignity of his calling; that he is a social servant set apart for the maintenance of proper social order and the securing of the right social growth.
- In this way the teacher always is the prophet of the true God and the usherer in of the true kingdom of God.

3

The Public School and the Immigrant Child

JANE ADDAMS

I AM ALWAYS DIFFIDENT WHEN I COME BEFORE a professional body of teachers, realizing as I do that it is very easy for those of us who look on to bring indictments against result; and realizing also that one of the most difficult situations you have to meet is the care and instruction of the immigrant child, especially as he is found where I see him, in the midst of crowded city conditions.

And yet in spite of the fact that the public school is the great savior of the immigrant district, and the one agency which inducts the children into the changed conditions of American life, there is a certain indictment which may justly be brought, in that the public school too often separates the child from his parents and widens that old gulf between fathers and sons which is never so cruel and so wide as it is between the immigrants who come to this country and their children who have gone to the public school and feel that they have there learned it all. The parents are thereafter subjected to certain judgment, the judgment of the young which is always harsh and in this instance founded upon the most superficial standard of Americanism. And yet there is a notion of culture which we would define as a knowledge of those things which have been long cherished by men, the things which men have loved because thru generations they have softened and interpreted life, and have endowed it with value and meaning. Could this standard have been given rather than the things which they see about them as the test of so-called success, then we might feel that the public school has given at least the beginnings of culture which the child ought to have. At present the Italian child goes back to its Italian home more or less disturbed and distracted by the contrast between the school and the home. If he throws off the control of the home because it does not represent the things which he has been taught to value he takes the first step toward the Juvenile Court and all the other operations of the law, because he has prematurely asserted himself long before he is ready to take care of his own affairs.

We find in the carefully prepared figures which Mr. Commons and other sociologists have published that while the number of arrests of immigrants is smaller than the arrests

Reprinted with permission from the National Education Association, *Journal of Proceedings and Addresses*, 1908, pp. 99–102.

of native born Americans, the number of arrests among children of immigrants is twice as large as the number of arrests among the children of native born Americans. It would seem that in spite of the enormous advantages which the public school gives to these children it in some way loosens them from the authority and control of their parents, and tends to send them, without a sufficient rudder and power of self-direction, into the perilous business of living. Can we not say, perhaps, that the schools ought to do more to connect these children with the best things of the past, to make them realize something of the beauty and charm of the language, the history, and the traditions which their parents represent. It is easy to cut them loose from their parents, it requires cultivation to tie them up in sympathy and understanding. The ignorant teacher cuts them off because he himself cannot understand the situation, the cultivated teacher fastens them because his own mind is open to the charm and beauty of that old-country life. In short, it is the business of the school to give to each child the beginnings of a culture so wide and deep and universal that he can interpret his own parents and countrymen by a standard which is world-wide and not provincial.

The second indictment which may be brought is the failure to place the children into proper relation toward the industry which they will later enter. Miss Arnold has told us that children go into industry for a very short time. I believe that the figures of the United States census show the term to be something like six years for the women in industry as over against twenty-four years for men, in regard to continuity of service. Yet you cannot disregard the six years of the girls nor the twenty-four years of the boys, because they are the immediate occupation into which they enter after they leave the school—even the girls are bound to go thru that period—that is, the average immigrant girls are—before they enter the second serious business of life and maintain homes of their own. Therefore, if they enter industry unintelligently, without some notion of what it means, they find themselves totally unprepared for their first experience with American life, they are thrown out without the proper guide or clue which the public school might and ought to have given to them. Our industry has become so international, that it ought to be easy to use the materials it offers for immigrant children. The very processes and general principles which industry represents give a chance to prepare these immigrant children in a way which the most elaborated curriculum could not present. Ordinary material does not give the same international suggestion as industrial material does.

Third, I do not believe that the children who have been cut off from their own parents are going to be those who, when they become parents themselves, will know how to hold the family together and to connect it with the state. I should begin to teach the girls to be good mothers by teaching them to be good daughters. Take a girl whose mother has come from South Italy. The mother cannot adjust herself to the changed condition of housekeeping, does not know how to wash and bake here, and do the other things which she has always done well in Italy, because she has suddenly been transported from a village to a tenement house. If that girl studies these household conditions in relation to the past and to the present needs of the family, she is undertaking the very best possible preparation for her future obligations to a household of her own. And to my mind she can undertake it in no better way. Her own children are mythical and far away, but the little brothers and sisters pull upon her affections and her loyalty, and she longs to have their needs recognized in the school so that the school may give her some help. Her mother complains that the baby is sick in America because she cannot milk her own goat; she insists if she had her own goat's milk the baby would be quite well and flourishing, as the children were in Italy. If that girl can be taught that the milk makes the baby ill because it is not clean and be provided with a simple test that she may know when milk is clean, it may take her into the study not only of the milk within the four walls of the tenement house, but into the inspection of the milk of her district. The milk, however, remains good educational material, it makes even more concrete the connection which you would be glad to use between the household and the affairs of the American city. Let her not follow the mother's example of complaining about changed conditions; let her rather make the adjustment for her mother's entire household. We cannot tell what adjustments the girl herself will be called upon to make ten years from now; but we can give her the clue and the aptitude to adjust the family with which she is identified to the constantly changing conditions of city life. Many of us feel that, splendid as the public schools are in their relation to the immigrant child, they do not understand all of the difficulties which surround that child—all of the moral and emotional perplexities which constantly harass him. The children long that the school teacher should know something about the lives their parents lead and should be able to reprove the hooting children who make fun of the Italian mother because she wears a kerchief on her head, not only because they are rude but also because they are stupid. We send young people to Europe to see Italy, but we do not utilize Italy when it lies about the schoolhouse. If the body of teachers in our great cities could take hold of the immigrant colonies, could bring out of them their handicrafts and occupations, their traditions, their folk songs and folk lore, the beautiful stories which every immigrant colony is ready to tell and translate; could get the children to bring these things into school as the material from which culture is made and the material upon which culture is based, they would discover that by comparison that which they give them now is a poor meretricious and vulgar thing. Give these children a chance to utilize the historic and industrial material which they see about them and they will begin to have a sense of ease in America, a first consciousness of being at home. I believe if these people are welcomed upon the basis of the resources which they represent and the contributions which they bring, it may come to pass that these schools which deal with immigrants will find that they have a wealth of cultural and industrial material which will make the schools in other neighborhoods positively envious. A girl living in a tenement household, helping along this tremendous adjustment, healing over this great moral upheaval which the parents have suffered and which leaves them bleeding and sensitive—such a girl has a richer experience and a finer material than any girl from a more fortunate household can have at the present moment.

I wish I had the power to place before you what it seems to me is the opportunity that the immigrant colonies present to the public school: the most endearing occupation of leading the little child, who will in turn lead his family, and bring them with him into the brotherhood for which they are longing. The immigrant child cannot make this demand upon the school because he does not know how to formulate it; it is for the teacher both to perceive it and to fulfil it.

4

Dare the School Build a New Social Order?

GEORGE S. COUNTS

3

If we may now assume that the child will be imposed upon in some fashion by the various elements in his environment, the real question is not whether imposition will take place, but rather from what source it will come. If we were to answer this question in terms of the past, there could, I think, be but one answer: on all genuinely crucial matters the school follows the wishes of the groups or classes that actually rule society; on minor matters the school is some-times allowed a certain measure of freedom. But the future may be unlike the past. Or perhaps I should say that teachers, if they could increase sufficiently their stock of courage, intelligence, and vision, might become a social force of some magnitude. About this eventuality I am not over sanguine, but a society lacking leadership as ours does, might even accept the guidance of teachers. Through powerful organizations they might at least reach the public conscience and come to exercise a larger measure of control over the schools than hitherto. They would then have to assume some responsibility for the more fundamental forms of imposition which, according to my argument, cannot be avoided.

That the teachers should deliberately reach for power and then make the most of their conquest is my firm conviction. To the extent that they are permitted to fashion the curriculum and the procedures of the school they will definitely and positively influence the social attitudes, ideals, and behavior of the coming generation. In doing this they should resort to no subterfuge or false modesty. They should say neither that they are merely teaching the truth nor that they are unwilling to wield power in their own right. The first position is false and the second is a confession of incompetence. It is my observation that the men and women who have affected the course of human events are those who have not hesitated to use the power that has come to them. Representing as they do, not the interests of the moment or of any special class, but rather the common and abiding interests of the

Chapters 3 and 4, in George S. Counts, *Dare the School Build a New Social Order?* New York: John Day, 1932. Reprinted by permission of Martha L. Counts. Copyright renewed 1959 by George S. Counts.

people, teachers are under heavy social obligation to protect and further those interests. In this they occupy a relatively unique position in society. Also since the profession should embrace scientists and scholars of the highest rank, as well as teachers working at all levels of the educational system, it has at its disposal, as no other group, the knowledge and wisdom of the ages. It is scarcely thinkable that these men and women would ever act as selfishly or bungle as badly as have the so-called "practical" men of our generation—the politicians, the financiers, the industrialists. If all of these facts are taken into account, instead of shunning power, the profession should rather seek power and then strive to use that power fully and wisely and in the interests of the great masses of the people.

The point should be emphasized that teachers possess no magic secret to power. While their work should give them a certain moral advantage, they must expect to encounter the usual obstacles blocking the road to leadership. They should not be deceived by the pious humbug with which public men commonly flatter the members of the profession. To expect ruling groups or classes to give precedence to teachers on important matters, because of age or sex or sentiment, is to refuse to face realities. It was one of the proverbs of the agrarian order that a spring never rises higher than its source. So the power that teachers exercise in the schools can be no greater than the power they wield in society. Moreover, while organization is necessary, teachers should not think of their problem primarily in terms of organizing and presenting a united front to the world, the flesh, and the devil. In order to be effective they must throw off completely the slave psychology that has dominated the mind of the pedagogue more or less since the days of ancient Greece. They must be prepared to stand on their own feet and win for their ideas the support of the masses of the people. Education as a force for social regeneration must march hand in hand with the living and creative forces of the social order. In their own lives teachers must bridge the gap between school and society and play some part in the fashioning of those great common purposes which should bind the two together.

This brings us to the question of the kind of imposition in which teachers should engage, if they had the power. Our obligations, I think, grow out of the social situation. We live in troublous times; we live in an age of profound change; we live in an age of revolution. Indeed it is highly doubtful whether man ever lived in a more eventful period than the present. In order to match our epoch we would probably have to go back to the fall of the ancient empires or even to that unrecorded age when men first abandoned the natural arts of hunting and fishing and trapping and began to experiment with agriculture and the settled life. Today we are witnessing the rise of a civilization quite without precedent in human history—a civilization founded on science, technology, and machinery, possessing the most extraordinary power, and rapidly making of the entire world a single great society. Because of forces already released, whether in the field of economics, politics, morals, religion, or art, the old molds are being broken. And the peoples of the earth are everywhere seething with strange ideas and passions. If life were peaceful and quiet and undisturbed by great issues, we might with some show of wisdom center our attention on the nature of the child. But with the world as it is, we cannot afford for a single instant to remove our eyes from the social scene or shift our attention from the peculiar needs of the age.

In this new world that is forming, there is one set of issues which is peculiarly fundamental and which is certain to be the center of bitter and prolonged struggle. I refer to those issues which may be styled economic. President Butler has well stated the case: "For a generation and more past," he says, "the center of human interest has been moving from the point which it occupied for some four hundred years to a new point which it bids fair to occupy for a time equally long. The shift in the position of the center of gravity in human interest has been from politics to economics; from considerations that had to do with forms of government, with the establishment and protection of individual liberty, to considerations that have to do with the production, distribution, and consumption of wealth."

Consider the present condition of the nation. Who among us, if he had not been reared amid our institutions, could believe his eyes as he surveys the economic situation, or his ears as he listens to solemn disquisitions by our financial and political leaders on the cause and cure of the depression! Here is a society that manifests the most extraordinary contradictions: a mastery over the forces of nature, surpassing the wildest dreams of antiquity, is accompanied by extreme material insecurity; dire poverty walks hand in hand with the most extravagant living the world has ever known; an abundance of goods of all kinds is coupled with privation, misery, and even starvation; an excess of production is seriously offered as the underlying cause of severe physical suffering; breakfastless children march to school past bankrupt shops laden with rich foods gathered from the ends of the earth; strong men by the million walk the streets in a futile search for employment and with the exhaustion of hope enter the ranks of the damned; great captains of industry close factories without warning and dismiss the workmen by whose labors they have amassed huge fortunes through the years; automatic machinery increasingly displaces men and threatens society with a growing contingent of the permanently unemployed; racketeers and gangsters with the connivance of public officials fasten themselves on the channels of trade and exact toll at the end of the machine gun; economic parasitism, either within or without the law, is so prevalent that the tradition of honest labor is showing signs of decay; the wages paid to the workers are too meager to enable them to buy back the goods they produce; consumption is subordinated to production and a philosophy of deliberate waste is widely proclaimed as the highest economic wisdom; the science of psychology is employed to fan the flames of desire so that men may be enslaved by their wants and bound to the wheel of production; a government board advises the cotton-growers to plow under every third row of cotton in order to bolster up the market; both ethical and aesthetic considerations are commonly over-ridden by "hard-headed business men" bent on material gain; federal aid to the unemployed is opposed on the ground that it would pauperize the masses when the favored members of society have always lived on a dole; even responsible leaders resort to the practices of the witch doctor and vie with one another in predicting the return of prosperity; an ideal of rugged individualism, evolved in a simple pioneering and agrarian order at a time when free land existed in abundance, is used to justify a system which exploits pitilessly and without thought of the morrow the natural and human resources of the nation and of the world. One can only imagine what Jeremiah would say if he could step out of the pages of the Old Testament and cast his eyes over this vast spectacle so full of tragedy and of menace.

The point should be emphasized, however, that the present situation is also freighted with hope and promise. The age is pregnant with possibilities. There lies within our grasp the most humane, the most beautiful, the most majestic civilization ever fashioned by any people. This much at least we know today. We shall probably know more tomorrow. At last men have achieved such a mastery over the forces of nature that wage slavery can follow chattel slavery and take its place among the relics of the past. No longer are there grounds for the contention that the finer fruits of human culture must be nurtured upon the toil and watered by the tears of the masses. The limits to achievement set by nature have been so extended that we are today bound merely by our ideals, by our power of self-discipline, by our ability to devise social arrangements suited to an industrial age. If we are to place any credence whatsoever in the word of our engineers, the full utilization of modern technology at its present level of development should enable us to produce several times as much goods as were ever produced at the very peak of prosperity, and with the working day, the working year, and the working life reduced by half. We hold within our hands the power to usher in an age of plenty, to make secure the lives of all, and to banish poverty forever from the land. The only cause for doubt or pessimism lies in the question of our ability to rise to the stature of the times in which we live.

Our generation has the good or the ill fortune to live in an age when great decisions must be made. The American people, like most of the other peoples of the earth, have come to the parting of the ways; they can no longer trust entirely the inspiration which came to them when the Republic was young; they must decide afresh what they are to do with their talents. Favored above all other nations with the resources of nature and the material instrumentalities of civilization, they stand confused and irresolute before the future. They seem to lack the moral quality necessary to quicken, discipline, and give direction to their matchless energies. In a recent paper Professor Dewey has, in my judgment, correctly diagnosed our troubles: "the schools, like the nation," he says, "are in need of a central purpose which will create new enthusiasm and devotion, and which will unify and guide all intellectual plans."

This suggests, as we have already observed, that the educational problem is not wholly intellectual in nature. Our Progressive schools therefore cannot rest content with giving children an opportunity to study contemporary society in all of its aspects. This of course must be done, but I am convinced that they should go much farther. If the schools are to be really effective, they must become centers for the building, and not merely for the contemplation, of our civilization. This does not mean that we should endeavor to promote particular reforms through the educational system. We should, however, give to our children a vision of the possibilities which lie ahead and endeavor to enlist their loyalties and enthusiasms in the realization of the vision. Also our social institutions and practices, all of them, should be critically examined in the light of such a vision.

4

In *The Epic of America* James Truslow Adams contends that our chief contribution to the heritage of the race lies not in the field of science, or religion, or literature, or art but rather in the creation of what he calls the "American Dream"—a vision of a society in which the lot of the common man will be made easier and his life enriched and ennobled. If this vision has been a moving force in our history, as I believe it has, why should we not set ourselves the task of revitalizing and reconstituting it? This would seem to be the great need of our age, both in the realm of education and in the sphere of public life, because men must have something for which to live. Agnosticism, skepticism, or even experimentalism, unless the last is made flesh through the formulation of some positive social program, constitutes an extremely meager spiritual diet for any people. A small band of intellectuals, a queer breed of men at best, may be satisfied with such a spare ration, particularly if they lead the sheltered life common to their class; but the masses, I am sure, will always demand something more solid and substantial. Ordinary men and women crave a tangible purpose towards which to strive and which lends richness and dignity and meaning to life. I would consequently like to see our profession come to grips with the problem of creating a tradition that has roots in American soil, is in harmony with the spirit of the age, recognizes the facts of industrialism, appeals to the most profound impulses of our people, and takes into account the emergence of a world society.[1]

The ideal foundations on which we must build are easily discernible. Until recently the very word America has been synonymous throughout the world with democracy and symbolic to the oppressed classes of all lands of hope and opportunity. Child of the revolutionary ideas and impulses of the eighteenth century, the American nation became the embodiment of bold social experimentation and a champion of the power of environment to develop the capacities and redeem the souls of common men and women. And as her stature grew, her lengthening shadow reached to the four corners of the earth and everywhere impelled the human will to rebel against ancient wrongs. Here undoubtedly is the finest jewel in our heritage and the thing that is most worthy of preservation. If America should lose her honest devotion to democracy, or if she should lose her revolutionary temper, she will no longer be America. In that day, if it has not already arrived, her spirit will have fled and she will be known merely as the richest and most powerful of the nations. If America is not to be false to the promise of her youth, she must do more than simply perpetuate the democratic ideal of human relationships: she must make an intelligent and determined effort to fulfill it. The democracy of the past was the chance fruit of a strange conjunction of forces on the new continent; the democracy of the future can only be the intended offspring of the union of human reason, purpose, and will. The conscious and deliberate achievement of democracy under novel circumstances is the task of our generation.

Democracy of course should not be identified with political forms and functions—with the federal constitution, the popular election of officials, or the practice of universal suffrage. To think in such terms is to confuse the entire issue, as it has been confused in the minds of the masses for generations. The most genuine expression of democracy in the United States has little to do with our political institutions: it is a sentiment with respect to the moral equality of men: it is an aspiration towards a society in which this sentiment will find complete fulfillment. A society fashioned in harmony with the American democratic tradition would combat all forces tending to produce social distinctions and classes; repress every form of privilege and economic parasitism; manifest a tender regard for the weak, the ignorant, and the unfortunate; place the heavier and more onerous social burdens on the backs of the strong; glory in every triumph of man in his timeless urge to express himself and to make the world more habitable; exalt human labor of hand and brain as the creator of all wealth and culture; provide adequate material and spiritual rewards for every kind of socially useful work; strive for genuine equality of opportunity among all races, sects, and occupations; regard as paramount the abiding interests of the great masses of the people; direct the powers of government to the elevation and the refinement of the life of the common man; transform or destroy all conventions, institutions, and special groups inimical to the underlying principles of democracy; and finally be prepared as a last resort, in either the defense or the realization of this purpose, to follow the method of revolution. Although these ideals have never been realized or perhaps even fully accepted anywhere in the United States and have always had to struggle for existence with contrary forces, they nevertheless have authentic roots in the past. They are the values for which America has stood before the world during most of her history and with which the American people have loved best to associate their country. Their power and authority are clearly revealed in the fact that selfish interests, when grasping for some special privilege, commonly wheedle and sway the masses by repeating the words and kneeling before the emblems of the democratic heritage.

It is becoming increasingly clear, however, that this tradition, if its spirit is to survive, will have to be reconstituted in the light of the great social trends of the age in which we live. Our democratic heritage was largely a product of the frontier, free land, and a simple agrarian order. Today a new and strange and closely integrated industrial economy is rapidly sweeping over the world. Although some of us in our more sentimental moments talk wistfully of retiring into the more tranquil society of the past, we could scarcely induce many of our fellow citizens to accompany us. Even the most hostile critics of industrialism would like to take with them in their retirement a few such fruits of the machine as electricity, telephones, automobiles, modern plumbing, and various labor-saving devices, or at least be assured of an abundant supply of slaves or docile and inexpensive servants. But all such talk is the most idle chatter. For better or for worse we must take industrial civilization as an enduring fact: already we have become parasitic on its institutions and products. The hands of the clock cannot be turned back.

If we accept industrialism, as we must, we are then compelled to face without equivocation the most profound issue which this new order of society has raised and settle that issue in terms of the genius of our people—the issue of the control of the machine. In whose interests and for what purposes are the vast material riches, the unrivaled industrial equipment, and the science and technology of the nation to be used? In the light of our democratic tradition there can be but one answer to the question: all of these resources must be dedicated to the promotion of the welfare of the great masses of the people. Even the classes in our society that perpetually violate this principle are compelled by the force of public opinion to pay lip-service to it and to defend their actions in its terms. No body of men, however powerful, would dare openly to flout it. Since the opening of the century the great corporations have even found it necessary to establish publicity departments or to employ extremely able men as public relations counselors in order to persuade the populace that regardless of appearances they are lovers of democracy and devoted servants of the people. In this they have been remarkably successful, at least until the coming of the Great Depression. For during the past generation there have been few things in America that could not be bought at a price.

If the benefits of industrialism are to accrue fully to the people, this deception must be exposed. If the machine is to serve all, and serve all equally, it cannot be the property of the few. To ask these few to have regard for the common weal, particularly when under the competitive system they are forced always to think first of themselves or perish, is to put too great a strain on human nature. With the present concentration of economic power in the hands of a small class, a condition that is likely to get worse before it gets better, the survival or development of a society that could in any sense be called democratic is unthinkable. The hypocrisy which is so characteristic of our public life today is due primarily to our failure to acknowledge the fairly obvious fact that America is the scene of an irreconcilable conflict between two opposing forces. On the one side is the democratic tradition inherited from the past; on the other is a system of economic arrangements which increasingly partakes of the nature of industrial feudalism. Both of these forces cannot survive: one or the other must give way. Unless the democratic tradition is able to organize and conduct a successful attack on the economic system, its complete destruction is inevitable.

If democracy is to survive, it must seek a new economic foundation. Our traditional democracy rested upon small-scale production in both agriculture and industry and a rather general diffusion of the rights of property in capital and natural resources. The driving force at the root of this condition, as we have seen, was the frontier and free land. With the closing of the frontier, the exhaustion of free land, the growth of population, and the coming of large-scale production, the basis of ownership was transformed. If property rights are to be diffused in industrial society, natural resources and all important forms of capital will have to be collectively owned. Obviously every citizen cannot hold title to a mine, a factory, a railroad, a department store, or even a thoroughly mechanized farm. This clearly means that, if democracy is to survive in the United States, it must abandon its individualistic affiliations in the sphere of economics. What precise form a democratic society will take in the age of science and the machine, we cannot know with any assurance today. We must, however, insist on two things: first, that technology be released from the fetters and the domination of every type of special privilege; and, second, that the resulting system of production and distribution be made to serve directly the masses of the people. Within these limits, as I see it, our democratic tradition must of necessity evolve and gradually assume an essentially collectivistic pattern. The only conceivable alternative is the abandonment of the last vestige of democracy and the frank adoption of some modern form of feudalism.

NOTE

1. In the remainder of the argument I confine attention entirely to the domestic situation. I do this, not because I regard the question of international relations unimportant, but rather because of limitations of space. All I can say here is that any proper conception of the world society must accept the principle of the moral equality of races and nations.

5

The Rise of Scientific Curriculum-Making and Its Aftermath

Herbert M. Kliebard

When Boyd Bode published *Modern Educational Theories* in 1927, he took on what had already become the entrenched establishment of the curriculum world. With his trenchant criticism of Franklin Bobbitt in the chapter, "Curriculum Construction and Consensus of Opinion" and of W. W. Charters in the succeeding chapter, "Curriculum Making and the Method of Job Analysis," Bode was attacking not only the work of two men who had established themselves as the prototypes of the curriculum specialist, but the very foundations on which curriculum as a field of specialization had been based. Bode probably did not suspect, however, that the notion of careful pre-specification of educational objectives (with variations in terminology and technique) and the notion of activity analysis as the means toward their "discovery" (also with variations in terminology and technique) would become the foundations on which, almost half a century later, many books would be written, Ph.D.s awarded, careers established, and millions of dollars expended. Certainly Bode never dreamed that legislation embodying these principles would be enacted across the United States and that the very ideas he was attacking would become semi-official doctrine in federal and state agencies as well as in many educational institutions.

THE SCIENTIFIC CURRICULUM MAKING OF BOBBITT AND CHARTERS

Bobbitt and Charters lived in auspicious times. Mental discipline as a theoretical basis for the curriculum was almost dead by the early twentieth century. The bright flame of American Herbartianism, which had for a time captured the imagination of the educational world, was flickering. An educational ideology true to the times was needed, and nothing was more appropriate than scientific curriculum making. This doctrine, with its promise of precision and objectivity, had an immediate appeal. Certainly there was no reason why scientific principles applied to education would not meet with the same success as science applied to business in the form of scientific management. The general notion of applied

Reprinted by permission of Blackwell Publishers, from *Curriculum Theory Network*, Vol. 5, No. 1, 1975, pp. 27–38.

science, as well as the particular model of scientific arrangement, is in fact evident throughout the work of Bobbitt and Charters.

Of the two, Bobbitt was perhaps the first to strike this rich vein. As a young instructor in educational administration at the University of Chicago, he effectively drew the parallel between business techniques and education in a lengthy article in the *Twelfth Yearbook of the National Society for the Study of Education* (Bobbitt 1913). But Bobbitt, unlike other educators who turned to scientific management, was not content merely to apply certain management techniques to education, such as maximum utilization of the school plant; he provided the professional educators in the twentieth century with the concepts and metaphors—indeed, the very language—that were needed to create an aura of technical expertise without which the hegemony of professional educators could not be established. Science was not simply a tool with which to carve out exactitude in educational affairs generally and in the curriculum in particular; it was a means by which one could confer professional status and exclude the uninitiated. Even the term "curriculum specialist" implied a particular set of technical skills unavailable to the untrained. While the notion of science implies a certain aura of exclusiveness, Bobbitt was probably not explicitly aware of such a political use of his technical language. In his two major works, *The Curriculum* (1918) and *How to Make a Curriculum* (1924), as well as in numerous articles on the techniques of curriculum making, he seems simply to have believed that science had the key that idle speculation and even philosophy failed to provide.

Like Bobbitt, W. W. Charters was already a major leader in education by the time Bode's work was published. Charters had written *Methods of Teaching* in 1909 and *Teaching the Common Branches* in 1913, both popular books; but with *Curriculum Construction* in 1923, he established himself in the forefront of curriculum thinking. (In the preface to this book, Charters gives particular thanks to his "former colleague, B. H. Bode" for "his criticism of theoretical principles.") Like Bobbitt also, Charters approached the problems of curriculum from the perspective of functional efficiency. Through the method of activity analysis (or job analysis, as it was also called), Charters was able to apply professional expertise to the development of curricula in many diverse fields, including secretarial studies, library studies, pharmacy, and especially teacher education (with *The Commonwealth Teacher-Training Study* in 1929). Activity analysis was so universally applicable a technique of curriculum development that Charters was even able to use it to develop a curriculum for being a woman. As with other occupations, one simply had to analyze the particular activities that defined the role and then place these in relationship to the ideals that would control these activities. The training involved in performing the activities well would then become the curriculum (Charters 1921, 1925). Out of the work and thought of Bobbitt and Charters, as well as their contemporaries and disciples, arose a new rationale and a modus operandi for the curriculum field that were to prevail to the present day. So dominant did scientific curriculum making become that Bode's *Modern Educational Theories* stands as one of the few direct assaults on some of its principal tenets and certainly the most important.

PREPARING FOR ADULTHOOD

One of the most basic tenets of scientific curriculum making is a principle enunciated early in Bobbitt's *How to Make a Curriculum*: "Education is primarily for adult life, not for child life. Its fundamental responsibility is to prepare for the fifty years of adulthood, not for the twenty years of childhood and youth" (1924, p. 8). Education, in other words, consists in preparing to become an adult. There is probably no more crucial notion in the entire theory. Without it, there would be no point, for example, in such careful analysis of adult activities and their ultimate transformation into minute and explicit curricular objectives. Moreover, much curriculum policy, such as the strong emphasis on curriculum differentiation with its basis in predicting the probable destination of children as to their adult lives, rests squarely on education as preparation. If education is for what lies ahead, then it becomes of utmost importance to state with reasonable accuracy what that future holds. Bode's criticism is most telling in making the distinction between a prediction by, for example, an astronomer as to the curve of a comet and an educator constructing a future ideal in schooling. Curriculum making, in other words, is a form of utopian thinking, not of crystal-ball gazing. But Dewey, whom Bode cites favorably in this context, had gone even further in attacking the notion of preparation. In "My Pedagogic Creed," Dewey took pains to define education as "a process of living and not a preparation for future living" (1929, p. 292), and he undertook specifically in *Democracy and Education* to point up other deficiencies in the idea. To think of children as merely getting ready for a remote and obscure world, Dewey thought, is to remove them as social members of the community. "They are looked upon as candidates," he said; "they are placed on the waiting list" (1916, p. 63). Furthermore, since children are not directed and stimulated by what is so remote in time, the educator must introduce, on a large scale, extrinsic rewards and punishments. Bode's criticism of education as preparation rests largely on the assumption that it would lead to a social status quo rather than social improvement. While Dewey would no doubt agree, his criticism is more far-reaching and devastating. He considered not only its social significance but its impact on the child and the pedagogical process itself.

A curious sidelight to the importance of education as preparation in scientific curriculum making is Bobbitt's own developing ambivalence toward the idea. In setting forth his curriculum theory in the epic *Twenty-Sixth Yearbook of the National Society for the Study of Education,* Bobbitt says, "Education is not primarily to prepare for life at some future time. Quite the reverse; it purposes to hold high the current living. . . . In a very true sense, life cannot be 'prepared for.' It can only be lived" (1926, p. 43). Later, when asked to write his summary theory of curriculum, Bobbitt declared, "While there are general guiding principles that enable parents and teachers to foresee in advance the long general course that is normally run, yet they cannot foresee or foreknow the specific and concrete details of the course that is to be actualized" (1934, p. 4). In these passages, he sounds more like Kilpatrick than himself. But if Bobbitt was ambivalent, even self-contradictory, on the subject of education as preparation, his disciples and present intellectual heirs are not. If anything is ingrained in curriculum thinking today, it is the notion that it is the job of curriculum planners to anticipate the exact skills, knowledge, and—to use today's most fashionable term—"competencies" that will stand one in good stead at an imagined point in the future. These predictions about what one will need in the future become the bases of curriculum planning.

Specificity of Objectives

A concomitant of the emphasis on preparation is the insistence that the end products of the curriculum be stated with great particularity. Vague Delphic prophecies simply won't do. "'Ability to care for one's health' . . ." declared Bobbitt, "is too general to be useful. It must be reduced to particularity: ability to manage the ventilation of one's sleeping room, ability to protect one's self against micro-organisms, ability to care for the teeth, and so on" (1924, p. 32). If science is to be identified with exactitude, then scientific curriculum making must demonstrate its elevated status through the precision with which objectives are stated. It is at this point that Bode's criticism is both astute and telling. He points out, for example, that under the guise of scientific objectivity, Bobbitt inserts a submerged ideology. Scientific objectivity, it turns out, becomes a way of preserving the tried and true values of the society as well as making explicit the prevailing practical skills of the contemporary world.

Bode, of course, would not object to a philosophy of education governing curriculum; his objection is that the values of the scientific curriculum makers are disguised and covert. Furthermore, even a cursory examination of Bobbitt's most famous list of objectives would indicate wide latitude in the degree of specificity with which the objectives are stated. Alongside "the ability to keep one's emotional serenity, in the face of circumstances however trying" (1924, p. 25), "an attitude and desire of obedience to the immutable and eternal laws which appear to exist in the nature of things," and "confidence in the beneficence of these laws" (1924, p. 26), we find "ability to read and interpret facts expressed by commonly used types of graphs, diagrams, and statistical tables" (1924, p. 12), as well as "ability to care properly for the feet" (1924, p. 14). Although the injunction to be specific and explicit is unqualified, there seems to be some difficulty in carrying it out simply as a practical matter. In considering the efficient functioning of the human body, for example, we have no guidance as to whether to begin with the leg, the foot, the toe, or the toenail. The same problem would arise if we were dealing with the ability to swing a hammer or the ability to solve quadratic equations. The scientific curriculum makers' allegiance to specificity was allied to Thorndike's conception of the mind as consisting of multitudinous separate and individual functions (1901, p. 249), whereas Bode seems committed to a much broader conception of thought processes as well as a more optimistic view of transfer of training.

Making a Choice

If the practical problem of specificity were somehow resolved, perhaps by extending the list of objectives into the thousands or the hundreds of thousands, another issue would become even more apparent: how would we decide, objectively of course, which objectives to keep and which to leave out? As Bode indicates, one of Bobbitt's solutions was to throw the matter open to a vote or at least to a panel. In his famous Los Angeles study, Bobbitt asserted that his list of objectives "represent[ed] the practically unanimous judgment of some twenty-seven hundred well-trained and experienced adults" (1924, p. 10), a claim about which Bode is clearly skeptical. As Bode points out, the twelve hundred Los Angeles teachers, who were charged with reviewing the list drawn up by the fifteen hundred graduate students at the University of Chicago, were in a dilemma. All of the objectives listed unquestionably represented desirable traits and skills, from "keeping razor in order" (Bobbitt 1922, p. 21) to "ability to tell interesting stories interestingly—and many of them" (p. 26).

The wide agreement, Bode suspects, was probably achieved by a combination of specificity when practical and clearly desirable skills were involved and vagueness or ambiguity when value issues were broached. Inspection of Bobbitt's list of objectives indicates that Bode is essentially correct, thereby accounting in part for the obvious discrepancies in the level of specificity with which the objectives are stated as well as the near unanimity of agreement among twenty-seven hundred adult human beings. State legislators, educators, and the general public frequently find themselves in the same position today when they are asked to give their assent to such educational goals as "self-realization" and "mental health." One can hardly be against them.

A STANDARD FOR LIVING

Although Bode's criticism of the method of consensus is certainly convincing, he considers only indirectly another of Bobbitt's ways of dealing with the seemingly limitless scope of a curriculum defined by the full range of human activity. While the task of the "curriculum discoverer" did involve, according to Bobbitt, a full catalog of the activities of mankind, Bobbitt was careful to indicate that much of what has to be learned is acquired by "undirected experience." "*The curriculum of the directed training*," Bobbitt insisted, "*is to be discovered in the shortcomings of individuals after they have had all that can be given by the undirected training*" (1918, p. 45, original emphasis). Bobbitt's understanding of "shortcomings," actually, is quite similar to the contemporary notion of "needs." A standard is set, a norm; and the curriculum consists of the ways of treating deviations from the standard. Thus the curriculum seems cut down to manageable proportions without resort to the method of consensus. (It is a deceptively simple solution.) The fundamental issue, however, is not whether the list of objectives is derived from this or that method: more basic is the question of whether objectives ought to be prespecified at all. One might argue, therefore, that Bode, in skillfully demolishing the method of consensus, did not quite strike the jugular vein of scientific curriculum making. The central question is whether the curriculum should be a blueprint for what people should be like, not how the blueprint is drawn.

But even if one were to concede prespecification of objectives in such areas as arithmetic, grammar, and spelling, how far could one go in justifying the "social shortcomings" of which Bobbitt speaks (1918, p. 50)? As many of Bobbitt's objectives imply, there was literally no activity of mankind—social, intellectual, or practical—that was not potentially, at least, a curricular objective. Bode correctly identified Herbert Spencer as having anticipated the trend toward specificity in stating objectives, but of at least equal importance is Spencer's role in identifying the scope of the school curriculum with life itself. Spencer, like Bobbitt and Charters, considered the best curriculum to be the one that demonstrated the highest utility. Spencer, it should be remembered, asked the question, "What knowledge is of most worth?," not merely, "What shall the schools teach?" In a subtle way, then, he was reconstructing a basic curriculum question. To the scientific curriculum makers, the two questions were essentially the same; thus by posing their question in this way, scientific curriculum makers were determining the kind of answer that could be given. The answer to the scientific curriculum maker is likely to be phrased in terms of high survival value and functional utility rather than in terms of intellectual virtues. In this sense, the curriculum became the ultimate survival kit for the modern world. For example, in the state of Oregon today, certain districts have instituted requirements for high school graduation of such "survival" skills as listing birth-control methods in order of effectiveness, or demonstrating ability to officiate at two different sports and perform two basic dance steps (*Newsweek*, January 25, 1975, p. 69). Any sense of a distinctive function for the schools is lost.

Limitations of the School

Two serious but often unexamined questions are raised by such a conception of the school curriculum. The first relates to the extent to which the school as one institution of society can as a purely practical matter devote itself to the full range of human activity that man engages in. A second question, perhaps even more fundamental than the first, is whether all activity can be reduced to particular components.

From the days of the *Cardinal Principles* report to the present, the conventional way to begin the process of curriculum development has been to agree on a set of broad goals which in fact represents a categorization of human activity generally. The next step, of course, is to "operationalize" these goals by translating them into numerous minute and specific objectives—in effect, creating a catalog of human activity. Surely if Charters were able to identify the activities that constitute being a secretary or a librarian, it was only a step further to identify all the other activities of mankind. In this way the most urgent of these activities may be identified (e.g., earning a living) and the most pressing social problems addressed (e.g., drug addiction).

The missing ingredient in all this is some attention to the nature of the school. If there is one serious omission in Bode's analysis, it is the failure to recognize the limitations of the institution of schooling. The knowledge that is of the most worth may not be the kind of knowledge that can be transmitted in a school context. The place of the school in the social structure, the makeup of its inhabitants, and the characteristic activities that take place within its boundaries must be considered along with the power of schooling as we know it to produce fundamental and direct changes in human attitudes and behavior. Hence if curriculum makers do not temper the question of what is most important to know with the question of what schools can accomplish, their claims for programs designed to reduce crime, improve human relations, prevent drunken driving, ensure economic independence, or remove sex inhibitions are unreliable.

Analyzing Human Activity

Furthermore, while it may be true that a limited number of human activities may be anticipated and therefore practiced in advance, the extension of the method of job analysis from the limited realm of routine and replicative behavior into the full universe of human activity represents perhaps the most fundamental fallacy in the whole scientific curriculum-making movement. The source of this assumption, as is the case with other elements of scientific curriculum making, is the example of industry. Just as the global and complex process of building an automobile can be broken down into a series of minute and simple operations, so presumably can the activities of a mother or a teacher. But we do not learn language, for example, by anticipating all of the sentences we will utter in our adult lives and then rehearsing them as part of our preparation to become adults. Instead, we learn or assimilate or perhaps even inherit the governing principles of language that permit us to create or invent sentences that we have never before heard expressed. Similarly, in mathematics we do not scientifically catalog all of the mathematical operations we will perform as adults as a direct rehearsal for the performance of those mathematical operations.

Here Bode's criticism of job analysis as the universal technique of curriculum making is particularly cogent. The analogy between definite operations which imply simply replicative activity and activities that involve, let us say, judgment, simply will not hold. As he puts it, friendliness, courtesy, and honesty "are not reducible to 'definite operations'" (Bode 1927, p. 109). The process of educating a teacher to conduct himself or herself wisely and judiciously in the classroom is not, as current programs of teacher training so often imply, a process of first anticipating the particular situations that will arise in the classroom and then directing the teachers to conduct themselves in a particular way relative to these specific situations. Rather, teacher education can involve the examination, analysis, and adaptation of some broad principles which at some unknown point in the future and in some unanticipated circumstances may provide a guide to keen judgment and wise action.

SCIENTIFIC CURRICULUM MAKING IN TEACHER EDUCATION

Bode's astute criticism of the scientific curriculum makers notwithstanding, it should be clear to anyone familiar with the current state of the art in the curriculum world that the scientific curriculum movement, with few adaptations and modifications, has been triumphant. It is true that behaviorism has provided a few refinements of language in stating objectives, and certain so-called academic subjects such as mathematics and science have perhaps more respectability than in the days of Bobbitt and Charters. But the key ingredients and analogies remain the same. While this modern version of scientific curriculum making is well established in virtually all sectors of the curriculum world, it exists, not surprisingly, in its most virulent form in the area of teacher education. The vogue movements which go under the names of competency-based teacher education (CBTE) and performance-based teacher education (PBTE) are prime examples of what has evolved from the basic principles enunciated by Bobbitt and Charters. Charters himself helped direct a major study begun in 1925 which had all the earmarks of the PBTE (or CBTE) ideology.

The Commonwealth Teacher-Training Study

As is the case with the current programs, the *Commonwealth Teacher-Training Study* was to be based on scientific research into the teaching process as opposed to mere speculation and tradition. As a first step, Charters and Waples "ascertained the traits that characterize excellent teachers" (1929, p. 4). Adapting the consensus approach, the investigators used two methods: analyzing the professional literature and interviewing "expert judges." Working from a list of eighty-three traits, ranging alphabetically from Accuracy through Foresight and Magnetism all the way to Wittiness (pp. 56–61), "translators" were given the task of interpreting statements made in writing or in the interviews. Thus, "knows how to meet people" could become translated into the traits, "adaptability" or "approachability." Reliability among the translators was determined by applying the Spearman prophecy formula. Finally, after some of the original traits of teachers were telescoped, scientifically determined lists were prepared indicating that senior high school teachers should be characterized by twenty-six traits including Good Taste and Propriety, junior high school teachers by Conventionality (morality) and Open-mindedness, and so on.

Next, in an adaptation of the job analysis technique, the investigators collected a master list of 1,001 teacher activities. Perhaps one of these activities is worth quoting in its entirety:

788. Securing cordial relations with superintendent
Maintaining cordial relations with superintendent. This involves being loyal to and respecting the superintendent. Becoming acquainted with superintendent and working in harmony with him. Performing friendly acts for superintendent; remembering superintendent at Christmas; making designs and drawings for superintendent; making lamp shades for superintendent's wife. [Charters and Waples 1929, p. 423]

Thus, after three years of research by trained investigators and a grant of $42,000 from the Commonwealth Fund, was a blow dealt to fuzzy thinking in teacher education and a major stride taken in the direction of a scientifically determined teacher-education curriculum.

THE CONTEMPORARY AFTERMATH

One of the most persistent and puzzling questions in this, the aftermath of the scientific curriculum-making movement, is why we retain, even revere, the techniques and assumptions we have inherited from Bobbitt and Charters, at the same time as we reject, implicitly at least, the actual outcomes of their research. Few people read Bobbitt's famous study, *Curriculum-Making in Los Angeles*, or his magnum opus, *How to Make a Curriculum*, or have even heard of Charters and Waples's *Commonwealth Teacher-Training Study*. If they did read these works, the most likely reaction would be one of amusement. And yet we pursue with sober dedication the techniques on which these works are based. Admittedly, performance-based teacher education may just be a slogan system resting only on a foundation of high-sounding rhetoric and pious promises and covered with a gloss of false novelty; but if it means anything, it surely implies that one can identify the particular components of teaching activity that make for good teachers and that these characteristics (Charters would call them traits) or behaviors (Charters would call them activities) can form the basis of a program of teacher training. Research takes the form of identifying the particular components of teaching that will ensure success. While there seems to be some caution in stating the characteristics and behaviors with the same degree of conviction as Bobbitt and Charters did, an abiding faith in the efficacy of the approach remains. The persistence of this faith in the face of a record of over a half century of failure is a mystery that probably even Bode could not fathom.

Is Teaching a Technology?

At the heart of some of our most fundamental problems in the field of curriculum and of teacher education as well is the question of whether teaching is a technology by which carefully fashioned products in the form of learning or behavior are made. These products would have to be designed with the exactitude and specificity that Bobbitt and Charters called for. Teaching would be the application of standardized means by which predictable results would be achieved, and curriculum development the specification of the end-products and the rules for their efficient manufacture. Teacher education, in turn, would be the process by which persons are transformed into efficient manufacturers. The research evidence that presumably would support such an analogy between the teaching and the manufacturing process, however, has been disappointing to the proponents. For example, a recent thorough examination of the research basis for performance-based teacher education led to the conclusion that eleven process variables previously identified as "promising"—such as "clarity," "variability," and "enthusiasm"—were indeed notably unpromising, leading the authors to conclude that "an empirical basis for performance-based teacher education does not exist" (Heath and Nielson 1974, p. 475). Moreover, pessimism about the ultimate success of the approach was not based simply on flaws in statistical analysis or research design. The more fundamental problem was the framework in which such research was cast—a framework which, by the way, has held sway since the days of Bobbitt, Charters, and the scientific curriculum-making movement.

Bode as Prophet

The point of all this is not simply that Bobbitt, Charters, and their likeminded contemporaries were mistaken in their faith in a given approach; the age in which they lived was one where optimism about the power of science to solve a multitude of human and social problems was near its peak. If they were naive or mistaken, one can hardly blame them. What is almost unforgivable, however, is that the half century since the zenith of their influence has produced little more by way of sophistication and refinement. With few exceptions, Bode's criticism of 1927 would carry as much force today were it directed against the present-day heirs of scientific curriculum making.

Particularly disappointing are the precipitous efforts to convert highly tentative and limited research findings into immediate prescriptions. This may be a function of the large constituency of teachers and school administrators who want immediate and concrete answers to such global questions as What is a good teacher? and What is a good curriculum? Part of the problem, undoubtedly, with the era of the scientific curriculum makers and with ours is the failure to recognize the complexity of the phenomena with which we deal. There is the same confusion between science and desert empiricism, the same naiveté about the nature of the teaching process, the same neglect of conceptual analysis. To be critical of scientific curriculum making, as Bode was, is not to be critical of science or even the importance of scientific inquiry into educational processes: it is to be critical of a simplistic and vulgar scientism. Its persistence is a source of embarrassment.

REFERENCES

Bobbitt, Franklin. "Some General Principles of Management Applied to the Problems of City-School Systems." In *The Supervision of City Schools. Twelfth Yearbook of the National Society for the Study of Education,* Part 1, pp. 7–96. Bloomington, Ill.: Public School Publishing Co., 1913.

———. *The Curriculum.* Boston: Houghton Mifflin, 1918.

———. *Curriculum-making in Los Angeles.* Supplementary Educational Monographs, no. 20. Chicago: University of Chicago Press, 1922.

———. *How to Make a Curriculum.* Boston: Houghton Mifflin, 1924.

———. "The Orientation of the Curriculum-maker." In *The Foundations and Technique of Curriculum-construction. Twenty-Sixth Yearbook of the National Society for the Study of Education,* Part 2, pp. 41–55. Bloomington, Ill.: Public School Publishing Co., 1926.

———. "A Summary Theory of the Curriculum." *Society for Curriculum Study News Bulletin* 5 (January 12, 1934): 2–4.

Bode, Boyd H. *Modern Educational Theories.* New York: Macmillan, 1927.

Charters, Werrett W. *Methods of Teaching: Developed from a Functional Standpoint.* Chicago: Row, Peterson & Co., 1909.

———. *Teaching the Common Branches.* Boston: Houghton Mifflin, 1913.

———. "The Reorganization of Women's Education." *Educational Review* 62 (October 1921): 224–231.

———. *Curriculum Construction.* New York: Macmillan, 1923.

———. "Curriculum for Women." In *Proceedings of the High School Conference.* Urbana, Ill.: University of Illinois, 1925.

Charters, Werrett W., and Waples, Douglas. *The Commonwealth Teacher-training Study.* Chicago: University of Chicago Press, 1929.

Dewey, John. *Democracy and Education: An Introduction to the Philosophy of Education.* New York: Macmillan, 1916.

———. "My Pedagogic Creed." *Journal of the National Education Association* 18, no. 9 (December 1929): 291–295.

Heath, Robert W., and Nielson, Mark A. "The Research Basis for Performance-based Teacher Education." *Review of Educational Research* 44, no. 4 (Fall 1974): 463–484.

National Education Association Commission on the Reorganization of Secondary Education. *Cardinal Principles of Secondary Education: A Report.* Washington: Government Printing Office, 1918.

Spencer, Herbert. "What Knowledge Is of Most Worth?" In *Education: Intellectual, Moral and Physical,* pp. 1–96. New York: D. Appleton and Co., 1860.

"Survival Test." *Newsweek,* January 25, 1975, p. 69.

Thorndike, E. L., and Woodworth, R. S. "The Influence of Improvement in One Mental Function upon the Efficiency of Other Functions," Part 1. *Psychological Review* 8, no. 3 (May 1901): 247–261.

II

CURRICULUM AT EDUCATION'S CENTER STAGE

THE READINGS IN THIS PART OF THE BOOK LEAD INTO and reflect the reform efforts of the 1950s and 1960s. This era witnessed unprecedented federal and private support for curriculum development projects. The life cycle of these projects alternated between crisis and optimism. The crisis, set against the backdrop of Cold War politics, was a crisis of national security and academic rigor. Mathematics, science, and foreign language curricula were perceived as directly relevant to national defense, and thus the first to receive attention. While these school subjects were widely judged deficient, the period's optimism affirmed the possibilities of redemption. In particular, this faith stemmed from the belief that subject matter experts, armed with specialized knowledge and modern techniques, could set American schools back on track. But the era ended in controversy all the same. Its political aftermath is symbolized by what eventually came to be an open attack on the National Science Foundation for its role in the development of an elementary social studies curriculum, "Man: A Course of Study." Although this program had been designed to teach processes and skills, its content came to be seen as a repudiation of mainstream American values (Schaffarzick, 1979). Scholarly rather than political controversy came from within academe, symbolized by Joseph Schwab's pronouncement in 1969 that for all practical purposes, the curriculum field had reached a moribund state.

We begin this section with Ralph Tyler's *Basic Principles of Curriculum and Instruction*, which is far from the turmoil of the late 1960s. Tyler's slim book, a mere 128 pages cover to cover, was published in 1949. At that time it served as both a precursor to national reform and a culmination of Progressive educational thought. In particular, Tyler's rationale reaches back to the work of Franklin Bobbitt and others who sought to bring the field into the modern, scientific age. Their strategy for doing so was to develop curricula using a means-ends model. Tyler specifically organized the process around four questions: What are the purposes of an educational program? What experiences will further these purposes? How shall the program be organized? And, how shall it be evaluated?

These questions represent four design elements, the first of which Tyler gives special emphasis. "All aspects of the educational program," he writes, "are really means to accomplish basic educational purposes" (this volume). Tyler's book does not venture to suggest specific aims, but almost half of its pages are devoted to describing sources of information that support the selection of aims. Three primary sources are discussed early on. The first is the study of learners, including their social and psychological needs. The second source includes studies of contemporary life to help identify "critical knowledge" and aid in the transfer of training. The third source of information includes suggestions from subject matter specialists. Tyler cites the Committee of Ten as an example, but not as an exemplar, of using subject matter specialists to identify educational objectives. This committee was formed in 1892 by the National Education Association, and it was charged with the task of recommending standards for secondary education. The committee organized its work around particular subjects such as geography, mathematics, and Latin. In this sense, subject matter expertise was foregrounded. However, more recent scholars have argued that the Committee of Ten represented a perspective that included both essentialist and Progressive thinking (see, for example, Kliebard, 2002; Bohan, 2003).

With or without historical precedent, subject matter specialists played a key role in the national reform efforts of the 1950s and 1960s. John I. Goodlad makes this point in the pages we have extracted from his book, *School Curriculum Reform in the United States*. Goodlad's aim is to survey and critique the then-current national reform projects "from the viewpoint of a curriculum generalist" (this volume). The reform movement, according to Goodlad, had already taken on several distinctive characteristics. They included: (1) the financial support of private foundations and federal agencies; (2) the widespread involvement of discipline-based scholars; (3) the affiliation of projects with national organizations such as the American Mathematical Society and the American Association for the Advancement of Science; (4) the focus of projects on subject-centered curriculum; and 5. their top-down approach to curriculum planning.

Goodlad describes sixteen "illustrative projects" in subject areas ranging from social studies and the English language arts to mathematics and science. We have extracted four projects to represent high school mathematics, high school physics, elementary school mathematics, and elementary school science. Following these descriptions is a "potpourri" section that briefly identifies related trends. The arts are noted in this potpourri section largely for their absence, albeit they would eventually join the reform movement in their own time and on their own terms. Two other trends mentioned were less conspicuous at the time, at least to the discipline-based scholars who had initiated the reform projects. These trends focus on reorganizing schools to achieve more "cooperative teaching arrangements" and recognizing issues of student diversity.

While these trends are mentioned largely as an afterthought, Goodlad recognized them as perennial concerns. Specifically, the movement's subject-centered approach generally assumed the value of academic content and the ability of students to learn that content. These assumptions take for granted and thus provide little justification for answering two of the most fundamental questions in curriculum planning: What determines content worth learning, and how should that content be taught? Furthermore, Goodlad situates the Achilles heel of national curriculum reform within the historical context of the movement itself, arguing that its subject-centered approach should be viewed as a reaction to the earlier trends introduced in Part I of this volume. Dewey (1938), for example, had argued that content as conceived by subject matter experts was likely to be inappropriate if not outright harmful to children. Thus, Goodlad saw this tension in terms of a cycle. In his words, "To the extent that this reaction to child-centered and society-oriented theories is itself perceived to be an overemphasis on subject matter in determining curricular ends and means, today's movement already is breeding tomorrow's counter-reaction" (this volume).

Both Tyler's rationale and Goodlad's critique of national reform serve to underscore questions of educational purpose, and doing so sets the stage for the next pair of readings. These readings represent the great objectives debate. By the late 1960s, this debate had come to focus not on whether specific objectives should be used in curriculum planning, but on how objectives should be used, the form they should take, and the functions they should be expected to serve. The dominant camp again worked from a means-ends perspective that required curriculum developers to clearly state the objectives of a program prior to deciding its content or organization. Proponents of this approach, such as W. James Popham and others (Mager, 1962), argued that prespecified, clearly stated, and measurable objectives are essential to curriculum planning for at least two reasons. First, educators without such objectives would not know the outcomes they seek to realize, and thus have little basis for deciding how to select or organize classroom activities. Second, without objectives, an evaluator would not know what to look for in determining a program's success or failure. Under the influence of this logic, thousands of American teachers learned to write behavioral objectives in the 1970s using standardized and tightly specified formats.

A dissenting position to the objectives movement is represented by Elliot W. Eisner's article, "Educational Objectives: Help or Hindrance?" Eisner questioned both the practicality of prespecified objectives and the underlying assumptions on which they are based. On the practical side, he saw two problems. First, the potential outcomes of instruction are usually so numerous that it would be difficult to anticipate all of these objectives with a high degree of specificity. Second, the objectives-first sequence does not seem to be borne out in practice. That is, while teachers often begin with explicit aims, they also allow the selection of content and activities to inform and modify aims as instructional activities unfold in the classroom. To put this another way, Eisner argued that the rationality of teaching is more dynamic, more interactive, and less mechanistic than the proponents of behavioral objectives had assumed. Moreover, Eisner asserts that evaluators have confused objectives with standards. Standards can be applied in a fairly routine manner, but using objectives as criteria for assessment always entails an element of judgment on the part of the evaluator.

A related criticism was that the objectives movement jumped too quickly from aims to outcomes, thereby bypassing practice altogether. This concern made Philip W. Jackson's book, *Life in Classrooms*, particularly distinctive. Jackson did not vault over classrooms, but jumped right into them. In the brief excerpts we have taken from his book, Jackson offers a number of arguments for why the daily routines of practice should be of paramount concern for those interested in school curriculum. These routines are often overshadowed because they are commonplace, repetitive, and ordinary. Herein we find an interesting paradox; if Jackson is right, practice is ignored for the very reasons that it is important. Classroom routines have an enduring influence specifically because they are commonplace, repetitive, and ordinary. In addition, Jackson argues that these routines are more than simply ways of delivering subject matter or acquiring academic skills. Rather, "the daily grind" itself teaches a hidden curriculum of unspoken expectations, and these expectations are what most often determine a student's school success or failure. If researchers or evaluators were to examine an educational program solely on the basis of its stated objectives, the hidden curriculum would in all likelihood remain just that—hidden.

The final reading in this section is Joseph J. Schwab's article, "The Practical: A Language for Curriculum." It is the first of his four articles published between 1970 and 1983 in which Schwab examines a range of issues related to developments within the field and to "the practical arts" of curriculum deliberation. We have included the first of these essays in our collection partly because of its broad scope. It is an essay that can be viewed in several ways: as a critique of the field at large; as an effort to reframe the relationship between theory and practice; and as a call for problem-based, collaborative forms of curriculum development. For its time, the article also reflects a heightened level of self-consciousness about the field's past, present, and future trends.

Schwab's place in curriculum history and his overall contributions to the field are two questions on which scholars currently disagree. Jackson (1992), for example, views Schwab's work as moving away from systematic approaches as conceived in the past, but still offering a version of the dominant perspective that had already been well established in the work of people such as Bobbitt and Tyler. In this view, Schwab was working with variations on the theme. Others, such as William Reid (1993), argue that Schwab's work be placed in a category by itself, as an alternative to the dominant perspective rather than as a modified version of earlier approaches. Nothing inherent in systematic methods (i.e., Bobbitt's approach) would seem to automatically exclude the forms of deliberation and the practical arts on which Schwab focused his work. Yet, as Reid argues, these are precisely the aspects of curriculum development on which earlier traditions of scholarship provide little if any guidance.

REFERENCES

Dewey, John. (1938). *Experience and Education*. New York: Collier Books.

Jackson, J.W. (1992). "Conceptions of Curriculum and Curriculum Specialists." In P.W. Jackson (Ed.), Handbook of Research on Curriculum (pp. 3–40). New York: Macmillan.

Mager, R.F. (1962). *Preparing Instructional Objectives*. Palo Alto, CA: Fearon.

Reid, W.A. (1993). "Does Schwab Improve on Tyler? A Response to Jackson." *Journal of Curriculum Studies*, 25, 499–510.

Schaffarzick, J. (1979). "Federal Curriculum Reform: A Crucible for Value Conflict." In J. Schaffarzick and G. Sykes (Eds.), *Value Conflicts and Curriculum Issues* (pp. 1–24). Berkeley, CA: McCutchan.

6

Basic Principles of Curriculum and Instruction

INTRODUCTION

This small book attempts to explain a rationale for viewing, analyzing and interpreting the curriculum and instructional program of an educational institution. It is not a textbook, for it does not provide comprehensive guidance and readings for a course. It is not a manual for curriculum construction since it does not describe and outline in detail the steps to be taken by a given school or college that seeks to build a curriculum. This book outlines one way of viewing an instructional program as a functioning instrument of education. The student is encouraged to examine other rationales and to develop his own conception of the elements and relationships involved in an effective curriculum.

The rationale developed here begins with identifying four fundamental questions which must be answered in developing any curriculum and plan of instruction. These are:

1. What educational purposes should the school seek to attain?
2. What educational experiences can be provided that are likely to attain these purposes?
3. How can these educational experiences be effectively organized?
4. How can we determine whether these purposes are being attained?

This book suggests methods for studying these questions. No attempt is made to answer these questions since the answers will vary to some extent from one level of education to another and from one school to another. Instead of answering the questions, an explanation is given of procedures by which these questions can be answered. This constitutes a rationale by which to examine problems of curriculum and instruction.

1. WHAT EDUCATIONAL PURPOSES SHOULD THE SCHOOL SEEK TO ATTAIN?

Many educational programs do not have clearly defined purposes. In some cases one may ask a teacher of science, of English, of social studies, or of some other subject what

From Ralph W. Tyler, *Basic Principles of Curriculum and Instruction*. Chicago: University of Chicago Press, 1949: pp. 1–7, 16–19, 25–33. Reprinted by permission.

objectives are being aimed at and get no satisfactory reply. The teacher may say in effect that he aims to develop a well-educated person and that he is teaching English or social studies or some other subject because it is essential to a well-rounded education. No doubt some excellent educational work is being done by artistic teachers who do not have a clear conception of goals but do have an intuitive sense of what is good teaching, what materials are significant, what topics are worth dealing with and how to present material and develop topics effectively with students. Nevertheless, if an educational program is to be planned and if efforts for continued improvement are to be made, it is very necessary to have some conception of the goals that are being aimed at. These educational objectives become the criteria by which materials are selected, content is outlined, instructional procedures are developed and tests and examinations are prepared. All aspects of the educational program are really means to accomplish basic educational purposes. Hence, if we are to study an educational program systematically and intelligently we must first be sure as to the educational objectives aimed at.

But how are objectives obtained? Since they are consciously willed goals, that is, ends that are desired by the school staff, are they not simply matters of personal preference of individuals or groups? Is there any place for a systematic attack upon the problem of what objectives to seek?

It is certainly true that in the final analysis objectives are matters of choice, and they must therefore be the considered value judgments of those responsible for the school. A comprehensive philosophy of education is necessary to guide in making these judgments. And, in addition, certain kinds of information and knowledge provide a more intelligent basis for applying the philosophy in making decisions about objectives. If these facts are available to those making decisions, the probability is increased that judgments about objectives will be wise and that the school goals will have greater significance and greater validity. For this reason, a large part of the so-called scientific study of the curriculum during the past thirty years has concerned itself with investigations that might provide a more adequate basis for selecting objectives wisely. The technical literature of the curriculum field includes hundreds of studies that collected information useful to curriculum groups in selecting objectives.

Accepting the principle that investigations can be made which will provide information and knowledge useful in deciding about objectives, the question is then raised what sources can be used for getting information that will be helpful in this way. A good deal of controversy goes on between essentialists and progressives, between subject specialists and child psychologists, between this group and that school group over the question of the basic source from which objectives can be derived. The progressive emphasizes the importance of studying the child to find out what kinds of interests he has, what problems he encounters, what purposes he has in mind. The progressive sees this information as providing the basic source for selecting objectives. The essentialist, on the other hand, is impressed by the large body of knowledge collected over many thousands of years, the so-called cultural heritage, and emphasizes this as the primary source for deriving objectives. The essentialist views objectives as essentially the basic learnings selected from the vast cultural heritage of the past.

Many sociologists and others concerned with the pressing problems of contemporary society see in an analysis of contemporary society the basic information from which objectives can be derived. They view the school as the agency for helping young people to deal effectively with the critical problems of contemporary life. If they can determine what these contemporary problems are then the objectives of the school are to provide those knowledges, skills, attitudes, and the like that will help people to deal intelligently with these contemporary problems. On the other hand, the educational philosophers recognize that there are basic values in life, largely transmitted from one generation to another by means of education. They see the school as aiming essentially at the transmission of the basic values derived by comprehensive philosophic study and hence see in educational philosophy the basic source from which objectives can be derived.

The point of view taken in this course is that no single source of information is adequate to provide a basis for wise and comprehensive decisions about the objectives of the school. Each of these sources has certain values to commend it. Each source should be given some consideration in planning any comprehensive curriculum program. Hence, we shall turn to each of the sources in turn to consider briefly what kinds of information can be obtained from the source and how this information may suggest significant educational objectives.

Studies of the Learners Themselves as a Source of Educational Objectives

Education is a process of changing the behavior patterns of people. This is using behavior in the broad sense to include thinking and feeling as well as overt action. When education is viewed in this way, it is clear that educational objectives, then, represent the kinds of changes in behavior that an educational institution seeks to bring about in its students. A study of the learners themselves would seek to identify needed changes in behavior patterns of the students which the educational institution should seek to produce.

An investigation of children in the elementary school in a certain community may reveal dietary deficiency and inadequate physical condition. These facts may suggest objectives in health education and in social studies but they suggest objectives only when viewed in terms of some conception of normal or desirable physical condition. In a society which takes dietary deficiencies for granted, there would be little likelihood of inferring any educational objectives from such data. Correspondingly, studies of adolescence during the depression indicated that a considerable number were greatly perturbed over the possibility that they would be unable to find work upon graduation. This does not automatically suggest the need for vocational guidance or occupational preparation. Studies of the learner suggest educational objectives only when the information about the learner is compared with some desirable standards, some conception of acceptable norms, so that the difference between the present condition of the learner and the acceptable norm can be identified. This difference or gap is what is generally referred to as a need.

There is another sense in which the term "need" is used in the psychological writings of Prescott, Murray, and others. They view a human being as a dynamic organism, an energy system normally in equilibrium between internal forces produced by the energy of the oxidation of food and external conditions. To keep the system in equilibrium it is necessary that certain "needs" be met. That is, certain tensions are produced which result in disequilibrium unless these tensions are relieved. In this sense every organism is continually meeting its needs, that is, reacting in such a way as to relieve these forces that bring about imbalance. In these terms one of the problems of education is to channel the means by which these needs are met so that the resulting behavior is socially acceptable, yet at the same time the needs are met and the organism is not under continuous, unrelieved tensions. Prescott classifies these needs into three types: physical needs such as the need for food, for water, for activity, for sex and the like; social needs such as the need for affection, for belonging, for status or respect from this social group; and integrative needs, the need to relate one's self to something larger and beyond one's self, that is, the need for a philosophy of life. In this sense all children have the same needs and it is the responsibility of the school as with every other social institution to help children to get these needs met in a way which is not only satisfying but provides the kind of behavior patterns that are personally and socially significant. A study of such needs in a given group of children would involve identifying those needs that are not being properly satisfied and an investigation of the role the school can play in helping children to meet these needs. This may often suggest educational objectives in the sense of indicating certain knowledge, attitudes, skills, and the like, the development of which would help children to meet these needs more effectively. These studies may also suggest ways in which the school can help to give motivation and meaning to its activities by providing means for children to meet psychological needs that are not well satisfied outside the school.

Studies of Contemporary Life Outside the School

The effort to derive objectives from studies of contemporary life largely grew out of the difficulty of accomplishing all that was laid upon the schools with the greatly increased body of knowledge which developed after the advent of science and the Industrial Revolution. Prior to this time the body of material that was considered academically respectable was sufficiently small so that there was little problem in selecting the elements of most importance from the cultural heritage. With the tremendous increase in knowledge accelerating with each generation after the advent of science, the schools found it no longer possible to include in their program all that was accepted by scholars. Increasingly the question was raised as to the contemporary significance of particular items of knowledge or particular skills and abilities. Herbert Spencer in his essay on *What Knowledge Is of Most Worth?* attempted to deal with this problem in a way that has characterized many of the efforts over the past century. Although this represented the interpretation of informal observations rather than systematic studies, the technique used by Spencer in some respects is very similar to techniques used by investigators today.

When the first World War required the training of a large number of people in the skilled trades, training that must take place in a relatively short period of time, the older and slower apprentice systems were no longer adequate. The idea of job analysis developed and was widely used to work out training programs in World War I which would speed up the training of people for the skilled trades and various types of technology. In essence, job analysis is simply a method of analyzing the activities carried on by a worker in a particular field in order that a training program can be focused upon those critical activities performed by this worker. In essence, most studies of contemporary life have a somewhat similar "logic."

Today there are two commonly used arguments for analyzing contemporary life in order to get suggestions for educational objectives. The first of these arguments is that because contemporary life is so complex and because life is continually changing, it is very necessary to focus educational efforts upon the critical aspects of this complex life and upon those aspects that are of importance today so that we do not waste the time of students in learning things that were important fifty years ago but no longer have significance at the same time that we are neglecting areas of life that are now important and for which the schools provide no preparation.

A second argument for the study of contemporary life grows out of the findings relating to transfer of training. As long as educators believed that it was possible for a student to train his mind and the various faculties of the mind in general and that he could use these faculties under whatever conditions might be appropriate, there was less need for analyzing contemporary life to suggest objectives. According to this view the important objectives were to develop the several faculties of the mind and as life developed the student would be able to use this trained mind to meet the conditions that he encountered. Studies of transfer of training, however, indicated that the student was much more likely to apply his learning when he recognized the similarity between the situations encountered in life and the situations in which the learning took place. Furthermore, the student was more likely to perceive the similarity between the life situations and the learning situations when two conditions were met: (1) the life situations and the learning situations were obviously alike in many respects, and (2) the student was given practice in seeking illustrations in his life outside of school for the application of things learned in school. These findings are used to support the value of analyzing contemporary life to identify learning objectives for the school that can easily be related to the conditions and opportunities of contemporary life for use of these kinds of learning.

Using studies of contemporary life as a basis for deriving objectives has sometimes been criticized particularly when it is the sole basis for deriving objectives. One of the most frequent criticisms has been that the identification of contemporary activities does not in itself indicate their desirability. The finding, for example, that large numbers of people are engaged in certain activities does not per se indicate that these activities should be taught to students in the school. Some of these activities may be harmful and in place of being taught in the school some attention might need to be given to their elimination. The second type of criticism is the type made by essentialists who refer to studies of contemporary life as the cult of "presentism." These critics point out that because life is continually changing, preparing students to solve the problems of today will make them unable to deal with the problems they will encounter as adults because the problems will have changed. A third kind of criticism is that made by some progressives who point out that some of the critical problems of contemporary life and some of the common activities engaged in by adults are not in themselves interesting to children nor of concern to children, and to assume that they should become educational objectives for children of a given age neglects the importance of considering the children's interests and children's needs as a basis for deriving objectives.

These criticisms in the main apply to the derivation of objectives solely from studies of contemporary life. When objectives derived from studies of contemporary life are checked against other sources and in terms of an acceptable educational philosophy, the first criticism is removed. When studies of contemporary life are used as a basis for indicating important areas that appear to have continuing importance, and when the studies of contemporary life suggest areas in which students can have opportunity to practice what they learn in school, and also when an effort is made to develop in students an intelligent understanding of the basic principles involved in these matters, the claim that such a procedure involves a worship of "presentism" is largely eliminated. Finally, if studies of contemporary life are used to indicate directions in which educational objectives may aim, while the choice of particular objectives for given children takes into account student interests and needs, these studies of contemporary life can be useful without violating relevant criteria of appropriateness for students of particular age levels. Hence, it is worthwhile to utilize data obtained from studies of contemporary life as one source for suggesting possible educational objectives.

Suggestions About Objectives from Subject Specialists

This is the source of objectives most commonly used in typical schools and colleges. School and college textbooks are usually written by subject specialists and largely reflect their views. Courses of study prepared by school and college groups are usually worked out by subject specialists and represent their conception of objectives that the school should attempt to attain. The reports of the Committee of Ten that appeared at the turn of the century had a most profound effect upon American secondary education for at least twenty-five years. Its reports were prepared by subject specialists and the objectives suggested by them were largely aimed at by thousands of secondary schools.

Many people have criticized the use of subject specialists on the grounds that the objectives they propose are too technical, too specialized, or in other ways are inappropriate for a large number of the school students. Probably the inadequacy of many previous lists of objectives suggested by subject specialists grows out of the fact that these specialists have not been asked the right questions. It seems quite clear that the Committee of Ten thought it was answering the question: What should be the elementary instruction for students who are later to carry on much more advanced work in the field? Hence, the report in History, for example, seems to present objectives for the beginning courses for persons who are training to be historians. Similarly the report in Mathematics outlines objectives for the beginning courses in the training of a mathematician. Apparently each committee viewed its job as outlining the elementary courses with the idea that these students taking these courses would go on for more and more advanced work, culminating in major specialization at the college or university level. This is obviously not the question that subject specialists should generally be asked regarding the secondary school curriculum. The question which they should be asked runs somewhat like this: What can your subject contribute to the education of young people who are not going to be specialists in your field; what can your subject contribute to the layman, the garden variety of citizen? If subject specialists can present answers to this question, they can make an important contribution, because, presumably, they have a considerable knowledge of the specialized field and many of them have had opportunity both to see what this subject has done for them and for those with whom they work. They ought to be able to suggest possible contributions, knowing the field as well as they do, that it might make to others in terms of its discipline, its content, and the like.

Some of the more recent curriculum reports do indicate that subject specialists can make helpful suggestions in answers to this question. The various reports published by the Commission on the Secondary School Curriculum of the Progressive Education Association beginning with "Science in General Education," including "Mathematics in General Education," "Social Studies in General Education," and other titles have been very useful and have thrown some light on the question, "What can this subject contribute to the education of young people who are not to specialize in it?" Other groups have recently prepared somewhat similar reports which also seem promising. Committee reports from the National Council of Mathematics Teachers, the National Council of English Teachers, the National Council of Social Studies Teachers, are cases in point. In general, they recognize much more clearly than did the committee preparing reports for the Committee of Ten that the subject is expected to make contributions to a range of students not considered in the earlier reports. In general, the more recent reports will be found useful as an additional source for suggestions about objectives.

Most of the reports of subject groups do not stop with objectives and many of them do not list objectives specifically. Most of them begin with some outline indicating their conception of the subject field itself and then move on to indicate ways in which it can be used for purposes of general education. Persons working on the curriculum will find it necessary to read the reports in some detail and at many places draw inferences from the statements regarding objectives implied. In general, two kinds of suggestions can be got from the reports as far as objectives are concerned. The first is a list of suggestions regarding the broad functions a particular subject can serve, the second is with regard to particular contributions the subject can make to other large functions which are not primarily functions of the subject concerned.

Let me illustrate these two types of suggestions that can be got from these reports. Recent reports of English groups, for example, have suggested educational functions of English as a study of language. The first function is to develop effective communication including both the communication of meaning and the communication of form. The second type of contribution is to effective expression, including in expression the effort of the individual to make internal adjustments to various types of internal and external pressures. A third function of language is to aid in the clarification of thought as is provided, for example, by the use of basic English as a means of aiding students to see whether they understand ideas clearly enough to translate them into operational words. This last function of clarification of thought is well illustrated by the statement of George Herbert Palmer that when confused he used to write himself clearheaded.

In the realm of literature these English committees see various kinds of contributions in terms of major functions literature can serve. Some emphasize its value in personal exploration. Literature in this sense can provide an opportunity for the individual to explore kinds of life and living far beyond his power immediately to participate in, and also give him a chance to explore vicariously kinds of situations which are too dangerous, too fraught with consequences for him to explore fully in reality. A number of committee reports speak of the general function of literature in providing greater extension to the experience of young people, not limited by geographic opportunities, nor limited in time nor limited in social class or types of occupations or social groups with which they can participate. In this case literature becomes the means of widely extending the horizon of the reader through vicarious experience. Another function of literature is to develop reading interests and habits that are satisfying and significant to the reader. Some English committees stress as an important objective to develop increasing skill in interpreting literary material, not only skill in analyzing the logical development and exposition of ideas but also the whole range of things including human motives which are formulated in written language and can therefore be subject to study and critical interpretation. Finally, some English committees propose that literature serves the function of appreciation, including both an opportunity for significant emotional reactions to literary forms and also opportunities for critical appraisal both of form and content, and a means thereby of developing standards of taste in literature.

These suggestions with regard to possible major functions of language and literature provide large headings under which to consider possible objectives which the school can aim at through language and literature. Such an analysis indicates the pervasive nature of the contribution that language and literature might possibly make to the development of children, adolescents, or adults. They suggest objectives that are more than knowledge, skills, and habits; they involve modes of thinking, or critical interpretation, emotional reactions, interests and the like.

Another illustration of the suggestions of major functions a subject may serve can be obtained from recent reports of science committees. One such report suggests three major functions science can serve for the garden variety of citizen. The first of these is to contribute to the improvement of health, both the individual's health and public health. This includes the development of health practices, of health attitudes, and of health knowledge, including an understanding of the way in which disease is spread and the precautions that can be taken by the community to protect itself from disease and from other aspects of poor health. The second suggested function of science is the use and conservation of natural resources; that is, science can contribute to an understanding of the resources of matter and energy that are available, the ways in which matter and energy can be obtained and utilized so as not greatly to deplete the total reserves, an understanding of the efficiency of various forms of energy transformation, and an understanding of plant and animal resources and the ways in which they can be effectively utilized. The third function of science is to provide a satisfying world-picture, to get clearer understanding of the world as it is viewed by the scientist and man's relation to it, and the place of the world in the larger universe. From these suggested functions of science, again it is possible to infer a good many important objectives in the science field, objectives relating to science, knowledge, attitudes, ability to solve problems, interests and the like.

Recent art reports illustrate another example of suggestions regarding major functions a subject might serve in general education. Some five functions have been proposed in these reports. The first, and in terms of Monroe's writing the most important, is the function of art in extending the range of perception of the student. Through art one is able to see things more clearly, to see them through the eyes of the artist, and thus to get a type of perception he is not likely to obtain in any other way. Both art production and art criticism are likely to extend perception. A second function proposed for art is the clarification of ideas and feelings through providing another medium for communication in addition to verbal media. There are students who find it possible to express themselves and communicate more effectively through art forms than through writing or speaking. For them this is an important educational function of art. A third function is personal integration. This refers to the contribution art has sometimes made to the relieving of tensions through symbolic expression. The making of objects in the studio and shop and expression through dancing and through music have long been known to produce an opportunity for personal expression and personal release from tension that is important in providing for the better integration of some young people. A fourth function is the development of interests and values. It is maintained that aesthetic values are important both as interesting qualities for the student and also as expressing very significant life values in the same category with the highest ultimate values of life. On this basis the contribution art can make in providing satisfaction of these interests and in developing an understanding of and desire to obtain these art values is an important educational function of art. Finally, a fifth function of art is the development of technical competence, a means of acquiring skill in painting or drawing or music, or some other art form which can have meaning and significance to the art student. These art reports are another illustration of material from which a number of significant suggestions regarding educational objectives can be inferred from a statement of functions.

A second type of suggestion that can be got from reports of subject specialists are the particular contributions that a subject can make to other large educational functions, that may not be thought of as unique functions of the subject itself. *The Report of the Committee on Science in General Education* is an excellent illustration of this type of suggestion. This report is organized in terms of suggested contributions science can make in each of the major areas of human relationships. In personal living, for example, suggestions are made as to ways in which science can help to contribute to personal health, to the need for self assurance, to a satisfying world picture, to a wide range of personal interests, and to aesthetic satisfaction. In the area of personal-social relations, suggestions are made as to ways in which science may help to meet student needs for increasingly mature relationships in home and family life and with adults outside the family, and for successful and increasingly mature relationships with age mates of both sexes. In the area of social-civic relations suggestions are made as to how science may help to meet needs for responsible participation in socially significant activities, and to acquire social recognition. In the area of economic relations suggestions are made as to how science may help to meet needs for emotional assurance of progress toward adult status, to meet the need for guidance in choosing an occupation and for vocational preparation, to meet the need for the wise selection and use of goods and services, and to meet the needs for effective action in solving basic economic problems.

The volume *Science in General Education* then goes on to outline the ways in which science can be taught to encourage reflective thinking and to develop other characteristics of personality such as creative thinking, aesthetic appreciation, tolerance, social sensitivity, self-direction. Critics have questioned the depths of contributions that science might make on a number of these points, but it is clear that these suggestions are useful in indicating possible objectives that a school might wish to aim at, using science or other fields as a means for attaining these objectives. Other subject groups have, in similar fashion, made suggestions regarding specific contributions these subjects might make to areas that are not uniquely the responsibility of these subjects. It is then through the drawing of inferences from reports of this sort regarding both the major functions that specialists think the subject can make and also the more specific contributions that the subject might make to other major functions that one is able to infer objectives from the reports of subject specialists.

I would suggest in order to get some taste of the kind of thing that can be obtained from these reports that you read at least one subject report at the level in which you are interested and jot down your interpretation of the major functions the committee believes that this subject can serve and the more specific contributions it can make to other educational functions. Then, formulate a list of the educational objectives you infer from these statements. This will give you some idea of the kinds of objectives that are likely to be suggested by the reports that are being made by various subject groups.

7

School Curriculum Reform in the United States

John I. Goodlad

THE REFORM MOVEMENT

Talk of the "new" mathematics, the "new" physics, and the "new" biology is commonplace today. Various groups and individuals, handsomely supported by the National Science Foundation—and, to a lesser degree, by several private philanthropic foundations—have developed new courses and instructional materials to go with them for high-school mathematics, physics, chemistry, biology, economics, geography, anthropology, English, and foreign languages, and for several subjects taught in elementary schools. Thousands of teachers and students have participated in the preparation and trial use of these materials. Clearly, a massive reformulation of what is to be taught and learned in the schools of the United States of America is under way.

The beginnings of the current curriculum reform movement are commonly identified with the successful launching of the first Russian satellite in the fall of 1957. This spectacular event set off blasts of charges and countercharges regarding the effectiveness of our schools and accelerated curriculum revision, notably in mathematics and the physical sciences. But the roots of change go back further, to the years immediately following World War II. The recruitment of young men for the armed services had revealed shocking inadequacies in the science and mathematics programs of high-school graduates. The problem was partly the limited quantity of work in these fields, partly the quality of what had been taught. The secondary-school curriculum too often reflected knowledge of another era, instead of the scientific advances of the twentieth century. Recognizing their responsibility for this unhappy state of affairs, scholars in a few fields began to participate actively in what has now become a major curriculum reform movement.

Sometimes the initiative came from an individual, sometimes from a learned society, such as the American Mathematical Society, for example. In either case, the subsequent course of events was surprisingly similar from project to project. First, a group of scholars

Public domain, from John I. Goodlad, *School Curriculum Reform in the United States.* New York: The Fund for the Advancement of Education, 1964: pp. 9–12, 14–16, 20–21, 23–25, 40–42, 50–51, 54–56.

met to review the need for pre-collegiate curriculum change in their field. Then, in subsequent summers, scholars and teachers invited from the schools planned course content and wrote materials. These materials were tried out in cooperating schools during the school year and revised in the light of this experience. Meanwhile, in summer and year-long institutes, teachers were educated in the new content and methodology. Throughout, participants seemed in agreement that new materials are central to a basic curriculum change.

The current curriculum reform movement is too far advanced to still warrant the adjective "new." In some fields, notably mathematics, the first wave of change is about to be followed by a second; the "new" new mathematics is in the offing.

It is dangerous, however, to assume that curriculum change has swept through all of our 85,000 public elementary and 24,000 public secondary schools during this past decade of reform. Tens of thousands of schools have scarcely been touched, or not been touched at all, especially in areas of very sparse or very dense population. Tens of thousands of teachers have had little opportunity to realize what advances in knowledge and changes in subject fields mean for them. Tens of thousands hold emergency certificates or teach subjects other than those in which they were prepared. In elementary schools, teachers with backgrounds in science and mathematics constitute a species that is about as rare as the American buffalo.

Suburban schools, with their ability to provide resources for in-service education, and for attracting qualified teachers, have fared better by comparison.

Curriculum planning is a political process, just as it is an ideological process of determining ends and means for education. Proposals either find their way through the political structure into educational institutions, or slip into obscurity. The unique and sensitive relationship among local, state, and federal governments in the support and conduct of school affairs has materially affected the ways in which the various curriculum projects have entered the bloodstream of American education.

Almost without exception, these projects have had their genesis outside of the formal political structure. They have been conceived primarily by scholars in colleges and universities who were joined by teachers from elementary and secondary schools. Projects have been supported by funds that are predominantly federal in origin, attesting to the fact that the education of its youth is a primary interest of the nation. Conditions of the grants have cautioned recipients against promoting their wares in any way; project directors have been limited to descriptive information, articles and, on request, speeches. But their efforts are in vain unless the results find their way to local schools and school systems. It is not surprising, therefore, that products, largely in the form of textbooks, often have been turned over to commercial publishers who have their own effective means of reaching state and local school authorities.

The strengths and weaknesses of the several projects stem in part from the structure of the American educational system and its characteristic strengths and weaknesses. For example, instead of having one set of clearly defined aims for America's schools, we have many. Consequently, each curriculum project is free to formulate objectives for its own particular segment of the curriculum. Rarely are these objectives defined with such precision that one would know exactly what to evaluate in determining the success of a given project. It might be argued that those undertaking the various curriculum activities have no responsibility for the formulation of objectives but that this should be done by the local school districts.

Each project, then, is responsible only for specifying what should be taught in a given subject. But can ends and means of curriculum planning be thus separated?

The curriculum reform movement so far has been focused on single subjects—planned, generally, from the top down. This focus and the "national" character of the projects have attracted first-rate scholars into pre-collegiate curriculum planning. But these characteristics have also attracted scholars from fields normally outside of pre-collegiate schooling who sense, apparently, an opportunity to include their particular roads to the good life in the curriculum of elementary or secondary schools.

This competition among fields places severe burdens upon instructional time. Just how all of the subjects will share in the available time remains to be seen. Demands will exceed time, even if the school day, week and year should be lengthened. Some subjects will have to be combined or left out—there is not enough room for twenty academic disciplines in the kindergarten. Arguments for the root nature and basic value of a discipline notwithstanding, problems of which subject should prevail are generally solved in the political realm at federal, state, and local levels of educational responsibility. National concerns tend to dominate today but, with any appreciable reduction in world tension, the humanities and social sciences should be gaining increasing favor.

SOME ILLUSTRATIVE PROJECTS ...

University of Illinois Committee on School Mathematics (UICSM)

The Committee on School Mathematics developed as a result of the interest of three colleges (Education, Engineering, and Liberal Arts and Sciences) at the University of Illinois in improving their freshman courses. This interest subsequently shifted to high-school mathematics. From 1951 through 1961, the work of the committee was supported by funds from the University of Illinois, the United States Office of Education, the National Science Foundation (for summer institutes), and the Carnegie Corporation. During these ten years, materials for grades 9 through 12 were produced and tested. The second phase of this program, the preparation of materials for grades 7 through 12, has just begun and is being supported by the National Science Foundation. Materials from the first phase will be used only if they satisfy criteria for the second. Max Beberman, project director, estimates expenditures of approximately $1,000,000 annually after 1963–64.

The committee set out to present mathematics as a consistent, unified discipline; to lead students to "discover" principles for themselves; and to assure the development of those manipulative skills necessary for problem-solving. The UICSM program emphasizes "learning by discovery," with the student *doing* (rather than being told about) mathematics. The student need not verbalize his discovery; in fact, early verbalization is discouraged for fear that premature or incorrect verbalization of a generalization may hinder its use. "Precision in exposition is something we expect of the textbook and the teacher, rather than of the learner. Precise communication is a characteristic of a good textbook and a good teacher; correct *action* is a characteristic of a good learner."[1] Verbalization, for communication and proof, is to come only after the student has become thoroughly familiar with the generalization and has had adequate opportunity to test and refine it.

A four-year sequential program has been developed through eleven units as follows: (1) the arithmetic of real numbers; (2) pronumerals, generalizations, and algebraic manipulations, (3) equations and inequations, applications; (4) ordered pairs and graphs; (5)

relations and functions; (6) geometry; (7) mathematical induction; (8) sequences; (9) exponential and logarithmic functions; (10) circular functions and trigonometry; and (11) polynomial functions and complex numbers. Units 1–4 are intended for the first year (grade 9), units 5–6 for the second, units 7–8 for the third, and units 9–11 for the fourth (grade 12). There is a teachers' edition for each unit, consisting of the students' edition plus commentary pages, providing mathematical background material and teaching suggestions, together with answers to the problems in the text. Both teachers' and students' editions are published by the University of Illinois Press.

The UICSM program is designed for *all* students, but it is assumed that many students will drop mathematics after a year or two, leaving only those who are somewhat more interested in mathematics for the last two years. Some schools report satisfactory use of the ninth-grade materials with gifted eighth-grade students. Material to be developed in the second phase of the project will reach up to the first two years of the present college curriculum, and will branch sideways into a variety of applications. Beberman is much interested in programmed materials for self-instruction (and such materials already have been developed) but is reluctant to use them to the point of eliminating the "electric charge," as he calls it, of group interaction. He believes that students are motivated and stimulated through the realization that other students are "getting something" they don't yet see.

The sequence of units and accompanying pedagogy virtually necessitate the special training of teachers. Until 1958, textbooks were available only to teachers who had received special training in their use and who were willing to assist in their evaluation. Even today, teachers planning to use the materials are urged to consult colleagues who have had such special training and to seek it for themselves. Both summer institutes and pedagogical films are available for this purpose. The committee urges use of the complete sequence, and discourages the use of single units, either by themselves or in conjunction with other materials.

The effectiveness of the UICSM program, as the effectiveness of other projects in the current curriculum reform movement, has not been fully tested. This is due partly to the difficulty entailed in evaluating such goals, for example, as "an intuitive grasp of fundamental principles," partly to the absence of criteria for comparing programs. Students in the UICSM courses, however, do about as well as students in traditional mathematics on tests designed for the latter. What the UICSM has produced so far is but a beginning. The group has embarked upon computer analyses of programmed materials and of "systems" approaches to the teaching-learning situation that should prove valuable in further curriculum revision . . . .

The Suppes Experimental Project in the Teaching of Elementary-School Mathematics

Patrick Suppes of Stanford University is developing a mathematics program for kindergarten and the first three grades (and perhaps the fourth), and a program in mathematical logic for able fifth- and sixth-grade children. Only the first of the programs is described here.

The central concept in the materials developed for the primary years is that of a set. According to Suppes, "all mathematics can be developed from the concept of set and operations upon sets."[2] He views sets as appropriate for young children because sets are more concrete than numbers and, in addition, facilitate mathematically precise definitions.

The project is experimental and involves a great deal of comparison between children using the Suppes materials, and those in regular, control classes. The aim is to develop a program that is both mathematically sound and pedagogically simple. Although the major emphasis is on the concepts, laws, and skills of arithmetic, content from both algebra and geometry is included. The materials stress precise and exact mathematical language. Experience has shown that a young child easily learns a technical vocabulary when the idea represented is clear. A fundamental assumption throughout this project is that children in the primary grades can learn much more mathematics than is traditionally assumed.

Workbooks for kindergarten and the first three grades have been written and used with selected classes. Production, at least in the initial stages, has been virtually a one-man job, with Suppes writing the exercises from his personal conception of what is mathematically desirable and feasible for the children. Experimental classes were taught by regular classroom teachers, with no special background or presupposed training. The teachers were brought together for a general orientation period at the beginning of the school year and met monthly thereafter to discuss problems and progress. The preparation of workbooks and teachers' manuals has been supported by a grant from the Carnegie Corporation.

Testing, supported by a grant from the National Science Foundation, has sought to determine the difference in children's learning of the experimental material and of traditional arithmetic. For example, a test designed to measure content in most first-grade arithmetic books was used in comparing experimental and non-experimental (control) classes. Over-all accomplishment favored the experimental group, especially on items involving arithmetical operations. There were no significant differences on items involving simple recognition of Arabic numerals, sequence of numerals, and telling of time.

A major phase of the work, supported by a grant from the Office of Education, involves detailed analysis of how children form and learn mathematical concepts. Studies of individual children under controlled experimental conditions seek to uncover, for example, the courses of greatest difficulty in the workbook exercises. The Suppes effort goes far beyond the reorganization of conventional content into both a tentative program of new content and a search for the kind and amount of mathematics that can be handled successfully by elementary-school children . . . .

Physical Science Study Committee (PSSC)

The Physical Science Study Committee, in developing a first physics course for high-school students, has acted as a pioneer in many areas of the curriculum reform movement: in the effective involvement of scholars and teachers, in the search for truly fundamental concepts, in the development of films, and in the packaging of an instructional program. PSSC's activities, initially centered at the Massachusetts Institute of Technology, led to the formation of Educational Services Incorporated (Watertown, Mass.), a non-profit corporation which now administers them. Major grants to support the committee's work have come from the National Science Foundation; smaller grants from the Sloan Foundation and the Ford Foundation's Fund for the Advancement of Education.

The PSSC course emphasizes the basic structure of physics, the acquisition of new physical knowledge, and the necessity for understanding rather than memorizing basic physics concepts. A central concept is the laboratory in which students gain first-hand experience in discovering and verifying physical phenomena. The program contains fewer facts than are usually included in an elementary physics course, but concepts are to be understood and used, not just asserted. The committee has worked out a comprehensive set of means for achieving the purposes of its course: a textbook, laboratory experiments and simplified apparatus, films, achievement tests, books on special topics, and a teacher's guide to classroom and laboratory activities.

The course consists of four parts, each one building on the preceding part. Part I deals with the fundamental concepts of time, space, and matter; part II with a detailed examination of light; part III with motion; and part IV with electricity and the physics of the atom. Students count, measure, observe; learn about, construct, and test conceptual models; and finally arrive at the modern model of atoms. They come to see that physics is not fixed or static but that it evolves from the inquiries and basic research of scientists.

Where textbook, class discussion and the laboratory leave off, films take over. The films are not of the usual "enrichment" sort. Some introduce the student to an area which he will traverse later; others present a simple experiment for him to duplicate; some include experiments which cannot be completed in the school laboratory, and still others present the more difficult portions of the course. The viewer is struck by the painstaking care that has gone into the production of each film, be it the portrayal of physical phenomena or of investigators at work.

Teacher institute during the summer and school year have been an integral part of the PSSC physics program from its inception. Since the first year of operation, 1957–58, when eight teachers and 300 students used the course, it has mushroomed. Approximately 4,000 teachers and 170,000 students, or 40 to 45 per cent of all secondary-school students enrolled in physics classes in the United States, participated during 1963–64. Hundreds more teachers used parts of the course materials in conjunction with conventional physics textbooks, and interest has even spread to foreign countries. Translations of the textbook into Spanish and Japanese are completed and translations into French, Italian, Danish, Swedish, Norwegian, Hebrew, Portuguese, and Turkish are in process.

Evaluation of the program confronts the common query: can its effectiveness be appraised by using conventional tests. The committee's answer is an emphatic "No." Mimeographed articles contrast objectives of the PSSC course with objectives of conventional physics courses, stressing the limitations of conventional tests in attempting evaluative comparisons. An examination prepared and administered by the College Entrance Examination Board has been used to compare students in PSSC with those in conventional physics classes.

Students coming through this new physics course, like students coming through other new high-school curricula, move on to college courses geared more closely to the old materials. There is no evidence to suggest that these high-school graduates are in any way at a disadvantage, although they sometimes have indicated a dissatisfaction with their college fare. The Physical Science Study Committee points to the need for revising the college physics curriculum if PSSC students are to be adequately challenged, and if college courses are to keep pace with current thought in the realm of physics education. There are increasing signs that this collegiate reform has started . . . .

Science—A Process Approach

During the summer, 1963, a writing group under the Commission on Science Education of the American Association for the Advancement of Science prepared a teachers' manual and a number of course content outlines in science for the early years of elementary schooling. The experimental edition of the content outlines has appeared in five paperbook sections. The effort is financed by a grant from the National Science Foundation.

Fundamental assumptions underlying the proposed courses are that science is much more than a simple encyclopedic collection of facts, and that children in the primary grades can benefit from acquiring certain basic skills and competencies essential to the learning of science. These competencies have been identified as follows: observation, classification, recognition and use of space-time relations, recognition and use of numbers and number relations, measurement, communication, inference, and prediction. The expectation is that the ability to use scientific processes will remain after many of the details of science have been forgotten. These competencies are advocated as appropriate for virtually all levels of science education and are not confined to the primary grades.

Four major areas of content, designated as appropriate for the first ten years of school, give some guidance in the selection of specific topics through which scientific behavior is to be achieved. These are: the universe—its galaxies, our solar system, the earth and the immediate environment, and measurements used to describe astronomical and geological phenomena; the structure and reactions of matter—compounds and mixtures, large and small molecules, elements, atoms, protons, neutrons, and electrons; the conservation and transformation of energy—the electro magnetic spectrum, motion and potential energy, electrical energy and chemical energy, force and work, and gravitational and magnetic fields; the interaction between living things and their environment—animal and human behavior, the relation between biological structure and function, reproduction, development, genetics, evolution, and the biological units of cell, organism, and population.

All of the books currently available are for teachers. The teachers' guide is an overall view of the rationale of curriculum organization, of the topics, and of recommended instructional procedures. The other books outline the specific content and activities to be used by the teacher. Each of them lists a dozen or more topics, organized so as to remind the reader that they be used in developing student ability to observe, measure, classify, and communicate. Each topic is designed with two or three particular objectives in mind. Thus, the first topic of the first book, "Recognizing Regular Shapes," specifically states that, with completion of instruction, the children should be able to recognize common two-dimensional shapes and to identify common shapes as components of complex objects. At the end of each topic, ways and means are suggested to evaluate whether or not these aims have been achieved. This procedure is followed for all the topics covered by the booklets.

In view of the fact that these preliminary materials were prepared in an eight-weeks' writing session during the summer, 1963, and have been tried out in only a very preliminary way, an appraisal of the specific content and suggested activities would be premature. The booklets have recently been introduced into selected cooperating schools, a step which will probably result in a substantial revision.

This project is noteworthy, furthermore, in that it recognizes the many persistent curricular problems and attempts to solve them. Clearly, the current stand is that no single science discipline should prevail but that topics from many sciences and from mathematics should be woven into a unified whole, the goal being the development of a basic scientific behavior in the student.

The advice to teachers to begin with part I in the first grade (if there is no kindergarten), part II in the second grade, part III in the third grade, etc., raises some questions about how individual differences are to be taken care of. However, the project supplies a check list to help teachers determine pupil accomplishment so that they can adjust their teaching accordingly. How subsequent individualization of instruction is to be provided is not made clear, but it is anticipated that the feedbacks from trial use will influence adjustments for differences in ability . . . .

POTPOURRI

The foregoing descriptions of projects and activities in various subject fields are a representative sample of current curriculum reform in the United States. They are proof of the steadily increasing interest in improving the curriculum by constructing new courses and producing more effective teaching materials. The many other curricular and instructional efforts—too numerous to be included here—are additional evidence of the intense efforts on the part of educators and laymen alike to raise the quality of American education.

Noteworthy among the less formalized endeavors are recommendations suggesting that the fine and applied arts—virtually pushed aside as "frills" during the past decade—may, one day, have a place in the curriculum, along with science, mathematics, and foreign languages. The arts, it is believed, can not only contribute to the understanding and attitude needed to stay an ever-threatening holocaust but can also contribute significantly to man's quality of living in a world which, hopefully, will survive.

The work on creativity by psychologists such as Guilford, Taylor, Torrance, Getzels, and Jackson, and on inquiry and inquiry training by Bruner and Suchman, is closely related to the current curriculum reform movement. Undoubtedly, these men and others have been instrumental in creating the growing interest that many subject-matter specialists have lately displayed in having their students learn fundamental concepts and processes in preference to their merely memorizing facts. Psychologists and educators involved in various aspects of programmed instruction have had a major part in stimulating the curricular reformers to arrange subject matter in more meaningful sequences, and to base whole sections of courses entirely on auto-instructional techniques.

The growing popularity of plans that reorganize schools vertically into multi-graded or non-graded programs, and horizontally into various cooperative teaching arrangements, is closely tied to curriculum revision. The non-graded scheme of school organization is compatible with a curriculum planned around themes, principles, concepts, generalizations, and modes of inquiry that will be developed over many years of schooling, replacing a curriculum consisting of bits and pieces and daily or weekly time blocks of instruction. Team teaching has grown, at least in part, out of a recognized need to provide students with teachers who possess a thorough knowledge of their subject field as well as a real understanding of the school's function.

Greater awareness of the fact that a large number of students do not seem to profit from the fare the schools offer has resulted in a plethora of proposals to educate the slow learners, the academically talented, and the physically handicapped. The realization that automation is bringing about employment problems of a kind never experienced before has helped to revitalize the field of vocational and technical education.

In all this agitation—some of it denoting progress, some of it not—a faint glimmer of light is growing stronger; the belief that, increasingly, curriculum reform will be based on the cultivation of the individual and the assurance of a self-renewing society, whereas the curriculum revisions of the past were largely a result of pressures for societal preservation . . . .

ANALYSIS: PROBLEMS AND ISSUES

Curricular Problems and Issues Within Courses

AIMS AND OBJECTIVES. There is a striking similarity in the aims and objectives of nearly all projects. Objectives, as they are defined in various descriptive documents, stress the importance of understanding the structure of the discipline, the purposes and methods of the field, and the part that creative men and women played in developing the field. One of the major aims is that students get to explore, invent, discover, as well as sense some of the feelings and satisfactions of research scholars, and develop some of the tools of inquiry appropriate to the field. When more remote aims are implied, the impression is created that the student should prepare for intellectual and academic survival in a complex, scientific world. Such social aims as preparation for citizenship or intelligent participation in decisions facing the community are only rarely mentioned.

Objectives of the programs appear to rest on the assumption that any significant behavior which can be derived from analysis of an academic discipline can be learned by students of a given age and is, therefore, worth learning. Such an assumption almost automatically implies that those subjects already well established in the curriculum determine what the schools ought to teach. The schools' curriculum, then, is closed to new subjects, and to old subjects that have been poorly represented in the political market place. The goals of schooling, therefore, would be determined by those subjects that have been most successful in finding their way through the political structure into the schools!

It should be stated, though, in defense of all those who are involved with the various curriculum projects, that neither are they nor should they be charged with the responsibility of determining the aims of America's schools. This responsibility falls to the citizenry as a whole. The fact that our communities have, generally speaking, not assumed this responsibility has resulted in a lack of broadly accepted aims against which the validity of the projects' objectives may be checked. The objectives of the several subject-field projects become, therefore—by default as it were—the educational aims of the communities adopting the various project courses.

> How does a community decide which value patterns are to be taught in its schools and are to be used as a basis for curricular and instructional decisions? ... One possible answer is that a pluralistic society wishes for an obvious and open decision never to occur. A struggle of this sort would be divisive, indicating quite clearly to a number of subgroups that their views were not being adopted by the society as a whole. Thus a pluralistic society may prefer to ignore this question as long as possible in the hope that it will not become too troublesome. Some aspects of our present educational situation suggest that in part we have more or less consciously adopted this answer.[14]

To determine what students *ought* to learn on the basis of what is significant to the discipline and what *can* be learned by a majority of the students, causes some difficulty. Concepts of energy, number, and evolution certainly are significant to physics, mathematics, and biology, respectively. Further, they can be learned in an academically respectable way by young children. (The optimum time for learning them, however, still remains to be empirically determined.) But suppose we find that a range of concepts, running the gamut of twenty or more disciplines, *can* be learned by young children? Since limitations in time necessitate choice, what criteria do we use to guide our choices? Clearly, some more fundamental validation than the ability of children to learn certain concepts is needed to help us choose among a number of alternatives. The problem is no less pressing at the high-school level where, in order to set up a social studies curriculum, criteria other than student capability are required to arrive at an intelligent choice among history, geography, economics, political science, sociology, and anthropology.

The long-term solution to this dilemma may be that those state and local (and perhaps federal) agencies, that are entrusted with responsibility for the schools, begin to formulate the aims. Once this has been done, curriculum groups could go to work to determine the best curricular patterns to achieve these aims. But these agencies are not now assuming this responsibility nor does it seem likely that they will do so in the near future.[15] There might, however, be a place in our pluralistic society for independent centers—preferably attached to universities—which would engage in a systematic study of all data relating to a school's aims and other curricular problems.

These centers would not determine the aims for the communities but would present and analyze alternatives, support bases for alternatives, and point out possible consequences of adopting any given aim. The work of such centers would have the virtue of eschewing any particular subject as both the road to and the end of the good life.

The short-term answer is for project committees to try and justify goals beyond the parochial limits of disciplines and children's abilities to learn them. And some projects are moving in just that direction. Project directors have become increasingly sensitive to the human processes which appear to transcend the methods presumed to be unique to the discipline. John Mayor, for example (University of Maryland Mathematics Project), lauds cultivation of such fundamental processes as observing, classifying, measuring, drawing inferences, speculating, and experimenting. These appear not to be unique to mathematics but to be equally appropriate to the enjoyment of literature and artistic performance—and to the full development of man's rational powers.

NOTES

1. Max Beberman and Herbert Vaughan, *Unit 1 of High School Mathematics (Teacher's Edition)*, Introduction. Urbana, Illinois: University of Illinois Press, 1960.
2. Patrick Suppes, "Sets and Numbers," an Experimental Project in the Teaching of Elementary School Mathematics, 1962–1963. (Mimeographed, Stanford: Institute for Mathematical Studies in the Social Sciences, January, 1963), p. 2.
14. Harold B. Dunkel, "Value Decisions and the Public Schools," *School Review* 70 (Summer, 1962), p. 165.
15. Ammons, for example, was hard pressed to find, within a 300-mile radius of Chicago, more than a handful of schools with anything that might reasonably be called a set of aims. See Margaret P. Ammons, "Educational Objectives: The Relation between the Process Used in Their Development and Their Quality" (Unpublished doctoral dissertation, University of Chicago, 1961).

8

Objectives

W. James Popham

A KEY FEATURE OF ANY RATIONAL PLANNING, educational or otherwise, is the possession of some idea of what is to be accomplished. Educators, of course, characteristically describe these intended accomplishments as their goals or objectives. Some people use the terms "goal" or "objective" interchangeably, as well as such synonyms as "aims," "intents," etc. Other people employ a much more distinctive meaning of the terms, using "goal" to describe a broader description of intent and "objective" to denote a more specific spelling out of the goal. Because there is currently no overwhelmingly preferred usage of these terms, be sure to seek clarification from an educator regarding the manner in which he is using the many terms which may be employed to describe educational goals. In this guidebook, the terms will be employed interchangeably.

MEASURABILITY AND CLARITY

One of the most prominent arenas of educational activity during the 1960's concerned the form in which instructional objectives should be stated. As a consequence of the programmed instruction movement which captured the attention of many educators during the early sixties, we heard more and more about the merits of stating objectives in precise, measurable terms. Programmed instruction enthusiasts pointed out again and again that such objectives were requisite for a proper instructional design. A number of other instructional specialists also began to support the worth of explicitly stated objectives. What was the point of this activity?

For years educators have been specifying their objectives in rather general language such as, "At the end of the year the student will become familiar with important literary insights." There is nothing intrinsically wrong with such an objective, for it probably provides one with a general idea of what is to be done during the year. However, for instructional or evaluation purposes, such an objective is almost useless since it identifies no specific

Public domain, Chapter 2 from W. James Popham, *An Evaluation Guidebook: A Set of Practical Guidelines for the Educational Evaluator*. Los Angeles: The Instructional Objectives Exchange, 1972.

indicator for determining whether or not the objective has been achieved. As a consequence, in recent years an increasing number of educators have urged that in order for objectives to function effectively in instructional and evaluation situations, they must be stated in terms of *measurable learner behavior*. In other words, since educational systems are designed to improve the learner in some way, an educational objective should describe the particular kind of behavior changes which will reflect such improvement. An example of objectives which would satisfy this measurability criterion would be the following: "When given previously unencountered selections from different authors, the student can, by style and other cues, correctly name the writer." The main attribute of a properly stated instructional objective is that it describes what the learner *will do* or is *able to do* at the end of instruction which he could not prior to instruction. Another way of putting it is that a usefully stated objective will invariably be measurable in such a way that an unequivocal determination can be made as to whether the objective has been accomplished.

The major advantages of such objectives is that they promote increased *clarity* regarding educational intents, whereas vague and unmeasurable objectives yield considerable ambiguity and, as a consequence, the possibility of many interpretations not only of what the objective means but, perhaps more importantly, whether it has been accomplished.

During the past several years many books and papers and audiovisual aids have been published[1] which guide the practitioner regarding how instructional objectives should be stated. Some of these guides focus considerable attention on the choice of verb used to describe the hoped-for post-instruction status of the learner. For instance, instead of saying "The learner *will know* the chief battles of the Civil War," the educator is advised to put it this way: "The learner *will list* in writing the chief battles of the Civil War." Note that the only difference is that in the second objective a verb is employed which describes a specific type of action or *behavior* on the part of the learner, in contrast to the verb "know" which can mean many things to many people. In the preferred objective a phrase, "in writing," has also been added which ties down the meaning of the objective even more. Since the essential feature of a properly stated objective is that it unambiguously communicates an educational intent, we might also have used such phrases as:

> will recite aloud
> will select from a list
> will write the names of the opposing generals

One can think of different verbs which might be employed to communicate what is intended in an objective. At a very general level there are "internal state" verbs such as "understand." At a more specific level we can think of action verbs such as "identify" or "distinguish." But even these verbs permit some difference in interpretations as to the precise manner in which the learner will identify or distinguish. Even more specific behavioral phrases such as "pointing to" or "reciting aloud" further reduce the ambiguity. In general, the evaluator should employ phrases with sufficient specificity for the task at hand. Usually, that will mean more rather than less specific language.

Because a well formed instructional objective describes the type of learner behavior which is to be produced by the instructional treatment, such statements have often been referred to as *behavioral objectives* or *performance objectives*. The reason why so many educators have recently been advocating such goal statements is that the reduced ambiguity of the objectives yields a significant increase in the clarity needed both for (1) deciding on the *worth* of the objective and (2) determining whether the objective has been *achieved*.

Another important attribute of a well stated instructional objective is that it refers to the *learner's* behavior, not that of the *teacher*. Statements such as "the teacher will introduce the class to the basic elements of set theory" do not qualify as educational objectives, for they merely describe the nature of the educational treatment (in this case provided by the teacher), not what that treatment is to accomplish in terms of modifications in the learner.

An additional element of a usefully formulated instructional objective is that it should refer to the learner's *post-instruction* behavior, not his behavior during instruction. For instance, we might imagine a group of children working furiously on practice problems in a mathematics class. Now it is not on the basis of the learners' skill with these practice problems that the teacher will judge the adequacy of his instruction, but on later problems given as part of an end-of-unit or end-of-course examination. Thus, the type of learner behavior to be described in a properly stated educational objective must definitely occur after the instruction designed to promote it.

The term "post-instruction" should be clarified, however. Certainly we are interested in what is happening to learners during the course of a school year, not merely at its conclusion. Thus, we test or otherwise observe pupils at numerous points during the year. Similarly, we might conceive of a one week or single day instructional period for our treatment. A useful objective, useful in the sense that we can determine whether it has been achieved by the learner, might be promoted by an extremely short instructional period.

Guideline Number 1. The educational evaluator should encourage the use of instructional objectives which provide explicit descriptions of the post-instruction behavior desired of learners.

All, or Nothing at All?

As the evaluator becomes conversant with the advantages of measurable goals he sometimes becomes excessive in his advocacy of such objectives. Educators will ask him, "Must *all* my goals be stated in measurable terms? Aren't there some objectives that I can pursue even if I can't describe precisely how I will measure them?"

For *evaluation purposes*, the response should be that unmeasurable goals are of little or no use. Yet, for instructional purposes a more conciliatory response is warranted. There are undoubtedly some objectives, e.g., promoting a student's appreciation of art, which may currently be unassessable yet are so intrinsically meritorious that they are worth the risk of some instructional investment. Such high-risk high-gain goals might reasonably command a segment of our instructional time, but it is the *proportion* of instruction devoted to the pursuit of such goals which is at issue. Currently, the vast majority of our educational efforts are devoted to the pursuit of such non-measurable aims. We need to alter the proportion so that most of our goals are of a measurable nature, thus permitting us to determine whether they have been accomplished and, consequently, allowing us to get better at achieving them. Some proportion of instructional resources might, on the other hand, because of great potential dividends, be devoted to the pursuit of non-measurable objectives. From an evaluator's point of view, the unmeasurable goals will be of no use, thus he should attempt to reduce the proportion of such non-behavioral goals to a reasonable number. At the same time, of course, we should increase our sophistication in measuring those goals which are important but currently elusive so that in the future we can measure even these.

Guideline Number 2. While recognizing that non-measurable goals will be of limited use for his purposes, the educational evaluator must be aware that instructors may wish to devote a reasonable proportion of their efforts to the pursuit of important but currently unassessable objectives.

Selected and Constructed Learner Responses

When describing the myriad forms of learner behavior which educators might be interested in achieving you will find that the learner is engaging in acts which can be classified under two headings, that is, he is either *selecting* from alternatives or *constructing*. He is *selecting* when he chooses "true" or "false" to describe a statement or when he picks the answer to a multiple choice question. He is *constructing* when he writes an essay, gives an impromptu speech, or performs a free exercise routine in a gymnastics class. In a sense the difference between selected and constructed responses is somewhat similar to the difference between "recognition" and "recall" as used by measurement specialists in connection with customary achievement testing. When the learner is asked to recognize a correct answer from among multiple choice alternatives, he must select the correct response. When he is asked to recall a correct answer, he must construct his own response, presumably based on his recollection of what the correct answer should be. Beyond this difference, however, the selection versus construction distinction can be applied to all types of learner response, noncognitive as well as cognitive, and therefore is more useful.

The distinction between selected and constructed responses becomes important when we realize that with selected response objectives it is relatively simple to determine whether the learner's responses are acceptable, for we merely identify in advance which alternatives are the correct ones. With constructed responses, however, the task is far more difficult since we must identify in advance the criteria by which we will distinguish between acceptable and unacceptable learner responses. To illustrate, if the objective concerns the learner's skill in writing essays, then unless we can specify the standard which all acceptable essays must satisfy, we have an objective which is difficult if not impossible to measure.

The importance of this point cannot be overemphasized, for many educators who zealously proclaim the merits of measurable objectives end up by offering the following type of goal as an example of a well written objective:

> At the conclusion of the course the student will describe the major contributions of each novelist studied during the semester.

The difficulty with such objectives is that the elements needed to render a description satisfactory are not delineated. How will the teacher, in examining the various descriptions prepared by her students, decide which ones are good enough? This should not suggest that such criteria cannot be isolated or described. They definitely can, but it is hard work. Many teachers who rely heavily on constructed response student behavior prefer the work-evading tactic of relying on a "general impression" of the quality of a student's efforts. The unreliability of such general impressions, of course, has been amply documented through the years.

The major point of this discussion is that if an objective is based upon a learner's constructed response, the *criteria of adequacy must be given*, that is, the standards for judging the acceptability of a learner's response must be supplied. The criteria of adequacy should be included in the objective, or at least referred to in the objective. For example, the following objective would be acceptable:

> The learner will deliver a 15 minute extemporaneous speech violating no more than two of the twelve "rules for oral presentation" supplied in class, as judged by a panel of three randomly selected classmates using the standard rating form.

Ideally, the evaluator would prefer a set of crisply stated criteria by which to determine the adequacy of a constructed response. In practice, however, it may be necessary to state such criteria in terms of a group of judges being satisfied. For instance, even without explicating a single criterion, one can frame a satisfactory objective which indicates that a judge (or judges) will consider satisfactory greater proportions of post-instruction learner responses than those which occurred prior to instruction.

An example of this stratagem may prove helpful. Suppose an elementary teacher wants to improve her pupils' abilities to prepare watercolor prints, but has difficulty in describing criteria of adequacy for determining the quality of colors. She might give a particular assignment at the start of instruction, next teach the children, then give an *identical* watercolor assignment after instruction. The two productions of each child are then randomly paired after first having been secretly coded so that the teacher knows which was pre-instruction and which was post-instruction. The pairs are then given to a competent judge who is asked simply to designate which of any pair is better. No criteria at all need be described. The hope, of course, would be that more of the post-instruction watercolors would be judged superior. The objective for such a situation might be phrased like this:

> When compared with pre-instruction watercolor preparations based on an identical assignment, at least 75 per cent of the pupils' post-instruction watercolor productions will be considered superior by an external judge who is not aware of the point at which the watercolors were prepared.

It is important to use an external judge in these situations to avoid bias, conscious or subconscious, on the part of the teacher or, for that matter, anyone involved heavily in the instruction.

Anytime anyone engaged in educational evaluation encounters a constructed response objective without clearly explicated criteria of adequacy, the deficiency should be remedied or the objective discarded.

Guideline Number 3. The educational evaluator must identify criteria of adequacy when using instructional objectives which require constructed responses from learners.

Content Generality

In the early 1960's any objective which explicitly described the learner's post-instruction behavior was considered to be an acceptable goal statement. Such objectives as the following were frequently found in sets of recommended goals:

> The pupil will be able to identify at least three elements in *Beowulf* which are characteristic of the epic form.

Yet, upon examining such objectives it becomes clear that the statement is nothing more than a test item concerning the particular literary work, *Beowulf.* Such objectives, while sufficiently precise, are not very economical to use. To teach a semester or year long course with this type of objectives one might be obliged to have dozens or even hundreds of such statements. At any rate, what most educators wish to accomplish is not so limited in scope, but covers a broad range of learner behaviors, behaviors which hopefully can be employed profitably in many situations. Professor Eva Baker[2] has offered a useful distinction between objectives according to whether they possess content *generality* or *test* item *equivalence.* The former *Beowulf* example, since it dealt with a single test item, possessed test item equivalence and is of limited utility. To possess content generality, that is, to describe a broader range of learner behavior, the objective could be rewritten as follows:

> The pupil will be able to identify at least three elements in any epic which are characteristic of that form.

By referring to *any epic*, rather than a particular epic, the objective takes on a more general form, and, as such, can be more parsimoniously employed by educational evaluators. If only to avoid the necessity of dealing with innumerable objectives, educational evaluators should foster the use of content general objectives and eschew the use of test item equivalent goals.

One of the most vexing problems for those who work with instructional objectives is deciding *just how specific* or *just how general* they should be stated. Although there are no absolute guides here, or even consensus preference, it has become clear that the level of generality for objectives should probably vary from situation to situation. A teacher in the classroom may wish to use extremely explicit objectives. Yet, if the evaluator is attempting to secure reactions from community people regarding their estimates of the worth of certain objectives, then more general statements may be preferable. There are experimental techniques which can be used to cope with the generality level question, but until we have definitive evidence regarding what level works best in given situations, it would be wise for the evaluator to remain flexible on this point.

Guideline Number 4. The educational evaluator should foster the use of measurable objectives which possess content generality rather than test item equivalence.

Proficiency Levels

Once a measurable objective has been formulated, there is another question which should be answered by those framing the objective, namely, *how well* should the learner perform the behavior specified in the objectives. A convenient way of thinking about this question is to consider two kinds of minimal proficiency levels which can be associated with an objective.

First, we are interested in the degree of proficiency which must be displayed by an individual learner. This is called the *student minimal level* and is illustrated by the *italicized* section in the following objective:

> The learner will be able to multiply correctly *at least nine out of ten* of any pair of two digit multiplication problems randomly generated by the instructor.

This student minimal level asserts that the learner must perform with at least a 90 per cent proficiency.

A second decision needs to be made with respect to the proportion of the *group* of learners who must master the objective. Does everyone need to achieve the objective? Only half the class? This is established through the *class minimal level* which is illustrated by the *italicized* section of the following objective:

> *Eighty per cent or more* of the learners will be able to multiply correctly at least nine out of ten of any pair of two digit multiplication problems randomly generated by the instructor.

Here we see that for the objective to be achieved at the desired levels of proficiency at least 80 per cent of the learners must perform 90 per cent or better on the multiplication problems. Sometimes this is referred to as an 80–90 proficiency level.

Now the advantage, particularly to the evaluator, of specifying class and student minimal levels *prior to instruction* is that the power of the instructional treatment can then be tested against such standards in producing the hoped-for results. Too often the designers of an instructional system will, after instruction, settle for mediocre levels of proficiency. By pre-setting performance standards those involved in the design and implementation of the instructional treatment are forced to put their pedagogical proficiency on the line.

But it's easier to say how to state minimal proficiency levels than it is to decide just what they should be. Too many educators merely pluck them from the air if they're used at all, e.g., "We want 90–90 levels on all our objectives." Obviously, this would be unthinking, for there are certain objectives which we would hope that *all* of our learners would achieve with 100 per cent proficiency. Examples of these might be in the field of health, rudimentary intellectual skills, etc.

Probably the best we can do now is to seek the wisdom of many people, certainly including those who have experience in the education of the learners with whom we are working. Careful analysis of how well learners have done in the past, coupled with our most insightful appraisal of how well each individual *should* perform with respect to the objective, can yield an approximation of defensible class and student minimal levels.

An important consideration for establishing some proficiency levels is the initial skill of the learner prior to instruction, sometimes referred to as his "entry behavior." For certain instructional situations, e.g., remedial math, learners who commence an instructional sequence with abysmally low entry behaviors might not be expected to perform as well at the close of instruction as other learners who headed into the instruction with an advantage. For other situations, the criterion levels are not so malleable, thus we would expect students in a driver training course to achieve the desired minimal levels irrespective of their entry behavior.

Now it is always possible, of course, to alter performance standards after the instructional treatment has either proven to be ineffectual or more effective than we thought. But this should be done very cautiously, only after pushing the instructional treatment to the limits of its potency.

Guideline Number 5. Prior to the introduction of the instructional treatment educational evaluators should strive to establish minimal proficiency levels for instructional objectives.

The Taxonomies of Educational Objectives

A technique for analyzing objectives which many evaluators find useful stems from the work of Benjamin Bloom and a group of university examiners who in 1956 published a scheme[3] for classifying educational objectives according to the kinds of learner behavior they were attempting to promote. An extension of the classification scheme by David Krathwohl and others appeared in 1964.[4] These two *taxonomies* (classification schemes) of educational objectives first divided instructional goals into three groups or *domains*, the cognitive, affective, and psychomotor. *Cognitive* objectives deal with intellectual learner outcomes such as whether a pupil can analyze sentences into their component parts or can recall the names of the 50 states. *Affective* objectives are concerned with attitudinal, valuing, emotional learner actions such as promoting a pupil's interest in literature or strengthening his esteem for democratic processes. *Psychomotor* objectives describe intended learner outcomes of a largely physical skill nature such as learning to use a typewriter or how to swim the breast stroke.

Each of these three domains has been further subdivided into several levels of learner behaviors which are sought in each domain. For instance, in the cognitive domain we find *knowledge* objectives which, briefly, describe those goals that require the learner to recall information of one sort or another. Another type of objective in the cognitive domain is *analysis* which refers to the learner's ability to subdivide a complex whole into its constituent segments. Within each domain the several levels of objectives are arranged more or less hierarchically so that, for example, analysis objectives are ranked higher than knowledge objectives. Lower levels within a domain are generally considered prerequisite to higher levels.

To the evaluator, the major utility of a taxonomic analysis of the objectives with which he is dealing is that he can detect unsuspected omissions or overemphasis. For example, he might subject a group of objectives under consideration by a school faculty to an analysis according to the taxonomies and discover that there were no affective objectives present or that all of the cognitive objectives were at the lowest levels of the cognitive domain. Once apprised of this situation the school faculty might wish to select the objectives anyway, but at least they have a better idea of the types of goals they are adopting.

Although each of the three domains has been broken down into multiple levels, six for the cognitive, five for the affective and five for the psychomotor,[5] the evaluator may find the use of all of these levels too sophisticated for some of the tasks he must accomplish. Many educators report sufficient utility is gained by using the three major domain headings, i.e., cognitive, affective, and psychomotor, coupled with a rough two-level breakdown in each domain, such as "lowest level" and "higher than lowest level." However, there may be some situations in which a more fine grained analysis is required.[6] Accordingly, brief descriptions of each level in each of the three domains are presented below. An evaluator should, however, regroup the levels into a system of sufficient precision for the task at hand.

Cognitive Domain

The cognitive domain has six levels. They move from knowledge, the lowest level, to evaluation, the highest level.

Knowledge. Knowledge involves the recall of specifics or universals, the recall of methods and processes, or the recall of a pattern, structure, or setting. It will be noted that the essential attribute at this level is *recall*. For assessment purposes, a recall situation involves little more than "bringing to mind" appropriate material.

Comprehension. This level represents the lowest form of understanding and refers to a kind of apprehension that indicates that a student knows what is being communicated and can make use of the material or idea without necessarily relating it to other material or seeing it in its fullest implications.

Application. Application involves the use of abstractions in particular or concrete situations. The abstractions used may be in the form of procedures, general ideas, or generalized methods. They may also be ideas, technical principles, or theories that must be remembered and applied to novel situations.

Analysis. Analysis involves the breakdown of a communication into its constituent parts such that the relative hierarchy within that communication is made clear, that the relations between the expressed ideas are made explicit, or both. Such analyses are intended to clarify the communication, to indicate how it is organized and the way in which the communication managed to convey its effects as well as its basis and arrangement.

Synthesis. Synthesis represents the combining of elements and parts so that they form a whole. This operation involves the process of working with pieces, parts, elements, and so on, and arranging them so as to constitute a pattern or structure not clearly present before.

Evaluation. Evaluation requires judgments about the value of material and methods for given purposes. Quantitative and qualitative judgments are made about the extent to which material and methods satisfy criteria. The criteria employed may be those determined by the learner or those given to him.

Affective Domain

The affective domain is subdivided into five levels. These levels, in particular, may cause the evaluator much difficulty in classifying objectives. Once more, the five levels may have some value in that they encourage one to think about different forms of objectives, but it is not recommended that the evaluator devote too much time in attempting to classify various objectives within these levels.

Receiving (Attending). The first level of the affective domain is concerned with the learner's sensitivity to the existence of certain phenomena and stimuli, that is, with his willingness to receive or to attend to them. This category is divided into three subdivisions which reflect three different levels of attending to phenomena—namely, awareness of the phenomena, willingness to receive phenomena, and controlled or selected attention to phenomena.

Responding. At this level one is concerned with responses that go beyond merely attending to phenomena. The student is sufficiently motivated that he is not just "willing to attend," but is actively attending.

Valuing. This category reflects the learner's holding of a particular value. The learner displays behavior with sufficient consistency in appropriate situations that he actually is perceived as holding this value.

Organization. As the learner successively internalizes values, he encounters situations in which more than one value is relevant. This requires the necessity of organizing his values into a system such that certain values exercise greater control.

Characterization by a Value or Value Complex. At this highest level of the affective taxonomy internalization has taken place in an individual's value hierarchy to the extent that we can actually characterize him as holding a particular value or set of values.

Psychomotor Domain

Simpson's psychomotor taxonomy, although not as widely used as the cognitive and affective taxonomies, rounds out our three domain picture. Like the affective taxonomy, this domain consists of five levels.

Perception. The first step in performing a motor act is the process of becoming aware of objects, qualities or relations by way of the sense organs. It is the main portion of the situation-interpretation-action chain leading to motor activity.

Set. Set is a preparatory adjustment for a particular kind of action or experience. Three distinct aspects of set have been identified, namely, mental, physical, and emotional.

Guided Response. This is an early step in the development of a motor skill. The emphasis is upon the abilities that are components of the more complex skill. Guided response is the overt behavioral act of an individual under the guidance of another individual.

Mechanism. At this level the learner has achieved a certain confidence and degree of skill in the performance of an act. The habitual act is a part of his repertoire of possible responses to stimuli and the demands of situations where the response is appropriate.

Complex Overt Response. At this level, the individual can perform a motor act that is considered complex because of the movement pattern required. The act can be carried out efficiently and smoothly, that is, with minimum expenditure of energy and time.

Another way in which these taxonomies may be of use to the evaluator is as an aid in generating new objectives. The evaluator may suggest to the educator who is formulating objectives a wider variety of learner behaviors which might be incorporated in the objectives.

Guideline Number 6. The educational evaluator will often find the Taxonomies of Educational Objectives useful both in describing instructional objectives under consideration and in generating new objectives.

Constructing Versus Selecting Objectives

Thus far in the discussion it has been emphasized that the educational evaluator will find the use of measurable instructional objectives invaluable in his work. Recalling that the two major roles of educational evaluation occur in connection with needs assessment and assessing treatment adequacy, the evaluator will find that measurable goals are literally indispensable in properly carrying out either of these two roles. As we continue to examine additional techniques which may be used by evaluators this will become even more evident. Yet, there is a major problem to be faced by the evaluator, namely, where do such measurable goals come from?

Suppose, for example, that an evaluation consultant is called upon by a local school district to help in determining whether a new treatment, in this case a series of new text books, is sufficiently effective. The first thing he does is to ask what objective the treatment is supposed to accomplish. If he discovers that no objectives arise, at least none beyond a few nebulous general goals, what is he to do? Should he refuse to assist the district until they put their objectives in order? Obviously not. Should he prepare the objectives himself? Well, for any extended treatment that requires a tremendous amount of work and, besides, the school staff may not agree with the objectives he constructs. Should he give the school faculty a crash course in how to write objectives, then help them as they spell out their own measurable goals? So far, this seems like the best alternative, but the evaluator had best recognize that most school personnel—teachers through administrators—are already heavily committed to other assignments. Too many evaluators who have used this "help them construct their own objectives" approach will recount frustrating experiences in getting already harassed teachers to write out their own measurable objectives.

A better alternative would seem to be to ask the school faculty to *select* objectives from a set of alternatives rather than to ask them to construct their own. Selecting measurable objectives from a wide ranging set of alternatives represents a task that can reasonably be accomplished by most educators. Asking those same educators to *construct* their own measurable objectives is, generally speaking, an unrealistic request.

During the past few years several agencies have been established to collect large pools of instructional objectives and test measures. In general, these item banks and objectives banks have been assembled to permit educators to employ their resources in activities related to instruction or evaluation. A directory of extant collections of instructional objectives[7] is now available and should be of considerable use to an educational evaluator.

Illustrative of agencies established to collect and distribute educational objectives is the Instructional Objectives Exchange (IOX), founded in 1968. The Exchange has assembled an extensive collection of measurable instructional objectives in grades K-12 in all fields. These objectives were usually contributed to IOX by school districts, Title III projects, curriculum development teams, or individual teachers. Some were developed in the Instructional Objectives Exchange. As soon as a reasonably extensive group of objectives have been assembled in a given field at a given grade range, these are published as an IOX *collection*. Each collection consists of a set of objectives plus one or more measuring devices which may be used to assess the attainment of each objective. The Exchange intends to have at least a half dozen or so test items (broadly defined) for all their objectives so that they can be readily used to constitute pretests, posttests, etc.

By consulting the current listing of IOX objective collections[8] an evaluator can secure a set of alternative objectives from which the educators with whom he is working can select those appropriate for their own instructional situations. It is assumed that only a portion of any collection will be selected. Of course, if all the objectives which are sought are not included in a collection, the local educators can augment those available by writing some of their own. Since this should, in general, be a reasonably small number, the objective construction task should therefore not be too onerous.

Either for needs assessment or assessing treatment adequacy the use of extant objectives collections can prove invaluable. Although we shall be examining the specifics of the process in more detail later, it can be seen how in assessing the current perceptions of students, teachers, and community representatives regarding needed objectives, reactions to a list of possible objectives (selected from extant collections) would represent an economic way to secure such perceptions. Similarly, in assessing the adequacy of a new instructional procedure it should be relatively straightforward to select from an available collection those objectives which the procedure seemed best suited to accomplish. Since in many of the agencies currently distributing objectives a number of test items accompany each objective, it is apparent that it would be relatively simple to assess whether the objective had been accomplished.

Objective 87   Collection: Language Arts
                                                                   Grades 4–6

Major Category: Mechanics and Conventions
Sub-Category: Capitalization

OBJECTIVE: Given a set of sentences containing uncapitalized proper nouns, the student will identify nouns that should be capitalized.

SAMPLE ITEM: Rewrite all words that should be capitalized in the following sentences.

    1. Some emerald mines in colombia, central america, are more than four hundred years old.

    2. venezuela, colombia, argentina and peru have many oil wells.

    3. brasilia is a large modern city in brazil.

ANSWER: 1. Colombia; Central America

    2. Venezuela; Colombia; Argentina; Peru

    3. Brasilia; Brazil

FIGURE 1. Sample objective and item from an IOX collection.

To give the reader some idea of the kinds of materials available in these collections, Figure 1 includes an example from one of the IOX collections. Although the objectives from other objective pools may be organized somewhat differently, they are essentially comparable. In Figure 2 some affective objectives from two recently developed[9] collections, namely, (1) attitude toward school and (2) self-concept, are presented to illustrate the type of non-cognitive goals available in such collections.

Although the objective collections currently available at various locations throughout the country represent an extremely useful resource for the educational evaluator, there may be situations for which an evaluator finds no already prepared objectives available. The most likely alternatives for him to follow have been previously described, and they usually require his heavy involvement in construction of the objectives. Another option, however, is to try to pool the resources of several groups who have similar interests in order to produce a new objective pool. For instance, several of the health professions, notably nursing and dental education, have lately shown considerable interest in establishing objective banks which are specifically designed for their own instructional situations.

As these recently developed objective collections are revised and updated, as different forms of data (e.g., consumer value ratings) are assembled to guide the selector, and as more sophisticated storage and retrieval systems (e.g., computer-based) are established, these objectives/measures banks should provide an increasingly useful set of tools for an educational evaluator.

Guideline Number 7. The educational evaluator should consider the possibility of selecting measurable objectives from extant collections of such objectives.

In reviewing the section regarding the uses of instructional objectives by educational evaluators, we have examined (1) the role of measurability as an aid to clarity, (2) selected versus constructed learner responses, (3) content general versus test item equivalent objectives,

Attitude Toward School

(Attitude Toward School Subjects) Students will indicate relative preferences for five subject areas (aesthetics—art and music; language arts—spelling, oral participation, listening, writing; mathematics; reading; science), when given sets of three verbal descriptions of classroom activities in specific subject areas and three corresponding pictures, by marking one of the pictures to indicate in which activity they would most like to participate.

(General Attitude) Students will indicate favorable attitudes toward school, in a global sense, by incurring a minimum of absenteeism from school during a specified time period, as observed from teacher or school records.

(Attitude Toward School Subjects) Students will reveal relative preferences for seven subject areas (English, arithmetic, social studies, art, music, physical education, science) by selecting, from among sets of seven "headlines" (each representing one of the subject areas noted above), those that appear most and least interesting to read about.

Self Concept

Given a contrived situation in which the teacher describes several factitiously esteemed students, class members will demonstrate positive self concepts by voluntarily identifying themselves as students who have won the teacher's esteem.

The students will display unconditionally positive self concepts by responding to a 10-item inventory, entitled *Parental Approval Index*, which asks how the child's mother would feel about him as a person if he engaged in certain actions which would normally be expected to yield disapproval of the act.

Students will display an expectation for future success by checking a higher percentage of want ad job requests from the *Choose a Job Inventory* which offer more prestigious, socially approved occupations.

FIGURE 2. Examples of objectives from two IOX collections in the affective domain

(4) the proportion of objectives which must be measurable, (5) performance standards, (6) taxonomic analysis of objectives, and (7) selecting objectives from extant collections. For each of those points a guideline was presented which, briefly, suggested a course of action for educational evaluators.

NOTES

1. See, for example, Popham, W.J. and Baker, E.L. *Establishing Instructional Goals*, Prentice Hall, Inc., Englewood Cliffs, N.J., 1970, as well as the numerous citations in the selected references section of this guidebook. A series of filmstrip-tape programs distributed by Vimcet Associates, P.O. Box 24714, Los Angeles, California 90024, will also be helpful for training evaluation personnel.
2. Baker, E.L. *Defining Content for Objectives*, Vimcet Associates, Box 24714, Los Angeles, California, 1968.
3. Bloom, Benjamin, et al. *The Taxonomy of Educational Objectives, Handbook I: The Cognitive Domain*, David McKay, New York, 1956.
4. Krathwohl, David, et al. *The Taxonomy of Educational Objectives, Handbook II: The Affective Domain*, David McKay, New York, 1964.

5. Simpson, Elizabeth J. *The Classification of Educational Objectives: Psychomotor Domain*, Research Project No. OE-5-85-104, University of Illinois, Urbana, 1966.

6. It should be noted that in order to make accurate classifications according to the *Taxonomies* it is often necessary to know the nature of the instructional events preceding the point at which the learner's behavior is measured. For example, a given learner behavior might reflect only recall if the topic had been previously treated, but something quite different if not previously encountered in class.

7. The *Directory of Measurable Objectives Sources* at one time could be obtained from the Upper Midwest Regional Educational Laboratory in Minneapolis, Minnesota or in care of Mr. Arthur Olson, Colorado State Department of Education, State Office Building, Denver, Colorado 80203. Objectives and related tests of the Wisconsin Design for Reading Skill Development, an individualized reading system, are also available from National Computer Systems, 4401 West 76th St., Minneapolis, Minnesota 55435.

8. Available from IOX, Box 24095, Los Angeles, California 90024.

9. Support for the development of these affective objective collections was contributed in a cooperative effort of the state level ESEA Title III programs of the following states: Arizona, Colorado, Florida, Hawaii, Idaho, Iowa, Kansas, Massachusetts, Minnesota, Missouri, Montana, North Dakota, Ohio, Rhode Island, South Carolina, Texas and Wisconsin.

9

Educational Objectives— Help or Hindrance?[1]

ELLIOT W. EISNER

IF ONE WERE TO RANK THE VARIOUS BELIEFS or assumptions in the field of curriculum that are thought most secure, the belief in the need for clarity and specificity in stating educational objectives would surely rank among the highest. Educational objectives, it is argued, need to be clearly specified for at least three reasons: first, because they provide the goals toward which the curriculum is aimed; second, because once clearly stated they facilitate the selection and organization of content; third, because when specified in both behavioral and content terms they make it possible to evaluate the outcomes of the curriculum.

It is difficult to argue with a rational approach to curriculum development—who would choose irrationality? And, if one is to build curriculum in a rational way, the clarity of premise, end or starting point, would appear paramount. But I want to argue in this paper that educational objectives clearly and specifically stated can hamper as well as help the ends of instruction and that an unexamined belief in curriculum as in other domains of human activity can easily become dogma which in fact may hinder the very functions the concept was originally designed to serve.

When and where did beliefs concerning the importance of educational objectives in curriculum development emerge? Who has formulated and argued their importance? What effect has this belief had upon curriculum construction? If we examine the past briefly for data necessary for answering these questions, it appears that the belief in the usefulness of clear and specific educational objectives emerged around the turn of the century with the birth of the scientific movement in education.

Before this movement gained strength, faculty psychologists viewed the brain as consisting of a variety of intellectual faculties. These faculties, they held, could be strengthened if exercised in appropriate ways with particular subject matters. Once strengthened, the faculties could be used in any area of human activity to which they were applicable.

Reprinted by permission of the University of Chicago Press, from *School Review*, Vol. 75, No. 3, 1967: pp. 250–260. Copyright University of Chicago Press.

Thus, if the important faculties could be identified and if methods of strengthening them developed, the school could concentrate on this task and expect general intellectual excellence as a result.

This general theoretical view of mind had been accepted for several decades by the time Thorndike, Judd, and later Watson began, through their work, to chip away the foundations upon which it rested. Thorndike's work especially demonstrated the specificity of transfer. He argued theoretically that transfer of learning occurred if and only if elements in one situation were identical with elements in the other. His empirical work supported his theoretical views, and the enormous stature he enjoyed in education as well as in psychology influenced educators to approach curriculum development in ways consonant with his views. One of those who was caught up in the scientific movement in education was Franklin Bobbitt, often thought of as the father of curriculum theory. In 1918 Bobbitt published a signal work titled simply, *The Curriculum*.[2] In it he argued that educational theory is not so difficult to construct as commonly held and that curriculum theory is logically derivable from educational theory. Bobbitt wrote in 1918:

> The central theory is simple. Human life, however varied, consists in its performance of specific activities. Education that prepares for life is one that prepares definitely and adequately for these specific activities. However numerous and diverse they may be for any social class, they can be discovered. This requires that one go out into the world of affairs and discover the particulars of which these affairs consist. These will show the abilities, habits, appreciations, and forms of knowledge that men need. These will be the objectives of the curriculum. They will be numerous, definite, and particularized. The curriculum will then be that series of experiences which childhood and youth must have by way of attaining those objectives.[3]

In *The Curriculum*, Bobbitt approached curriculum development scientifically and theoretically: study life carefully to identify needed skills, divide these skills into specific units, organize these units into experiences, and provide these experiences to children. Six years later, in his second book, *How To Make a Curriculum*,[4] Bobbitt operationalized his theoretical assertions and demonstrated how curriculum components—especially educational objectives—were to be formulated. In this book Bobbitt listed nine areas in which educational objectives are to be specified. In these nine areas he listed 160 major educational objectives which run the gamut from "Ability to use language in all ways required for proper and effective participation in community life" to "Ability to entertain one's friends, and to respond to entertainment by one's friends."[5]

Bobbitt was not alone in his belief in the importance of formulating objectives clearly and specifically. Pendleton, for example, listed 1,581 social objectives for English, Guiler listed more than 300 for arithmetic in grades 1–6, and Billings prescribed 888 generalizations which were important for the social studies.

If Thorndike was right, if transfer was limited, it seemed reasonable to encourage the teacher to teach for particular outcomes and to construct curriculums only after specific objectives had been identified.

In retrospect it is not difficult to understand why this movement in curriculum collapsed under its own weight by the early 1930's. Teachers could not manage fifty highly specified objects, let alone hundreds. And, in addition, the new view of the child, not as a complex machine but as a growing organism who ought to participate in planning his own educational program, did not mesh well with the theoretical views held earlier.[6]

But, as we all know, the Progressive movement too began its decline in the forties, and by the middle fifties, as a formal organization at least, it was dead.

By the late forties and during the fifties, curriculum specialists again began to remind us of the importance of specific educational objectives and began to lay down guidelines for their formulation. Rationales for constructing curriculums developed by Ralph Tyler[7] and Virgil Herrick[8] again placed great importance on the specificity of objectives. George Barton[9] identified philosophic domains which could be used to select objectives. Benjamin Bloom and his colleagues[10] operationalized theoretical assertions by building a taxonomy of educational objectives in the cognitive domain; and in 1964, Krathwohl, Bloom, and Masia[11] did the same for the affective domain. Many able people for many years have spent a great deal of time and effort in identifying methods and providing prescriptions for the formulation of educational objectives, so much so that the statement "Educational objectives should be stated in behavioral terms" has been elevated—or lowered—to almost slogan status in curriculum circles. Yet, despite these efforts, teachers seem not to take educational objectives seriously—at least as they are prescribed from above. And when teachers plan curriculum guides, their efforts first to identify over-all educational aims, then specify school objectives, then identify educational objectives for specific subject matters, appear to be more like exercises to be gone through than serious efforts to build tools for curriculum planning. If educational objectives were really useful tools, teachers, I submit, would use them. If they do not, perhaps it is not because there is something wrong with the teachers but because there might be something wrong with the theory.

As I view the situation, there are several limitations to theory in curriculum regarding the functions educational objectives are to perform. These limitations I would like to identify.

Educational objectives are typically derived from curriculum theory, which assumes that it is possible to predict with a fair degree of accuracy what the outcomes of instruction will be. In a general way this is possible. If you set about to teach a student algebra, there is no reason to assume he will learn to construct sonnets instead. Yet, the outcomes of instruction are far more numerous and complex for educational objectives to encompass. The amount, type, and quality of learning that occurs in a classroom, especially when there is interaction among students, are only in small part predictable. The changes in pace, tempo, and goals that experienced teachers employ when necessary and appropriate for maintaining classroom organization are dynamic rather than mechanistic in character. Elementary school teachers, for example, are often sensitive to the changing interests of the children they teach, and frequently attempt to capitalize on these interests, "milking them" as it were for what is educationally valuable.[12] The teacher uses the moment in a situation that is better described as kaleidoscopic than stable. In the very process of teaching and discussing, unexpected opportunities emerge for making a valuable point, for demonstrating an interesting idea, and for teaching a significant concept. The first point I wish to make, therefore, is that the dynamic and complex process of instruction yields outcomes far too numerous to be specified in behavioral and content terms in advance.

A second limitation of theory concerning educational objectives is its failure to recognize the constraints various subject matters place upon objectives. The point here is brief. In some subject areas, such as mathematics, languages, and the sciences, it is possible to specify with great precision the particular operation or behavior the student is to perform after instruction. In other subject areas, especially the arts, such specification is frequently not possible, and when possible may not be desirable. In a class in mathematics or spelling, uniformity in response is desirable, at least insofar as it indicates that students are able to perform a particular operation adequately, that is, in accordance with accepted procedures. Effective instruction in such areas enables students to function with minimum error in these fields. In the arts and in subject matters where, for example, novel or creative responses are desired, the particular behaviors to be developed cannot easily be identified. Here curriculum and instruction should yield behaviors and products which are unpredictable. The end achieved ought to be something of a surprise to both teacher and pupil. While it could be argued that one might formulate an educational objective which specified novelty, originality, or creativeness as the desired outcome, the particular referents for these terms cannot be specified in advance; one must judge after the fact whether the product produced or the behavior displayed belongs in the "novel" class. This is a much different procedure than is determining whether or not a particular word has been spelled correctly or a specific performance, that is, jumping a 3-foot hurdle, has been attained. Thus, the second point is that theory concerning educational objectives has not taken into account the particular relationship that holds between the subject matter being taught and the degree to which educational objectives can be predicted and specified. This, I suppose, is in part due to the fact that few curriculum specialists have high degrees of intimacy with a wide variety of subject matters and thus are unable to alter their general theoretical views to suit the demands that particular subject matters make.

The third point I wish to make deals with the belief that objectives stated in behavioral and content terms can be used as criteria by which to measure the outcomes of curriculum and instruction. Educational objectives provide, it is argued, the standard against which achievement is to be measured. Both taxonomies are built upon this assumption since their primary function is to demonstrate how objectives can be used to frame test items appropriate for evaluation. The assumption that objectives can be used as standards by which to measure achievement fails, I think, to distinguish adequately between the application of a standard and the making of a judgment. Not all—perhaps not even most—outcomes of curriculum and instruction are amenable to measurement. The application of a standard requires that some arbitrary and socially defined quantity be designated by which other qualities can be compared. By virtue of socially defined rules of grammar, syntax, and logic, for example, it is possible to quantitatively compare and measure error in a discursive or mathematical statement. Some fields of activity, especially those which are qualitative in character, have no comparable rules and hence are less amenable to quantitative assessment. It is here that evaluation must be made, not primarily by applying a socially defined standard, but by making a human qualitative judgment. One can specify, for example, that a student shall be expected to know how to extract a square root correctly and in an unambiguous way, through the application of a standard, determine whether this end has been achieved. But it is only in a metaphoric sense that one can measure the extent to which a student has been able to produce an aesthetic object or an expressive narrative. Here standards are unapplicable; here judgment is required. The making of a judgment in distinction to the application of a standard implies that valued qualities are not merely socially defined and arbitrary in character. The judgment by which a critic determines the value of a poem, novel, or play is not achieved merely by applying standards already known to the particular product being judged; it requires that the critic—or teacher—view the product with respect to the unique properties it displays and then, in relation to his experience and sensibilities, judge its value in terms which are incapable of being reduced to quantity or rule.

This point was aptly discussed by John Dewey in his chapter on "Perception and Criticism" in *Art as Experience*.[13] Dewey was concerned with the problem of identifying the means and ends of criticism and has this to say about its proper function:

> The function of criticism is the reeducation of perception of works of art; it is an auxiliary process, a difficult process, of learning to see and hear. The conception that its business is to appraise, to judge in the legal and moral sense, arrests the perception of those who are influenced by the criticism that assumes this task.[14]

Of the distinction that Dewey makes between the application of a standard and the making of a critical judgment, he writes:

> There are three characteristics of a standard. It is a particular physical thing existing under specifiable conditions; it is *not* a value. The yard is a yard-stick, and the meter is a bar deposited in Paris. In the second place, standards are measures of things, of lengths, weights, capacities. The things measured are not values, although it is of great social value to be able to measure them, since the properties of things in the way of size, volume, weight, are important for commercial exchange. Finally, as standards of measure, standards define things with respect to *quantity*. To be able to measure quantities is a great aid to further judgments, but it is not a mode of judgment. The standard, being an external and public thing, is applied *physically*. The yard-stick is physically laid down upon things to determine their length.[15]

And I would add that what is most educationally valuable is the development of that mode of curiosity, inventiveness, and insight that is capable of being described only in metaphoric or poetic terms. Indeed, the image of the educated man that has been held in highest esteem for the longest period of time in Western civilization is one which is not amenable to standard measurement. Thus, the third point I wish to make is that curriculum theory which views educational objectives as standards by which to measure educational achievement overlooks those modes of achievement incapable of measurement.

The final point I wish to make deals with the function of educational objectives in curriculum construction.

The rational approach to curriculum development not only emphasizes the importance of specificity in the formulation of educational objectives but also implies when not stated explicitly that educational objectives be stated prior to the formulation of curriculum activities. At first view, this seems to be a reasonable way to proceed with curriculum construction: one should know where he is headed before embarking on a trip. Yet, while the procedure of first identifying objectives before proceeding to identify activities is logically defensible, it is not necessarily the most psychologically efficient way to proceed. One can, and teachers often do, identify activities that seem useful, appropriate, or rich in educational opportunities, and from a consideration of what can be done in class, identify the objectives or possible consequences of using these activities. MacDonald argues this point cogently when he writes:

> Let us look, for example, at the problem of objectives. Objectives are viewed as directives in the rational approach. They are identified prior to the instruction or action and used to provide a basis for a screen for appropriate activities.
>
> There is another view, however, which has both scholarly and experiential referents. This view would state that our objectives are only known to us in any complete sense after the completion of our act of instruction. No matter what we thought we were attempting to do, we can only know what we wanted to accomplish after the fact. Objectives by this rationale are heuristic devices which provide initiating consequences which become altered in the flow of instruction.
>
> In the final analysis, it could be argued, the teacher in actuality asks a fundamentally different question from "What am I trying to accomplish?" The teacher asks "What am I going to do?" and out of the doing comes accomplishment.[16]

Theory in curriculum has not adequately distinguished between logical adequacy in determining the relationship of means to ends when examining the curriculum as a *product* and the psychological processes that may usefully be employed in building curriculums. The method of forming creative insights in curriculum development, as in the sciences and arts, is as yet not logically prescribable. The ways in which curriculums can be usefully and efficiently developed constitute an empirical problem; imposing logical requirements upon the process because they are desirable for assessing the product is, to my mind, an error. Thus, the final point I wish to make is that educational objectives need not precede the selection and organization of content. The means through which imaginative curriculums can be built is as open-ended as the means through which scientific and artistic inventions occur. Curriculum theory needs to allow for a variety of processes to be employed in the construction of curriculums.

I have argued in this paper that curriculum theory as it pertains to educational objectives has had four significant limitations. First, it has not sufficiently emphasized the extent to which the prediction of educational outcomes cannot be made with accuracy. Second, it has not discussed the ways in which the subject matter affects precision in stating educational objectives. Third, it has confused the use of educational objectives as a standard for measurement when in some areas it can be used only as a criterion for judgment. Fourth, it has not distinguished between the logical requirement of relating means to ends in the curriculum as a product and the psychological conditions useful for constructing curriculums.

If the arguments I have formulated about the limitations of curriculum theory concerning educational objectives have merit, one might ask: What are their educational consequences? First, it seems to me that they suggest that in large measure the construction of curriculums and the judgment of its consequences are artful tasks. The methods of curriculums development are, in principle if not in practice, no different from the making of art— be it the art of painting or the art of science. The identification of the factors in the potentially useful educational activity and the organization or construction of sequence in curriculum are in principle amenable to an infinite number of combinations. The variable teacher, student, class group, require artful blending for the educationally valuable to result.

Second, I am impressed with Dewey's view of the functions of criticism—to heighten one's perception of the art object—and believe it has implications for curriculum theory. If the child is viewed as an art product and the teacher as a critic, one task of the teacher would be to reveal the qualities of the child to himself and to others. In addition, the teacher as critic would appraise the changes occurring in the child. But because the teacher's task includes more than criticism, he would also be responsible, in part, for the improvement of the work of art. In short, in both the construction of educational means (the curriculum) and the appraisal of its consequences, the teacher would become an artist, for criticism itself when carried to its height is an art. This, it seems to me, is a dimension to which curriculum theory will someday have to speak.

NOTES

1. This is a slightly expanded version of a paper presented at the fiftieth annual meeting of the American Educational Research Association, Chicago, February, 1966.
2. Franklin Bobbitt, *The Curriculum* (Boston: Houghton Mifflin Co., 1918).
3. *Ibid.*, p. 42.
4. Franklin Bobbitt, *How To Make a Curriculum* (Boston: Houghton Mifflin Co., 1924).
5. *Ibid.*, pp. 11–29.
6. For a good example of this view of the child and curriculum development, see *The Changing Curriculum, Tenth Yearbook,* Department of Supervisors and Directors of Instruction, National Education Association and Society for Curriculum Study (New York: Appleton-Century Crofts Co., 1937).
7. Ralph W. Tyler, *Basic Principles of Curriculum and Instruction* (Chicago: University of Chicago Press, 1951).
8. Virgil E. Herrick, "The Concept of Curriculum Design," *Toward Improved Curriculum Theory*, ed. Virgil E. Herrick and Ralph W. Tyler (Supplementary Educational Monographs, No. 71 [Chicago: University of Chicago Press, 1950]), pp. 37–50.
9. George E. Barton, Jr., "Educational Objectives: Improvement of Curriculum Theory about Their Determination," *ibid.*, pp. 26–35.
10. Benjamin Bloom et al. (ed.), *Taxonomy of Educational Objectives, Handbook I:* The Cognitive Domain (New York: Longmans, Green & Co., 1956).
11. David Krathwohl, Benjamin Bloom, and Bertram Masia, *Taxonomy of Educational Objectives, Handbook II: The Affective Domain* (New York: David McKay, Inc., 1964).
12. For an excellent paper describing educational objectives as they are viewed and used by elementary school teachers, see Philip W. Jackson and Elizabeth Belford, "Educational Objectives and the Joys of Teaching," *School Review,* LXXIII (1965), 267–91.
13. John Dewey, *Art as Experience* (New York: Minton, Balch & Co., 1934).
14. *Ibid.*, p. 324.
15. *Ibid.*, p. 307.
16. James B. MacDonald, "Myths about Instruction," *Educational Leadership,* XXII, No. 7 (May, 1965), 613–14.

10

The Daily Grind

Philip W. Jackson

On a typical weekday morning between September and June some 35 million Americans kiss their loved ones goodby, pick up their lunch pails and books, and leave to spend their day in that collection of enclosures (totalling about one million) known as elementary school classrooms. This massive exodus from home to school is accomplished with a minimum of fuss and bother. Few tears are shed (except perhaps by the very youngest) and few cheers are raised. The school attendance of children is such a common experience in our society that those of us who watch them go hardly pause to consider what happens to them when they get there. Of course our indifference disappears occasionally. When something goes wrong or when we have been notified of his remarkable achievement, we might ponder, for a moment at least, the meaning of the experience for the child in question, but most of the time we simply note that our Johnny is on his way to school, and now, it is time for our second cup of coffee.

Parents are interested, to be sure, in how *well* Johnny does while there, and when he comes trudging home they may ask him questions about what happened today or, more generally, how things went. But both their questions and his answers typically focus on the highlights of the school experience—its unusual aspects—rather than on the mundane and seemingly trivial events that filled the bulk of his school hours. Parents are interested, in other words, in the spice of school life rather than in its substance.

Teachers, too, are chiefly concerned with only a very narrow aspect of a youngster's school experience. They, too, are likely to focus on specific acts of misbehavior or accomplishment as representing what a particular student did in school today, even though the acts in question occupied but a small fraction of the student's time. Teachers, like parents, seldom ponder the significance of the thousands of fleeting events that combine to form the routine of the classroom.

Reprinted by permission of the publisher, from Philip W. Jackson, *Life in Classrooms* (New York: Teachers College Press © 1990 by Teachers College, Columbia University. All rights reserved.), pp. 3–11, 33–37. (Originally published 1968.)

And the student himself is no less selective. Even if someone bothered to question him about the minutiae of his school day, he would probably be unable to give a complete account of what he had done. For him, too, the day has been reduced in memory into a small number of signal events—"I got 100 on my spelling test," "We went to gym," "We had music." His spontaneous recall of detail is not much greater than that required to answer our conventional questions.

This concentration on the highlights of school life is understandable from the standpoint of human interest. A similar selection process operates when we inquire into or recount other types of daily activity. When we are asked about our trip down-town or our day at the office we rarely bother describing the ride on the bus or the time spent in front of the watercooler. Indeed, we are more likely to report that nothing happened than to catalogue the pedestrian actions that took place between home and return. Unless something interesting occurred there is little purpose in talking about our experience.

Yet from the standpoint of giving shape and meaning to our lives these events about which we rarely speak may be as important as those that hold our listener's attention. Certainly they represent a much larger portion of our experience than do those about which we talk. The daily routine, the "rat race," and the infamous "old grind" may be brightened from time to time by happenings that add color to an otherwise drab existence, but the grayness of our daily lives has an abrasive potency of its own. Anthropologists understand this fact better than do most other social scientists, and their field studies have taught us to appreciate the cultural significance of the humdrum elements of human existence. This is the lesson we must heed as we seek to understand life in elementary classrooms.

I

School is a place where tests are failed and passed, where amusing things happen, where new insights are stumbled upon, and skills acquired. But it is also a place in which people sit, and listen, and wait, and raise their hands, and pass out paper, and stand in line, and sharpen pencils. School is where we encounter both friends and foes, where imagination is unleashed and misunderstanding brought to ground. But it is also a place in which yawns are stifled and initials scratched on desktops, where milk money is collected and recess lines are formed. Both aspects of school life, the celebrated and the unnoticed, are familiar to all of us, but the latter, if only because of its characteristic neglect, seems to deserve more attention than it has received to date from those who are interested in education.

In order to appreciate the significance of trivial classroom events it is necessary to consider the frequency of their occurrence, the standardization of the school environment, and the compulsory quality of daily attendance. We must recognize, in other words, that children are in school for a long time, that the settings in which they perform are highly uniform, and that they are there whether they want to be or not. Each of these three facts, although seemingly obvious, deserves some elaboration, for each contributes to our understanding of how students feel about and cope with their school experience.

The amount of time children spend in school can be described with a fair amount of quantitative precision, although the psychological significance of the numbers involved is another matter entirely. In most states the school year legally comprises 180 days. A full session on each of those days usually lasts about six hours (with a break for lunch), beginning somewhere around nine o'clock in the morning and ending about three o'clock in the afternoon. Thus, if a student never misses a day during the year, he spends a little more than one thousand hours under the care and tutelage of teachers. If he has attended kindergarten and was reasonably regular in his attendance during the grades, he will have logged a little more than seven thousand classroom hours by the time he is ready for junior high school.

The magnitude of 7,000 hours spread over six or seven years of a child's life is difficult to comprehend. On the one hand, when placed beside the total number of hours the child has lived during those years it is not very great—slightly more than one-tenth of his life during the time in question, about one-third of his hours of sleep during that period. On the other hand, aside from sleeping, and perhaps playing, there is no other activity that occupies as much of the child's time as that involved in attending school. Apart from the bedroom (where he has his eyes closed most of the time) there is no single enclosure in which he spends a longer time than he does in the classroom. From the age of six onward he is a more familiar sight to his teacher than to his father, and possibly even to his mother.

Another way of estimating what all those hours in the classroom mean is to ask how long it would take to accumulate them while engaged in some other familiar and recurring activity. Church attendance provides an interesting comparison. In order to have had as much time in church as a sixth grader has had in classrooms we would have to spend all day at a religious gathering every Sunday for more than 24 years. Or, if we prefer our devotion in smaller doses, we would have to attend a one-hour service every Sunday for 150 years before the inside of a church became as familiar to us as the inside of a school is to a twelve-year-old.

The comparison with church attendance is dramatic, and perhaps overly so. But it does make us stop and think about the possible significance of an otherwise meaningless number. Also, aside from the home and the school there is no physical setting in which people of all ages congregate with as great a regularity as they do in church.

The translation of the child's tenure in class into terms of weekly church attendance serves a further purpose. It sets the stage for considering an important similarity between the two institutions: school and church. The inhabitants of both are surrounded by a stable and highly stylized environment. The fact of prolonged exposure in either setting increases in its meaning as we begin to consider the elements of repetition, redundancy, and ritualistic action that are experienced there.

A classroom, like a church auditorium, is rarely seen as being anything other than that which it is. No one entering either place is likely to think that he is in a living room, or a grocery store, or a train station. Even if he entered at midnight or at some other time when the activities of the people would not give the function away, he would have no difficulty understanding what was *supposed* to go on there. Even devoid of people, a church is a church and a classroom, a classroom.

This is not to say, of course, that all classrooms are identical, anymore than all churches are. Clearly there are differences, and sometimes very extreme ones, between any two settings. One has only to think of the wooden benches and planked floor of the early American classroom as compared with the plastic chairs and tile flooring in today's suburban schools. But the resemblance is still there despite the differences, and, more important, during any particular historical period the differences are not that great. Also, whether the student moves from first to sixth grade on floors of vinyl tile or oiled wood, whether he spends his days in front of a black blackboard or a green one, is not as important as the fact that the environment in which he spends these six or seven years is highly stable.

In their efforts to make their classrooms more homelike, elementary school teachers often spend considerable time fussing with the room's decorations. Bulletin boards are changed, new pictures are hung, and the seating arrangement is altered from circles to rows and back again. But these are surface adjustments at best, resembling the work of the inspired housewife who rearranges the living room furniture and changes the color of the drapes in order to make the room more "interesting." School bulletin boards may be changed but they are never discarded, the seats may be rearranged but thirty of them are there to stay, the teacher's desk may have a new plant on it but there it sits, as ubiquitous as the roll-down maps, the olive drab waste-basket, and the pencil sharpener on the window ledge.

Even the odors of the classroom are fairly standardized. Schools may use different brands of wax and cleaning fluid, but they all seem to contain similar ingredients, a sort of universal smell which creates an aromatic background that permeates the entire building. Added to this, in each classroom, is the slightly acrid scent of chalk dust and the faint hint of fresh wood from the pencil shavings. In some rooms, especially at lunch time, there is the familiar odor of orange peels and peanut butter sandwiches, a blend that mingles in the late afternoon (following recess) with the delicate pungency of children's perspiration. If a person stumbled into a classroom blindfolded, his nose alone, if he used it carefully, would tell him where he was.

All of these sights and smells become so familiar to students and teachers alike that they exist dimly, on the periphery of awareness. Only when the classroom is encountered under somewhat unusual circumstances, does it appear, for a moment, a strange place filled with objects that command our attention. On these rare occasions when, for example, students return to school in the evening, or in the summer when the halls ring with the hammers of workmen, many features of the school environment that have merged into an undifferentiated background for its daily inhabitants suddenly stand out in sharp relief. This experience, which obviously occurs in contexts other than the classroom, can only happen in settings to which the viewer has become uncommonly habituated.

Not only is the classroom a relatively stable physical environment, it also provides a fairly constant social context. Behind the same old desks sit the same old students, in front of the familiar blackboard stands the familiar teacher. There are changes, to be sure— some students come and go during the year and on a few mornings the children are greeted at the door by a strange adult. But in most cases these events are sufficiently uncommon to create a flurry of excitement in the room. Moreover, in most elementary classrooms the social composition is not only stable, it is also physically arranged with considerable regularity. Each student has an assigned seat and, under normal circumstances, that is where he is to be found. The practice of assigning seats makes it possible for the teacher or a student to take attendance at a glance. A quick visual sweep is usually sufficient to determine who is there and who is not. The ease with which this procedure is accomplished reveals more eloquently than do words how accustomed each member of the class is to the presence of every other member.

An additional feature of the social atmosphere of elementary classrooms deserves at least passing comment. There is a social intimacy in schools that is unmatched elsewhere in our society. Buses and movie theaters may be more crowded than classrooms, but people rarely stay in such densely populated settings for extended periods of time and while there, they usually are not expected to concentrate on work or to interact with each other.

Even factory workers are not clustered as close together as students in a standard class-room. Indeed, imagine what would happen if a factory the size of a typical elementary school contained three or four hundred adult workers. In all likelihood the unions would not allow it. Only in schools do thirty or more people spend several hours each day literally side by side. Once we leave the classroom we seldom again are required to have contact with so many people for so long a time. This fact will become particularly relevant in a later chapter in which we treat the social demands of life in school.

A final aspect of the constancy experienced by young students involves the ritualistic and cyclic quality of the activities carried on in the classroom. The daily schedule, as an instance, is commonly divided into definite periods during which specific subjects are to be studied or specific activities engaged in. The content of the work surely changes from day to day and from week to week, and in this sense there is considerable variety amid the constancy. But spelling still comes after arithmetic on Tuesday morning, and when the teacher says, "All right class, now take out your spellers," his announcement comes as no surprise to the students. Further, as they search in their desks for their spelling textbooks, the children may not know what new words will be included in the day's assignment, but they have a fairly clear idea of what the next twenty minutes of class time will entail.

Despite the diversity of subject matter content, the identifiable forms of classroom activity are not great in number. The labels: "seatwork," "group discussion," "teacher demonstration," and "question-and-answer period" (which would include work "at the board"), are sufficient to categorize most of the things that happen when class is in session. "Audiovisual display," "testing session," and "games" might be added to the list, but in most elementary classrooms they occur rarely.

Each of these major activities are performed according to rather well-defined rules which the students are expected to understand and obey—for example, no loud talking during seatwork, do not interrupt someone else during discussion, keep your eyes on your own paper during tests, raise your hand if you have a question. Even in the early grades these rules are so well understood by the students (if not completely internalized) that the teacher has only to give very abbreviated signals ("Voices, class," "Hands, please.") when violations are perceived. In many classrooms a weekly time schedule is permanently posted so that everyone can tell at a glance what will happen next.

Thus, when our young student enters school in the morning he is entering an environment with which he has become exceptionally familiar through prolonged exposure. Moreover, it is a fairly stable environment—one in which the physical objects, social relations, and major activities remain much the same from day to day, week to week, and even, in certain respects, from year to year. Life there resembles life in other contexts in some ways, but not all. There is, in other words, a uniqueness to the student's world. School, like church and home, is someplace special. Look where you may, you will not find another place quite like it.

There is an important fact about a student's life that teachers and parents often prefer not to talk about, at least not in front of students. This is the fact that young people have to be in school, whether they want to be or not. In this regard students have something in common with the members of two other of our social institutions that have involuntary attendance: prisons and mental hospitals. The analogy, though dramatic, is not intended to be shocking, and certainly there is no comparison between the unpleasantness of life for inmates of our prisons and mental institutions, on the one hand, and the daily travails of a first or second grader, on the other. Yet the school child, like the incarcerated adult, is, in a sense, a prisoner. He too must come to grips with the inevitability of his experience. He too must develop strategies for dealing with the conflict that frequently arises between his natural desires and interests on the one hand and institutional expectations on the other. Several of these strategies will be discussed in the chapters that follow. Here it is sufficient to note that the thousands of hours spent in the highly stylized environment of the elementary classroom are not, in an ultimate sense, a matter of choice, even though some children might prefer school to play. Many seven-year-olds skip happily to school, and as parents and teachers we are glad they do, but we stand ready to enforce the attendance of those who are more reluctant. And our vigilance does not go unnoticed by children.

In sum, classrooms are special places. The things that happen there and the ways in which they happen combine to make these settings different from all others. This is not to say, of course, that there is no similarity between what goes on in school and the students' experiences elsewhere. Classrooms are indeed like homes and churches and hospital wards in many important respects. But not in all.

The things that make schools different from other places are not only the paraphernalia of learning and teaching and the educational content of the dialogues that take place there, although these are the features that are usually singled out when we try to portray what life in school is really like. It is true that nowhere else do we find blackboards and teachers and textbooks in such abundance and nowhere else is so much time spent on reading, writing, and arithmetic. But these obvious characteristics do not constitute all that is unique about this environment. There are other features, much less obvious though equally omnipresent, that help to make up "the facts of life," as it were, to which students must adapt. From the standpoint of understanding the impact of school life on the student some features of the classroom that are not immediately visible are fully as important as those that are.

The characteristics of school life to which we now turn our attention are not commonly mentioned by students, at least not directly, nor are they apparent to the casual observer. Yet they are as real, in a sense, as the unfinished portrait of Washington that hangs above the cloakroom door. They comprise three facts of life with which even the youngest student must learn to deal and may be introduced by the key words: *crowds, praise,* and *power.*

Learning to live in a classroom involves, among other things, learning to live in a crowd. This simple truth has already been mentioned, but it requires greater elaboration. Most of the things that are done in school are done with others, or at least in the presence of others, and this fact has profound implications for determining the quality of a student's life.

Of equal importance is the fact that schools are basically evaluative settings. The very young student may be temporarily fooled by tests that are presented as games, but it doesn't take long before he begins to see through the subterfuge and comes to realize that school, after all, is a serious business. It is not only what you do there but what others think of what you do that is important. Adaptation to school life requires the student to become used to living under the constant condition of having his words and deeds evaluated by others.

School is also a place in which the division between the weak and the powerful is clearly drawn. This may sound like a harsh way to describe the separation between teachers and students, but it serves to emphasize a fact that is often overlooked, or touched upon gingerly at best. Teachers are indeed more powerful than students, in the sense of having greater responsibility for giving shape to classroom events, and this sharp difference in authority is another feature of school life with which students must learn how to deal.

In three major ways then—as members of crowds, as potential recipients of praise or reproof, and as pawns of institutional authorities—students are confronted with aspects of reality that at least during their childhood years are relatively confined to the hours spent in classrooms. Admittedly, similar conditions are encountered in other environments. Students, when they are not performing as such, must often find themselves lodged within larger groups, serving as targets of praise or reproof, and being bossed around or guided by persons in positions of higher authority. But these kinds of experiences are particularly frequent while school is in session and it is likely during this time that adaptive strategies having relevance for other contexts and other life periods are developed.

In the sections of this chapter to follow, each of the three classroom qualities that have been briefly mentioned will be described in greater detail. Particular emphasis will be given to the manner in which students cope with these aspects of their daily lives. The goal of this discussion, as in the preceding chapters, is to deepen our understanding of the peculiar mark that school life makes on us all. . . .

V

As implied in the title of this chapter, the crowds, the praise, and the power that combine to give a distinctive flavor to classroom life collectively form a hidden curriculum which each student (and teacher) must master if he is to make his way satisfactorily through the school. The demands created by these features of classroom life may be contrasted with the academic demands—the "official" curriculum, so to speak—to which educators traditionally have paid the most attention. As might be expected, the two curriculums are related to each other in several important ways.

As has already been suggested in the discussion of praise in the classroom, the reward system of the school is linked to success in both curriculums. Indeed, many of the rewards and punishments that sound as if they are being dispensed on the basis of academic success and failure are really more closely related to the mastery of the hidden curriculum. Consider, as an instance, the common teaching practice of giving a student credit for trying. What do teachers mean when they say a student tries to do his work? They mean, in essence, that he complies with the procedural expectations of the institution. He does his homework (though incorrectly), he raises his hand during class discussion (though he usually comes up with the wrong answer), he keeps his nose in his book during free study period (though he doesn't turn the page very often). He is, in other words, a "model" student, though not necessarily a good one.

It is difficult to imagine any of today's teachers, particularly those in elementary schools, failing a student who tries, even though his mastery of course content is slight. Indeed, even at higher levels of education rewards sometimes go to the meek as well as the mighty. It is certainly possible that many of our valedictorians and presidents of our honor societies owe their success as much to institutional conformity as to intellectual prowess. Although it offends our sensibilities to admit it, no doubt that bright-eyed little girl who stands trembling before the principal on graduation day arrived there at least in part because she typed her weekly themes neatly and handed her homework in on time.

This manner of talking about educational affairs may sound cynical and may be interpreted as a criticism of teachers or as an attempt to subvert the virtues of neatness, punctuality, and courteous conduct in general. But nothing of that kind is intended. The point is simply that in schools, as in prisons, good behavior pays off.

Just as conformity to institutional expectations can lead to praise, so can the lack of it lead to trouble. As a matter of fact, the relationship of the hidden curriculum to student difficulties is even more striking than is its relationship to student success. As an instance, consider the conditions leading to disciplinary action in the classroom. Why do teachers scold students? Because the student has given a wrong answer? Because, try as he might, he fails to grasp the intricacies of long division? Not usually. Rather, students are commonly scolded for coming into the room late or for making too much noise or for not listening to the teacher's directions or for pushing while in line. The teacher's wrath, in other words, is more frequently triggered by violations of institutional regulations and routines than by signs of his students' intellectual deficiencies.

Even when we consider the more serious difficulties that clearly entail academic failure, the demands of the hidden curriculum lurk in the background. When Johnny's parents are called in to school because their son is not doing too well in arithmetic, what explanation is given for their son's poor performance? Typically, blame is placed on motivational deficiencies in Johnny rather than on his intellectual shortcomings. The teacher may even go so far as to say that Johnny is *un*motivated during arithmetic period. But what does this mean? It means, in essence, that Johnny does not even try. And not trying, as we have seen, usually boils down to a failure to comply with institutional expectations, a failure to master the hidden curriculum.

Testmakers describe a person as "test-wise" when he has caught on to the tricks of test construction sufficiently well to answer questions correctly even though he does not know the material on which he is being examined. In the same way one might think of students as becoming "school-wise" or "teacher-wise" when they have discovered how to respond with a minimum amount of pain and discomfort to the demands, both official and unofficial, of classroom life. Schools, like test items, have rules and traditions of their own that can only be mastered through successive exposure. But with schools as with tests all students are not equally adroit. All are asked to respond but not everyone catches on to the rules of the game.

If it is useful to think of there being two curriculums in the classroom, a natural question to ask about the relationship between them is whether their joint mastery calls for compatible or contradictory personal qualities. That is, do the same strengths that contribute to intellectual achievement also contribute to the student's success in conformity to institutional expectations? This question likely has no definite answer, but it is thought-provoking and even a brief consideration of it leads into a thicket of educational and psychological issues.

It is probably safe to predict that general ability, or intelligence, would be an asset in meeting all of the demands of school life, whether academic or institutional. The child's ability to understand causal relationships, as an instance, would seem to be of as much service as he tries to come to grips with the rules and regulations of classroom life as when he grapples with the rudiments of plant chemistry. His verbal fluency can be put to use as easily in "snowing" the teacher as in writing a short story. Thus, to the extent that the demands of classroom life call for rational thought, the student with superior intellectual ability would seem to be at an advantage.

But more than ability is involved in adapting to complex situations. Much also depends upon attitudes, values, and life style—upon all those qualities commonly grouped under the term: *personality*. When the contribution of personality to adaptive strategy is considered, the old adage of "the more, the better," which works so well for general ability, does not suffice. Personal qualities that are beneficial in one setting may be detrimental in another. Indeed, even a single setting may make demands that call upon competing or conflicting tendencies in a person's makeup.

We have already seen that many features of classroom life call for patience, at best, and resignation, at worst. As he learns to live in school our student learns to subjugate his own desires to the will of the teacher and to subdue his own actions in the interest of the common good. He learns to be passive and to acquiesce to the network of rules, regulations, and routines in which he is embedded. He learns to tolerate petty frustrations and accept the plans and policies of higher authorities, even when their rationale is unexplained and their meaning unclear. Like the inhabitants of most other institutions, he learns how to shrug and say, "That's the way the ball bounces."

But the personal qualities that play a role in intellectual mastery are very different from those that characterize the Company Man. Curiosity, as an instance, that most fundamental of all scholarly traits, is of little value in responding to the demands of conformity. The curious person typically engages in a kind of probing, poking, and exploring that is almost antithetical to the attitude of the passive conformist. The scholar must develop the habit of challenging authority and of questioning the value of tradition. He must insist on explanations for things that are unclear. Scholarship requires discipline, to be sure, but this discipline serves the demands of scholarship rather than the wishes and desires of other people. In short, intellectual mastery calls for sublimited forms of aggression rather than for submission to constraints.

This brief discussion likely exaggerates the real differences between the demands of institutional conformity and the demands of scholarship, but it does serve to call attention to points of possible conflict. How incompatible are these two sets of demands? Can both be mastered by the same person? Apparently so. Certainly not all of our student council presidents and valedictorians can be dismissed as weak-willed teacher's pets, as academic Uriah Heeps. Many students clearly manage to maintain their intellectual aggressiveness while at the same time acquiescing to the laws that govern the social traffic of our schools. Apparently it *is* possible, under certain conditions, to breed "docile scholars," even though the expression seems to be a contradiction in terms. Indeed, certain forms of scholarship have been known to flourish in monastic settings, where the demands for institutional conformity are extreme.

Unfortunately, no one seems to know how these balances are maintained, nor even how to establish them in the first place. But even more unfortunate is the fact that few if any school people are giving the matter serious thought. As institutional settings multiply and become for more and more people the areas in which a significant portion of their life is enacted, we will need to know much more than we do at present about how to achieve a reasonable synthesis between the forces that drive a person to seek individual expression and those that drive him to comply with the wishes of others. Presumably what goes on in classrooms contributes significantly to this synthesis. The school is the first major institution, outside the family, in which almost all of us are immersed. From kindergarten onward, the student begins to learn what life is really like in The Company.

The demands of classroom life discussed in this chapter pose problems for students and teachers alike. As we have seen, there are many methods for coping with these demands and for solving the problems they create. Moreover, each major adaptive strategy is subtly transformed and given a unique expression as a result of the idiosyncratic characteristics of the student employing it. Thus, the total picture of adjustment to school becomes infinitely complex as it is manifested in the behavior of individual students.

Yet certain commonalities do exist beneath all the complexity created by the uniqueness of individuals. No matter what the demand or the personal resources of the person facing it there is at least one strategy open to all. This is the strategy of psychological withdrawal, of gradually reducing personal concern and involvement to a point where neither the demand nor one's success or failure in coping with it is sharply felt. In order to better understand student tactics, however, it is important to consider the climate of opinion from which they emerge. Before focusing on what they do in the classroom, we must examine how students feel about school.

11

The Practical: A Language for Curriculum[1]

Joseph J. Schwab

I SHALL HAVE THREE POINTS. THE FIRST IS THIS: that the field of curriculum is moribund, unable by its present methods and principles to continue its work and desperately in search of new and more effective principles and methods.

The second point: the curriculum field has reached this unhappy state by inveterate and unexamined reliance on theory in an area where theory is partly inappropriate in the first place and where the theories extant, even where appropriate, are inadequate to the tasks which the curriculum field sets them. There are honorable exceptions to this rule but too few (and too little honored) to alter the state of affairs.

The third point, which constitutes my thesis: there will be a renaissance of the field of curriculum, a renewed capacity to contribute to the quality of American education, only if the bulk of curriculum energies are diverted from the theoretic to the practical, to the quasi-practical and to the eclectic. By "eclectic" I mean the arts by which unsystematic, uneasy, but usable focus on a body of problems is effected among diverse theories, each relevant to the problems in a different way. By the "practical" I do *not* mean the curbstone practicality of the mediocre administrator and the man on the street, for whom the practical means the easily achieved, familiar goals which can be reached by familiar means. I refer, rather, to a complex discipline, relatively unfamiliar to the academic and differing radically from the disciplines of the theoretic. It is the discipline concerned with choice and action, in contrast with the theoretic, which is concerned with knowledge. Its methods lead to defensible decisions, where the methods of the theoretic lead to warranted conclusions, and differ radically from the methods and competences entailed in the theoretic. I shall sketch some of the defining aspects of practical discipline at the appropriate time.

A CRISIS OF PRINCIPLE

The frustrated state of the field of curriculum is not an idiopathology and not a condition which warrants guilt or shame on the part of its practitioners. All fields of systematic

Reprinted by permission of the University of Chicago Press, from *School Review*, Vol. 78, No. 1, 1969: pp. 1–23. Published by the University of Chicago Press.

intellectual activity are liable to such crises. They are so because any intellectual discipline must begin its endeavors with untested principles. In its beginnings, its subject matter is relatively unknown, its problems unsolved, indeed unidentified. It does not know what questions to ask, what other knowledge to rest upon, what data to seek or what to make of them once they are elicited. It requires a preliminary and necessarily untested guide to its enquiries. It finds this guide by borrowing, by invention, or by analogy, in the shape of a hazardous commitment to the character of its problems or its subject matter and a commitment to untried canons of evidence and rules of enquiry. What follows these commitments is years of their application, pursuit of the mode of enquiry demanded by the principles to which the field has committed itself. To the majority of practitioners of any field, these years of enquiry appear only as pursuit of knowledge of its subject matter or solution of its problems. They take the guiding principles of the enquiry as givens. These years of enquiry, however, are something more than pursuit of knowledge or solution or problems. They are also tests, reflexive and pragmatic, of the principles which guide the enquiries. They determine whether, in fact, the data demanded by the principles can be elicited and whether, if elicited, they can be made to constitute knowledge adequate to the complexity of the subject matter, or solutions which, in fact, do solve the problems with which the enquiry began.

In the nature of the case, these reflexive tests of the principles of enquiry are, more often than not, partially or wholly negative, for, after all, the commitment to these principles was made before there was well-tested fruit of enquiry by which to guide the commitment. The inadequacies of principles begin to show, in the case of theoretical enquiries, by failures of the subject matter to respond to the questions put to it, by incoherencies and contradictions in data and in conclusions which cannot be resolved, or by clear disparities between the knowledge yielded by the enquiries and the behaviors of the subject matter which the knowledge purports to represent. In the case of practical enquiries, inadequacies begin to show by incapacity to arrive at solutions to the problems, by inability to realize the solutions proposed, by mutual frustrations and cancellings out as solutions are put into effect.

Although these exhaustions and failures of principles may go unnoted by practitioners in the field, at least at the conscious level, what may not be represented in consciousness is nevertheless evidenced by behavior and appears in the literature and the activities of the field as signs of the onset of a crisis of principle. These signs consist of a large increase in the frequency of published paper and colloquia marked by a *flight from the subject of the field*. There are usually six signs of this flight or directions in which the flight occurs.

SIGNS OF CRISIS

The first and most important, though often least conspicuous, sign is a flight of the field itself, a translocation of its problems and the solving of them from the nominal practitioners of the field to other men. Thus one crucial frustration of the science of genetics was resolved by a single contribution from an insurance actuary. The recent desuetude of academic physiology has been marked by a conspicuous increase in the frequency of published solutions to physiological problems by medical researchers. In similar fashion, the increasing depletion of psychoanalytic principles and methods in recent years was marked by the onset of contributions to its lore by internists, biochemists, and anthropologists.

A second flight is a flight upward, from discourse about the subject of the field to discourse about the discourse of the field, from *use* of principles and methods to *talk* about them, from grounded conclusions to the construction of models, from theory to metatheory and from metatheory to metametatheory.

A third flight is downward, an attempt by practitioners to return to the subject matter in a state of innocence, shorn not only of current principles but of all principles, in an effort to take a new, a pristine and unmediated look at the subject matter. For example, one conspicuous reaction to the warfare of numerous inadequate principles in experimental psychology has been the resurgence of ethology, which begins as an attempt to return to a pure natural history of behavior, to intensive observation and recording of the behavior of animals undisturbed in their natural habitat, by observers, equally undisturbed by mediating conceptions, attempting to record anything and everything they see before them.

A fourth flight is to the sidelines, to the role of observer, commentator, historian, and critic of the contributions of others to the field.

A fifth sign consists of marked perseveration, a repetition of old and familiar knowledge in new languages which add little or nothing to the old meanings as embodied in the older and familiar language, or repetition of old and familiar formulations by way of criticisms or minor additions and modifications.

The sixth is a marked increase in eristic, contentious, and *ad hominem* debate.

I hasten to remark that these signs of crisis are not all or equally reprehensible. There is little excuse for the increase in contentiousness nor much value in the flight to the sidelines or in perseveration, but the others, in one way or another, can contribute to resolution of the crisis. The flight of the field itself is one of the more fruitful ways by which analogical principles are disclosed, modified, and adapted to the field in crisis. The flight upward, to models and metatheory, if done responsibly, which means with a steady eye on the actual problems and conditions of the field for which the models are ostensibly constructed, becomes, in fact, the proposal and test of possible new principles for the field. The flight backward, to a state of innocence, is at least an effort to break the grip of old habits of thought and thus leave space for needed new ones, though it is clear that in the matter of enquiry, as elsewhere, virginity, once lost, cannot be regained.

In the present context, however, the virtue or vice of these various flights is beside the point. We are concerned with them as signs of collapse of principles in a field, and it is my contention, based on a study not yet complete, that most of these signs may now be seen in the field of curriculum. I shall only suggest, not cite, my evidence.

THE CASE OF CURRICULUM

With respect to flight of the field itself, there can be little doubt. Of the five substantial high school science curricula, four of them—PSSC, BSCS, Chems and CBA—were instituted and managed by subject-matter specialists; the contribution of educators was small and that of curriculum specialists near vanishing point. Only Harvard Project Physics, at this writing not yet available, appears to be an exception. To one of two elementary science projects, a psychologist appears to have made a substantial contribution but curriculum specialists very little. The other—the Elementary Science Study—appears to have been substantially affected (to its advantage) by educators with one or both feet in curriculum. The efforts of the Commission of Undergraduate Education in the Biological Sciences have been carried on almost entirely by subject-matter specialists. The English Curriculum Study Centers appear to be in much the same state as the high school science curricula: overwhelmingly centered on subject specialists. Educators contribute expertise only in the area of test construction and evaluation, with here and there a contribution by a psychologist. Educators, including curriculum specialists, were massively unprepared to cope with the problem of integrated education and only by little, and late, and by trial and error, put together the halting solutions currently known as Head Start. The problems posed by the current drives toward ethnicity in education find curriculum specialists even more massively oblivious and unprepared. And I so far find myself very much alone with respect to the curriculum problems immanent in the phenomena of student protest and student revolt. (Of the social studies curriculum efforts, I shall say nothing at this time.)

On the second flight—upward—I need hardly comment. The models, the metatheory, and the metametatheory are all over the place. Many of them, moreover, are irresponsible—concerned less with the barriers to continued productivity in the field of curriculum than with exploitation of the exotic and the fashionable among forms and models of theory and metatheory: systems theory, symbolic logic, language analysis. Many others, including responsible ones, are irreversible flights upward or sideways. That is, they are models or metatheories concerned not with the judgment, the reasoned construction, or reconstruction of curriculums but with other matters—for example, how curriculum changes occur or how changes can be managed.

The flight downward, the attempt at return to a pristine, unmediated look at the subject matter, is, for some reason, a missing symptom in the case of curriculum. There are returns—to the classroom, if not to other levels or aspects of curriculum—with a measure of effort to avoid preconceptions (e.g., Smith, Bellack, and studies of communication nets and lines), but the frequency of such studies has not markedly increased. The absence of this symptom may have significance. In general, however, it is characteristic of diseases that the whole syndrome does not appear in all cases. Hence, pending further study and thought, I do not count this negative instance as weakening the diagnosis of a crisis of principle.

The fourth flight—to the sidelines—is again a marked symptom of the field of curriculum. Histories, anthologies, commentaries, criticisms, and proposals of curriculums multiply.

Perseveration is also marked. I recoil from counting the persons and books whose lives are made possible by continuing restatement of the Tyler rationale, of the character and case for behavioral objectives, of the virtues and vices of John Dewey.

The rise in frequency and intensity of the eristic and *ad hominem* is also marked. Thus one author climaxes a series of petulances by the remark that what he takes to be his own forte "has always been rare—and shows up in proper perspective the happy breed of educational reformer who can concoct a brand new, rabble-rousing theory of educational reform while waiting for the water to fill the bathtub."

There is little doubt, in short, that the field of curriculum is in a crisis of principle.

A crisis of principle arises, as I have suggested, when principles are exhausted—when the questions they permit have all been asked and answered—or when the efforts at enquiry instigated by the principles have at last exhibited their inadequacy to the subject matter and the problems which they were designed to attack. My second point is that the latter holds in the case of curriculum: the curriculum movement has been inveterately theoretic, and its theoretic bent has let it down. A brief conspectus of instances will suggest the extent of this theoretic bent and what is meant by "theoretic."

CHARACTERISTICS OF THEORY

Consider first the early, allegedly Herbartian efforts (recently revived by Bruner). These efforts took the view that ideas were formed by children out of received notions and experiences of things, and that these ideas functioned thereafter as discriminators and organizers of what was later learned. Given this view, the aim of curriculum was to discriminate the right ideas (by way of analysis of extant bodies of knowledge), determine the order in which they could be learned by children as they developed, and thereafter present these ideas at the right times with clarity, associations, organization, and application. A theory of mind and knowledge thus solves by one mighty coup the problem of what to teach, when and how; and what is fatally theoretic here is not the presence of a theory of mind and a theory of knowledge, though their presence is part of the story, but the dispatch, the sweeping appearance of success, the vast simplicity which grounds this purported solution to the problem of curriculum. And lest we think that this faith in the possibility of successful neatness, dispatch, and sweeping generality is mark of the past, consider the concern of the National Science Teachers Association only four years ago "with identifying the broad principles that can apply to any and all curriculum development efforts in science," a concern crystallized in just seven "conceptual schemes" held to underlie all science. With less ambitious sweepingness but with the same steadfast concern for a single factor—in this case, supposed fixed structure of knowledge—one finds similar efforts arising from the Association of College Teachers of Education, from historians, even from teachers of literature.

Consider, now, some of the numerous efforts to ground curriculum in derived objectives. One effort seeks the ground of its objectives in social need and finds its social needs in just those facts about its culture which are sought and found under the aegis of a single conception of culture. Another grounds its objectives in the social needs identified by a single theory of history and of political evolution.

A third group of searches for objectives are grounded in theories of personality. The persuasive coherence and plausibility of Freudianism persuaded its followers to aim to supply children with adequate channels of sublimation of surplus libido, appropriate objects and occasions for aggressions, a properly undemanding ego ideal, and an intelligent minimum of taboos. Interpersonal theories direct their adherents to aim for development of abilities to relate to peers, "infeers," and "supeers," in relations nurturant and receiving, adaptive, vying, approving and disapproving. Theories of actualization instruct their adherents to determine the salient potentialities of each child and to see individually to the development of each.

Still other searches for objectives seek their aims in the knowledge needed to "live in the modern world," in the attitudes and habits which minimize dissonance with the prevailing mores of one's community or social class, in the skills required for success in a trade or vocation, in the ability to participate effectively as member of a group. Still others are grounded in some quasi-ethics, some view of the array of goods which are good for man.

Three features of these typical efforts at curriculum making are significant here, each of which has its own lesson to teach us. First, each is grounded in a theory as such. We shall return to this point in a moment. Second, each is grounded in a theory from the social or behavioral sciences: psychology, psychiatry, politics, sociology, history. Even the ethical bases and theories of "mind" are behavioral. To this point, too, we shall return in a moment.

Third, they are theories concerning *different* subject matters. One curriculum effort is grounded in concern for the individual, another in concern for groups, others in concern for cultures, communities, societies, minds, or the extant bodies of knowledge.[2]

NEED FOR AN ECLECTIC

The significance of this third feature is patent to the point of embarrassment: no curriculum grounded in but one of these subjects can possibly be adequate, defensible. A curriculum based on theory about individual personality, which thrusts society, its demands and its structure, far into the background or ignores them entirely, can be nothing but incomplete and doctrinaire, for the individuals in question are in fact members of a society and must meet its demands to some minimum degree since their existence and prosperity as individuals depend on the functioning of their society. In the same way, a curriculum grounded only in a view of social need or social change must be equally doctrinaire and incomplete, for societies do not exist only for their own sakes but for the prosperity of their members as individuals as well. In the same way, learners are not only minds or knowers but bundles of affects, individuals, personalities, earners of livings. They are not only group interactors but possessors of private lives.

It is clear, I submit, that a defensible curriculum or plan of curriculum must be one which somehow takes account of all these subsubjects which pertain to man. It cannot take only one and ignore the others; it cannot even take account of many of them and ignore one. Not only is each of them a constituent and a condition for decent human existence but each interpenetrates the others. That is, the character of human personalities is a determiner of human society and the behavior of human groups. Conversely, the conditions of group behavior and the character of societies determine in some large part the personalities which their members develop, the way their minds work, and what they can learn and use by way of knowledge and competence. These various "things" (individuals, societies, cultures, patterns of enquiry, "structures" of knowledge or of enquiries, apperceptive masses, problem solving), though discriminable as separate subjects of differing modes of enquiry, are nevertheless parts or affectors of one another, or coactors. (Their very separation for purposes of enquiry is what marks the outcomes of such enquiries as "theoretic" and consequently incomplete.) In practice, they constitute one complex, organic agency. Hence, a focus on only one not only ignores the others but vitiates the quality and completeness with which the selected one is viewed.

It is equally clear, however, that there is not, and will not be in the foreseeable future, one theory of this complex whole which is other than a collection of unusable generalities. Nor is it true that the lack of a theory of the whole is due to the narrowness, stubbornness, or merely habitual specialism of social and behavioral scientists. Rather, their specialism and the restricted purview of their theories are functions of their subject, its enormous complexity, its vast capacity for difference and change. Man's competence at the construction of theoretical knowledge is so far most inadequate when applied to the subject of man. There have been efforts to conceive principles of enquiry which would encompass the whole variety and complexity of humanity, but they have fallen far short of adequacy to the subject matter or have demanded the acquisition of data and modes of interpretation of data beyond our capabilities. There *are* continuing efforts to find bridging terms which would relate the principles of enquiry of one subfield of the social sciences to another and thus begin to effect connections among our knowledges of each, but successful bridges are so far few and narrow and permit but a trickle of connection. As far, then, as theoretical knowledge is concerned, we must wrestle as best we can with numerous, largely unconnected, separate theories of these many, artificially discriminated subsubjects of man.

I remarked in the beginning that renewal of the field of curriculum would require diversion of the bulk of its energies from theory to the practical, the quasi-practical, and the eclectic. The state of affairs just described, the existence and the necessarily continuing existence of separate theories of separate subsubjects distributed among the social sciences, constitutes the case for one of these modes, the necessity of an eclectic, of arts by which a usable focus on a common body of problems is effected among theories which lack theoretical connection. The argument can be simply summarized. A curriculum grounded in but one or a few subsubjects of the social sciences is indefensible; contributions from all are required. There is no foreseeable hope of a unified theory in the immediate or middle future, nor of a metatheory which will tell us how to put those subsubjects together or order them in a fixed hierarchy of importance to the problems of curriculum. What remains as a viable alternative is the unsystematic, uneasy, pragmatic, and uncertain unions and connections which can be effected in an eclectic. And I must add, anticipating our discussion of the practical, that *changing* connections and *differing* orderings at different times of these separate theories, will characterize a sound eclectic.

The character of eclectic arts and procedures must be left for discussion on another occasion. Let it suffice for the moment that witness of the high effectiveness of eclectic methods and of their accessibility is borne by at least one field familiar to us all—Western medicine. It has been enormously effective, and the growth of its competence dates from its disavowal of a single doctrine and its turn to eclecticism.

THE PLACE OF THE PRACTICAL

I turn now, from the fact that the theories which ground curriculum plans pertain to different subsubjects of a common field, to the second of the three features which characterize our typical instances of curriculum planning—the fact that the ground of each plan is a theory, a theory as such.

The significance of the existence of theory as such at the base of curricular planning consists of what it is that theory does not and cannot encompass. All theories, even the best of them in the simplest sciences, necessarily neglect some aspects and facets of the facts of the case. A theory covers and formulates the *regularities* among the things and events it subsumes. It abstracts a general or ideal case. It leaves behind the nonuniformities, the particularities, which characterize each concrete instance of the facts subsumed. Moreover, in the process of idealization, theoretical enquiry may often leave out of consideration conspicuous facets of *all* cases because its substantive principles of enquiry or its methods cannot handle them. Thus the constantly accelerating body of classical mechanics was the acceleration of a body in "free" fall, fall in a perfect vacuum, and the general or theoretical rule formulated in classical mechanics is far from describing the fall of actual bodies in actual mediums—the only kinds of fall then known. The force equation of classical dynamics applied to bodies of visible magnitudes ignores friction. The rule that light varies inversely as the square of the distance holds exactly only for an imaginary point source of light. For real light sources of increasing expanse, the so-called law holds more and more approximately, and for very large sources it affords little or no usable information. And what is true of the best of theories in the simplest sciences is true a fortiori in the social sciences. Their subject matters are apparently so much more variable, and clearly so much more complex, that their theories encompass much less of their subjects than do the theories of the physical and biological sciences.

Yet curriculum is brought to bear not on ideal or abstract representatives but on the real thing, on the concrete case in all its completeness and with all its differences from all other concrete cases on which the theoretic abstraction is silent. The materials of a concrete curriculum will not consist merely of portions of "science," of "literature," of "process." On the contrary, their constituents will be particular assertions about selected matters couched in a particular vocabulary, syntax, and rhetoric. They will be particular novels, short stories, or lyric poems, each, for better or for worse, with its own flavor. They will be particular acts upon particular matters in a given sequence. The curriculum will be brought to bear not in some archetypical classroom but in a particular locus in time and space with smells, shadows, seats, and conditions outside its walls which may have much to do with what is achieved inside. Above all, the supposed beneficiary is not the generic child, not even a class or kind of child out of the psychological or sociological literature pertaining to the child. The beneficiaries will consist of very local kinds of children and, within the local kinds, individual children. The same diversity holds with respect to teachers and what they do. The generalities about science, about literature, about children in general, about children or teachers of some specified class or kind, may be true. But they attain this status in virtue of what they leave out, and the omissions affect what remains. A Guernsey cow is not only something more than cow, having specific features omitted from description of the genus; it is also cowy in ways differing from the cowiness of a Texas longhorn. The specific not only adds to the generic; it also modulates it.

These ineluctable characteristics of theory and the consequent ineluctable disparities between real things and their representation in theory constitute one argument for my thesis, that a large bulk of curriculum energies must be diverted from the theoretic, not only to the eclectic but to the practical and the quasi-practical. The argument, again, can be briefly summarized. The stuff of theory is abstract or idealized representations of real things. But curriculum in action treats real things: real acts, real teachers, real children, things richer and different from their theoretical representations. Curriculum will deal badly with its real things if it treats them merely as replicas of their theoretic representations. If, then, theory is to be used well in the determination of curricular practice, it requires a supplement. It requires arts which bring a theory to its application: first, arts which identify the disparities between real thing and theoretic representation; second, arts which modify the theory in the course of its application, in the light of the discrepancies; and, third, arts which devise ways of taking account of the many aspects of the real thing which the theory does not take into account. These are some of the arts of the practical.

THEORIES FROM SOCIAL SCIENCES

The significance of the third feature of our typical instances of curriculum work—that their theories are mainly theories from the social and behavioral sciences—will carry us to the remainder of the argument for the practical. Nearly all theories in all the behavioral sciences are marked by the coexistence of competing theories. There is not one theory of personality but twenty, representing at least six radically different choices of what is relevant and important in human behavior. There is not one theory of groups but several.

There is not one theory of learning but half a dozen. All the social and behavioral sciences are marked by "schools," each distinguished by a different choice of principle of enquiry, each of which selects from the intimidating complexities of the subject matter the small fraction of the whole with which it can deal.

The theories which arise from enquiries so directed are, then, radically incomplete, each of them incomplete to the extent that competing theories take hold of different aspects of the subject of enquiry and treat it in a different way. Further, there is perennial invention of new principles which bring to light new facets of the subject matter, new relations among the facets and new ways of treating them. In short, there is every reason to suppose that any one of the extant theories of behavior is a pale and incomplete representation of actual behavior. There is similar reason to suppose that if all the diversities of fact, the different aspects of behavior treated in each theory, were somehow to be brought within the bounds of a single theory, that theory would still fall short of comprehending the whole of human behavior—in two respects. In the first place, it would not comprehend what there may be of human behavior which we do not see by virtue of the restricted light by which we examine behavior. In the second place, such a single theory will necessarily interpret its data in the light of its one set of principles, assigning to these data only one set of significances and establishing among them only one set of relations. It will remain the case, then, that a diversity of theories may tell us more than a single one, even though the "factual" scope of the many and the one are the same.

It follows, then, that such theories are not, and will not be, adequate by themselves to tell us what to do with human beings or how to do it. What they variously suggest and the contrary guidances they afford to choice and action must be mediated and combined by eclectic arts and must be massively supplemented, as well as mediated, by knowledge of some other kind derived from another source.

Some areas of choice and action with respect to human behavior have long since learned this lesson. Government is made possible by a lore of politics derived from immediate experience of the vicissitudes and tangles of legislating and administering. Institution of economic guidances and controls owes as much to unmediated experience of the marketplace as it does to formulas and theories. Even psychotherapy has long since deserted its theories of personality as sole guides to therapy and relies as much or more on the accumulated, explicitly nontheoretic lore accumulated by practitioners, as it does on theory or eclectic combinations of theory. The law has systematized the accumulation of direct experience of actual cases in its machinery for the recording of cases and opinions as precedents which continuously monitor, supplement, and modify the meaning and application of its formal "knowledge," its statutes. It is this recourse to accumulated lore, to experience of actions and their consequences, to action and reaction at the level of the concrete case, which constitutes the heart of the practical. It is high time that curriculum do likewise.

THE PRACTICAL ARTS

The arts of the practical are onerous and complex; hence only a sampling must suffice to indicate the character of this discipline and the changes in educational investigation which would ensue on adoption of the discipline. I shall deal briefly with four aspects of it.

The practical arts begin with the requirement that existing institutions and existing practices be preserved and altered piecemeal, not dismantled and replaced. It is further necessary that changes be so planned and so articulated with what remains unchanged that the functioning of the whole remain coherent and unimpaired. These necessities stem from the very nature of the practical—that it is concerned with the maintenance and improvement of patterns of purposed action, and especially concerned that the effects of the pattern through time shall retain coherence and relevance to one another.

This is well seen in the case of the law. Statutes are repealed or largely rewritten only as a last resort, since to do so creates confusion and diremption between old judgments under the law and judgments to come, confusion which must lead either to weakening of law through disrepute or a painful and costly process of repairing the effects of past judgments so as to bring them into conformity with the new. It is vastly more desirable that changes be instituted in small degrees and in immediate adjustment to the peculiarities of particular new cases which call forth the change.

The consequence, in the case of the law, of these demands of the practical is that the servants of the law must know the law through and through. They must know the statutes themselves, the progression of precedents and interpretations which have effected changes in them, and especially the present state of affairs—the most recent decisions under the law and the calendar of cases which will be most immediately affected by contemplated additions to precedent and interpretation.

The same requirements would hold for a practical program of improvement of education. It, too, would effect its changes in small progressions, in coherence with what remains unchanged, and this would require that we know *what is and has been going on in American schools.*

At present, we do not know. My own incomplete investigations convince me that we have not the faintest reliable knowledge of how literature is taught in the high schools, or what actually goes on in science classrooms. There are a dozen different ways in which the novel can be read. Which ones are used by whom, with whom, and to what effect? What selections from the large accumulation of biological knowledge are made and taught in this school system and that, to what classes and kinds of children, to what effect? To what extent is science taught as verbal formulas, as congeries of unrelated facts, as so-called principles and conceptual structures, as outcomes of enquiry? In what degree and kind of simplification and falsification is scientific enquiry conveyed, if it is conveyed at all?

A count of textbook adoptions will not tell us, for teachers select from textbooks and alter their treatment (often quite properly) and can frustrate and negate the textbook's effort to alter the pattern of instruction. We cannot tell from lists of objectives, since they are usually so vastly ambiguous that almost anything can go on under their aegis or, if they are not ambiguous, reflect pious hopes as much as actual practice. We cannot tell from lists of "principles" and "conceptual structures," since these, in their telegraphic brevity are also ambiguous and say nothing of the shape in which they are taught or the extent.

What is wanted is a totally new and extensive pattern of *empirical* study of classroom action and reaction; a study, not as basis for theoretical concerns about the nature of the teaching or learning process, but as a basis for beginning to know what we are doing, what we are not doing, and to what effect—what changes are needed, which needed changes can be instituted with what costs or economies, and how they can be effected with minimum tearing of the remaining fabric of educational effort.

This is an effort which will require new mechanisms of empirical investigation, new methods of reportage, a new class of educational researchers, and much money. It is an effort without which we will continue largely incapable of making defensible decisions about curricular changes, largely unable to put them into effect and ignorant of what real consequences, if any, our efforts have had.

A very large part of such a study would, I repeat, be direct and empirical study of action and reaction in the classroom itself, not merely the testing of student change. But one of the most interesting and visible alterations of present practice which might be involved is a radical change in our pattern of testing students. The common pattern tries to determine the extent to which *intended* changes have been brought about. This would be altered to an effort to find out what changes have occurred, to determine side effects as well as mainline consequences, since the distinction between these two is always in the eye of the intender and side effects may be as great in magnitude and as fatal or healthful for students as the intended effects.

A second facet of the practical: its actions are undertaken with respect to identified frictions and failures in the machine and inadequacies evidenced in felt shortcomings of its products. This origin of its actions leads to two marked differences in operation from that of theory. Under the control of theory, curricular changes have their origin in new notions of person, group or society, mind or knowledge, which give rise to suggestions of new things curriculum might be or do. This is an origin which, by its nature, takes little or no account of the existing effectiveness of the machine or the consequences to this effectiveness of the institution of novelty. If there is concern for what may be displaced by innovation or for the incoherences which may ensue on the insertion of novelty, the concern is gratuitous. It does not arise from the theoretical considerations which commend the novelty. The practical, on the other hand, because it institutes changes to repair frictions and deficiencies, is commanded to determine the whole array of possible effects of proposed change, to determine what new frictions and deficiencies the proposed change may unintentionally produce.

The other effective difference between theoretical and practical origins of deliberate change is patent. Theory, by being concerned with new things to do, is unconcerned with the successes and failures of present doings. Hence present failures, unless they coincide with what is repaired by the proposed innovations, go unnoticed—as do present successes. The practical, on the other hand, is directly and deliberately concerned with the diagnosis of ills of the curriculum.

These concerns of the practical for frictions and failures of the curricular machine would, again, call for a new and extensive pattern of enquiry. The practical requires curriculum study to seek its problems where its problems lie—in the behaviors, misbehaviors, and nonbehaviors of its students as they begin to evince the effects of the training they did and did not get. This means continuing assessment of students as they leave primary grades for the secondary school, leave secondary school for jobs and colleges. It means sensitive and sophisticated assessment by way of impressions, insights, and reactions of the community which sends its children to the school; employers of students, new echelons of teachers of students; the wives, husbands, and cronies of exstudents; the people with whom exstudents work; the people who work under them. Curriculum study will look into the questions of what games exstudents play; what, if anything, they do about politics and crime in the streets; what they read, if they do; what they watch on television and what they make of what they watch, again, if anything. Such studies would be undertaken, furthermore, not as mass study of products of the American school, taken in toto, but as studies of significantly separable schools and school systems—suburban and inner city, Chicago and Los Angeles, South Bend and Michigan City.

I emphasize sensitive and sophisticated assessment because we are concerned here, as in the laying of background knowledge of what goes in schools, not merely with the degree to which avowed objectives are achieved but also with detecting the failures and frictions of the machine: what it has not done or thought of doing, and what side effects its doings have had. Nor are we concerned with successes and failures only as measured in test situations but also as evidenced in life and work. It is this sort of diagnosis which I have tried to exemplify in a recent treatment of curriculum and student protest.[3]

A third facet of the practical I shall call the anticipatory generation of alternatives. Intimate knowledge of the existing state of affairs, early identification of problem situations, and effective formulation of problems are necessary to effective practical decision but not sufficient. It requires also that there be available to practical deliberation the greatest possible number and fresh diversity of alternative solutions to the problem. The reason for this requirement, in one aspect, is obvious enough: the best choice among poor and shopworn alternatives will still be a poor solution to the problem. Another aspect is less obvious. The problems which arise in an institutional structure which has enjoyed good practical management will be novel problems, arising from changes in the times and circumstances and from the consequences of previous solutions to previous problems. Such problems, with their strong tincture of novelty, cannot be solved by familiar solutions. They cannot be well solved by apparently new solutions arising from old habits of mind and old ways of doing things.

A third aspect of the requirement for anticipatory generation of alternatives is still less obvious. It consists of the fact that practical problems do not present themselves wearing their labels around their necks. Problem situations, to use Dewey's old term, present themselves to consciousness, but the character of the problem, its formulation, does not. This depends on the eye of the beholder. And this eye, unilluminated by possible fresh solutions to problems, new modes of attack, new recognitions of degrees of freedom for change among matters formerly taken to be unalterable, is very likely to miss the novel features of new problems or dismiss them as "impractical." Hence the requirement that the generation of problems be anticipatory and not await the emergence of the problem itself.

To some extent, the *theoretical* bases of curricular change—such items as emphasis on enquiry, on discovery learning, and on structure of the disciplines—contribute to this need but not sufficiently or with the breadth which permits effective deliberation. That is, these theoretic proposals tend to arise in single file, out of connection with other proposals which constitute alternatives, or, more important, constitute desiderata or circumstances which affect the choice or rejection of proposals. Consider, in regard to the problem of the "single file," only one relation between the two recent proposals subsumed under "creativity" and "structure of knowledge." If creativity implies some measure of invention, and "structure of knowledge" implies (as it does in one version) the systematic induction of conceptions as soon as children are ready to grasp them, an issue is joined. To the extent that the latter is timely and well done, scope for the former is curtailed. To the extent that children can be identified as more or less creative, "structure of knowledge" would be brought to bear on different children at different times and in different ways.

A single case, taken from possible academic resources of education, will suggest the new kind of enquiry entailed in the need for anticipatory generation of alternatives. Over the years, critical scholarship has generated, as remarked earlier, a dozen different conceptions of the novel, a dozen or more ways in which the novel can be read, each involving its own emphases and its own arts of recovery of meaning in the act of reading. Novels can be read, for example, as bearers of wisdom, insights into vicissitudes of human life and ways of enduring them. Novels can also be read as moral instructors, as sources of vicarious experience, as occasions for aesthetic experience. They can be read as models of human creativity, as displays of social problems, as political propaganda, as revelations of diversities of manners and morals among different cultures and classes of people, or as symptoms of their age.

Now what, in fact, is the full parade of such possible uses of the novel? What is required by each in the way of competences of reading, discussion, and thought? What are the rewards, the desirable outcomes, which are likely to ensue for students from each kind of reading or combinations of them? For what kinds or classes of students is each desirable? There are further problems demanding anticipatory consideration. If novels are chosen and read as displays of social problems and depictions of social classes, what effect will such instruction in literature have on instruction in the social studies? What will teachers need to know and be able to do in order to enable students to discriminate and appropriately connect the *apercus* of artists, the accounts of historians, and the conclusions of social scientists on such matters? How will the mode of instruction in science (e.g., as verified truths) and in literature (as "deep insights" or artistic constructions or matters of opinion) affect the effects of each?

The same kinds of questions could be addressed to history and to the social studies generally. Yet, nowhere, in the case of literature, have we been able to find cogent and energetic work addressed to them. The journals in the field of English teaching are nearly devoid of treatment of them. College and university courses, in English or education, which address such problems with a modicum of intellectual content are as scarce as hen's teeth. We cannot even find an unbiased conspectus of critical theory more complete than *The Pooh Perplex*, and treatments of problems of the second kind (pertaining to interaction of literature instruction with instruction in other fields) are also invisible.

Under a soundly practical dispensation in curriculum the address of such questions would be a high priority and require recruitment to education of philosophers and subject-matter specialists of a quality and critical sophistication which it has rarely, if ever, sought.

As the last sampling of the practical, consider its method. It falls under neither of the popular platitudes: it is neither deductive nor inductive. It is deliberative. It cannot be inductive because the target of the method is not a generalization or explanation but a decision about action in a concrete situation. It cannot be deductive because it deals with the concrete case, not abstractions from cases, and the concrete case cannot be settled by mere application of a principle. Almost every concrete case falls under two or more principles, and every concrete case will possess some cogent characteristics which are encompassed in no principle. The problem of selecting an appropriate man for an important post is a case in point. It is not a problem of selecting a representative of the appropriate personality type who exhibits the competences officially required for the job. The man we hire is more than a type and a bundle of competences. He is a multitude of probable behaviors which escape the net of personality theories and cognitive scales. He is endowed with prejudices, mannerisms, habits, tics, and relatives. And all of these manifold particulars will affect his work and the work of those who work for him. It is deliberation which operates in such cases to select the appropriate man.

COMMITMENT TO DELIBERATION

Deliberation is complex and arduous. It treats both ends and means and must treat them as mutually determining one another. It must try to identify, with respect to both, what facts may be relevant. It must try to ascertain the relevant facts in the concrete case. It must try to identify the desiderata in the case. It must generate alternative solutions. It must make every effort to trace the branching pathways of consequences which may flow from each alternative and affect desiderata. It must then weigh alternatives and their costs and consequences against one another and choose, not the right alternative, for there is no such thing, but the best one.

I shall mention only one of the new kinds of activity which would ensue on commitment to deliberation. It will require the formation of a new public and new means of communication among its constituent members. Deliberation requires consideration of the widest possible variety of alternatives if it is to be most effective. Each alternative must be viewed in the widest variety of lights. Ramifying consequences must be traced to all parts of the curriculum. The desirability of each alternative must be felt out, "rehearsed," by a representative variety of all those who must live with the consequences of the chosen action. And a similar variety must deal with the identification of problems as well as with their solution.

This will require penetration of the curtains which now separate educational psychologist from philosopher, sociologist from test constructor, historian from administrator; it will require new channels connecting the series from teacher, supervisor, and school administrator at one end to research specialists at the other. Above all, it will require renunciation of the specious privileges and hegemonies by which we maintain the fiction that problems of science curriculum, for example, have no bearing on problems of English literature or the social studies. The aim here is *not* a dissolving of specialization and special responsibilities. Quite the contrary: if the variety of lights we need are to be obtained, the variety of specialized interests, competences, and habits of mind which characterize education must be cherished and nurtured. The aim, rather, is to bring the members of this variety to bear on curriculum problems by communication with one another.

Concretely, this means the establishment of new journals, and education of educators so that they can write for them and read them. The journals will be forums where possible problems of curriculum will be broached from many sources and their possible importance debated from many points of view. They will be the stage for display of anticipatory solutions to problems, from a similar variety of sources. They will constitute deliberative assemblies in which problems and alternative solutions will be argued by representatives of all for the consideration of all and for the shaping of intelligent consensus.

Needless to say, such journals are not alone sufficient. They stand as only one concrete model of the kind of forum which is required. Similar forums, operating viva voce and in the midst of curriculum operation and curriculum change, are required: of the teachers, supervisors, and administrators of a school; of the supervisors and administrators of a school system; of representatives of teachers, supervisors, and curriculum makers in subject areas and across subject areas; of the same representatives and specialists in curriculum, psychology, sociology, administration, and the subject-matter fields.[4]

The education of educators to participate in this deliberative process will be neither easy nor quickly achieved. The education of the present generation of specialist researchers to speak to the schools and to one another will doubtless be hardest of all, and on this hardest problem I have no suggestion to make. But we could begin within two years to initiate the preparation of teachers, supervisors, curriculum makers, and graduate students of education in the uses and arts of deliberation—and we should.

For graduate students, this should mean that their future enquiries in educational psychology, philosophy of education, educational sociology, and so on, will find more effective focus on enduring problems of education, as against the attractions of the current foci of the parent disciplines. It will begin to exhibit to graduate students what their duties are to the future schoolmen whom they will teach. For teachers, curriculum makers, and others close to the classroom, such training is of special importance. It will not only bring immediate experience of the classroom effectively to bear on problems of curriculum but enhance the quality of that experience, for almost every classroom episode is a stream of situations requiring discrimination of deliberative problems and decision thereon.

By means of such journals and such an education, the educational research establishment might at last find a means for channeling its discoveries into sustained improvement of the schools instead of into a procession of ephemeral bandwagons.

NOTES

1. Copyright 1969 by Joseph J. Schwab. All rights reserved. A version of this paper was delivered to Section B of the American Educational Research Association, Los Angeles, February 1969. This paper has been prepared as part of a project supported by a grant from the Ford Foundation.
2. It should be clear by now that "theory" as used in this paper does *not* refer only to grand schemes such as the general theory of relativity, kinetic-molecular theory, the Bohr atom, the Freudian construction of a tripartite psyche. The attempt to give an account of human maturation by the discrimination of definite states (e.g., oral, anal, genital), an effort to aggregate human competences into a small number of primary mental abilities—these too are theoretic. So also are efforts to discriminate a few large classes of persons and to attribute to them defining behaviors: e.g., the socially mobile, the culturally deprived, the creative.
3. *College Curriculum and Student Protest* (Chicago: University of Chicago Press, 1969).
4. It will be clear from these remarks that the conception of curricular method proposed here is immanent in the Tyler rationale. This rationale calls for a diversity of talents and insists on the practical and eclectic treatment of a variety of factors. Its effectiveness in practice is vitiated by two circumstances. Its focus on "objectives," with their massive ambiguity and equivocation, provides far too little of the concrete matter required for deliberation and leads only to delusive consensus. Second, those who use it are not trained for the deliberative procedures it requires.

III

RECONCEPTUALIZING CURRICULUM THEORY

As the curriculum reform movement was drawing to a close with the 1960s, Joseph J. Schwab (see Part II) famously declared that the curriculum field was "moribund." While the death of the curriculum field turned out to be an exaggeration, he was surely correct that it was ripe for new directions. An important manifestation of change was attention in the 1970s through the mid-1980s, the times treated in the Part III, to why the preceding ambitious curriculum change efforts had failed to effect reform in the ways envisaged (e.g., McLaughlin, this volume). Schwab's call for an emphasis on deliberation, on the "practical" for "sustained improvement of the schools," was also to attract attention (e.g., Walker, 1971); however, he seems to have been more accurate about new directions for the curriculum field emerging than their exact paths. For example, one emphasis, which attracted considerable attention in the 1970s, that Schwab does not appear to have anticipated was the salience of personal experience in how students interacted with curricula. As Maxine Greene (this volume) wrote in 1971:

> Curriculum, from the learner's standpoint, ordinarily represents little more than an arrangement of subjects, a structure of socially prescribed knowledge, or a complex system of meanings which may or may not fall within his grasp. Rarely does it signify possibility for him as an existing person, mainly concerned with making sense of his own life-world.

Perhaps the times treated here in Part III of the *Reader* are best characterized as a period of experimentation with the products and wake of the curriculum reform movement. Looking back, Nel Noddings (2001) listed some of the significant experiments: continuous progress programs, modular scheduling, media-centered education, individualized instruction, behavioral objectives, mastery learning, discovery learning, interdisciplinary studies, and learning centers (pp. 38–39). By the 1970s, as the preceding list possibly implies, experimentation increasingly stressed curricular choice rather than uniformity. Students were often provided, for example, with multiple courses, even "mini-courses," which they could elect to meet standard requirements in academic subjects.

Thus one of the themes most important in Part III is choice, of students having some significant say in what they study or how they study or both. Choice suggests its alternative, curriculum standardization. Since what schools teach is a political as well as an educational decision, intertwined with issues of choice or standardization are questions of power, as George S. Counts had so well understood (see Part I). Curriculum scholars in the 1970s returned with greater vigor to issues of power than had been evident since the Great Depression. Power became a complementary theme to choice–standardization for this period. In a sense, then, the period from the late 1960s until the aftermath of the alarmist *A Nation at Risk* (1983) was a competition between the forces of curriculum standardization and curriculum choice. The powers of standardization won.

The battles over who controlled what schools teach overshadowed the possibilities unleashed by experimentation. In the circumstances, innovations may have been insufficiently tested to establish if they "worked." Some innovations, as is evident in the readings, harked back to the centrality John Dewey (this volume) ascribed to individualization of instruction: "What a child gets out of any subject presented to him is simply the images which he himself forms with regard to it." Unlike the standards movement and its associated testing movement, which secured dominance in U.S. public education in the 1990s, many of the curricular innovations of the 1970s valued the diverse outcomes that resulted from diversification of standard curricula in the interests of personal relevance. Subsequent insistence by policy-makers on the desirability of a standardized curriculum with uniform outcomes has been widely criticized as a policy, particularly concerning what outcomes should be valued, how it should be implemented, whether it is properly aligned with tests, and so forth. Oddly, however, less attention seems to have been devoted to questioning the premises of standardization, with questions such as why uniform outcomes are desirable in the first place and what opportunity costs they entail (see Eisner, 1998). The readings in Part III could contribute to a critique of these premises.

The first reading is by Paulo Freire, who had longtime involvement with social movements and adult education, particularly in his native Brazil and other parts of Latin America. By the 1970s his writings were becoming widely read in the United States where he attracted a devoted and enduring set of disciples. Freire's curriculum thought is not easily summarized. Indeed, Freire was always worried that his ideas would become a recipe-like method to be followed uncritically (Apple et al., 2001, p. 132). His overarching aim was to teach the oppressed classes to bring about social justice in capitalist societies. He vigorously opposed transmission models of curriculum as simple reinforcements of established knowledge already used to oppress the disadvantaged. Rather, he believed "emancipatory" curriculum must grow out of lived experience and social circumstances. There is no clear dividing line, Freire believed, between education and politics:

> The starting point for organizing the program content of education or political action must be the present, existential, concrete situation, reflecting the aspirations of the people. Utilizing certain basic contradictions, we must pose this existential, concrete, present situation to the people as a problem which challenges them and requires a response—not just at the intellectual level, but at the level of action. (this volume)

The next reading, by Maxine Greene, also displays open disenchantment with conventional curriculum design. As noted, she believed existing school programs were largely irrelevant to the existential desire for meaning and direction salient in the lives of young people. Moreover, such desires could not be quenched by rearrangement of the existing curriculum or its better presentation. Instead, Greene argued that the curriculum must engage students in an "interior journey." She continued:

> Not only may it [an interior journey] result in the effecting of new syntheses within experience; it may result in an awareness of the process of knowing, of believing, of perceiving. It may even result in an understanding of the ways in which meanings have been sedimented in an individual's own personal history . . . . But then there opens up the possibility of presenting curriculum in such a way that it does not impose or enforce. (this volume)

The next essay, by William F. Pinar, rounds out what might be considered the first group of essays of Part III, in which established approaches to curriculum were found either inadequate or incomplete or both. While maintaining that established approaches to curriculum were "reliant" on each other, Pinar was in the forefront of a new "reconceptualist" movement. He argued that the two other main currents of curriculum thought, perspectives of "traditionalists" and "conceptual-empiricists" (or employers of a "social science" perspective), were inherently incomplete. Two important elements of reconceptualist curriculum theory, Pinar argued, were its "value-laden perspective" and its "politically emancipatory intent." In large part, however, he distinguishes the movement by what it is "not."

According to Pinar, traditionalists, working in the wake of Franklin Bobbitt and Ralph Tyler, were immersed in the assumptions of schools and society as they are—their task was to describe how curriculum improvement could be secured without fundamental alterations in existing institutional and societal arrangements. To do so, Pinar maintained, traditionalists engaged in curriculum theorizing that "is theoretical only in the questionable sense that it is abstract and usually at variance with what occurs in schools" (this volume).

Pinar described conceptual-empiricists as curriculum scholars who applied the questions and methods of social science to curricular phenomena. Although he saw this group as an "heir" or successor to the traditionalists, he found their attention to the normative element of their work perfunctory, as conceptual-empirical "research in education, in many instances, has become indistinguishable from social science research" (this volume). Pinar seems have held out hope that the conceptual-empiricists might move toward the reconceptualist position. For instance, he credited the conceptual-empiricist Decker Walker with building on Schwab's call for deliberation rather than remaining preoccupied with "prescriptive curriculum theories" such as the Tyler rationale. Pinar also praised Walker's work because, even though it incorporated traditionalist elements such as "the practical concerns of school people and school curriculum," Walker's use of anthropological research methods placed "his work . . . closer to some reconceptualists than . . . other mainstream conceptual-empiricists." Pinar, in other words, urged "value-laden," politicized curriculum theorizing, which he thought more likely to occur through anthropological means than in "pure" social sciences such as "political science or psychology" (this volume).

Mortimer Adler, the philosopher who contributes the next essay, was basically interested in curriculum theorizing insofar as asserting what for him was its unquestioned basis: the "best" knowledge. He thus stood in contrast to the more varied and multifaceted concerns of the preceding three contributors to Part III, who nonetheless agreed the tradi-tional intellectual foundations of the "best" knowledge were an insufficient basis for sound curriculum theorizing. Adler was a perennialist, boldly declaring that the best knowledge was unchanging and concerned with the same great questions such as what is the nature of justice. He quoted his one-time associate, Robert Maynard Hutchins (1953), for the central plank of his beliefs: "The best education for the best is the best education for all."

Because, in Adler's words, "we are a politically classless society," he believed all young people in a democracy should study the same curriculum of the "best" knowledge. Adler asserted that this democratic view of schooling has been generally agreed upon in American education, exemplified by thinkers such as Hutchins, Dewey, and Horace Mann. Thus, Adler (and Hutchins) argued the curriculum traditionally preserved for the elite was best for everyone: "The innermost meaning of social equality is: substantially the same quality of life for all. That calls for: the same quality of schooling for all." Although Adler acknowledged the curriculum needed to be taught well and "children are educable in vary-ing degrees," he still insisted choice in the curriculum was to allow "a certain number of students to voluntarily downgrade their own education" (this volume).

In the next essay, the philosopher of education Nel Noddings roundly disputes Adler's theory of curriculum. To begin with, she disputes that we, except in the most narrow, tech-nical sense, live in a politically classless society. So for Adler to imply that giving everyone the same knowledge appreciably compensates for other inequalities, Noddings thinks, is misleading, even dangerous. Moreover, she notes, as Adler must have known but fails to mention, Dewey and Hutchins vigorously disagreed about curriculum. Further, she con-tests that social equality should be equated with everyone living (or being educated) in the same way. In fact, Noddings contends along with Dewey that equality suggests individual differences should be respected and education build on these legitimate differences.

Noddings allows that Adler's recommendations "follow inexorably" from his assump-tions, but she challenges his assumptions. She takes issue, for instance, with Adler's as-sumption that the "intellectually best" person is the ideal for all persons: "What the schools need to do, instead, is to legitimize multiple models of excellence," with the most impor-tant thing being "ethical goodness," which "we need far more urgently than intellectual prowess." Moreover, Noddings rejects Adler's dismissal of divergence from his prescribed subjects in the curriculum as the equivalent of "downgrading" of education:

> I am simply pointing out what John Dewey counseled again and again: Any subject freely un-dertaken as an occupation—as a set of tasks requiring goal-setting, means-ends analysis, choice of appropriate tools and materials, exercise of skills, living through the consequences, and evaluating the results—is educative . . . . It is not the subjects offered that make a curricu-lum properly a part of education but how those subjects are taught, how they connect to the personal interests and talents of the students who study them, and how skillfully they are laid out against the whole continuum of human experience. (this volume)

Unlike the preceding essays in Part III, the main concern of the next reading is less on the aims and construction of curricula than on their implementation. Milbrey Wallin McLaughlin was writing in the aftermath of the curriculum reform movement (see Part II) that was generally judged to have failed in meeting its objectives. McLaughlin explained that most of the curricular innovations had concentrated on "technological" change. She suggested that "organizational" change in the structure of the institutional setting or the culture of the school might be a more significant factor in effecting educational change. "Innovations in classroom organization such as open education, multiage grouping, integrated day, differentiated staffing, and team teaching," McLaughlin noted by way of illustration, "are not based on a 'model' of classroom organization change to be strictly followed, but a common set of convictions about the nature of learning and the purpose of teaching." Rather than the conventional assumption that implementation consists of "the direct and straightforward application of an educational technology or plan," McLaughlin was suggesting change that matters is associated with "mutual adaptation" or "modification of both the project design and changes in the institutional setting and individual participants during the course of implementation" (this volume).

McLaughlin's conclusions are instructive on the nature of meaningful curriculum change. To illustrate, she used open education projects in two settings. The settings were "similar in almost every aspect—resources, support and interest, target group, background characteristics"—but differed significantly in implementation strategy and implementation outcomes:

> The Eastown open education project had extensive and ongoing staff training, spent a lot of staff time and energy on materials development, arranged for staff to meet regularly, and engaged in regular formative evaluation. This project was also well implemented, ran smoothly, and met its objectives . . . . Implementation in this [the Seaside] project was only pro forma—largely because of the absence of implementation strategies that would allow learning, growth, and development or mutual adaptation to take place. (this volume)

The final reading in Part III, by Michael W. Apple, evokes themes from earlier essays on reconceptualism. Perhaps as significantly, however, it presents another view of implementation than the one presented by McLaughlin. Whereas McLaughlin examined curriculum change as potentially beneficial and dependent on teacher "ownership" of the innovation, Apple was looking at what he saw as ominous attempts to impoverish curricula and force acquiescence from teachers. Of course, Apple was writing a decade after McLaughlin, and educational policy-making had turned decidedly more conservative. He contends that teacher discretion over the curriculum, which McLaughlin considered both desirable and inescapable, was diminishing and had come to be deemed undesirable by authorities. Furthermore, McLaughlin tacitly portrays teachers as exercising a good deal of professional autonomy as curricular-instructional gatekeepers (Thornton, 1991), whereas Apple decries teachers having been "de-skilled" as workers by patriarchal, undemocratic policymakers. Teachers' work, he argued, had intensified while their control over its quality had declined. Certainly much of what Apple described here in the mid-1980s subsequently became, as is apparent in Part IV, even more widely discussed questions of the relationship of teachers to the curriculum in the 1990s and since:

> I claimed that they [teachers] were more and more faced with the prospect of being deskilled because of the encroachment of technical control procedures into the curriculum. The integration together of management systems, reductive behaviorally based curricula, pre-specified teaching "competencies" and procedures and student responses, and pre and post testing, was leading to a loss of control and a separation of conception from execution. (this volume)

REFERENCES

Apple, M.W., Gandin, L.A., and Hypolito, A.M. (2001). "Paulo Freire, 1921–1997." In J. Palmer (Ed.), *Fifty Modern Thinkers on Education:From Piaget to the Present* (pp. 128–133). London: Routledge.

Hutchins, R.M. (1953). *The Conflict in Education in a Democratic Society.* New York: Harper.

National Commission on Excellence in Education (1983). *A Nation at Risk: The Imperative for Educational Reform.* Washington: U.S. Department of Education.

Noddings, N. (2001). "Care and Coercion in School Reform." *Journal of Educational Change,* 2, 35–43.

Thornton, S.J. (1991). "Teacher as Curricular-Instructional Gatekeeper in Social Studies." In J.P. Shaver (Ed.), *Handbook of Research on Social Studies Teaching and Learning* (pp. 237–248). New York: Macmillan.

Walker, D.F. (1971). "A Naturalistic Model for Curriculum Development." *School Review,* 80, 51–65.

12

Pedagogy of the Oppressed

PAULO FREIRE

AS WE ATTEMPT TO ANALYZE DIALOGUE AS A HUMAN PHENOMENON, we discover something which is the essence of dialogue itself: *the word*. But the word is more than just an instrument which makes dialogue possible; accordingly, we must seek its constitutive elements. Within the word we find two dimensions, reflection and action, in such radical interaction that if one is sacrificed—even in part—the other immediately suffers. There is no true word that is not at the same time a praxis.[1] Thus, to speak a true word is to transform the world.[2]

An unauthentic word, one which is unable to transform reality, results when dichotomy is imposed upon its constitutive elements. When a word is deprived of its dimension of action, reflection automatically suffers as well; and the word is changed into idle chatter, into *verbalism*, into an alienated and alienating "blah." It becomes an empty word, one which cannot denounce the world, for denunciation is impossible without a commitment to transform, and there is no transformation without action.

On the other hand, if action is emphasized exclusively, to the detriment of reflection, the word is converted into *activism*. The latter—action for action's sake—negates the true praxis and makes dialogue impossible. Either dichotomy, by creating unauthentic forms of existence, creates also unauthentic forms of thought, which reinforce the original dichotomy.

Human existence cannot be silent, nor can it be nourished by false words, but only by true words, with which men transform the world. To exist, humanly, is to *name* the world, to change it. Once named, the world in its turn reappears to the namers as a problem and requires of them a new *naming*. Men are not built in silence,[3] but in word, in work, in action-reflection.

But while to say the true word—which is work, which is praxis—is to transform the world, saying that word is not the privilege of some few men, but the right of every man.

From Paulo Freire, *Pedagogy of the Oppressed*. New York: Continuum, 1970: pp. 75–86, 95–100. Reprinted by permission.

Consequently, no one can say a true word alone—nor can he say it *for* another, in a prescriptive act which robs others of their words.

Dialogue is the encounter between men, mediated by the world, in order to name the world. Hence, dialogue cannot occur between those who want to name the world and those who do not wish this naming—between those who deny other men the right to speak their word and those whose right to speak has been denied them. Those who have been denied their primordial right to speak their word must first reclaim this right and prevent the continuation of this dehumanizing aggression.

If it is in speaking their word that men, by naming the world, transform it, dialogue imposes itself as the way by which men achieve significance as men. Dialogue is thus an existential necessity. And since dialogue is the encounter in which the united reflection and action of the dialoguers are addressed to the world which is to be transformed and humanized, this dialogue cannot be reduced to the act of one person's "depositing" ideas in another, nor can it become a simple exchange of ideas to be "consumed" by the discussants. Nor yet is it a hostile, polemical argument between men who are committed neither to the naming of the world, nor to the search for truth, but rather to the imposition of their own truth. Because dialogue is an encounter among men who name the world, it must not be a situation where some men name on behalf of others. It is an act of creation; it must not serve as a crafty instrument for the domination of one man by another. The domination implicit in dialogue is that of the world by the dialoguers; it is conquest of the world for the liberation of men.

Dialogue cannot exist, however, in the absence of a profound love for the world and for men. The naming of the world, which is an act of creation and re-creation, is not possible if it is not infused with love.[4] Love is at the same time the foundation of dialogue and dialogue itself. It is thus necessarily the task of responsible Subjects and cannot exist in a relation of domination. Domination reveals the pathology of love: sadism in the dominator and masochism in the dominated. Because love is an act of courage, not of fear, love is commitment to other men. No matter where the oppressed are found, the act of love is commitment to their cause—the cause of liberation. And this commitment, because it is loving, is dialogical. As an act of bravery, love cannot be sentimental; as an act of freedom, it must not serve as a pretext for manipulation. It must generate other acts of freedom; otherwise, it is not love. Only by abolishing the situation of oppression is it possible to restore the love which that situation made impossible. If I do not love the world—if I do not love life—if I do not love men—I cannot enter into dialogue.

On the other hand, dialogue cannot exist without humility. The naming of the world, through which men constantly re-create that world, cannot be an act of arrogance. Dialogue, as the encounter of men addressed to the common task of learning and acting, is broken if the parties (or one of them) lack humility. How can I dialogue if I always project ignorance onto others and never perceive my own? How can I dialogue if I regard myself as a case apart from other men—mere "its" in whom I cannot recognize other "I"s? How can I dialogue if I consider myself a member of the in-group of "pure" men, the owners of truth and knowledge, for whom all non-members are "these people" or "the great unwashed?" How can I dialogue if I start from the premise that naming the world is the task of an elite and that the presence of the people in history is a sign of deterioration, thus to be avoided? How can I dialogue if I am closed to—and even offended by—the contribution of others? How can I dialogue if I am afraid of being displaced, the mere possibility causing me torment and weakness? Self-sufficiency is incompatible with dialogue. Men who lack humility (or have lost it) cannot come to the people, cannot be their partners in naming the world. Someone who cannot acknowledge himself to be as mortal as everyone else still has a long way to go before he can reach the point of encounter. At the point of encounter there are neither utter ignoramuses nor perfect sages; there are only men who are attempting, together, to learn more than they now know.

Dialogue further requires an intense faith in man, faith in his power to make and remake, to create and re-create, faith in his vocation to be more fully human (which is not the privilege of an elite, but the birthright of all men). Faith in man is an *a priori* requirement for dialogue; the "dialogical man" believes in other men even before he meets them face to face. His faith, however, is not naïve. The "dialogical man" is critical and knows that although it is within the power of men to create and transform, in a concrete situation of alienation men may be impaired in the use of that power. Far from destroying his faith in man, however, this possibility strikes him as a challenge to which he must respond. He is convinced that the power to create and transform, even when thwarted in concrete situations, tends to be reborn. And that rebirth can occur—not gratuitously, but in and through the struggle for liberation—in the supersedence of slave labor by emancipated labor which gives zest to life. Without this faith in man, dialogue is a farce which inevitably degenerates into paternalistic manipulation.

Founding itself upon love, humility, and faith, dialogue becomes a horizontal relationship of which mutual trust between the dialoguers is the logical consequence. It would be a contradiction in terms if dialogue—loving, humble, and full of faith—did not produce this climate of mutual trust, which leads the dialoguers into ever closer partnership in the naming of the world. Conversely, such trust is obviously absent in the anti-dialogics of the banking method of education. Whereas faith in man is an *a priori* requirement for dialogue, trust is established by dialogue. Should it founder, it will be seen that the preconditions were lacking. False love, false humility, and feeble faith in man cannot create trust. Trust is contingent on the evidence which one party provides the others of his true, concrete intentions; it cannot exist if that party's words do not coincide with his actions. To say one thing and do another—to take one's own word lightly—cannot inspire trust. To glorify democracy and to silence the people is a farce; to discourse on humanism and to negate man is a lie.

Nor yet can dialogue exist without hope. Hope is rooted in men's incompletion, from which they move out in constant search—a search which can be carried out only in communion with other men. Hopelessness is a form of silence, of denying the world and fleeing from it. The dehumanization resulting from an unjust order is not a cause for despair but for hope, leading to the incessant pursuit of the humanity denied by injustice. Hope, however, does not consist in crossing one's arms and waiting. As long as I fight, I am moved by hope; and if I fight with hope, then I can wait. As the encounter of men seeking to be more fully human, dialogue cannot be carried on in a climate of hopelessness. If the dialoguers expect nothing to come of their efforts, their encounter will be empty and sterile, bureaucratic and tedious.

Finally, true dialogue cannot exist unless the dialoguers engage in critical thinking— thinking which discerns an indivisible solidarity between the world and men and admits of no dichotomy between them—thinking which perceives reality as process, as transformation, rather than as a static entity—thinking which does not separate itself from action, but constantly immerses itself in temporality without fear of the risks involved. Critical thinking contrasts with naïve thinking, which sees "historical time as a weight, a stratification of the acquisitions and experiences of the past,"[5] from which the present should emerge normalized and "well-behaved." For the naïve thinker, the important thing is accommodation to this normalized "today." For the critic, the important thing is the continuing transformation of reality, in behalf of the continuing humanization of men. In the words of Pierre Furter:

The goal will no longer be to eliminate the risks of temporality by clutching to guaranteed space, but rather to temporalize space. . . . The universe is revealed to me not as space, imposing a massive presence to which I can but adapt, but as a scope, a domain which takes shape as I act upon it.[6]

For naïve thinking, the goal is precisely to hold fast to this guaranteed space and adjust to it. By thus denying temporality, it denies itself as well.

Only dialogue, which requires critical thinking, is also capable of generating critical thinking. Without dialogue there is no communication, and without communication there can be no true education. Education which is able to resolve the contradiction between teacher and student takes place in a situation in which both address their act of cognition to the object by which they are mediated. Thus, the dialogical character of education as the practice of freedom does not begin when the teacher-student meets with the students-teachers in a pedagogical situation, but rather when the former first asks himself *what* he will dialogue with the latter *about*. And preoccupation with the content of dialogue is really preoccupation with the program content of education.

For the anti-dialogical banking educator, the question of content simply concerns the program about which he will discourse to his students; and he answers his own question, by organizing his own program. For the dialogical, problem-posing teacher-student, the program content of education is neither a gift nor an imposition—bits of information to be deposited in the students—but rather the organized, systematized, and developed "re-presentation" to individuals of the things about which they want to know more.[7]

Authentic education is not carried on by "A" *for* "B" or by "A" *about* "B," but rather by "A" *with* "B," mediated by the world—a world which impresses and challenges both parties, giving rise to views or opinions about it. These views, impregnated with anxieties, doubts, hopes, or hopelessness, imply significant themes on the basis of which the program content of education can be built. In its desire to create an ideal model of the "good man," a naïvely conceived humanism often overlooks the concrete, existential, present situation of real men. Authentic humanism, in Pierre Furter's words, "consists in permitting the emergence of the awareness of our full humanity, as a condition and as an obligation, as a situation and as a project."[8] We simply cannot go to the laborers—urban or peasant[9]—in the banking style, to give them "knowledge" or to impose upon them the model of the "good man" contained in a program whose content we have ourselves organized. Many political and educational plans have failed because their authors designed them according to their own personal views of reality, never once taking into account (except as mere objects of their action) the *men-in-a-situation* to whom their program was ostensibly directed.

For the truly humanist educator and the authentic revolutionary, the object of action is the reality to be transformed by them together with other men—not other men themselves. The oppressors are the ones who act upon men to indoctrinate them and adjust them to a reality which must remain untouched. Unfortunately, however, in their desire to obtain the support of the people for revolutionary action, revolutionary leaders often fall for the banking line of planning program content from the top down. They approach the peasant or urban masses with projects which may correspond to their own view of the world, but not to that of the people.[10] They forget that their fundamental objective is to fight alongside the people for the recovery of the people's stolen humanity, not to "win the people over" to their side. Such a phrase does not belong in the vocabulary of revolutionary leaders, but in that of the oppressor. The revolutionary's role is to liberate, and be liberated, with the people—not to win them over.

In their political activity, the dominant elites utilize the banking concept to encourage passivity in the oppressed, corresponding with the latter's "submerged" state of consciousness, and take advantage of that passivity to "fill" that consciousness with slogans which create even more fear of freedom. This practice is incompatible with a truly liberating course of action, which, by presenting the oppressors' slogans as a problem, helps the oppressed to "eject" those slogans from within themselves. After all, the task of the humanists is surely not that of pitting their slogans against the slogans of the oppressors, with the oppressed as the testing ground, "housing" the slogans of first one group and then the other. On the contrary, the task of the humanists is to see that the oppressed become aware of the fact that as dual beings, "housing" the oppressors within themselves, they cannot be truly human.

This task implies that revolutionary leaders do not go to the people in order to bring them a message of "salvation," but in order to come to know through dialogue with them both their *objective situation* and their *awareness* of that situation—the various levels of perception of themselves and of the world in which and with which they exist. One cannot expect positive results from an educational or political action program which fails to respect the particular view of the world held by the people. Such a program constitutes cultural invasion,[11] good intentions notwithstanding.

The starting point for organizing the program content of education or political action must be the present, existential, concrete situation, reflecting the aspirations of the people. Utilizing certain basic contradictions, we must pose this existential, concrete, present situation to the people as a problem which challenges them and requires a response—not just at the intellectual level, but at the level of action.[12]

We must never merely discourse on the present situation, must never provide the people with programs which have little or nothing to do with their own preoccupations, doubts, hopes, and fears—programs which at times in fact increase the fears of the oppressed consciousness. It is not our role to speak to the people about our own view of the world, not to attempt to impose that view on them, but rather to dialogue with the people about their view and ours. We must realize that their view of the world, manifested variously in their action, reflects their *situation* in the world. Educational and political action which is not critically aware of this situation runs the risk either of "banking" or of preaching in the desert.

Often, educators and politicians speak and are not understood because their language is not attuned to the concrete situation of the men they address. Accordingly, their talk is just alienated and alienating rhetoric. The language of the educator or the politician (and it seems more and more clear that the latter must also become an educator, in the broadest sense of the word), like the language of the people, cannot exist without thought; and neither language nor thought can exist without a structure to which they refer. In order to communicate effectively, educator and politician must understand the structural conditions in which the thought and language of the people are dialectically framed.

It is to the reality which mediates men, and to the perception of that reality held by educators and people, that we must go to find the program content of education. The investigation of what I have termed the people's "thematic universe"[13]—the complex of their "generative themes"—inaugurates the dialogue of education as the practice of freedom. The methodology of that investigation must likewise be dialogical, affording the opportunity both to discover generative themes and to stimulate people's awareness in regard to these themes. Consistent with the liberating purpose of dialogical education, the object of the investigation is not men (as if men were anatomical fragments), but rather the thought-language with which men refer to reality, the levels at which they perceive that reality, and their view of the world, in which their generative themes are found.

Equally appropriate for the methodology of thematic investigation and for problem-posing education is this effort to present significant dimensions of an individual's contextual reality, the analysis of which will make it possible for him to recognize the interaction of the various components. Meanwhile, the significant dimensions, which in their turn are constituted of parts in interaction, should be perceived as dimensions of total reality. In this way, a critical analysis of a significant existential dimension makes possible a new, critical attitude towards the limit-situations. The perception and comprehension of reality are rectified and acquire new depth. When carried out with a methodology of *conscientização* the investigation of the generative theme contained in the minimum thematic universe (the generative themes in interaction) thus introduces or begins to introduce men to a critical form of thinking about their world.

In the event, however, that men perceive reality as dense, impenetrable, and enveloping, it is indispensable to proceed with the investigation by means of abstraction. This method does not involve reducing the concrete to the abstract (which would signify the negation of its dialectical nature), but rather maintaining both elements as opposites which interrelate dialectically in the act of reflection. This dialectical movement of thought is exemplified perfectly in the analysis of a concrete, existential, "coded" situation.[21] Its "decoding" requires moving from the abstract to the concrete; this requires moving from the part to the whole and then returning to the parts; this in turn requires that the Subject recognize himself in the object (the coded concrete existential situation) and recognize the object as a situation in which he finds himself, together with other Subjects. If the decoding is well done, this movement of flux and reflux from the abstract to the concrete which occurs in the analysis of a coded situation leads to the supersedence of the abstraction *by* the critical perception of the concrete, which has already ceased to be a dense, impenetrable reality.

When an individual is presented with a coded existential situation (a sketch or photograph which leads by abstraction to the concreteness of existential reality), his tendency is to "split" that coded situation. In the process of decoding, this separation corresponds to the stage we call the "description of the situation," and facilitates the discovery of the interaction among the parts of the disjoined whole. This whole (the coded situation), which previously had been only diffusely apprehended, begins to acquire meaning as thought flows back to it from the various dimensions. Since, however, the coding is the representation of an existential situation, the decoder tends to take the step from the representation to the very concrete situation in which and with which he finds himself. It is thus possible to explain conceptually why individuals begin to behave differently with regard to objective reality, once that reality has ceased to look like a blind alley and has taken on its true aspect: a challenge which men must meet.

In all the stages of decoding, men exteriorize their view of the world. And in the way they think about and face the world—fatalistically, dynamically, or statically—their generative themes may be found. A group which does not concretely express a generative thematics—a fact which might appear to imply the nonexistence of themes—is, on the contrary, suggesting a very dramatic theme: *the theme of silence.* The theme of silence suggests a structure of mutism in face of the overwhelming force of the limit-situations.

I must re-emphasize that the generative theme cannot be found in men, divorced from reality; nor yet in reality, divorced from men; much less in "no man's land." It can only be apprehended in the men-world relationship. To investigate the generative theme is to investigate man's thinking about reality and man's action upon reality, which is his praxis. For precisely this reason, the methodology proposed requires that the investigators and the people (who would normally be considered objects of that investigation) should act as *co-investigators.* The more active an attitude men take in regard to the exploration of their thematics, the more they deepen their critical awareness of reality and, in spelling out those thematics, take possession of that reality.

Some may think it inadvisable to include the people as investigators in the search for their own meaningful thematics: that their intrusive influence (N.B., the "intrusion" of those who are most interested—or ought to be—in their own education) will "adulterate" the findings and thereby sacrifice the objectivity of the investigation. This view mistakenly presupposes that themes exist, in their original objective purity, outside men—as if themes were *things.* Actually, themes exist in men in their relations with the world, with reference to concrete facts. The same objective fact could evoke different complexes of generative themes in different epochal sub-units. There is, therefore, a relation between the given objective fact, the perception men have of this fact, and the generative themes.

A meaningful thematics is expressed by men, and a given moment of expression will differ from an earlier moment, if men have changed their perception of the objective facts to which the themes refer. From the investigator's point of view, the important thing is to detect the starting point at which men visualize the "given" and to verify whether or not during the process of investigation any transformation has occurred in their way of perceiving reality. (Objective reality, of course, remains unchanged. If the perception of that reality changes in the course of the investigation, that fact does not impair the validity of the investigation.)

We must realize that the aspirations, the motives, and the objectives implicit in the meaningful thematics are *human* aspirations, motives, and objectives. They do not exist "out there" somewhere, as static entities; *they are occurring.* They are as historical as men themselves; consequently, they cannot be apprehended apart from men. To apprehend these themes and to understand them is to understand both the men who embody them and the reality to which they refer. But—precisely because it is not possible to understand these themes apart from men—it is necessary that the men concerned understand them as well. Thematic investigation thus becomes a common striving towards awareness of reality and towards self-awareness, which makes this investigation a starting point for the educational process or for cultural action of a liberating character.

The real danger of the investigation is not that the supposed objects of the investigation, discovering themselves to be co-investigators, might "adulterate" the analytical results. On the contrary, the danger lies in the risk of shifting the focus of the investigation from the meaningful themes to the people themselves, thereby treating the people as objects of the investigation. Since this investigation is to serve as a basis for developing an educational program in which teacher-student and students-teachers combine their cognitions of the same object, the investigation itself must likewise be based on reciprocity of action.

Thematic investigation, which occurs in the realm of the human, cannot be reduced to a mechanical act. As a process of search, of knowledge, and thus of creation, it requires the investigators to discover the interpenetration of problems, in the linking of meaningful themes. The investigation will be most educational when it is most critical, and most critical when it avoids the narrow outlines of partial or "focalized" views of reality, and sticks to the comprehension of *total* reality. Thus, the process of searching for the meaningful thematics should include a concern for the links between themes, a concern to pose these themes as problems, and a concern for their historical-cultural context.

Just as the educator may not elaborate a program to present *to* the people, neither may the investigator elaborate "itineraries" for researching the thematic universe, starting from points which *he* has predetermined. Both education and the investigation designed to support it must be "sympathetic" activities, in the etymological sense of the word. That is, they must consist of communication and of the common experience of a reality perceived in the complexity of its constant "becoming."

The investigator who, in the name of scientific objectivity, transforms the organic into something inorganic, what is becoming into what is, life into death, is a man who fears change. He sees in change (which he does not deny, but neither does he desire) not a sign of life, but a sign of death and decay. He does want to study change—but in order to stop it, not in order to stimulate or deepen it. However, in seeing change as a sign of death and in making people the passive objects of investigation in order to arrive at rigid models, he betrays his own character as a killer of life.

NOTES

1. $\left.\begin{matrix} \text{Action} \\ \text{Reflection} \end{matrix}\right\}$ word = work = praxis

   Sacrifice of action = verbalism

   Sacrifice of reflection = activism

2. Some of these reflections emerged as a result of conversations with Professor Ernani Maria Fiori.

3. I obviously do not refer to the silence of profound meditation, in which men only apparently leave the world, withdrawing from it in order to consider it in its totality, and thus remaining with it. But this type of retreat is only authentic when the meditator is "bathed" in reality; not when the retreat signifies contempt for the world and flight from it, in a type of "historical schizophrenia."

4. I am more and more convinced that true revolutionaries must perceive the revolution, because of its creative and liberating nature, as an act of love. For me, the revolution, which is not possible without a theory of revolution—and therefore science— is not irreconcilable with love. On the contrary: the revolution is made by men to achieve their humanization. What, indeed, is the deeper motive which moves men to become revolutionaries, but the dehumanization of man? The distortion imposed on the word "love" by the capitalist world cannot prevent the revolution from being essentially loving in character, nor can it prevent the revolutionaries from affirming their love of life. Guevara (while admitting the "risk of seeming ridiculous") was not afraid to affirm it: "Let me say, with the risk of appearing ridiculous, that the true revolutionary is guided by strong feelings of love. It is impossible to think of an authentic revolutionary without this quality." *Venceremos—The Speeches and Writings of Che Guevara*, edited by John Gerassi (New York, 1969), p.398.

5. From the letter of a friend.

6. Pierre Furter, *Educação e Vida* (Rio, 1966), pp. 26–27.

7. In a long conversation with Malraux, Mao-Tse-Tung declared, "You know I've proclaimed for a long time: we must teach the masses clearly what we have received from them confusedly." André Malraux, *Anti-Memoirs* (New York, 1968), pp. 361–362. This affirmation contains an entire dialogical theory of how to construct the program content of education, which cannot be elaborated according to what the *educator* thinks best for *his* students.

8. Furter, *op. cit.*, p. 165.

9. The latter, usually submerged in a colonial context, are almost umbilically linked to the world of nature, in relation to which they feel themselves to be component parts rather than shapers.

10. "Our cultural workers must serve the people with great enthusiasm and devotion, and they must link themselves with the masses, not divorce themselves from the masses. In order to do so, they must act in accordance with the needs and wishes of the masses. All work done for the masses must start from their needs and not from the desire of any individual, however well-intentioned. It often happens that objectively the masses need a certain change, but subjectively they are not yet conscious of the need, not yet willing or determined to make the change. In such cases, we should wait patiently. We should not make the change until, through our work, most of the masses have become conscious of the need and are willing and determined to carry it out. Otherwise we shall isolate ourselves from the masses. . . . There are two principles here: one is the actual needs of the masses rather than what we fancy they need, and the other is the wishes of the masses, who must make up their own minds instead of our making up their minds for them." From the *Selected Works of Mao-Tse-Tung*, Vol. III. "The United Front in Cultural Work" (October 30, 1944) (Peking, 1967), pp. 186–187.

11. This point will be analyzed in detail in Chapter 4.

12. It is as self-contradictory for true humanists to use the banking method as it would be for rightists to engage in problem-posing education. (The latter are always consistent—they never use a problem-posing pedagogy.)

13. The expression "meaningful thematics" is used with the same connotation.

21. The coding of an existential situation is the representation of that situation, showing some of its constituent elements in interaction. Decoding is the critical analysis of the coded situation.

13

Curriculum and Consciousness

Maxine Greene

CURRICULUM, FROM THE LEARNER'S STANDPOINT, ordinarily represents little more than an arrangement of subjects, a structure of socially prescribed knowledge, or a complex system of meanings which may or may not fall within his grasp. Rarely does it signify possibility for him as an existing person, mainly concerned with making sense of his own life-world. Rarely does it promise occasions for ordering the materials of that world, for imposing "configurations"[1] by means of experiences and perspectives made available for personally conducted cognitive action. Sartre says that "knowing is a moment of praxis," opening into "what has not yet been."[2] Preoccupied with priorities, purposes, programs of "intended learning"[3] and intended (or unintended) manipulation, we pay too little attention to the individual in quest of his own future, bent on surpassing what is merely "given," on breaking through the everyday. We are still too prone to dichotomize: to think of "disciplines" or "public traditions" or "accumulated wisdom" or "common culture" (individualization despite) as objectively existent, external to the knower—there to be discovered, mastered, learned.

Quite aware that this may evoke Dewey's argument in *The Child and the Curriculum*, aware of how times have changed since 1902, I have gone in search of contemporary analogies to shed light on what I mean. ("Solution comes," Dewey wrote, "only by getting away from the meaning of terms that is already fixed upon and coming to see the conditions from another point of view, and hence in a fresh light."[4]) My other point of view is that of literary criticism, or more properly philosophy of criticism, which attempts to explicate the modes of explanation, description, interpretation, and evaluation involved in particular critical approaches. There is presently an emerging philosophic controversy between two such approaches, one associated with England and the United States, the other with the Continent, primarily France and Switzerland; and it is in the differences in orientation that I have found some clues.

From *Teachers College Record*, Vol. 73, No. 2, 1971: pp. 253–269. Reprinted by permission.

These differences are, it will be evident, closely connected to those separating what is known as analytic or language philosophy from existentialism and phenomenology. The dominant tendency in British and American literary criticism has been to conceive literary works as objects or artifacts, best understood in relative isolation from the writer's personal biography and undistorted by associations brought to the work from the reader's own daily life. The new critics on the Continent have been called "critics of consciousness."[5] They are breaking with the notion that a literary work can be dealt with objectively, divorced from experience. In fact, they treat each work as a manifestation of an individual writer's experience, a gradual growth of consciousness into expression. This is in sharp contrast to such a view as T.S. Eliot's emphasizing the autonomy and the "impersonality" of literary art. "We can only say," he wrote in an introduction to *The Sacred Wood*, "that a poem, in some sense, has its own life; that its parts form something quite different from a body of neatly ordered biographical data; that the feeling, or emotion, or vision resulting from the poem is something different from the feeling or emotion or vision in the mind of the poet."[6] Those who take this approach or an approach to a work of art as "a self-enclosed isolated structure"[7] are likely to prescribe that purely aesthetic values are to be found in literature, the values associated with "significant form"[8] or, at most, with the contemplation of an "intrinsically interesting possible."[9] M.H. Abrams has called this an "austere dedication to the poem *per se*,"[10] for all the enlightening analysis and explication it has produced. "But it threatens also to commit us," he wrote, "to the concept of a poem as a language game, or as a floating Laputa, insulated from life and essential human concerns in a way that accords poorly with our experience in reading a great work of literature."

For the critic of consciousness, literature is viewed as a genesis, a conscious effort on the part of an individual artist to understand his own experience by framing it in language. The reader who encounters the work must recreate it in terms of *his* consciousness. In order to penetrate it, to experience it existentially and empathetically, he must try to place himself within the "interior space"[11] of the writer's mind as it is slowly revealed in the course of his work. Clearly, the reader requires a variety of cues if he is to situate himself in this way; and these are ostensibly provided by the expressions and attitudes he finds in the book, devices which he must accept as orientations and indications—"norms," perhaps, to govern his recreation. *His* subjectivity is the substance of the literary object; but, if he is to perceive the identity emerging through the enactments of the book, he must subordinate his own personality as he brackets out his everyday, "natural" world.[12] His objective in doing so, however, is not to analyze or explicate or evaluate; it is to extract the experience made manifest by means of the work. Sartre says this more concretely:

> Reading seems, in fact, to be the synthesis of perception and creation. . . . The object is essential because it is strictly transcendent, because it imposes its own structures, and because one must wait for it and observe it; but the subject is also essential because it is required not only to disclose the object (that is, to make *there be* an object) but also that this object might *be* (that is, to produce it). In a word, the reader is conscious of disclosing in creating, of creating by disclosing. . . . If he is inattentive, tired, stupid, or thoughtless most of the relations will escape him. He will never manage to "catch on" to the object (in the sense in which we see that fire "catches" or "doesn't catch"). He will draw some phrases out of the shadow, but they will appear as random strokes. If he is at his best, he will project beyond the words a synthetic form, each phrase of which will be no more than a partial function: the "theme," the "subject," or the "meaning."[13]

There must be, he is suggesting, continual reconstructions if a work of literature is to become meaningful. The structures involved are generated over a period of time, depending upon the perceptiveness and attentiveness of the reader. The reader, however, does not simply regenerate what the artist intended. His imagination can move him beyond the artist's traces, "to project beyond the words a synthetic form," to constitute a new totality. The autonomy of the art object is sacrificed in this orientation; the reader, conscious of lending his own life to the book, discovers deeper and more complex levels than the level of "significant form." (Sartre says, for instance, that "Raskolnikov's waiting is *my* waiting, which I lend him. Without this impatience of the reader he would remain only a collection of signs. His hatred of the police magistrate who questions him is my hatred which has been solicited and wheedled out of me by signs, and the police magistrate himself would not exist without the hatred I have for him via Raskolnikov."[14])

DISCLOSURE, RECONSTRUCTION, GENERATION

The reader, using his imagination, must move within his own subjectivity and break with the common sense world he normally takes for granted. If he could not suspend his ordinary ways of perceiving, if he could not allow for the possibility that the horizons of daily life are not inalterable, he would not be able to engage with literature at all. As Dewey put it: "There is work done on the part of the percipient as there is on the part of the artist. The one who is too lazy, idle, or indurated in convention to perform this work will not see or hear. His 'appreciation' will be a mixture of scraps of learning with conformity to norms of conventional admiration and with a confused, even if genuine, emotional excitation."[15] The "work" with which we are here concerned is one of disclosure, reconstruction, generation. It is a work which culminates in a bringing something into being by the reader—in a "going beyond" what he has been.[16]

Although I am going to claim that learning, to be meaningful, must involve such a "going beyond," I am not going to claim that it must also be in the imaginative mode. Nor am I going to assert that, in order to surpass the "given," the individual is required to move into and remain within a sealed subjectivity. What I find suggestive in the criticism of consciousness is the stress on the gradual disclosure of structures by the reader. The process is, as I have said, governed by certain cues or norms perceived in the course of reading. These demand, if they are to be perceived, what Jean Piaget has called a "continual 'decentering' without which [the individual subject] cannot become free from his intellectual egocentricity."[17]

The difference between Piaget and those interested in consciousness is, of course, considerable. For one thing, he counts himself among those who prefer not to characterize the subject in terms of its "lived experience." For another thing, he says categorically that "the 'lived' can only have a very minor role in the construction of cognitive structures, for these do not belong to the subject's *consciousness* but to his operational *behavior*, which is something quite different."[18] I am not convinced that they are as different as he conceives them to be. Moreover, I think his differentiation between the "individual subject" and what he calls "the epistemic subject, that cognitive nucleus which is common to all subjects at the same level,"[19] is useful and may well shed light on the problem of curriculum, viewed from the vantage point of consciousness. Piaget is aware that his stress on the "epistemic subject" looks as if he were subsuming the individual under some impersonal abstraction;[20] but his discussion is not far removed from those of Sartre and the critics of consciousness, particularly when they talk of the subject entering into a process of generating structures whose being (like the structures Piaget has in mind) consists in their "coming to be."

Merleau-Ponty, as concerned as Piaget with the achievement of rationality, believes that there is a primary reality which must be taken into account if the growth of "intellectual consciousness" is to be understood. This primary reality is a perceived life-world; and the structures of the "perceptual consciousness"[21] through which the child first comes in contact with his environment underlie all the higher level structures which develop later in his life. In the prereflective, infantile stage of life he is obviously incapable of generating cognitive structures. The stage is characterized by what Merleau-Ponty calls "egocentrism" because the "me" is part of an anonymous collectivity, unaware of itself, capable of living "as easily in others as it does in itself."[22] Nevertheless, even then, before meanings and configurations are imposed, there is an original world, a natural and social world in which the child is involved corporeally and affectively. Perceiving that world, he effects certain relations within his experience. He organizes and "informs" it before he is capable of logical and predicative thought. This means for Merleau-Ponty that consciousness exists primordially—the ground of all knowledge and rationality.

The growing child assimilates a language system and becomes habituated to using language as "an open system of expression" which is capable of expressing "an indeterminate number of cognitions or ideas to come."[23] His acts of naming and expression take place, however, around a core of primary meaning found in "the silence of primary consciousness." This silence may be understood as the fundamental awareness of being present in the world. It resembles what Paulo Freire calls "background awareness"[24] of an existential situation, a situation actually lived before the codifications which make new perceptions possible. Talking about the effort to help peasants perceive their own reality differently (to enable them, in other words, to learn), Freire says they must somehow make explicit their "real consciousness" of their worlds, or what they experienced while living through situations they later learn to codify.

The point is that the world is constituted for the child (by means of the behavior called perception) prior to the "construction of cognitive structures." This does not imply that he lives his life primarily in that world. He moves outward into diverse realms of experience in his search for meaning. When he confronts and engages with the apparently independent structures associated with rationality, the so-called cognitive structures, it is likely that he does so as an "epistemic subject," bracketing out for the time his subjectivity, even his presence to himself.[25] But the awareness remains in the background; the original perceptual reality continues as the ground of rationality, the base from which the leap to the theoretical is taken.

Merleau-Ponty, recognizing that psychologists treat consciousness as "an object to be studied," writes that it is simply not accessible to mere factual observation:

> The psychologist always tends to make consciousness into just such an object of observation. But all the factual truths to which psychology has access can be applied to the concrete subject only after a philosophical correction. Psychology, like physics and the other sciences of nature, uses the method of induction, which starts from facts and then assembles them. But it is very evident that this induction will remain blind if we do not know in some other way, and indeed from the inside of consciousness itself, what this induction is dealing with.[26]

Induction must be combined "with the reflective knowledge that we can obtain from ourselves as conscious objects." This is not a recommendation that the individual engage in introspection. Consciousness, being intentional, throws itself outward *towards* the world. It is always consciousness of something—a phenomenon, another person, an object in the world: Reflecting upon himself as a conscious object, the individual—the learner, perhaps—reflects upon his relation to the world, his manner of comporting himself with respect to it, the changing perspectives through which the world presents itself to him. Merleau-Ponty talks about the need continually to rediscover "my actual presence to myself, the fact of my consciousness which is in the last resort what the word and the concept of consciousness mean."[27] This means remaining in contact with one's own perceptions, one's own experiences, and striving to constitute their meanings. It means achieving a state of what Schutz calls "*wide-awakeness . . .* a plane of consciousness of highest tension originating in an attitude of full attention to life and its requirements."[28] Like Sartre, Schutz emphasizes the importance of attentiveness for arriving at new perceptions, for carrying out cognitive projects. All this seems to me to be highly suggestive for a conception of a learner who is "open to the world,"[29] eager, indeed *condemned* to give meaning to it—and, in the process of doing so, recreating or generating the materials of a curriculum in terms of his own consciousness.

SOME ALTERNATIVE VIEWS

There are, of course, alternative views of consequence for education today. R.S. Peters, agreeing with his philosophic precursors that consciousness is the hallmark of mind and always "related in its different modes to objects," asserts that the "objects of consciousness are first and foremost objects in a public world that are marked out and differentiated by a public language into which the individual is initiated."[30] (It should be said that Peters is, *par excellence*, the exponent of an "objective" or "analytic" approach to curriculum, closely related to the objective approach to literary criticism.) He grants that the individual "represents a unique and unrepeatable viewpoint on this public world"; but his primary stress is placed upon the way in which the learning of language is linked to the discovery of that separately existing world of "objects in space and time." Consciousness, for Peters, cannot be explained except in connection with the demarcations of the public world which meaning makes possible. It becomes contingent upon initiation into public traditions, into (it turns out) the academic disciplines. Since such an initiation is required if modes of consciousness are to be effectively differentiated, the mind must finally be understood as a "product" of such initiation. The individual must be enabled to achieve a state of mind characterized by "a mastery of and care for the worthwhile things that have been transmitted, which are viewed in some kind of cognitive perspective."[31]

Philip H. Phenix argues similarly that "the curriculum should consist entirely of knowledge which comes from the disciplines, for the reason that the disciplines reveal knowledge in its teachable forms."[32] He, however, pays more heed to what he calls "the experience of reflective self-consciousness,"[33] which he associates specifically with "concrete existence in direct personal encounter."[34] The meanings arising out of such encounter are expressed, for him, in existential philosophy, religion, psychology, and certain dimensions of imaginative literature. They are, thus, to be considered as one of the six "realms of meaning" through mastery of which man is enabled to achieve self-transcendence. Self-transcendence, for Phenix, involves a duality which enables the learner to feel himself to be agent and knower, and at once to identify with what he comes to know. Self-transcendence is the ground of meaning; but it culminates in the engendering of a range of "essential meanings," the achievement of a hierarchy in which all fundamental patterns of meaning are related and through which human existence can be fulfilled. The inner life of generic man is clearly encompassed by this scheme; but what is excluded, I believe, is what has been called the "subjectivity of the actor," the *individual* actor ineluctably present to himself. What is excluded is the feeling of separateness, of strangeness when such a person is confronted with the articulated curriculum intended to counteract meaninglessness.

Schutz writes:

> When a stranger comes to the town, he has to learn to orientate in it and to know it. Nothing is self-explanatory for him and he has to ask an expert . . . to learn how to get from one point to another. He may, of course, refer to a map of the town, but even to use the map successfully he must know the meaning of the signs on the map, the exact point within the town where he stands and its correlative on the map, and at least one more point in order correctly to relate the signs on the map to the real objects in the city.[35]

The prestructured curriculum resembles such a map; the learner, the stranger just arrived in town. For the cartographer, the town is an "object of his science," a science which has developed standards of operation and rules for the correct drawing of maps. In the case of the curriculum-maker, the public tradition or the natural order of things is "the object" of his design activities. Here too there are standards of operation: the subject matter organized into disciplines must be communicable; it must be appropriate to whatever are conceived as educational aims. Phenix has written that education should be understood as "a guided recapitulation of the processes of inquiry which gave rise to the fruitful bodies of organized knowledge comprising the disciplines."[36] Using the metaphor of the map, we might say that this is like asking a newcomer in search of direction to recapitulate the complex processes by which the cartographer made his map. The map may represent a fairly complete charting of the town; and it may ultimately be extremely useful for the individual to be able to take a cartographer's perspective. When that individual first arrives, however, his peculiar plight ought not to be overlooked: his "background awareness" of being alive in an unstable world; his reasons for consulting the map; the interests he is pursuing as he attempts to orient himself when he can no longer proceed by rule of thumb. He himself may recognize that he will have to come to understand the signs on the map if he is to make use of it. Certainly he will have to decipher the relationship between those signs and "real objects in the city." But his initial concern will be conditioned by the "objects" he wants to bring into visibility, by the landmarks he needs to identify if he is to proceed on his way.

LEARNING—A MODE OF ORIENTATION

Turning from newcomer to learner (contemporary learner, in our particular world), I am suggesting that his focal concern is with ordering the materials of his own life-world when dislocations occur, when what was once familiar abruptly appears strange. This may come about on an occasion when "future shock" is experienced, as it so frequently is today. Anyone who has lived through a campus disruption, a teachers' strike, a guerilla theatre production, a sit-in (or a be-in, or a feel-in) knows full well what Alvin Toffler means when he writes about the acceleration of change. "We no longer 'feel' life as men did in the past," he says. "And this is the ultimate difference, the distinction that separates the truly contemporary man from all others. For this acceleration lies behind the impermanence—the transience—that penetrates and tinctures our consciousness, radically affecting the way we relate to other people, to things, to the entire universe of ideas, art and values."[37] Obviously, this does not happen in everyone's life; but it is far more likely to occur than ever before in history, if it is indeed the case that change has speeded up and that forces are being released which we have not yet learned to control. My point is that the contemporary learner is more likely than his predecessors to experience moments of strangeness, moments when the recipes he has inherited for the solution of typical problems no longer seem to work. If Merleau-Ponty is right and the search for rationality is indeed grounded in a primary or perceptual consciousness, the individual may be fundamentally aware that the structures of "reality" are contingent upon the perspective taken and that most achieved orders are therefore precarious.

The stage sets are always likely to collapse.[38] Someone is always likely to ask unexpectedly, as in Pinter's *The Dumb Waiter*, "Who cleans up after we're gone?"[39] Someone is equally likely to cry out, "You seem to have no conception of where we stand! You won't find the answer written down for you in the bowl of a compass—I can tell you that."[40] Disorder, in other words, is continually breaking in; meaninglessness is recurrently overcoming landscapes which once were demarcated, meaningful. It is at moments like these that the individual reaches out to reconstitute meaning, to close the gaps, to make sense once again. It is at moments like these that he will be moved to pore over maps, to disclose or generate structures of knowledge which may provide him unifying perspectives and thus enable him to restore order once again. His learning, I am saying, is a mode of orientation—or reorientation in a place suddenly become unfamiliar. And "place" is a metaphor, in this context, for a domain of consciousness, intending, forever thrusting outward, "open to the world." The curriculum, the structures of knowledge, must be presented to such a consciousness as possibility. Like the work of literature in Sartre's viewing, it requires a subject if it is to be disclosed; it can only *be* disclosed if the learner, himself engaged in generating the structures, lends the curriculum his life. If the curriculum, on the other hand, is seen as external to the search for meaning, it becomes an alien and an alienating edifice, a kind of "Crystal Palace" of ideas.[41]

There is, then, a kind of resemblance between the ways in which a learner confronts socially prescribed knowledge and the ways in which a stranger looks at a map when he is trying to determine where he is in relation to where he wants to go. In Kafka's novel, *Amerika*, I find a peculiarly suggestive description of the predicament of someone who is at once a stranger and a potential learner (although, it eventually turns out, he never succeeds in being taught). He is Karl Rossmann, who has been "packed off to America" by his parents and who likes to stand on a balcony at his Uncle Jacob's house in New York and look down on the busy street:

> From morning to evening and far into the dreaming night that street was a channel for the constant stream of traffic which, seen from above, looked like an inextricable confusion, forever newly improvised, of foreshortened human figures and the roofs of all kinds of vehicles, sending into the upper air another confusion, more riotous and complicated, of noises, dusts and smells, all of it enveloped and penetrated by a flood of light which the multitudinous

objects in the street scattered, carried off and again busily brought back, with an effect as palpable to the dazzled eye as if a glass roof stretched over the street were being violently smashed into fragments at every moment.[42]

Karl's uncle tells him that the indulgence of idly gazing at the busy life of the city might be permissible if Karl were traveling for pleasure; "but for one who intended to remain in the States it was sheer ruination." He is going to have to make judgments which will shape his future life; he will have, in effect, to be reborn. This being so, it is not enough for him to treat the unfamiliar landscape as something to admire and wonder at (as if it were a cubist construction or a kaleidoscope). Karl's habitual interpretations (learned far away in Prague) do not suffice to clarify what he sees. If he is to learn, he must identify what is questionable, try to break through what is obscure. Action is required of him, not mere gazing; *praxis*, not mere reverie.

If he is to undertake action, however, he must do so against the background of his original perceptions, with a clear sense of being present to himself. He must do so, too, against the background of his European experience, of the experience of rejection, of being "packed off" for reasons never quite understood. Only with that sort of awareness will he be capable of the attentiveness and commitment needed to engage with the world and make it meaningful. Only with the ability to be reflective about what he is doing will he be brave enough to incorporate his past into the present, to link the present to a future. All this will demand a conscious appropriation of new perspectives on his experience and a continual reordering of that experience as new horizons of the "Amerika" become visible, as new problems arise. The point is that Karl Rossmann, an immigrant in an already structured and charted world, must be conscious enough of himself to strive towards rationality; only if he achieves rationality will he avoid humiliations and survive.

As Kafka tells it, he never does attain that rationality; and so he is continually manipulated by forces without and within. He never learns, for example, that there can be no justice if there is no good will, even though he repeatedly and sometimes eloquently asks for justice from the authorities—always to no avail. The ship captains and pursers, the business men, the head waiters and porters all function according to official codes of discipline which are beyond his comprehension. He has been plunged into a public world with its own intricate prescriptions, idiosyncratic structures, and hierarchies; but he has no way of appropriating it or of constituting meanings. Throughout most of the novel, he clings to his symbolic box (with the photograph of his parents, the memorabilia of childhood and home). The box may be egocentrism; it may signify his incapacity to embark upon the "decentering" required if he is to begin generating for himself the structures of what surrounds.

In his case (and, I would say, in the case of many other people) the "decentering" that is necessary is not solely a cognitive affair, as Piaget insists it is. Merleau-Ponty speaks of a "lived decentering,"[43] exemplified by a child's learning" "to relativise the notions of the youngest and the eldest" (to learn, e.g., to become the eldest in relation to the newborn child) or by his learning to think in terms of reciprocity. This happens, as it would have to happen to Karl, through actions undertaken within the "vital order," not merely through intellectual categorization. It does not exclude the possibility that a phenomenon analogous to Piaget's "epistemic subject" emerges, although there appears to be no reason (except, perhaps, from the viewpoint of empirical psychology) for separating it off from the "individual subject." (In fact, the apparent difference between Piaget and those who talk of "lived experience" may turn upon a definition of "consciousness." Piaget, as has been noted,[44] distinguishes between "consciousness" and "operational behavior," as if consciousness did *not* involve a turning outward to things, a continuing reflection upon situationality, a generation of cognitive structures.) In any case, every individual who consciously seeks out meaning is involved in asking questions which demand essentially epistemic responses.[45] These responses, even if incomplete, are knowledge claims; and, as more and more questions are asked, there is an increasing "sedimentation" of meanings which result from the interpretation of past experiences looked at from the vantage point of the present. Meanings do not inhere in the experiences that emerge; they have to be constituted, and they can only be constituted through cognitive action.

Returning to Karl Rossmann and his inability to take such action, I have been suggesting that he *cannot* make his own "primary consciousness" background so long as he clings to his box; nor can he actively interpret his past experience. He cannot (to stretch Piaget's point somewhat) become or will himself to be an "epistemic subject." He is, as Freire puts it, submerged in a "dense, enveloping reality or a tormenting blind alley" and will be unless he can "perceive it as an objective-problematic situation."[46] Only then will he be able to intervene in his own reality with attentiveness, with awareness—to act upon his situation and make sense.

It would help if the looming structures which are so incomprehensible to Karl were somehow rendered cognitively available to him. Karl might then (with the help of a teacher willing to engage in dialogue with him, to help him pose his problems) reach out to question in terms of what he feels is thematically relevant or "worth questioning."[47] Because the stock of knowledge he carries with him does not suffice for a definition of situations in which porters manhandle him and women degrade him, in which he is penalized for every spontaneous action, he cannot easily refer to previous situations for clues. In order to cope with this, he needs to single out a single relevant element at first (from all the elements in what is happening) to transmute into a theme for his "knowing consciousness." There is the cruel treatment meted out to him, for example, by the Head Porter who feels it his duty "to attend to things that other people neglect." (He adds that, since he is in charge of all the doors of the hotel [including the "doorless exits"], he is "in a sense placed over everyone," and everyone has to obey him absolutely. If it were not for his repairing the omissions of the Head Waiter in the name of the hotel management, he believes, "such a great organization would be unthinkable."[48]) The porter's violence against Karl might well become the relevant element, the origin of a theme.

MAKING CONNECTIONS

"What makes the theme to be a theme." Schutz writes, "is determined by motivationally relevant interest-situations and spheres of problems. The theme which thus has become relevant has now, however, become a problem to which a solution, practical, theoretical, or emotional, must be given."[49] The problem for Karl, like relevant problems facing any individual, is connected with and a consequence of a great number of other perplexities, other dislocations in his life. If he had not been so badly exploited by authority figures in time past, if he were not so childishly given to blind trust in adults, if he were not so likely to follow impulse at inappropriate moments, he would never have been assaulted by the Head Porter. At this point, however, once the specific problem (the assault) has been determined to be thematically relevant for him, it can be detached from the motivational context out of which it derived. The mesh-work of related perplexities remains, however, as an outer horizon, waiting to be explored or questioned when necessary. The thematically relevant element can then be made interesting in its own right and worth questioning. In the foreground, as it were, the focus of concern, it can be defined against the background of the total situation. The situation is not in any sense obliterated or forgotten. It is *there*, at the fringe of Karl's attention while the focal problem is being solved; but it is, to an extent, "bracketed out." With this bracketing out and this foreground focusing, Karl may be for the first time in a condition of wide-awakeness, ready to pay active attention to what has become so questionable and so troubling, ready to take the kind of action which will move him ahead into a future as it gives him perspective on his past.

The action he might take involves more than what is understood as problem-solving. He has, after all, had some rudimentary knowledge of the Head Porter's role, a knowledge conditioned by certain typifications effected in the prepredicative days of early childhood. At that point in time, he did not articulate his experience in terms of sense data or even in terms of individual figures standing out against a background. He saw typical structures according to particular zones of relevancy. This means that he probably saw his father, or the man who was father, not only as bearded face next to his mother, not only as large figure in the doorway, but as over-bearing, threatening, incomprehensible Authority who was "placed over everyone" and had the right to inflict pain. Enabled, years later, to confront something thematically relevant, the boy may be solicited to recognize his present knowledge of the porter as the sediment of previous mental processes.[50] The knowledge of the porter, therefore, has a history beginning in primordial perceptions; and the boy may succeed in moving back from what is seemingly "given" through the diverse mental processes which constituted the porter over time. Doing so, he will be exploring both the inner and outer horizons of the problem, making connections within the field of his consciousness, interpreting his own past as it bears on his present, reflecting upon his own knowing.

And that is not all. Having made such connections between the relevant theme and other dimensions of his experience, he may be ready to solve his problem; he may even feel that the problem is solved. This, however, puts him into position to move out of his own inner time (in which all acts are somehow continuous and bound together) into the intersubjective world where he can function as an epistemic subject. Having engaged in a reflexive consideration of the activity of his own consciousness, he can now shift his attention back to the life-world which had been rendered so unrecognizable by the Head Porter's assault. Here too, meanings must be constituted; the "great organization" must be understood, so that Karl can orient himself once again in the everyday. Bracketing out his subjectivity for the time, he may find many ways of engaging as a theoretical inquirer with the problem of authority in hotels and the multiple socioeconomic problems connected with that. He will voluntarily become, when inquiring in this way, a partial self, an inquirer deliberately acting a role in a community of inquirers. I am suggesting that he could not do so as effectively or as authentically if he had not first synthesized the materials within his inner time, constituted meaning in his world.

The analogy to the curriculum question, I hope, is clear. Treating Karl as a potential learner, I have considered the hotels and the other structured organizations in his world as analogous to the structures of prescribed knowledge—or to the curriculum. I have suggested that the individual, in our case the student, will only be in a position to learn when he is committed to act upon his world. If he is content to admire it or simply accept it as given, if he is incapable of breaking with egocentrism, he will remain alienated from himself and his own possibilities; he will wander lost and victimized upon the road; he will be unable to learn. He may be conditioned; he may be trained. He may even have some rote memory of certain elements of the curriculum; but no matter how well devised is that curriculum, no matter how well adapted to the stages of his growth, learning (as disclosure, as generating structures, as engendering meanings, as achieving mastery) will not occur.

At once, I have tried to say that unease and disorder are increasingly endemic in contemporary life, and that more and more persons are finding the recipes they habitually use inadequate for sense-making in a changing world. This puts them more and more frequently, in the position of strangers or immigrants trying to orient themselves in an unfamiliar town. The desire, indeed the *need*, for orientation is equivalent to the desire to constitute meanings, all sorts of meanings, in the many dimensions of existence. But this desire, I have suggested, is not satisfied by the authoritative confrontation of student with knowledge structures (no matter how "teachable" the forms in which the knowledge is revealed). It is surely not satisfied when the instructional situation is conceived to be, as G.K. Plochmann has written, one in which the teacher is endeavoring "with respect to his subject matter, to bring the understanding of the learner in equality with his own understanding."[51] Described in that fashion, with "learner" conceived generically and the "system" to be taught conceived as preexistent and objectively real, the instructional situation seems to me to be one that alienates because of the way it ignores both existential predicament and primordial consciousness. Like the approach to literary criticism Abrams describes, the view appears to commit us to a concept of curriculum "as a floating Laputa, insulated from life and essential human concerns. . . ."[52]

The cries of "irrelevance" are still too audible for us to content ourselves with this. So are the complaints about depersonalization, processing, and compulsory socialization into a corporate, inhuman world. Michael Novak, expressing some of this, writes that what our institutions "decide is real is enforced as real." He calls parents, teachers, and psychiatrists (like policemen and soldiers) "the enforcers of reality"; then he goes on to say:

> When a young person is being initiated into society, existing norms determine what is to be considered real and what is to be annihilated by silence and disregard. The good, docile student accepts the norms; the recalcitrant student may lack the intelligence—or have too much; may lack maturity—or insist upon being his own man.[53]

I have responses like this in mind when I consult the phenomenologists for an approach to curriculum in the present day. For one thing, they remind us of what it means for an individual to be present to himself; for another, they suggest to us the origins of significant quests for meaning, origins which ought to be held in mind by those willing to enable students to be themselves.

If the existence of a primordial consciousness is taken seriously, it will be recognized that awareness begins perspectively, that our experience is always incomplete. It is true that we have what Merleau-Ponty calls a "prejudice" in favor of a world of solid, determinate objects, quite independent of our perceptions. Consciousness does, however, have the capacity to return to the precognitive, the primordial, by "bracketing out" objects as customarily seen. The individual can release himself into his own inner time and rediscover the ways in which objects arise, the ways in which experience develops. In discussing the possibility of Karl Rossmann exploring his own past, I have tried to show what this sort of interior journey can mean. Not only may it result in the effecting of new syntheses within experience; it may result in an awareness of the process of knowing, of believing, of perceiving. It may even result in an understanding of the ways in which meanings have been sedimented in an individual's own personal history. I can think of no more potent mode of combatting those conceived to be "enforcers of the real," including the curriculum designers.

But then there opens up the possibility of presenting curriculum in such a way that is does not impose or enforce. If the student is enabled to recognize that reason and order may represent the culminating step in his constitution of a world, if he can be enabled to see that what Schutz calls the attainment of a "reciprocity of perspectives"[54] signifies the achievement of rationality, he may realize what it is to generate the structures of the disciplines on his own initiative, against his own "background awareness." Moreover, he may realize that he is projecting beyond his present horizons each time he shifts his attention and takes another perspective on his world. "To say there exists rationality," writes Merleau-Ponty, "is to say that perspectives blend, perceptions confirm each other, a meaning emerges."[55] He points out that we witness at every moment "the miracles of related experiences, and yet nobody knows better than we do how this miracle is worked, for we are ourselves this network of relationships." Curriculum can offer the possibility for students to be the makers of such networks. The problem for their teachers is to stimulate an awareness of the questionable, to aid in the identification of the thematically relevant, to beckon beyond the everyday.

> I am a psychological and historical structure, and have received, with existence, a manner of existence, a style. All my actions and thoughts stand in a relationship to this structure, and even a philosopher's thought is merely a way of making explicit his hold on the world, and what he is. The fact remains that I am free, not in spite of, or on the hither side of these motivations, but by means of them. For this significant life, this certain significance of nature and history which I am, does not limit my access to the world, but on the contrary is my means of entering into communication with it. It is by being unrestrictedly and unreservedly what I am at present that I have a chance of moving forward; it is by living my time that I am able to understand other times, by plunging into the present and the world by taking on deliberately what I am fortuitously, by willing what I will and doing what I do, that I can go further.[56]

To plunge in; to choose; to disclose; to move: this is the road, it seems to me, to mastery.

NOTES

1. Maurice Merleau-Ponty, *The Primary of Perception.* James M. Edie, ed. Evanston, Ill.: Northwestern University Press, 1964, p. 99.
2. Jean Paul Sartre, *Search for a Method.* New York: Alfred A. Knopf, 1963, p. 92.
3. Ryland W. Crary, *Humanizing the School Curriculum: Development and Theory.* New York: Alfred A. Knopf, 1969, p. 13.
4. John Dewey, "The Child and the Curriculum," Martin S. Dworking, ed. *Dewey on Education.* New York: Teachers College Bureau of Publications, 1959, p. 91.
5. Sarah Lawall, *Critics of Consciousness.* Cambridge, Mass.: Harvard University Press, 1968.
6. T.S. Eliot, *The Sacred Wood.* New York: Barnes & Noble University Paperbacks, 1960, p. x.
7. Dorothy Walsh. "The Cognitive Content of Art." Francis J. Coleman, ed. *Aesthetics.* New York: McGraw-Hill, 1968, p. 297.
8. Clive Bell, *Art.* London: Chatto & Windus, 1914.

9. Walsh, *op. cit.*

10. M.H. Abrams, "Belief and the Suspension of Belief." M.H. Abrams, ed. *Literature and Belief.* New York: Columbia University Press, 1957, p. 9.

11. Maurice Blanchot. *L'Espace littéraire.* Paris: Gallimard, 1955.

12. See, e.g., Alfred Schutz, "Some Leading Concepts of Phenomenology," Maurice Natanson, ed. *Collected Papers I.* The Hague: Martinus Nijhoff, 1967, pp. 104–5.

13. Jean Paul Sartre. *Literature and Existentialism.* 3rd ed. New York: The Citadel Press, 1965, p. 43.

14. *Ibid.* p. 15.

15. John Dewey. *Art as Experience.* New York: Minton, Balch & Company, 1934, p. 54.

16. Sartre. *Search for a Method. op. cit.*, p. 91.

17. Jean Piaget. *Structuralism.* New York: Basic Books, 1970, p. 139.

18. *Ibid.*, p. 68.

19. *Ibid.*, p. 139.

20. *Ibid.*

21. Maurice Merleau-Ponty. *Phenomenology of Perception.* London: Routledge Kegan Paul Ltd., 1962.

22. Merleau-Ponty. *The Primacy of Perception, op. cit.*, p. 119.

23. *Ibid.*, p. 99.

24. Paulo Freire. *Pedagogy of the Oppressed.* New York: Herder and Herder, 1970, p. 108.

25. Schutz. "On Multiple Realities." *op. cit.*, p. 248.

26. Merleau-Ponty. *The Primacy of Perception, op. cit.*, p. 58.

27. Merleau-Ponty. *Phenomenology of Perception, op. cit.*, p. xvii.

28. Schutz. "On Multiple Realities." *op. cit.*

29. Merleau-Ponty, *op. cit.*, p. xv.

30. R.S. Peters. *Ethics and Education.* London: George Allen and Unwin, 1966, p. 50.

31. R.S. Peters. *Ethics and Education.* Glenview, Ill.: Scott Foresman and Co., 1967, p. 12.

32. Philip H. Phenix, "The Uses of the Disciplines as Curriculum Content," Donald Vandenberg, ed. *Theory of Knowledge and Problems of Education.* Urbana, Ill.: University of Illinois Press, 1969, p. 195.

33. Philip H. Phenix. *Realms of Meaning.* New York: McGraw-Hill, 1964, p. 25.

34. *Ibid.*

35. Schutz. "Problem of Rationality in the Social World." Natanson, ed. *Collected Papers II.* The Hague: Martinus Nijhoff, 1967, p. 66.

36. Phenix, "Disciplines as Curriculum Content," *op. cit.*, p. 195.

37. Alvin Toffler. *Future Shock.* New York: Random House, 1970, p. 18.

38. Albert Camus. *The Myth of Sisyphus.* New York: Alfred A. Knopf, 1955, p. 72.

39. Harold Pinter. *The Dumb Waiter.* New York: Grove Press, 1961, p. 103.

40. Tom Stoppard. *Rosencrantz and Guildenstern are Dead.* New York: Grove Press, 1967, pp. 58–59.

41. cf. Fyodor Dostoevsky. *Notes from Underground*, in *The Short Novels of Dostoevsky.* New York: Dial Press, 1945. "You believe in a palace of crystal that can never be destroyed . . . a palace at which one will not be able to put out one's tongue or make a long nose on the sly." p. 152.

42. Franz Kafka. *Amerika.* Garden City, N.Y.: Doubleday Anchor Books, 1946, p. 38.

43. Merleau-Ponty. *The Primacy of Perception, op. cit.*, p. 110.

44. Piaget, *op. cit.*

45. Richard M. Zaner. *The Way of Phenomenology.* New York: Pegasus Books, 1970, p. 27.

46. Freire, *op. cit.*, p. 100.

47. Schutz. "The Life-World." Natanson, ed. *Collected Papers, III.* The Hague: Martinus Nijhoff, 1967, p. 125.

48. Kafka, *op. cit.*, p. 201.

49. Schutz. "The Life-World." *op. cit.*, p. 124.

50. Schutz, "Leading Concepts of Phenomenology," *op. cit.*, p. 111.

51. G.K. Plochmann. "On the Organic Logic of Teaching and Learning." Vandenberg, *op. cit.*, p. 244.

52. cf. footnote 10.

53. Michael Novak. *The Experience of Nothingness.* New York: Harper & Row, 1970, p. 94.

54. Schutz. "Symbols, Reality, and Society." *Collected Papers I, op. cit.*, p. 315.

55. Merleau-Ponty, *Phenomenology of Perception, op. cit.*, p. xix.

56. *Ibid.*, pp. 455–56.

14

The Reconceptualization of Curriculum Studies

WILLIAM F. PINAR

WHAT SOME OBSERVERS HAVE DESIGNATED A "MOVEMENT" is visible in the field of curriculum studies in the United States. Some have termed it "reconceptualism," others "the new curriculum theory." Both terms suggest more thematic unity among the curriculum writing characterized as the "reconceptualization" than, upon close examination, appears to exist. Nonetheless, some thematic similarities are discernible, though insufficient in number to warrant a characterization like "ideology" or composite, agreed-upon point of view. What can be said, without dispute, is that by the summer of 1978, there will have been six conferences and five books[1] in the past six years which are indications of a socio-intellectual phenomenon in this field, and a phenomenon which clearly functions to reconceptualize the field of curriculum studies. Thus, while the writing published to date may be somewhat varied thematically, it is unitary in its significance for the field. If this process of transformation continues at its present rate, the field of curriculum studies will be profoundly different in 20 years time than it has been during the first 50 years of its existence.

What is this reconceptualization? The answer, at this point, is a slippery one, and to gain even an inchoate grip, one looks to the field as it is. This will indicate, in part, what is not. To a considerable extent, the reconceptualization is a reaction to what the field has been, and what it is seen to be at the present time.

TRADITIONALISTS

Most curricularists at work in 1977 can be characterized as *traditionalists*. Their work continues to make use of the "conventional wisdom" of the field, epitomized still by the work of Tyler. More important in identifying traditionalists than the allusion to Tyler is citing the *raison d'être* for traditional curriculum work. Above all, the reason for curriculum writing, indeed curriculum work generally, is captured in the phrase "service to practitioners." Curriculum work tends to be field-based and curriculum writing tends to have school teachers in mind. In short, traditional curriculum work is focused on the schools. Further,

Reprinted by permission. From *Journal of Curriculum Studies*, Vol. 10, No. 3, 1978: pp. 205–214.

professors of curriculum have tended to be former school people. In fact, school service of some sort, ordinarily classroom teaching, is still viewed as a prerequisite for a teaching post in the field in a college or university. To an extent not obvious in certain of the other sub-fields of education (for instance, philosophy and psychology of education, recently in ad-ministration and the "helping services"), curricularists are former school people whose intellectual and subcultural ties tend to be with school practitioners. They tend to be less interested in basic research, in theory development, in related developments in allied fields, than in a set of perceived realities of classrooms and school settings generally.

There is, of course, an historical basis for traditional curriculum work. Cremin suggests that it was after superintendent Newlon's work in curriculum revision, in the early 1920s in Denver, that the need for a curriculum specialist became clear.[2] It is plausible to imagine school administrators like Newlon asking teachers who demonstrated an interest in cur-riculum and its development to leave classroom teaching and enter an administrative of-fice from which they would attend full-time to matters curricular. There were no departments of curriculum in colleges of education in the 1920s; Newlon and other ad-ministrators could go nowhere else but to the classroom for curriculum personnel. When the training of curriculum personnel began at the university level in the 1930s, it surfaced in departments of administration and secondary education, indicating further the field's origin in and loyalty to the practical concerns of school personnel. This affiliation, more tenuous and complex at the present time than it was in the 1920s and 1930s, is evident in the programmes of the largest professional association of curricularists in the United States, the Association for Supervision and Curriculum Development. The programmes of ASCD annual meetings indicate a considerable and growing presence of school personnel. Further, the workshops and papers listed, the authors of which are university teachers, tend to have an explicit thematic focus on whatever school concerns are *au courant*.

There is another sense in which traditionalists carry forward the tradition of the field. The curriculum field's birth in the 1920s was understandably shaped by the intellectual character of that period. Above all it was a time of an emerging scientism when so-called scientific techniques from business and industry were finding their way into educational theory and practice. The early curricularist came to employ what Kliebard has termed the "bureaucratic model."[3] This model is characterized by its ameliorative orientation, ahis-torical posture, and an allegiance to behaviourism and to what Macdonald has termed a "technological rationality." The curriculum worker is dedicated to the "improvement" of schools. He honours this dedication by accepting the curriculum structure as it is. "Cur-riculum change" is measured by comparing resulting behaviours with original objectives. Even humanistic educators tend to accept many of these premises, as they introduce, per-haps, "values clarification" into the school curriculum. Accepting the curriculum structure as it is, and working to improve it, is what is meant by the "technician's mentality." In a cap-sule way, it can be likened to adjusting an automobile engine part in order to make it func-tion more effectively. This is also technological rationality, and its manifestations in school practice run the gamut from "competency-based teacher education" to "modular schedul-ing." The emphasis is on design, change (behaviourally observable), and improvement.

What has tended to be regarded as curriculum theory in the traditional sense, most no-tably Tyler's rationale,[4] is theoretical only in the questionable sense that it is abstract and usually at variance with what occurs in schools. Its intent is clearly to guide, to be of assis-tance to those in institutional positions who are concerned with curriculum. Of course, this is a broad concern. Most teachers share it, at least in terms of daily lesson planning. But as well as an element of teaching, curriculum is traditionally thought to include considerations such as evaluation, supervision, and also curriculum development and implementation. The boundaries of the field are fuzzy.

Thematically there is no unity. From Tyler to Taba and Saylor and Alexander to the current expression of this genre in Daniel and Laurel Tanner's book, Neil's and Zais' writing (all of which attempt an overview of considerations imagined pertinent to a curriculum worker) to the humanistic movement (for instance the work of such individuals as Fantini, Jordan, Simon, Weinstein) is a broad thematic territory.[5] What makes this work one territory is its fundamental interest in working with school people, with revising the curricula of schools. Traditional writing tends to be journalistic, necessarily so, in order that it can be readily accessible to a readership seeking quick answers to pressing, practical problems. The publications of the Association for Supervision and Curriculum Development also exemplify, to a considerable extent, this writing. ASCD is the traditionalists' professional organization. Relatively speaking, there exists a close relationship between traditional curricularists and school personnel.

CONCEPTUAL-EMPIRICISTS

A relationship between school personnel and the other two groups of curricularists— *conceptual-empiricists* and *reconceptualists*—also exists. But the nature of this relationship differs from the alliance historically characteristic of the field. This difference becomes clearer as we examine, momentarily, a second group of curricularists, a group which, until reconceptualists appeared, seemed to be the only heir to the field.

I use the word heir advisedly, for the traditional curriculum field has been declared terminally ill or already deceased by several influential observers, among them Schwab and Huebner.[6] What has caused, in the past 15 to 20 years, the demise of the field? A comprehensive answer to this important question is inappropriate in the present context. What can be pointed to is two-fold. First, the leadership of the so-called curriculum reform movement of the 1960s was outside the field. This bypass was a crippling blow to its professional status. If those whose work was curriculum development and implementation were called on primarily as consultants and only rarely at that, then clearly their claim to specialized knowledge and expertise was questionable. Second, the economic situation of the past six years has meant a drying up of funds for in-service work and for curriculum proposals generally. A field whose professional status was irreparably damaged now lost the material basis necessary for its functioning. How could curricularists work with school people without money or time for in-service workshops? How could curriculum proposals be implemented without requisite funds?

With the traditional, practical justification of the field attenuated—even teacher-training efforts have slowed dramatically—new justifications appeared. Curriculum and other education subfields have become increasingly vulnerable to criticisms regarding scholarly standards by colleagues in so-called cognate fields. Particularly the influence of colleagues in the social sciences is evident, paralleling the political ascendency of these disciplines in the university generally. In fact, research in education, in many instances, has become indistinguishable from social science research. The appearance and proliferation of conceptual-empiricists in the curriculum field is a specific instance of this general phenomenon. There remains, of course, the notion that research has implications for classroom practice, but it is usually claimed that many years of extensive research are necessary before significant implications can be obtained.

This development has gone so far that, examining the work done by a faculty in a typical American college of education, one has little sense of education as a field with its own identity. One discovers researchers whose primary identity is with the cognate field. Such individuals view themselves as primarily psychologists, philosophers, or sociologists with "research interests" in schools and education-related matters. By 1978, it is accurate to note that the education field has lost whatever (and it was never complete of course) intellectual autonomy it possessed in earlier years, and now is nearly tantamount to a colony of superior, imperialistic powers.

The view that education is not a discipline in itself but an area to be studied by the disciplines is evident in the work of those of curricularists I have called conceptual-empiricists. The work of this group can be so characterized, employing conceptual and empirical in the sense social scientists typically employ them. This work is concerned with developing hypotheses to be tested, and testing them in methodological ways characteristic of mainstream social science. This work is reported, ordinarily, at meetings of the American Educational Research Association. Just as the Association for Supervision and Curriculum Development is the traditionalists' organization, AERA tends to be the organization of conceptual-empiricists. (In relatively small numbers traditionalists and reconceptualists also read papers at AERA annual meetings.)

An illustrative piece of conceptual work from this second group of curricularists was published in the AERA-sponsored *Review of Educational Research*. It is George Posner's (with Kenneth Strike) "A categorization scheme for principles of sequencing content." A prefatory paragraph indicates that his view is a social scientist's one, reliant upon hypothesis-making, data collection, and interpretation.

> We have very little information, based on hard data, regarding the consequences of alternative content sequences and will need a good deal more research effort before we are able to satisfactorily suggest how content *should* be sequenced. Our intention here is to consider the question, What are the alternatives?[7]

The article is a conceptual one, concerned with what the authors view as logically defensible content sequencing alternatives, and it is empirical in its allegiance to the view of empirical research, one yielding "hard data," typical of social science at the present time.

In a recently published essay, Decker F. Walker, another visible conceptual-empiricist, moves away somewhat from strict social science as exemplified in Posner's work.[8] His essay, or case study as he terms it, is more anthropological in its methodological form, demonstrating a type of curriculum research which Walker's co-editor Reid endorses.[9] Anthropology, it should be noted, while regarded as not as "pure" a social science as political science or psychology, is nonetheless generally categorized as a social science.

Taking his cue from Schwab, Walker argues that prescriptive curriculum theories, (partly because they do not reflect the actual process of curriculum change), are not useful. Rather than focus on why curriculum developers did not follow the Tyler rationale, Walker concentrates on how, in fact, the developers did proceed. In his study he finds little use for terms like objectives and important use for terms such as platform and deliberation. He concludes that curricularists probably ought to abandon the attempt to make actual curriculum development mirror prescriptive theories, accept "deliberation" as a core aspect of the development process, and apply the intellectual resources of the field toward improving the quality of deliberation and employing it more effectively.

This work I find significant to the field in two ways. First it deals another hard blow to the Tyler rationale and its influence. Second, Walker is moving away from social science. His work remains social science, but it is closer to the work of some reconceptualists than it is to that of Posner, and other mainstream conceptual-empiricists. Walker retains the traditional focus upon the practical concerns of school people and school curriculum, and no doubt he has and will spend a portion of his professional time on actual curriculum projects. Further, his methods seem more nearly those of the ethnomethodologist whose approaches do not easily fit the picture of conventional theories of the middle range, as projected by individuals such as the sociologist Robert Merton, who has influenced so many conceptual-empirical studies in the field of sociology. Walker appears to be moving outside mainstream conceptual-empiricism.

Also in the Reid and Walker book is work by another visible conceptual-empiricist, Ian Westbury. With his co-author Lynn McKinney, Westbury studies the Gary, Indiana school system during the period 1940–1970.[10] Like Walker's study of the art project, McKinney and Westbury's study would seem to be outside mainstream conceptual-empiricism, even close to work characteristic of the humanities. The structure of the study, however, indicates its allegiance to social science, thus warranting its categorization as conceptual-empirical. The work is a historical study done in the service of generalization, work that has interest in the particular (the Gary district) as it contributes to understanding of the general. The "general" in this instance is the phenomenon of stability and change, which the authors "now believe are the two primary functions of the administrative structure which surround the schools."[11] Finally what the study demonstrates is "that a concern for goals without a concomitant concern for organizational matters addresses only a small part of the problem of conceiving new designs for schools."[12] This use of the specific to illustrate a general, ahistorical "law" is, of course, a fundamental procedure of mainstream social science.

RECONCEPTUALISTS

This concern for generalization is not abandoned in the work of the third group of curricularists, the reconceptualists. For example, at the fourth conference at the University of Wisconsin-Milwaukee, Professor Apple reported the results of a study he and a colleague conducted in a kindergarten, substantiating claims he has made before regarding the socio-political functions of classroom behaviour.[13] His case study is distinguishable from the work of a typical conceptual-empiricist in two significant respects: (1) his acknowledged "value-laden" perspective, and (2) a perspective with a politically emancipatory intent. That is, in contrast to the canon of traditional social science, which prescribes data collection, hypothesis substantiation or disconfirmation in the disinterested service of building a body of knowledge, a reconceptualist tends to see research as an inescapably political as well as intellectual act. As such, it works to suppress, or to liberate, not only those who conduct the research, and those upon whom it is conducted, but as well those outside the academic subculture. Mainstream social science research, while on the surface seemingly apolitical in nature and consequence, if examined more carefully can be seen as contributing to the maintenance of the contemporary social-political order, or contributing to its dissolution. Apple and Marxists and neo-Marxists go further and accept a teleological view of historical movement, allying themselves with the lower classes, whose final emergence from oppression is seen to be inevitable. A number of reconceptualists, while not Marxists, nonetheless accept some variation of this teleological historical view. And many of these, at least from a distance, would seem to be "leftists" of some sort. Nearly all accept that a political dimension is inherent in any intellectual activity.

This political emphasis distinguishes the work of Apple, Burton, Mann, Molnar, some of the work of Huebner and Macdonald, from the work of traditionalists and conceptual-empiricists.[14] It is true that Reid and Walker in their *Case Studies in Curriculum Change* acknowledge that curriculum development is political, but the point is never developed, and never connected with a view of history and the contemporary social order. The focus of Walker's case study and of other case studies in the book is limited to literal curriculum change, without historicizing this change, indicating its relationship to contemporary historical movement generally. In the 1975 ASCD year-book, on the other hand, which is edited by Macdonald and Zaret, with essays also by Apple, Burton, Huebner, and Mann, this siting of curriculum issues in the broad intellectual-historical currents of twentieth-century life is constant.[15] Macdonald speaks, for instance, of technological rationality, an intellectual mode comparable in its pervasiveness and taken-for-grantedness to the ascendency of technology in human culture at large.[16] Such individuals would argue that comprehension of curriculum issues is possible only when they are situated historically.

The 1975 ASCD year-book speaks to school people. It is not that reconceptualists do not speak to this constituency of the curriculum field. But there is a conscious abandonment of the "technician's mentality." There are no prescriptions or traditional rationales. What this year-book offers, instead, is heightened awareness of the complexity and historical significance of curriculum issues. Because the difficulties these reconceptualists identify are related to difficulties in the culture at large, they are not "problems" that can be "solved." That concept created by technological rationality, is itself problematic. Thus, what is necessary, in part, is fundamental structural change in the culture. Such an aspiration cannot be realized by "plugging into" the extant order. That is why an elective or two on Marx in high-school social studies classes, or the teaching of autobiographical reflection in English classes, bring indifference and often alarm to most reconceptualists. That "plugging into," "co-opting" it was termed in the 1960s during the student protests, accepts the social order as it is. What is necessary is a fundamental reconceptualization of what curriculum is, how it functions, and how it might function in emancipatory ways. It is this commitment to a comprehensive critique and theory development that distinguishes the reconceptualist phenomenon.

To understand more fully the efforts of the individuals involved in inquiry of this kind requires some understanding of metatheory and philosophy of science. Without such grounding, it is difficult, if not impossible, for curricularists to see clearly their work in the context of the growth of knowledge in general. Max van Manen's paper at the 1976 Wisconsin conference was a significant effort to analyse various structures of theoretic knowledge as they related to dominant modes of inquiry in the field of curriculum.[17] His work builds on basic analyses undertaken by philosophers of science such as Radnitzky and Feyerabend.[18] More work needs to be done along this line.

The reconceptualization, it must be noted, is fundamentally an intellectual phenomenon, not an interpersonal-affiliative one. Reconceptualists have no organized group, such as ASCD or AERA. Individuals at work, while sharing certain themes and motives, do not tend to share any common interpersonal affiliation. (In this one respect their work parallels that of the so-called romantic critics of the 1960s. But here any such comparison stops.) Conferences have been held yearly; the most recent on the campus of Rochester Institute of Technology, Rochester, New York. A journal and a press emphasizing this work are scheduled to appear by 1979.

CONCLUSION

As an interpreter of metatheories, Richard Bernstein recently analysed, in detail, individuals at work in four areas—empirical research, philosophical analysis, phenomenology and critical theory of society.[19] (The first category corresponds to conceptual-empirical, the third and fourth to reconceptualist work.) He ends his study with this conviction:

> In the final analysis we are not confronted with exclusive choices: either empirical or interpretative theory or critical theory. Rather there is an internal dialectic in the restructing of social political theory: when we work through any one of these movements we discover the others are implicated.[20]

This is so in the field of curriculum studies also. We are not faced with an exclusive choice: either the traditional wisdom of the field, or conceptual-empiricism, or the reconceptualization. Each is reliant upon the other. For the field to become vital and significant to American education it must nurture each "moment," its "internal dialectic." And it must strive for synthesis, for a series of perspectives on curriculum that are at once empirical, interpretative, critical, emancipatory.

But such nurturance and synthesis do not characterize, on the whole, the field today. Some of the issues raised by the British sociologist David Silverman are germane here.[21] As a prologue to more adequate social science theorizing, Silverman proposes that we learn how to read Castaneda's account of his apprenticeship to Don Juan in order that we may come to know the kinds of questions that need to be asked. He is convinced that mainstream conceptual-empiricists, regardless of field, do not now know what questions to ask, and are, indeed, intolerant of reconceptualizations that differ from their own. This intolerance is discernible in the American curriculum field. To some extent it can be found in each group of curricularists.

I am convinced that this intolerance among curricularists for work differing from one's own must be suspended to some extent if significant intellectual movement in the field is to occur. Becoming open to another genre of work does not mean loss of one's capacity for critical reflection. Nor does it mean, necessarily, loss of intellectual identity. One may remain a traditionalist while sympathetically studying the work of a reconceptualist. One's own point of view may well be enriched. Further, an intellectual climate may become established in which could develop syntheses of current perspectives, regenerating the field, and making more likely that its contribution to American education be an important one.

ACKNOWLEDGMENT

This is a revised version of a paper presented at the Annual Meeting of the American Educational Research Association in New York in April, 1977.

REFERENCE AND NOTES

1. Conferences have been held at the University of Rochester (1973), Xavier University of Cincinnati (1974), the University of Virginia (1975), the University of Wisconsin at Milwaukee (1976), Kent State University (1977), and the Rochester Institute of Technology (1978). Books include:

   Pinar, W. (Ed) *Heightened Consciousness, Cultural Revolution and Curriculum Theory* (McCutchan Publishing Corp., Berkeley, CA, 1974);

   IDEM, *Curriculum Theorizing: The Reconceptualists* (McCutchan Publishing Corp., Berkeley, CA, 1975);

   Pinar, W., and Grumet, M. R. *Toward a Poor Curriculum* (Kendall/Hunt Publishing Co., Dubuque, IA, 1976).

   At a 1976 conference held at the State University of New York at Geneseo; Professors Apple, Greene, Kliebard and Huebner read papers. Each of these persons has been associated with the reconceptualists although the chairmen of this meeting, Professors DeMarte and Rosarie, did not see this seminar as being in the tradition of the others. The papers from this seminar were published in *Curriculum Inquiry*, Vol. 6, No. 4 (1977).

2. Cremin, L. "Curriculum-making in the United States," In Pinar, W. (Ed), *Curriculum Theorizing*, pp. 19–35.

3. Kliebard, H. M. "Persistent curriculum issues in historical perspective," and "Bureaucracy and curriculum theory." In Pinar, W. (Ed) *Curriculum Theorizing*, pp. 39–69.

4. Tyler, R. W., *Basic Principles of Curriculum and Instruction* (University of Chicago Press, Chicago, 1950).

5. Taba, H. *Curriculum Development: Theory and Practice* (Harcourt, Brace and World, New York, 1962);

   Saylor, G., and Alexander, W. *Curriculum Planning for Modern Schools* (Holt, Rinehart and Winston, New York, 1966);

   Tanner, D., and Tanner, L. N. *Curriculum Development: Theory into Practice* (MacMillan, New York, 1975);

   Neil, J. D. *Curriculum: A Comprehensive Introduction* (Little, Brown and Co., Boston, 1977);

   Zais, R. S. *Curriculum: Principles and Foundations* (Thomas Y. Browell, New York, 1976);

   Weinstein, G., and Fantini, M. D. *Toward Humanistic Education: A Curriculum of Affect* (Praeger Publishers, New York, 1971);

   Simon, S., et al. *Values Clarification* (Hart, New York, 1972);

   Jordan, D. "The ANISA Model." Paper presented to conference on curriculum at the University of Virginia, 1975 (available from Charles W. Beegle, Curry Memorial School of Education, University of Virginia, Charlottesville, VA 22903, USA).

6. Schwab, J. J. *The Practical: A Language for Curriculum* (National Education Association, Washington, D.C., 1970);

   Huebner, D. "The moribund curriculum field: Its wake and our work." *Curriculum Inquiry*, Vol. 6, No. 2 (1976).

7. Posner, G. J. and Strike, K. A. "A categorization scheme for principles of sequencing content." *Review of Educational Research*, Vol. 46, No. 4 (1976).

8. Walker, D. F. "Curriculum development in an art project." In Reid, W. A., and Walker, D. F. (Eds) *Case Studies in Curriculum Change* (Routledge and Kegan Paul, London, 1975).

9. Reid, W. A. "The changing curriculum: theory and practice." In Reid and Walker, op. cit.

10. McKinney, W. L., and Westbury, I. "Stability and change; the public schools of Gary, Indiana, 1940–70." In Reid and Walker, op. cit.

11. Ibid., p. 44.

12. Ibid., p. 50.

13. Apple, M. W., and King, N. "What do schools teach?" Paper presented at the University of Wisconsin and Milwaukee Conference.

14. For discussion of this point see my prefatory remarks in *Curriculum Theorizing* (Note 1). See also:

    Klohr, P. R. "The State of the Field." Paper presented at the Xavier University Conference on Curriculum;

    Miller, J. L. "Duality: Perspectives on the reconceptualization." Paper presented to University of Virginia Conference;

    Macdonald, J. B. "Curriculum Theory as intentional activity." Paper presented to University of Virginia Conference (see Note 5);

Macdonald, J. B. "Curriculum Theory and human interests." In Pinar, W. (Ed) *Curriculum Theorizing*; Benham, B. J. "Curriculum Theory in the 1970s: the reconceptualist movement." Texas Technical University, 1976, unpublished paper.

15. Zaret, E., and Macdonald, J. B. *Schools in Search of Meaning* (Association for Supervision and Curriculum Development, Washington, D.C., 1975).

16. Macdonald, J. B. "The quality of everyday life in schools." In Zaret and Macdonald, op. cit.

17. Van Manen, M. "Linking ways of knowing with ways of being practical." *Curriculum Inquiry*, Vol. 6, No. 3 (1977).

18. Radnitzky, G. *Contemporary Schools of Metascience* (Henry Regnery Co., Chicago, 1973); Feyerbend P. K. "Against method; outline of an anarchist theory of knowledge." In *Minnesota Studies in the Philosophy of Science*, Vol. 4 (University of Minnesota Press, Minneapolis, 1970).

19. Bernstein, R. J. *The Restructuring of Social and Political Theory* (Harcourt, Brace, Jovanovich, New York, 1976).

20. Ibid., 235.

21. Silverman, D. *Reading Castaneda: A Prologue to the Social Sciences* (Routledge and Kegan Paul, London, 1975).

15

The Paideia Proposal

Mortimer J. Adler

DEMOCRACY AND EDUCATION

We are on the verge of a new era in our national life. The long-needed educational reform for which this country is at last ready will be a turning point toward that new era.

Democracy has come into its own for the first time in this century. Not until this century have we undertaken to give twelve years of schooling to all our children. Not until this century have we conferred the high office of enfranchised citizenship on all our people, regardless of sex, race, or ethnic origin.

The two—universal suffrage and universal schooling—are inextricably bound together. The one without the other is a perilous delusion. Suffrage without schooling produces mobocracy, not democracy—not rule of law, not constitutional government by the people as well as for them.

The great American educator, John Dewey, recognized this early in this century. In *Democracy and Education*, written in 1916, he first tied these two words together and let each shine light upon the other.

A revolutionary message of that book was that a democratic society must provide equal educational opportunity not only by giving to all its children the same quantity of public education—the same number of years in school—but also by making sure to give to all of them, all with no exceptions, the same quality of education.

The ideal Dewey set before us is a challenge we have failed to meet. It is a challenge so difficult that it is understandable, perhaps excusable, that we have so far failed. But we cannot continue to fail without disastrous consequences for all of us. For the proper working of our political institutions, for the efficiency of our industries and businesses, for the salvation of our economy, for the vitality of our culture, and for the ultimate good of our citizens as individuals, and especially our future citizens—our children—we must succeed.

Reprinted by permission From Mortimer J. Adler. 1982. *The Paideia Proposal: An Educational Manifesto*. New York: Collier Books.

We are all sufferers from our continued failure to fulfill the educational obligations of a democracy. We are all the victims of a school system that has only gone halfway along the road to realize the promise of democracy.

At the beginning of this century, fewer than 10 percent of those of an age eligible for high school entered such schools. Today, almost 100 percent of our children enter, but not all complete such secondary schooling; many drop out for many reasons, some of them understandable.

It has taken us the better part of eighty years to go halfway toward the goal our society must achieve if it is to be a true democracy. The halfway mark was reached when we finally managed to provide twelve years of basic public schooling for all our children. At that point, we were closer to the goal that Horace Mann set for us more than a century ago when he said: "Education is the gateway to equality."

But the democratic promise of equal educational opportunity, half fulfilled, is worse than a promise broken. It is an ideal betrayed. Equality of educational opportunity is not, in fact, provided if it means no more than taking all the children into the public schools for the same number of hours, days, and years. If once there they are divided into the sheep and the goats, into those destined solely for toil and those destined for economic and political leadership and for a quality of life to which all should have access, then the democratic purpose has been undermined by an inadequate system of public schooling.

It fails because it has achieved only the same quantity of public schooling, not the same quality. This failure is a downright violation of our democratic principles.

We are politically a classless society. Our citizenry as a whole is our ruling class. We should, therefore, be an educationally classless society.

We should have a one-track system of schooling, not a system with two or more tracks, only one of which goes straight ahead while the others shunt the young off onto sidetracks not headed toward the goals our society opens to all. The innermost meaning of social equality is: *substantially the same quality of life for all.* That calls for: *the same quality of schooling for all.*

We may take some satisfaction, perhaps, in the fact that we have won half the battle—the quantitative half. But we deserve the full development of the country's human potential. We should, therefore, be vexed that we have not yet gone further. We should be impatient to get on with it, in and through the schools.

Progress toward the fulfillment of democracy by means of our educational system should and can be accelerated. It need not and must not take another century to achieve uniform quality for all in our public schools.

There are signs on all sides that tell us the people want that move forward now. The time is ripe. Parents, teachers, leaders of government, labor unions, corporations—above all, the young themselves—have uttered passionate complaints about the declining quality of public schooling.

There is no acceptable reason why trying to promote equality should have led to a lessening or loss of quality. Two decades after John Dewey, another great American educator, Robert Maynard Hutchins, as much committed to democracy as Dewey was before him, stated the fundamental principle we must now follow in our effort to achieve a true equality of educational conditions. "The best education for the best," he said, "is the best education for all."

The shape of the best education for the best is not unknown to us. But we have been slow to learn how to provide it. Nor have we always been honest in our commitment to democracy and its promise of equality. A part of our population—and much too large a part—has harbored the opinion that many of the nation's children are not fully educable. Trainable for one or another job, perhaps, but not educable for the duties of self-governing citizenship and for the enjoyment of things of the mind and spirit that are essential to a good human life.

We must end that hypocrisy in our national life. We cannot say out of one side of our mouth that we are for democracy and all its free institutions including, preeminently, political and civil liberty for all; and out of the other side of our mouth, say that only some of the children—fewer than half—are educable for full citizenship and a full human life.

With the exception of a few suffering from irremediable brain damage, every child is educable up to his or her capacity. Educable—not just trainable for jobs! As John Dewey said almost a century ago, vocational training, training for particular jobs, is not the education of free men and women.

True, children are educable in varying degrees, but the variation in degree must be of the same kind and quality of education. If "the best education for the best is the best education for all," the failure to carry out that principle is the failure on the part of society—a failure of parents, of teachers, of administrators—not a failure on the part of the children.

There are no unteachable children. There are only schools and teachers and parents who fail to teach them.

THE SAME COURSE OF STUDY FOR ALL

To give the same quality of schooling to all requires a program of study that is both liberal and general, and that is, in several, crucial, overarching respects, one and the same for every child. All sidetracks, specialized courses, or elective choices must be eliminated. Allowing them will always lead a certain number of students to voluntarily downgrade their own education.

Elective choices are appropriate only in a curriculum that is intended for different avenues of specialization or different forms of preparation for the professions or technical careers. Electives and specialization are entirely proper at the level of advanced schooling—in our colleges, universities, and technical schools. They are wholly inappropriate at the level of basic schooling.

The course of study to be followed in the twelve years of basic schooling should, therefore, be completely required, with only one exception. That exception is the choice of a second language. In addition to competence in the use of English as everyone's primary language, basic schooling should confer a certain degree of facility in the use of a second language. That second language should be open to elective choice.

The diagram depicts in three columns three distinct modes of teaching and learning, rising in successive gradations of complexity and difficulty from the first to the twelfth year. All three modes are essential to the overall course of study.

These three columns are interconnected, as the diagram indicates. The different modes of learning on the part of the students and the different modes of teaching on the part of the teaching staff correspond to three different ways in which the mind can be improved—(1) by the acquisition of organized knowledge; (2) by the development of intellectual skills; and (3) by the enlargement of understanding, insight, and aesthetic appreciation.

In addition to the three main Columns of Learning, the required course of study also includes a group of auxiliary subjects, of which one is physical education and care of the body. This runs through all twelve years. Of the other two auxiliary subjects, instruction in a variety of manual arts occupies a number of years, but not all twelve; and the third consists of an introduction to the world of work and its range of occupations and careers. It is given in the last two of the twelve years.

	COLUMN ONE	**COLUMN TWO**	**COLUMN THREE**
Goals	ACQUISITION OF ORGANIZED KNOWLEDGE	DEVELOPMENT OF INTELLECTUAL SKILLS—SKILLS OF LEARNING	ENLARGED UNDERSTANDING OF IDEAS AND VALUES
	by means of	by means of	by means of
Means	DIDACTIC INSTRUCTION LECTURES AND RESPONSES TEXTBOOKS AND OTHER AIDS	COACHING, EXERCISES, AND SUPERVISED PRACTICE	MAIEUTIC OR SOCRATIC QUESTIONING AND ACTIVE PARTICIPATION
	in three areas of subject-matter	in the operations of	in the
Areas of Operations and Activities	LANGUAGE, LITERATURE, AND THE FINE ARTS, MATHEMATICS AND NATURAL SCIENCE, HISTORY, GEOGRAPHY, AND SOCIAL STUDIES	READING, WRITING, SPEAKING, LISTENING CALCULATING, PROBLEM-SOLVING, OBSERVING MEASURING, ESTIMATING EXERCISING CRITICAL JUDGMENT	DISCUSSION OF BOOKS (NOT TEXTBOOKS) AND OTHER WORKS OF ART AND INVOLVEMENT IN ARTISTIC ACTIVITIES e.g., MUSIC, DRAMA, VISUAL ARTS

THE THREE COLUMNS DO NOT CORRESPOND TO SEPARATE COURSES, NOR IS ONE KIND OF TEACHING AND LEARNING NECESSARILY CONFINED TO ANY ONE CLASS.

16

The False Promise of the Paideia: A Critical Review of The Paideia Proposal

Nel Noddings

The Paideia Proposal is offered as an educational prescription for all of America's children. It is based on two major premises: that "the shape of the best education for the best is not unknown to us" (p. 7) and that "the best education for the best . . . is the best education for all" (p. 6). Surely no humane and decent person finds it easy to counsel against a proposal that promises to provide the "same quality of schooling to all," and thereby to educate all of our children to their fullest potential. Hard as it is, however, I believe that we should reject the recommendations in *The Paideia Proposal*. I will argue that "equality of quality" in education cannot be achieved by forcing all students to take exactly the same course of study, nor can the ideal of a democratic, classless society be actualized by establishing only one model of excellence.

The *Paideia's* recommendations fall into two major categories: content and method. Those on method will be discussed at the end of this essay. The recommendations on content are encapsulated in this paragraph from the *Paideia*:

> The course of study to be followed in the twelve years of basic schooling should, therefore, be completely required, with only one exception. That exception is the choice of a second language. (p. 21)

There is little use in arguing directly against the *Paideia's* recommendations, because they follow inexorably from Mortimer Adler's two basic assumptions. But both of Adler's premises may be called into question as well as his strategy of persuasion: linking John Dewey and Robert Hutchins together as though no disagreement separated the two should cause thoughtful educators considerable uneasiness. I will start by examining that strategy, and then I will examine each of Adler's premises in turn.

Reprinted by permission of Caddo Gap Press, From *Journal of Thought*, Vol. 18, No. 4, 1983, pp. 81–91.

1

The Paideia Proposal is dedicated to Horace Mann, John Dewey, and Robert Hutchins, "who would have been our leaders were they alive today." This is a lovely dedication, but Adler fails to mention that, if Dewey and Hutchins were alive today, they would almost certainly be engaged in the continuing battle of method and principle that they so vigorously mounted during their actual lifetimes. Mr. Hutchins would be an eloquent and outspoken advocate of the *Paideia*: Mr. Dewey would be a softer spoken but rigorously thoughtful opponent of the program. To suggest, even tacitly, that the *Paideia* fulfills the dreams and recommendations of both John Dewey and Robert Hutchins does a monumental disservice to John Dewey. The man and his educational thought deserve better. Further, Adler is thoroughly informed on the differences I shall point out, and one wonders why he chose to omit their discussion. Perhaps he believes that it is high time for reconciliation between Hutchins and Dewey and that this reconciliation holds promise for real improvement in the system of public education that both men loved (in some ideal form) and that is now so terribly beset with problems. Granted this generous motive, he still cannot responsibly attempt to effect reconciliation by assimilating a worthy opponent to the position of his adversary without even mentioning the problems that opponent would encounter in considering such a reconciliation.

Dewey and Hutchins are linked in Adler's arguments through their manifest interests in democracy and "equality of quality" in education. But their views on both concepts differed radically. Adler refers to Dewey's *Democracy and Education* when he says:

> A revolutionary message of that book was that a democratic society must provide equal opportunity not only by giving to all its children the same quantity of public education—the same number of years in school—but also by making sure to give to all of them, all with no exceptions, the same quality of education. (*Paideia*, p. 4)

Now, it is clear that Dewey did advocate a substantial "equality of quality" in education for all children. But his ideas on this were very different from those of Hutchins. In *The School and Society*, Dewey said:

> What the best and wisest parent wants for his own child, that must the community want for all its children. Any other ideal for our schools is narrow and unlovely; acted upon, it destroys our democracy. (1899, p. 3)

Clearly, we have to ask what Dewey meant when he referred to "the best and wisest parent." It is crystal clear at the outset, however, that he meant by "best" something very different from the "best" of Hutchins in the initial premises cited by Adler. Yet Adler throws them together in the same paragraph as though both were advocates of the program under construction. He says:

> There is no acceptable reason why trying to promote equality should have led to a lessening or loss of quality. Two decades after John Dewey, another great American educator, Robert Maynard Hutchins, as much committed to democracy as Dewey was before him, stated the fundamental principle we must follow in our effort to achieve a true equality of educational conditions. "The best education for the best." he said, "is the best education for all." (*Paideia*, p. 6)

Dewey would certainly challenge this premise if "best" is interpreted as "intellectually best"—as it surely is in the writings of Hutchins and Adler. Further, Dewey *did* challenge both premises in direct rebuttal of Hutchins. In a series of 1937 articles in *The Social Frontier*, Dewey criticized the program of higher education that Hutchins proposed in *The Higher Learning in America*. Dewey made it clear in the ensuing exchange of views that, while he accepted and admired some of Hutchins' analysis, he rejected the proposed remedy. He said:

> The essence of the remedy . . . is emancipation of higher learning from . . . practicality, and its devotion to the cultivation of intellectuality for its own sake. (1937, p. 103)

Dewey's objections to the remedies suggested in *The Higher Learning* centered on two matters that he thought were at the heart of Hutchins' ideas: belief in "the existence of fixed and eternal authoritative principles" and the separation of "higher learning from contemporary social life." It is not an exaggeration to say that Dewey's voluminous writings over a lifetime of effort attacked these ideas again and again from a wide variety of perspectives. The separation of learning from contemporary social life was, indeed, a favorite target of his criticism. Exactly the same objections may be brought against the *Paideia*: It elevates intellectual life above that which it should serve (the social communion of human beings), and it assumes an essential sameness in human beings and values that suggests, logically, a sameness in education.

It would be fun (and instructive, too) to follow the Dewey-Hutchins debate further, but I cannot do that here. Suffice it to say that these two great educators did not really communicate with each other. Hutchins, indeed, began his rejoinder to Dewey by saying that he could not "in any real sense" respond to Dewey for

> Mr. Dewey has stated my position in such a way as to lead me to think that I cannot write, and has stated his own in such a way as to make me suspect that I cannot read. (1937, p. 137)

This sort of wit was a favorite gambit of Hutchins. He did not engage in *dialogue* with Dewey and continually side-stepped Dewey's most telling points, preferring to display verbal pyrotechnics and to persuade through rhetoric. The same charade is now being replayed. Adler offers us a tightly argued program based on rhetorical premises, themselves entirely unsupported by logical argumentation. Accept his premises and he has you, because he does not make errors in the logic of *developing* his program. What is sad is that so many educators are listening to Adler without a murmur of logical protest. He is right about one thing—and, paradoxically, it is working for him—the education of educators is not all that it should be.

2

Let me raise a murmur of logical protest. Put aside for the moment the premise that makes claims about the "shape of the best education," and let's concentrate on the other. The best education for the best is the best education for all.

The word "best" is used three times here. All three uses invite scrutiny, but the second deserves special attention. It is used elliptically as a noun. If we insist that the ellipsis be filled and that "best" be used as an adjective, what noun will it modify? It is clear that "best" is not meant to modify such nouns as "life" or "effort" or "performance" or the like. Both Hutchins and Adler are talking about *people* when they refer to "the best." Now what noun shall we insert: people? students? minds? It is eminently clear that Hutchins meant to refer to an *intellectually best* when he used the word and that an accurate filling in of the ellipsis would be, "The best education for the intellectually best students is the best education for all." Further, because the two premises have influenced each other historically, "intellectually best" has been narrowed to "academically best" in the traditional sense. Adler wants all children to receive an education that is, in content at least, the education designed for our academically best students.

Why should we consider doing this? Are the academically best the only group that should provide a model for school learning? Is the mission of the school to provide training or "education" only for the mind? Or are there many models of excellence that must be recognized in both society and school? In my own secondary schooling, I participated in a program very like the one Adler outlines. I loved it. I was completely captivated by Caesar's Gallic Wars, geometry, trigonometric identities, and even Cicero's essay on old age. It was not until years later that I learned about the utter misery most of my classmates endured in the "same" environment. Mr. Adler, to his great credit, would try to alleviate that misery by better classroom teaching and individual coaching, but he is mistaken in what he believes would be effected. No special effort or even genius in teaching would have brought most of my classmates into fair competition with me. Whatever they did, however they improved, I would have done more of it and at a higher level. It is not that I was "better" than they. I was *interested* in the sort of material the school wanted me to learn. Now one might claim a special benefit in this side effect: the academically able would be pushed through increased competition to surpass themselves. But then they would be engaged in academics (if they remained engaged) for largely the wrong reasons and with loss of the joy that accompanies doing what one has chosen out of love to do. We should consider the *Paideia*'s proposals, then, if we want this sort of effect.

Giving all of our children the *same* education, especially when that "sameness" is defined in a model of intellectual excellence, cannot equalize the quality of education. When parents and their children want the sort of education prescribed in the *Paideia*, it seems right to accommodate them, but to impose a plan such as this on all children in the name of equality is wrong. It proceeds in part from the stated assumption that we are "politically a classless society" and that we should, therefore, be an "educationally classless society." Mr. Adler has the cart before the horse. We are *not*, in any but the most technical sense, a classless society and to impose a uniform and compulsory form of education on all children is likely to aggravate an already unhealthy condition. When children must all study the same material and strive to meet the same standards, it becomes infinitely easier to sort and grade them like so many apples on a conveyor belt. Some children will be in the top quartile and some will be in the bottom quartile. Are we to say, then, that they all had an "equal chance" and that the "classes" thus established are, at least, objectivly and fairly established?

To put the horse properly before the cart, we would have to ask what education might do to help the society arrive at the classless ideal it has stated for itself. Many theorists insist that the schools can do very little to change the society: As institutions *of* the society, they are instruments for the reproduction of society as it is. We can certainly take a more hopeful view than this, but whatever view we take must be realistic at the outset. People in our society perform a huge variety of tasks, have hundreds of different interests, hold a variety of precious values. We do not offer equality when we ask them to model themselves after the traditional profile of an "intellectual best." What the schools need to do, instead, is to legitimize multiple models of excellence, e.g., mechanical, artistic, physical, productive, academic, and caretaking. Standing over all these should be the ethical, for what we need far more urgently than intellectual prowess is ethical goodness.

Many thoughtful planners shrink from the notion of "multiple models" of excellence because they believe the schools are already asked to accomplish too much. John Gardner, for example, in his influential *Excellence* (1961), lauded excellence in all its forms at the level of societal activity, but he charged the school with the task of promoting only academic excellence. It seems entirely right in a society such as ours to value "excellent plumbers above mediocre philosophers," but must we not also value the budding plumber—the youngster who will be a craftsman—while he or she is still a student? Gardner argued that the schools cannot do everything and that they are best organized to achieve *academic* excellence. The weakest part of his argument was revealed when he admitted that some youngsters (probably many) would not do well in a program so oriented. They would have to understand, he said, that the failure they had experienced in school was only *one form* of failure and that they might still achieve excellence in other enterprises. But I ask you this: How is a youngster who has been at the bottom of the heap for twelve years going "to understand" that his or her failure so far is only "one form" of failure? Surely, if we value plumbing, and farming, and dancing, and writing, and repairing electronic devices at the societal level, we can find ways of valuing the talents that lead to these occupations during school years. We really *have* to do this if our talk of equality is to be anything more than *mere* talk.

To be reasonable, however, we do have to consider Gardner's concern that demands on the schools have so proliferated that they cannot achieve any sort of excellence. I suggest that it is not subject and activity demands that have overburdened our schools but, rather, demands to solve the problems of a society unwilling to bear its burdens where they should properly be shouldered. A society unwilling to rid itself of racial prejudice asks the *schools* to achieve desegregation. A society unwilling to talk with its children about love, delight, and commitment asks the *schools* to teach sex education. A society unwilling to recognize the forms of excellence that Mr. Gardner identifies asks the *schools* to teach everyone algebra. The greatest burden of the schools, as a result, is trying to find some way to teach to adequately intelligent students things that they do not want to learn.

Acting on the *Paideia* would not produce a "classless education." The *Paideia* selects a form of education traditionally associated with an academically privileged class—"education for the best"—and prescribes it for all children, regardless of home influences, individual interests, special talents, or any realistic hope that all can participate in the sort of professional life that such an education has traditionally aspired to. Even if we were to deny the existence of classes in our current society, we would inevitably produce them under the *Paideia*. In this system, *everyone* is to be judged by the standards usually applied to the academically talented. I object to this. I object as a teacher, as a parent, and as a thoughtful human being. There is more to life, more to excellence, more to success, and more to devotion than can be captured in a single intellectual model of excellence.

To provide an equal quality of education for all our children requires, first, that we hold the variety of their talents and legitimate interests to be equally valuable. This does not mean that schools should provide no common learnings. Of course the schools should teach all children to read, write, and compute. But the schools should also teach all children how to operate the technical machinery and gadgets that fill our homes and offices; to care responsibly for living things; to develop their bodies for lifelong physical grace; to obtain and convey information; to use their hands in making and finishing things; to develop their receptive capacities in the arts; to develop a commitment to service in some capacity. This sounds like an impossible list—and it is almost certainly incomplete. But the beautiful truth is that when we take all of the valuable aspects of life into consideration and when we respect all of our children's legitimate interests in our educational planning, it becomes *easier* to teach the basic skills. They become obviously necessary to the satisfaction of real problems and actual tasks. The answer is not to spend more and more time on "basics" but to revitalize the basics in a broad scheme of general education that is laid out boldly along the entire continuum of human experience.

Now, I can imagine at least some of the advocates of *Paideia* saying: But that is exactly what we mean to do; that is what education for the best has traditionally done! It provides a broad, general education that aims to liberate the human mind; it conduces to the "examined life." It . . . "Whoa up!" I'd have to say. You are still talking about an essentially abstract and bookish sort of education. Consider this: Is it not at least possible that academic talent is *per se* a somewhat specialized talent? If it is, and I believe there is evidence to support the contention, then so long as our schooling is highly "intellectualized," we have a specialized curriculum no matter how many traditional subjects we force people to take in the name of breadth. Such a program can hardly meet the criteria for "equality of quality."

3

Now, consider the second premise. Adler claims that "the shape of the best education for the best is not unknown to us." If he means by this that we know what has been provided for an intellectually and socially privileged class in the past, the claim seems reasonable. The force of his argument would then be, "Let us now give all our children what we have given these privileged few in the past." But is the traditional "education for the best" really the "best" even for our academically most able students? On what grounds is it so judged? The *Paideia* aims at an education that will enable all children to earn a living in an intelligent and responsible fashion, to function as intelligent and responsible citizens, and to make both of these things serve the purpose of leading intelligent and responsible lives— to enjoy as fully as possible all the goods that make a human life as good as it can be (p. 18).

"To achieve these three goals," Adler writes:

> basic schooling must have for all a quality that can be best defined, *positively*, by saying that it must be general and liberal; and *negatively*, by saying that it must be nonspecialized and non-vocational. (p. 18)

There are at least two difficulties here. One has to do with the word "vocational" and its uses. Another is the meaning of "nonspecialized." I have already argued that the sort of abstract and bookish education recommended by the *Paideia* is itself—in spite of its internal breadth—a specialized curriculum. It is designed for those whose further education will be academic, and there is little evidence that it will promote continued learning across other fields of endeavor. One could design a "mechanical-technical" education every bit as broad (internally) as the *Paideia*'s "liberal" education (thus avoiding the rapid obsolescence of skills), and most of us would still consider it too highly specialized to be used exclusively and for all our children. One can imagine, however, several such beautifully designed curricula, equally valuable, each characterized by internal breadth, offered on equal levels and freely chosen by well-informed students. This sort of plan might realistically avoid premature specialization. Further, the freedom of choice provided seems appropriate preparation for democratic life.

In its own effort to prepare children "equally" for participation in "democracy," the *Paideia* sacrifices a first principle of democracy: In the pursuit of eventual freedom, it denies students any freedom whatsoever in the choice of their own studies.

The one-track system of public schooling that *The Paideia Proposal* advocates has the same objectives for all without exception (p. 15).

Further:

All sidetracks, specialized courses, or elective choices must be eliminated. Allowing them will always lead a certain number of students to voluntarily downgrade their own education. (p. 21)

Think what we are suggesting in making or accepting such a recommendation. Why should electives in cooking, photography, or science fiction constitute a "downgrading" of education? Is James Beard a failure? Is Edward Steichen? Is Ray Bradbury? Now I am not arguing for premature specialization. I am simply pointing out what John Dewey counseled again and again: Any subject freely undertaken as an occupation—as a set of tasks requiring goal-setting, means-ends analysis, choice of appropriate tools and materials, exercise of skills, living through the consequences, and evaluating the results—is educative. Cooking can be approached with high intelligence and elegant cultural interests or it can deteriorate to baking brownies and cleaning ovens: similarly, mathematics can be taught so as to require deep reflective and intuitive thinking or it can be taught as a mindless bag of tricks. It is not the subjects offered that make a curriculum properly a part of education but how those subjects are taught, how they connect to the personal interests and talents of the students who study them, and how skillfully they are laid out against the whole continuum of human experience.

We see in this discussion another area of great disagreement between John Dewey and the perennialists, and this involves the difficulty I mentioned concerning the word "vocational." It is true, as Adler points out, that Dewey argued against something called "vocational education." But Dewey was arguing against a narrow form of specialization that tended to downgrade the participants *as persons*. He was arguing against a form of schooling, not education at all, that labels some children fit only to do Vocation X, where X itself may be held in disdain. More importantly, however, he wanted all children to experience education *through* occupations or vocations more broadly construed. He said:

A vocation signifies any form of continuous activity which renders service to others and engages personal powers in behalf of the accomplishment of results. (1916, p. 319)

Dewey insisted that education could be conducted through occupations or vocations in the important sense we are considering here. He insisted upon the organic connection between education and personal experience and, thus, between education and contemporary social life. Students do not have to study exactly the same subject matter nor need they be deprived of choice in order to be truly educated. Dewey spoke favorably of Plato's fundamental principle of tailoring education to the abilities of students, but he drew back from the hierarchical evaluation connected with this form of education, saying:

His [Plato's] error was not in qualitative principle, but in his limited conception of the scope of vocations socially needed: a limitation of vision which reacted to obscure his perception of the infinite variety of capacities found in different individuals. (1916, p. 309)

Dewey wanted us to avoid two equally pernicious ideas in education: first, that education must consist of a set of prespecified material to be transmitted to everyone regardless of personal interest: second, that education should consist of a hierarchically ordered set of curricula—the "highest" given to the "best," the "lowest" to the "least." To provide "equality of quality" in education for all our children requires that we start with equal respect for their talents and aspirations and that we help them to choose wisely within the domain of their interests.

My main aim in this section has been to cast doubt on Mr. Adler's claim that "the shape of the best education for the best is not unknown to us." On the contrary. I believe that far more reflection and responsible experimentation are required before we can support such a claim.

4

I promised at the beginning of this essay to say something about the recommendations the *Paideia* makes concerning methods of instruction. Three modes of teaching are prescribed, and they are all useful. Each mode of teaching is connected to a mode of learning: for the acquisition of organized knowledge, didactic instruction is recommended; for the development of intellectual skills, coaching is to be employed; and for the enlargement of understanding, insight, and aesthetic appreciation, "maieutic" or Socratic methods are to be used. All three methods, properly implemented, are sound and useful, and education would take a giant step forward if teachers were skilled in each of them.

But the methods as they are described are somewhat warped by the prescribed subject matter. There is no mention of the enormous skill required of teachers in setting the environment so that children will formulate purposes and thus *seek* to acquire segments of organized knowledge. Nor is the choice of coach or the relation between coach and student mentioned. These are oversights that I need not belabor. The attitude of which I complain pervades the *Paideia*: Students are treated as "minds" to be filled equally with the same quality material. Nowhere is there proper consideration of the *persons* who are, in their essential freedom and infinite diversity, central and instrumental in their own education.

REFERENCES

Mortimer J. Adler. *The Paideia Proposal.* New York: Macmillan Publishing Co., Inc., 1982.

John Dewey. *The School and Society.* Chicago: The University of Chicago Press, 1915 (1899).

John Dewey. *Democracy and Education.* New York: The Free Press, 1916.

John Dewey. "President Hutchins' Proposals to Remake Higher Education," *The Social Frontier 3* (1937): 103–104.

John Dewey. "The Higher Learning in America." *The Social Frontier* 3 (1937): 167–169.

John Gardner. *Excellence: Can We Be Equal and Excellent Too?* New York: Harper. 1961.

Robert Maynard Hutchins. "Grammar, Rhetoric, and Mr. Dewey," *The Social Frontier* 3 (1937): 137–139.

NOTE

This paper is built upon an address to the Association of Colorado Independent Schools. Their sponsorship is gratefully acknowledged. It does not imply their endorsement of the ideas within.

17

Implementation as Mutual Adaptation: Change in Classroom Organization

Milbrey Wallin McLaughlin

Most observers believe that the educational innovations undertaken as part of the curriculum reform movement of the 1950s and early 1960s, as well as the innovations that comprised the initiatives of the "Education Decade," generally have failed to meet their objectives.[1] One explanation for these disappointments focuses on the type of innovations undertaken and points out that until recently few educators have elected to initiate innovations that require change in the traditional roles, behavior, and structures that exist within the school organization or the classroom. Instead, most innovative efforts have focused primarily on technological change, not organizational change. Many argue that without changes in the structure of the institutional setting, or the culture of the school, new practices are simply "more of the same" and are unlikely to lead to much significant change in what happens to students.

Since 1970, however, a number of educators have begun to express interest in practices that redefine the assumptions about children and learning that underlie traditional methods—new classroom practices that attempt to change the ways that students, teachers, parents, and administrators relate to each other. Encouraged and stimulated by the work of such writers as Joseph Featherstone, Charles Silberman, and William Glasser, some local schoolmen have undertaken innovations in classroom organization such as open education, multiage grouping, integrated day, differentiated staffing, and team teaching. These practices are not based on a "model" of classroom organization change to be strictly followed, but on a common set of convictions about the nature of learning and the purpose of teaching. These philosophical similarities, which can be traced to the work of the Swiss psychologist Piaget, are based on a belief that humanistic, individualized, and child-centered education requires more than incremental or marginal change in classroom organization, educational technology, or teacher behavior.

Because classroom organization projects require teachers to work out their own styles and classroom techniques within a broad philosophical framework, innovations of this

From *Teachers College Record*, Vol. 77, No. 3, 1976: pp. 339–351. Reprinted by permission.

type cannot be specified or packaged in advance. Thus, the very nature of these projects requires that implementation be a *mutually adaptive process* between the user and the institutional setting—that specific project goals and methods be made concrete over time by the participants themselves.

Classroom organization projects were among the local innovations examined as part of Rand's Change-Agent Study.[2] Of the 293 projects surveyed, eighty-five could be classified as classroom organization projects; five of our thirty field sites were undertaking innovation of this nature. The findings of the change-agent study suggest that the experience of these projects should be examined in some detail. At the most general level, the change study concluded that implementation—rather than educational treatment, level of resources, or type of federal funding strategy—dominates the innovative process and its outcomes. The study found that the mere adoption of a "better" practice did not automatically or invariably lead to "better" student outcomes. Initially similar technologies undergo unique alterations during the process of implementation and thus their outcomes cannot be predicted on the basis of treatment alone. Further, the process of implementation that is inherent in classroom organization projects was found to describe effective implementation generally. Specifically, the change-agent study concluded that *successful implementation is characterized by a process of mutual adaptation.*

Contrary to the assumptions underlying many change strategies and federal change policies, we found that implementation did not merely involve the direct and straightforward application of an educational technology or plan. Implementation was a dynamic organizational process that was shaped over time by interactions between project goals and methods, and the institutional setting. As such, it was neither automatic nor certain. Three different interactions characterized this highly variable process.

One, *mutual adaptation*, described successfully implemented projects. It involved modification of both the project design and changes in the institutional setting and individual participants during the course of implementation.

A second implementation process, *cooptation*, signified adaptation of the project design, but no change on the part of participants or the institutional setting. When implementation of this nature occurred, project strategies were simply modified to conform in a pro forma fashion to the traditional practices the innovation was expected to replace—either because of resistance to change or inadequate help for implementers.

The third implementation process, *nonimplementation*, described the experience of projects that either broke down during the course of implementation or were simply ignored by project participants.

Where implementation was successful, and where significant change in participant attitudes, skills and behavior occurred, implementation was characterized by a process of mutual adaptation in which project goals and methods were modified to suit the needs and interests of participants and in which participants changed to meet the requirements of the project. This finding was true even for highly technological and initially well specified projects: unless adaptations were made in the original plans or technologies, implementation tended to be superficial or symbolic and significant change in participants did not occur.

Classroom organization projects provided particularly clear illustration of the conditions and strategies that support mutual adaptation and thus successful implementation. They are especially relevant to understanding the operational implications of this change-agent study finding for policy and practice not only because mutual adaptation is intrinsic to change in classroom organization, but also because the question of institutional receptivity does not cloud the view of effective implementation strategies afforded by these projects.

The receptivity of the institutional setting to a proposed innovation varied greatly among the projects we examined—from active support to indifference to hostility. The amount of interest, commitment, and support evidenced by principal actors had a major influence on the prospects for successful project implementation. In particular, the attitudes and interest of central administrators in effect provided a "signal" to project participants as to how seriously they should take project goals and how hard they should work to achieve them. Unless participants perceived that change-agent projects represented a school and district educational priority, teachers were often unwilling to put in the extra time and emotional investment necessary for successful implementation. Similarly, the attitudes of teachers were critical. Unless teachers were motivated by professional concerns (as opposed to more tangible incentives such as extra pay or credit on the district salary scale, for example), they did not expend the extra time and energy requisite to the usually painful process of implementing an innovation.

Classroom organization projects were almost always characterized by high levels of commitment and support for their initiation, both at the district and at the building level. This is not surprising when we consider the risk and difficulty associated with these projects; it is unlikely that a district would elect to undertake a project of this nature unless they believed strongly in the educational approach and were committed to attempting the changes necessary to implement it.

In fact, classroom organization projects possess none of the features traditionally thought to encourage local decision makers to adopt a given innovation:

1. Ease of explanation and communication to others.
2. Possibility of a trial on a partial or limited basis.
3. Ease of use.
4. Congruence with existing values.
5. Obvious superiority over practices that existed previously.[3]

Innovations that focus on classroom organization are at odds with all five of these criteria. First, since there is no specific "model" to be followed, it is difficult to tell people how these approaches operate. Advocates can only offer general advice and communicate the philosophy or attitudes that underlie innovation in classroom organization and activities.

Second, although open classroom or team-teaching strategies can be implemented slowly, and can be installed in just one or two classrooms in a school, it is generally not possible to be "just a little bit" open or just a "sometime" part of a team-teaching situation. The method is based on fundamental changes which are hard to accomplish piecemeal.

Third, change in classroom organization is inherently very complex. Innovations of this nature require the learning of new attitudes, roles and behavior on the part of teachers and administrators—changes far more difficult to bring about than the learning of a new skill or gaining familiarity with a new educational technology. Classroom organization changes also typically require new arrangements of classroom space, the provision of new instructional materials, and usually new school scheduling and reporting practices.

Fourth, strategies of open education or team teaching are a radical departure from the traditional or standard practices of a school, district, or teacher. Change in classroom organization means changing deeply held attitudes and customary behavior. These projects, by attempting to change organizational structure and goals, attempt to affect the fundamental nature of the organization and are therefore basically incongruent with existing values.

Fifth, although proponents argue that humanistic, child-centered education represents a big advance, the objective evidence is ambiguous. Most evaluations of informal classrooms conclude that participating children do better on affective measures, but there is little evidence of significant cognitive differences that could confidently be attributed to open classrooms themselves. An administrator contemplating a change in classroom organization is confronted with a complicated innovation that shows no clear advantage over existing practices—at least in the ways that often matter most to school boards, voters, and anxious parents.

Thus, given the complex, unspecified, and inherently difficult nature of these projects, they were rarely initiated without the active support and commitment of district officials and participants. Consequently, the insufficient institutional support that negatively influenced implementation in other projects and so made it difficult to obtain a clear picture of the strategic factors affecting project implementation (i.e., did disappointing implementation result from a lack of enthusiasm or from inadequate training?) generally was not a problem for classroom organization projects. Variance in the implementation outcome of classroom organization projects, consequently, can be attributed in large measure to the project's particular implementation strategy.

For classroom organization projects, as for other change-agent projects, *institutional receptivity was a necessary but not a sufficient condition for successful implementation.* Unless project implementation strategies were chosen that allowed institutional support to be engaged and mutual adaptation to occur, project implementation foundered. A project's particular implementation strategy is the result of many local choices about how best to implement project goals and methods. What seems to be the most effective thing to do? What is possible given project constraints? What process fits best with local needs and conditions? Decisions about the type and amount of training, the planning necessary, and project participants are examples of such choices. They effectively define how a proposed innovation is put into practice. Implementation strategies are distinguishable from project treatment. That is, the educational method chosen for a project (i.e., team teaching, diagnostic/prescriptive reading) is different from the strategies selected for implementing the method. No two reading projects, for example, employ quite the same process or strategy for achieving their almost identical goals.

IMPLEMENTATION STRATEGY

Each project employs its own combination of strategies that effectively defines its *implementation strategy.* Thus, in addition to identifying especially effective component strategies, it is meaningful to examine how and why the various individual strategies interact with each other to form a "successful" implementation strategy and to promote mutual adaptation. The experience of classroom organization projects suggests at least three specific strategies that are particularly critical and that work together to form an adaptive implementation strategy: local materials development; ongoing and concrete staff training; iterative, on-line planning combined with regular and frequent staff meetings.

Local Material Development

In almost all of the classroom organization projects, the staff spent a substantial amount of time developing materials to use in the project classrooms. These materials either were developed from scratch or put together from bits of commercially-developed materials. Although these activities were sometimes undertaken because the staff felt they couldn't locate appropriate commercial materials, the real contribution lay not so much in "better pedagogical products" but in providing the staff with a sense of involvement and an opportunity to "learn-by-doing." Working together to develop materials for the project gave the staff a sense of pride in its own accomplishments, a sense of "ownership" in the project. It also broke down the traditional isolation of the classroom teacher and provided a sense of "professionalism" and cooperation not usually available in the school setting. But even more important, materials development provided an opportunity for users to think through the concepts which underlay the project, in practical, operational terms—an opportunity to engage in experience-based learning. Although such "reinvention of the wheel" may not appear efficient in the short run, it appears to be a critical part of the individual learning and development necessary for significant change.

Staff Training

All the classroom organization projects we visited included both formal and informal, preservice and inservice staff training. For example, one project's formal training took place in a two-week summer session before the project began; its informal development activities had been extensive, providing for almost constant interaction among project staff. Almost all of these projects provided preservice training that included observations in operating classrooms. One open classroom project staff even participated in a trip to observe British infant schools. All projects also conducted regular workshops throughout the first three years of project implementation.

One-shot training, or training heavily concentrated at the beginning of the project, was not effective. Although such training designs have the virtues of efficiency and lower cost, they ignore the critical fact that project implementors cannot know what it is they need to know until project operations are well underway. This is generally true for all innovative efforts, but particularly salient in the case of amorphous classroom organization projects. There is just so much that a would-be implementor can be taught or can understand until problems have arisen in the course of project implementation, and solutions must be devised. Training programs that attempt to be comprehensive and cover all contingencies at the outset are bound to miss their mark and also to be less than meaningful to project participants.

Project staffs agreed that staff development and training activities were a critical part of successful implementation. They also agreed that some kinds of training activities were more useful than others. With few exceptions, visits by outside consultants and other outside "experts" were not considered particularly helpful. Teachers in all the change-agent projects we examined complained that most visiting consultants could not relate to the particular problems they were experiencing in their classrooms, or that their advice was too abstract to be helpful. Where outside experts were considered useful, their participation was concrete and involved working closely with project teachers in their classrooms or in "hands-on" workshops. However, it was unusual for outside consultants to have either the time or the inclination to provide assistance in other than a lecture format. Such expert delivery of "truth and knowledge," however, was seldom meaningful to participants, and foreclosed more powerful learning opportunities.

The sessions participants thought most useful were regular meetings of the project staff with local resource personnel in which ideas were shared, problems discussed, and support given. Materials development often provided the focus for these concrete, how-to-do-it training sessions. Visits to other schools implementing similar projects were also considered helpful; the teachers felt that seeing a similar program in operation for just a few hours was worth much more than several days of consultants delivering talks on philosophy.

Some commentators on the outcomes of planned change contend that where innovations fail, particularly innovations in classroom organization, they fail because their planners overlooked the "resocialization" of teachers. Even willing teachers have to go through such a *learning (and unlearning) process* in order to develop new attitudes, behaviors, and skills for a radically new role. Concrete, inquiry-based training activities scheduled regularly over the course of project implementation provide a means for this developmental process to occur.

Adaptive Planning and Staff Meetings

Because of their lack of prior specification, almost all classroom organization projects engaged in adaptive or on-line planning. Planning of this nature is a continuous process that establishes channels of communication and solicits input from a representative group of project participants. It provides a forum for reassessing project goals and activities, monitoring project activities, and modifying practices in light of institutional and project demands. Planning of this nature has a firm base in project and institutional reality; thus issues can be identified and solutions determined before problems become crises. Just as one-shot training activities can neither anticipate the information needs of implementors over time nor be comprehensible to trainees in the absence of direct experience with particular problems, neither can highly structured planning activities that attempt extensive prior specification of operational procedures and objectives effectively address all contingencies in advance or foresee intervening local conditions. Often problems arise and events occur during the course of implementation that are unexpected and unpredictable. As a result, project plans drawn up at one point in time may or may not be relevant to project operations at a later date. Planning activities that are ongoing, adaptive, and congruent with the nature of the project and the changing institutional setting are better able to respond to these factors.

Frequent and regular staff meetings were often used as a way to carry out project planning on a continuous basis. Projects that made a point of scheduling staff meetings on a frequent and regular basis had fewer serious implementation problems and greater staff cohesiveness. Staff meetings not only provided a vehicle for articulating and working out problems, but they also gave staff a chance to communicate project information, share ideas, and provide each other with encouragement and support.

Finding time for these meetings or planning activities was a problem that some districts were able to solve and others were not. One classroom organization project, for example, arranged time off one afternoon a week for meetings. Project participants almost universally singled out these meetings as one of the most important factors contributing to project success. Such time to share ideas and problems was, in the view of all classroom organization respondents, especially important in the rough and exhausting first year of the project. Where meetings were infrequent or irregular, morale was noticeably lower and reports of friction within the project were higher.

Past research on implementation is almost unanimous in citing "unanticipated events" and "lack of feedback networks" as serious problems during project implementation.[4] Routinized and frequent staff meetings combined with ongoing, iterative planning can serve to institutionalize an effective project feedback structure, as well as provide mechanisms that can deal with the unanticipated events that are certain to occur.

TWO OPEN CLASSROOM PROJECTS[5]

The critical role that such elements of an adaptive implementation strategy play in project implementation and outcomes is best illustrated by describing the experiences of two open classroom projects that were similar in almost every respect—resources, support and interest, target group background characteristics—but differed significantly in implementation strategy and in implementation outcome. The Eastown open education project had extensive and ongoing staff training, spent a lot of staff time and energy on materials development, arranged for staff to meet regularly, and engaged in regular formative evaluation. This project was also well implemented, ran smoothly, and met its objectives. In fact, this project received validation as a national exemplary project in its second year—a year before it was theoretically eligible.

The very similar Seaside project, in contrast, did not employ such an implementation strategy. Because of late funding notification, there was little time for advance planning or preservice training; project teachers were asked to implement a concept that they supported but that few had actually seen in operation. The planning that was done subsequently was mainly administrative in nature. The inservice training was spotty and was offered almost totally by "outside experts." The Seaside project did no materials development but instead tried to convert traditional materials to the goals of open education. This project has not only been less successful than hoped, but in our judgment, its central percepts and objectives are yet to be fully implemented. Teacher classroom behavior exhibits only a very superficial understanding of the rhetoric of open education; our observations led to the conclusion that teachers have yet to understand the practical implications of the tenets of open education, and have made only symbolic use of the more standard methods. For example, in many of the classrooms we visited, although the teacher had set up interest centers, these centers had not been changed in six or seven months. Thus they failed to serve their purpose of providing a continually changing menu of material for students. Teachers in the Seaside project had dutifully rearranged their classroom furniture and acquired rugs— as befits the open classroom—but even in this changed physical space, they continued to conduct their classes in a traditional manner. A student teacher commented that many of the teachers in this school conducted their class in the small groups or individualized manner appropriate to this educational philosophy only on visitors' day. In our judgment, many of the teachers in the school honestly wanted to implement open education, and many sincerely believed that they had accomplished that goal. But, in our view, implementation in this project was only *pro forma*—largely because of the absence of implementation strategies that would allow learning, growth, and development or mutual adaptation to take place.

SUMMARY

In summary, overcoming the challenges and problems inherent to innovations in classroom organization contributes positively and significantly to their effective implementation. The amorphous yet highly complex nature of classroom organization projects tends to *require* or *dictate* an adaptive implementation strategy that permits goals and methods to be reassessed, refined and made explicit during the course of implementation, and that fosters "learning-by-doing."

The adaptive implementation strategies defined by effectively implemented local projects were comprised of three common and critical components—local materials development; concrete, ongoing training; on-line or adaptive planning and regular, frequent staff meetings. These elements worked together in concert to promote effective implementation. Where any one component was missing or weak, other elements of the overall implementation strategy were less effective than they might be. A most important characteristic these component strategies hold in common is their support of individual learning and development—development most appropriate to the user and to the institutional setting. The experience of classroom organization projects underlines the fact that the process of mutual adaptation is fundamentally a learning process.

General Implications

It is useful to consider the implications of the classroom organization projects and the general change-agent study findings in the context of the ongoing debate about the "implementation problem."

The change-agent study is not the first research to point to the primary importance of implementation in determining special project outcomes.[6] A number of researchers and theoreticians have come to recognize what many practitioners have been saying all along: Educational technology is not self-winding. Adoption of a promising educational technology is only the beginning of a variable, uncertain, and inherently local process. It is the unpredictability and inconsistency of this process that have generated what has come to be called the "implementation problem."

There is general agreement that a major component of the "implementation problem" has to do with inadequate operational specificity.[7] There is debate concerning *who* should make project operations more specific, *how* it can be done, and *when* specificity should be introduced.

One approach prescribes more specificity prior to local initiation. Adherents of this solution ask that project planners and developers spell out concrete and detailed steps or procedures that they believe will lead to successful project implementation. It is hoped that increased prior operational specificity will minimize the necessity for individual users to make decisions or choices about appropriate project strategies or resources as the project is implemented. This essentially technological approach to the "implementation problem"—exemplified at the extreme by "teacher-proof" packages—aims at standardizing project implementation across project sites. It is expected that user adherence to such standardized and well-specified implementation procedures will reduce local variability as project plans are translated into practice and so lead to predictable and consistent project outcomes, regardless of the institutional setting in which the project is implemented.

A second approach takes an organizational rather than a technological perspective and focuses primarily on the development of the user, rather than on the prior development of the educational treatment or product. This approach assumes that local variability is not only inevitable, but a good thing if a proposed innovation is to result in significant and sustained change in the local setting. This approach also assumes that the individual learning requisite to successful implementation can only occur through user involvement and direct experience in working through project percepts. Instead of providing packages which foreclose the necessity for individuals to make decisions and choices during the course of project implementation, proponents of this perspective maintain that implementation strategies should be devised that give users the skills, information, and learning opportunities necessary to make these choices effectively. This approach assumes that specificity of project methods and goals should evolve over time in response to local conditions and individual needs. This second solution to the "implementation problem," in short, assumes that mutual adaptation is the key to effective implementation.

The findings of the change-agent study strongly support this second perspective and its general approach to the "implementation problem." We found that *all* successfully implemented projects in our study went through a process of mutual adaptation to some extent. Even fairly straightforward, essentially technological projects were either adapted in some way to the institutional setting—or they were only superficially implemented and were not expected to remain in place after the withdrawal of federal funds. Where attempts were made to take short cuts in this process—out of concern for efficiency, for example—such efforts to speed up project implementation usually led to project breakdown or to only *pro forma* installation of project methods.

Viewed in the context of the debate over the "implementation problem," these findings have a number of implications for change-agent policies and practice. At the most general level, they suggest that adaptation, rather than standardization, is a more realistic and fruitful objective for policy makers and practitioners hoping to bring about significant change in local educational practice. Such an objective would imply change-agent policies that focused on implementation, not simply on adoption—policies that were concerned primarily with the development of users and support of adaptive implementation strategies. Specifically, the classroom organization projects suggest answers to the strategic issues of "who, how, and when" innovative efforts should be made operationally explicit, and how user development can be promoted.

Furthermore, the classroom organization projects, as well as other innovative efforts examined as part of the change-agent study, imply that the would-be innovator also must be willing to learn and be motivated by professional concerns and interests if development is to take place. Thus, change-agent policies would be well advised not only to address the user needs that are part of the implementation process *per se*, but also to consider the developmental needs of local educational personnel that are requisite to the initial interest and support necessary for change-agent efforts. It is not surprising that teachers or administrators who have not been outside their district for a number of years are less eager to change—or confident in their abilities to do so—than planners would hope. Internships and training grants for administrators, or travel money and released time for teachers to participate in innovative practices in other districts, are examples of strategies that may enable educational personnel to expand their horizons and generate enthusiasm for change.

The findings of the change-agent study and the experience of the classroom organization projects also have implications for the dissemination and expansion of "successful" change-agent projects. They suggest, for example, that an effective dissemination strategy should have more to do with people who could provide concrete "hands-on" assistance than with the transcription and transferral of specific successful project operations. It is somewhat ironic that staff of the "developer-demonstrator" projects who last year pointed to the central importance of local materials development are, in their dissemination year, packaging their project strategies and materials without a backward glance. Indeed, the change-agent findings concerning the importance of mutual adaptation and "learning by doing" raise a number of critical questions for educational planners and disseminators. For example, to what extent can this developmental process be telescoped as project accomplishments are replicated in a new setting? What kinds of "learning" or advice can be transferred? If adaptation is characteristic of effective implementation and significant change, what constitutes the "core" or essential ingredients of a successful project?

District administrators hoping to expand successful project operations face similar issues. Our findings suggest that—even within the same district—replication and expansion of "success" will require that new adopters replicate, in large measure, the developmental process of the original site. While there are, of course, general "lessons" that original participants can transfer to would-be innovators, there is much that the new user will have to learn himself.

In summary, the experience of classroom organization projects together with the general change-agent study findings suggest that adaptation should be seen as an appropriate goal for practice and policy—not an undesirable aberration. These findings suggest a shift in change-agent policies from a primary focus on the *delivery system* to an emphasis on the *deliverer*. An important lesson that can be derived from the change-agent study is that unless the developmental needs of the users are addressed, and unless project methods are modified to suit the needs of the user and the institutional setting, the promises of new technologies are likely to be unfulfilled. Although the implementation strategy that classroom organization projects suggest will be effective represent "reinvention of the wheel" to a great extent—an unpalatable prospect for program developers, fiscal planners, and impatient educational policy makers—the experience of these projects counsels us that a most important aspect of significant change is not so much the "wheel" or the educational technology but the process of "reinvention" or individual development. Though new education technologies are undoubtedly important to improved practices, they cannot be effective unless they are thoroughly understood and integrated by the user. The evidence we have seen strongly suggests that the developmental process mutual adaptation is the best way to ensure that change efforts are not superficial, trivial, or transitory.

NOTES

1. This essay is a revision of a paper presented at the March 1975 American Educational Research Association meeting in Washington, D.C. It is based on the data collected for The Rand Corporation study of federal programs supporting educational change. However, the interpretation and speculations offered in this paper are my sole responsibility and do not necessarily represent the views of The Rand Corporation, or the study's sponsor, the United States Office of Education, or my colleague Paul Berman, who has been so helpful in formulating this paper.

2. The conceptual model, methodology, and results of the first year of the Rand Change-Agent Study are reported in four volumes: Paul Berman and Milbrey Wallin McLaughlin. *Federal Programs Supporting Educational Change, Vol. I: A Model of Educational Change.* Santa Monica, Calif.: Rand Corporation, R-1589/1-HEW, April 1975; Paul Berman and Edward W. Pauly, *Federal Programs Supporting*

Educational Change, Vol. II: Factors Affecting Change Agent Projects. Santa Monica, Calif.: Rand Corporation, R-1589/2-HEW, April 1975; Peter W. Greenwood, Dale Mann, and Milbrey Wallin McLaughlin. *Federal Programs Supporting Educational Change, Vol. III: The Process of Change.* Santa Monica, Calif.: Rand Corporation, R-1589/3-HEW, April 1975; and Paul Berman and Milbrey Wallin McLaughlin. *Federal Programs Supporting Educational Change, Vol. IV: The Findings in Review.* Santa Monica, Calif.: Rand Corporation, R-1589/4-HEW, April 1975. Four technical appendices to Volume III describe in detail the federal program management approach, state education agency participation, and case studies for each of the programs in the study.

3. E. Rogers and F. Shoemaker. *Communication of Innovation.* New York, N.Y.: Free Press, 1962.

4. See for example, W. W. Charters et al. *Contrasts in the Process of Planning Change of the School's Institutional Organization, Program 20.* Eugene, Ore.: Center for the Advanced Study of Educational Administration, 1973; O. Carlson et al. *Change Processes in the Public Schools.* Eugene, Ore.: Center for the Advanced Study of Educational Administration, 1971; M. Fullan and A. Pomfret. *Review of Research on Curriculum Implementation.* Toronto, Ont.: The Ontario Institute for Studies in Education, April 1975; M. Shipman. *Inside a Curriculum Project.* London, Eng.: Methuen, 1974; N.C. Gross et al. *Implementing Organizational Innovations.* New York, N.Y.: Basic Books, 1971; and L.M. Smith and P.M. Keith. *Anatomy of Educational Innovations: An Organizational Analysis of an Elementary School.* New York, N.Y.: John Wiley, 1971.

5. Project and site names are fictitious.

6. See especially the analysis of this debate in Fullan and Pomfret, *op. cit.* See also E.C. Hargrove. *The Missing Link: The Study of the Implementation of Social Policy*, Washington, D.C.: The Urban Institute, 1975, paper 797–1; and W. Williams, "Implementation Analysis and Assessment," Public Policy Paper No. 8, Institute of Governmental Research, University of Washington, February 1975.

7. See Fullan and Pomfret, *op. cit.*

18

Controlling the Work of Teachers

Michael W. Apple

PROLETARIANIZATION: CLASS AND GENDER

An examination of changes in class composition over the past two decades points out something quite dramatically. The process of proletarianization has had a large and consistent effect. There has been a systematic tendency for those positions with relatively little control over their labor process to expand during this time period. At the same time, there was a decline in positions with high levels of autonomy.[1]

This should not surprise us. In fact, it would be unusual if this did not occur, especially now. In a time of general stagnation and of crises in accumulation and legitimation, we should expect that there will also be attempts to further rationalize managerial structures and increase the pressure to proletarianize the labor process. This pressure is not inconsequential to educators, both in regard to the kinds of positions students will find available (or not available) after completing (or not completing) schooling, and also in regard to the very conditions of working within education itself. The labor of what might be called "semi-autonomous employees" will certainly feel the impact of this. Given the fiscal crisis of the state, this impact will be felt more directly among state employees such as teachers as well. One should expect to see a rapid growth of plans and pressures for the rationalization of administration and labor within the state itself.[2] This is one of the times when one's expectations will not be disappointed.

In earlier work, I argued that teachers have been involved in a long but now steadily increasing restructuring of their jobs. I claimed that they were more and more faced with the prospect of being deskilled because of the encroachment of technical control procedures into the curriculum in schools. The integration together of management systems, reductive behaviorally based curricula, pre-specified teaching "competencies" and procedures and student responses, and pre- and post-testing, was leading to a loss of control and a separation of conception from execution. In sum, the labor process of teaching was becoming susceptible to processes similar to those that led to the proletarianization of many other

Chapter 2 in Michael W. Apple, *Teachers and Texts*, New York: Routledge & Kegan Paul, 1986. Reprinted by permission.

blue-, pink-, and white-collar jobs. I suggested that this restructuring of teaching had important implications given the contradictory class location of teachers.[3]

When I say that teachers have a contradictory class location, I am *not* implying that they are by definition within the middle classes, or that they are in an ambiguous position somehow "between" classes. Instead, along with Wright, I am saying that it is wise to think of them as located simultaneously in two classes. They thus share the interests of both the petty bourgeoisie and the working class.[4] Hence, when there is a fiscal crisis in which many teachers are faced with worsening working conditions, layoffs, and even months without being paid—as has been the case in a number of urban areas in the United States—and when their labor is restructured so that they lose control, it is possible that these contradictory interests will move closer to those of other workers and people of color who have historically been faced with the use of similar procedures by capital and the state.[5]

Yet, teachers are not only classed actors. They are gendered actors as well—something that is too often neglected by investigators. This is a significant omission. A striking conclusion is evident from the analyses of proletarianization. In every occupational category, *women* are more apt to be proletarianized than men. This could be because of sexist practices of recruitment and promotion, the general tendency to care less about the conditions under which women labor, the way capital has historically colonized patriarchal relations, the historical relation between teaching and domesticity, and so on. Whatever the reason, it is clear that a given position may be more or less proletarianized depending on its relationship to the sexual division of labor.[6]

In the United States, it is estimated that over 90 percent of women's (paid) work falls into four basic categories: (1) employment in "peripheral" manufacturing industries and retail trades, and considerably now in the expanding but low-paid service sector of the economy; (2) clerical work; (3) health and education; and (4) domestic service. Most women in, say, the United States and the United Kingdom are concentrated in either the lowest-paid positions in these areas or at the bottom of the middle-pay grades when there has been some mobility.[7] One commentator puts it both bluntly and honestly: "The evidence of discrimination against women in the labour market is considerable and reading it is a wearing experience."[8]

This pattern is, of course, largely reproduced within education. Even given the years of struggle by progressive women and men, the figures—most of which will be quite familiar to many of you—are depressing. While the overwhelming majority of school teachers are women (a figure that becomes even higher in the primary and elementary schools), many more men are heads or principals of primary and elementary schools, despite the proportion of women teachers.[9] As the vertical segregation of the workforce increased, this proportion actually increased in inequality. In the United States in 1928, women accounted for 55 percent of the elementary school principalships. Today, with nearly 90 percent of the teaching force in elementary schools being women, they account for only 20 percent of principals.[10] This pattern has strong historical roots—roots that cannot be separated from the larger structures of class and patriarchy outside the school.

In this chapter, I shall want to claim that unless we see the connections between these two dynamics—class and gender—we cannot understand the history of and current attempts at rationalizing education or the roots and effects of proletarianization on teaching itself. Not all teaching can be unpacked by examining it as a labor process or as a class phenomenon, though as I have tried to demonstrate in some of my previous work much of it is made clearer when we integrate it into theories of and changes in class position and the labor process. Neither can all of teaching be understood as totally related to patriarchy, though why it is structured the way it is is due in very large part to the history of male dominance and gender struggles,[11] a history I shall discuss in considerably more detail in the next chapter. The two dynamics of class and gender (with race, of course) are not reducible to each other, but intertwine, work off, and codetermine the terrain on which each operates. It is at the intersection of these two dynamics that one can begin to unravel some of the reasons why procedures for rationalizing the work of teachers have evolved. As we shall see, the ultimate effects of these procedures, with the loss of control that accompanies them, can bear in important ways on how we think about the "reform" of teaching and curriculum and the state's role in it.

ACADEMIC KNOWLEDGE AND CURRICULAR CONTROL

So far I have made a number of general claims about the relationship between proletarianization and patriarchy in the constitution of teaching. I want to go on to suggest ways we can begin to see this relationship in operation. Some sense of the state's role in sponsoring changes in curricular and teaching practice in the recent past is essential here.

The fact that schools have tended to be largely organized around male leadership and female teachers is simply that—a social fact—unless one realizes that this means that educational authority relations have been formally patriarchal. As in the home and the office, male dominance is there; but teachers—like wives, mothers, clerical workers, and other women engaged in paid and unpaid labor—have carved out spheres of power and control in their long struggle to gain some autonomy. This autonomy only becomes a problem for capital and the state when what education is for needs revision.

To take one example outside of education: in offices clerical work is in the process of being radically transformed with the introduction of word-processing technologies, video display terminals, and so on. Traditional forms of control—ones usually based on the dominance of the male boss—are being altered. Technical control, where one's work is deskilled and intensified by the "impersonal" machinery in the office, has made significant inroads. While certainly not eliminating patriarchal domination, it has in fact provided a major shift in the terrain on which it operates. Capital has found more efficient modes of control than overt patriarchal authority.[12]

Similar changes have occurred in schools. In a time when the needs of industry for technical knowledge and technically trained personnel intersect with the growth in power of the new petty bourgeoisie (those people in technical and middle management positions) and the reassertion of academic dominance in the curriculum, pressures for curricular reform can become quite intense. Patience over traditional forms of control will lessen.

Patriarchal relations of power, therefore, organized around the male principal's relations to a largely female teaching staff, will not necessarily be progressive for capital or the state. While they once served certain educational and ideological ends, they are less efficient than what has been required recently. Gender relations must be partly subverted to create a more efficient institution. Techniques of control drawn from industry will tend to replace older styles which depended more on a sexual division of power and labor within the school itself.

Perhaps an example will document the long and continuing history of these altered relationships. In the United States, for instance, during the late 1950s and the 1960s, there was rather strong pressure from academics, capital, and the state to reinstitute academic disciplinary knowledge as the most "legitimate" content for schools. In the areas of mathematics and science especially, it was feared that "real" knowledge was not being taught. A good deal of effort was given to producing curricular programs that were systematic, based on rigorous academic foundations, and, in the elementary school material in particular, were teacher-proof. Everything a teacher was to deal with was provided and prespecified. The cost of the development of such programs was socialized by the state (i.e., subsidized by tax dollars). The chance of their being adopted by local school districts was heightened by the National Defense Education Act, which reimbursed school districts for a large portion of the purchase cost. That is, if a school system purchased new material of this type and the technology which supported it, the relative cost was minimal. The bulk of the expense was repaid by the state. Hence, it would have seemed irrational not to buy the material—irrational in two ways: (1) the chance of getting new curricula at low cost is clearly a rational management decision within industrial logic, and (2) given its imprimatur of science and efficiency, the material itself seemed rational.

All of this is no doubt familiar to anyone who lived through the early years of this movement, and who sees the later, somewhat less powerful, effects it had in, say, England and elsewhere. Yet this is not only the history of increasing state sponsorship of and state intervention in teaching and curriculum development and adoption. *It is the history of the state, in concert with capital and a largely male academic body of consultants and developers, intervening at the level of practice into the work of a largely female workforce.* That is, ideologies of gender, of sex-appropriate knowledge, need to be seen as having possibly played a significant part here. The loss of control and rationalization of one's work forms part of a state/class/gender "couplet" that works its way out in the following ways. Mathematics and science teaching are seen as abysmal. "We" need rapid change in our economic responsiveness and in "our" emerging ideological and economic struggle with the Soviet Union.[13] Teachers (who just happen to be almost all women at the elementary level) aren't sophisticated enough. Former ways of curricular and teaching control are neither powerful nor efficient enough for this situation. Provide both teacher-proof materials and financial incentives to make certain that these sets of curricula actually reach the classroom.

One must integrate an analysis of the state, changes in the labor process of state employees, and the politics of patriarchy to comprehend the dynamics of this history of curriculum. It is not a random fact that one of the most massive attempts at rationalizing curricula and teaching had as its target a group of teachers who were largely women. I believe that one cannot separate out the fact of a sexual division of labor and the vision of who has what kinds of competence from the state's attempts to revamp and make more "productive" its educational apparatus. In so doing, by seeing these structurally generated relationships, we can begin to open up a door to understanding part of the reasons behind what happened to these curriculum materials when they were in fact introduced.

As numerous studies have shown, when the material was introduced into many schools, it was not unusual for the "new" math and "new" science to be taught in much the same manner as the old math and old science. It was altered so that it fitted into both the existing regularities of the institution and the prior practices that had proven successful in teaching.[14] It is probably wise to see this as not only the result of a slow-to-change bureaucracy or a group of consistently conservative administrators and teachers. Rather, I think it may be just as helpful to think of this more structurally in labor process and gender terms. The supposed immobility of the institution, its lack of significant change in the face of the initial onslaught of such material, is at least partly tied to the resistances of a female workforce against external incursions into the practices they had evolved over years of labor. It is in fact more than a little similar to the history of ways in which other women employees in the state and industry have reacted to past attempts at altering traditional modes of control of their own labor.[15]

A NOTE ON THE STATE

The points I have just made about the resistances of the people who actually work in the institutions, about women teachers confronted by external control, may seem straightforward. However, these basic arguments have very important implications not only about how we think about the history of curriculum reform and control, but more importantly about how many educators and political theorists have pictured the larger issue of the state's role in supporting capital. In the historical example I gave, state intervention on the side of capital and for "defense" is in opposition to other positions within the state itself. The day-to-day interests of one occupational position (teachers) contradict the larger interests of the state in efficient production.[16] Because of instances such as this, it is probably inappropriate to see the state as a homogeneous entity, standing above day-to-day conflicts.

Since schools *are* state apparatuses, we should expect them to be under intense pressure to act in certain ways, especially in times of both fiscal and ideological crises. Even so, this does not mean that people employed in them are passive followers of policies laid down from above. As Roger Dale has noted:

> Teachers are not merely "state functionaries" but do have some degree of autonomy, and [this] autonomy will not necessarily be used to further the proclaimed ends of the state apparatus. Rather than those who work there fitting themselves to the requirements of the institutions, there are a number of very important ways in which the institution has to take account of the interests of the employees and fit itself to them. It is here, for instance, that we may begin to look for the sources of the alleged inertia of educational systems and schools, that is to say what appears as inertia is not some immutable characteristic of bureaucracies but is due to various groups within them having more immediate interests than the pursuit of the organization's goals.[17]

Thus, the "mere" fact that the state wishes to find "more efficient" ways to organize teaching does not guarantee that this will be acted upon by teachers who have a long history of work practices and self-organization once the doors to their rooms are closed. As we shall see in a moment, however, the fact that it is primarily women employees who have faced these forms of rationalization has meant that the actual outcomes of these attempts to retain control of one's pedagogic work can lead to rather contradictory ideological results.

LEGITIMATING INTERVENTION

While these initial attempts at rationalizing teaching and curricula did not always produce the results that were anticipated by their academic, industrial, and governmental proponents, they did other things that were, and are, of considerable import. The situation is actually quite similar to the effects of the use of Tayloristic management strategies in industry.

As a management technology for deskilling workers and separating conception from execution, Taylorism was less than fully successful. It often generated slowdowns and strikes, exacerbated tensions, and created new forms of overt and covert resistance. Yet, its ultimate effect was to legitimate a particular ideology of management and control both to the public and to employers and workers.[18] Even though it did not succeed as a set of techniques, it ushered in and finally brought acceptance of a larger body of ideological practices to deskill pink-, white-, and blue-collar workers and to rationalize and intensify their labor.

This too was one of the lasting consequences of these earlier curriculum "reform" movements. While they also did not completely transform the practice of teaching, while patriarchal relations of authority which paradoxically "gave" teachers some measure of freedom were not totally replaced by more efficient forms of organizing and controlling their day-to-day activity, they legitimated both new forms of control and greater state intervention using industrial and technical models and brought about a new generation of more sophisticated attempts at overcoming teacher "resistance." Thus, this new generation of techniques that are being instituted in so many states in the United States and elsewhere currently—from systematic integration of testing, behavioral goals and curriculum, competency-based instruction and prepackaged curricula, to management by objectives, and so forth—has not sprung out of nowhere, but, like the history of Taylorism, has grown out of the failures, partial successes, and resistances that accompanied the earlier approaches to control. As I have claimed, this is not only the history of the control of state employees to bring about efficient teaching, but a rearticulation of the dynamics of patriarchy and class in one site, the school.

INTENSIFICATION AND TEACHING

In the first half of this chapter, we paid particular attention to the historical dynamics operating in the schools. I would like now to focus on more current outgrowths of this earlier history of rationalization and control.

The earlier attempts by state bureaucrats, industry, and others to gain greater control of day-to-day classroom operation and its "output" did not die. They have had more than a decade to grow, experiment, and become more sophisticated. While gender will be less visible in the current strategies (in much the same way that the growth of management strategies in industry slowly covered the real basis of power in factories and offices), as we shall see it will be present in important ways once we go beneath the surface to look at changes in the labor process of teaching, how some teachers respond to current strategies, and how they interpret their own work.

Since in previous work I have focused on a number of elements through which curricula and teaching are controlled—on the aspects of deskilling and reskilling of labor, and on the separation of conception from execution in teachers' work—here I shall want to concentrate more on something which accompanies these historically evolving processes: what I shall call *intensification*. First, let me discuss this process rather generally.

Intensification "represents one of the most tangible ways in which the work privileges of educational workers are eroded." It has many symptoms, from the trivial to the more complex—ranging from being allowed no time at all even to go to the bathroom, have a cup of coffee or relax, to having a total absence of time to keep up with one's field. We can see intensification most visibly in mental labor in the chronic sense of work overload that has escalated over time.[19]

This has had a number of notable effects outside of education. In the newspaper industry, for example, because of financial pressures and the increased need for efficiency in operation, reporters have had their story quotas raised substantially. The possibility of doing non-routine investigative reporting, hence, is lessened considerably. This has had the effects of increasing their dependence "on prescheduled, preformulated events" in which they rely more and more on bureaucratic rules and surface accounts of news provided by official spokespersons.[20]

Intensification also acts to destroy the sociability of non-manual workers. Leisure and self-direction tend to be lost. Community tends to be redefined around the needs of the labor process. And, since both time and interaction are at a premium, the risk of isolation grows.[21]

Intensification by itself "does not necessarily reduce the range of skills applied or possessed by educated workers." It may, in fact, cause them to "cut corners" by eliminating what seems to be inconsequential to the task at hand. This has occurred with doctors, for instance; many examinations now concentrate only on what seems critical. The chronic work overload has also caused some non-manual workers to learn or relearn skills. The financial crisis has led to shortages of personnel in a number of areas. Thus, a more diverse array of jobs must be done that used to be covered by other people—people who simply do not exist within the institution any more.[22]

While this leads to a broader range of skills having to be learned or relearned, it can lead to something mentioned earlier—the loss of time to keep up with one's field. That is, what might be called "skill diversification" has a contradiction built into it. It is also part of a dynamic of intellectual deskilling[23] in which mental workers are cut off from their own fields and again must rely even more heavily on ideas and processes provided by "experts."

While these effects are important, one of the most significant impacts of intensification may be in reducing the *quality*, not the quantity, of service provided to people. While, traditionally, "human service professionals" have equated doing good work with the interests of their clients or students, intensification tends to contradict the traditional interest in work well done, in both a quality product and process.[24]

As I shall document, a number of these aspects of intensification are increasingly found in teaching, especially in those schools which are dominated by behaviorally prespecified curricula, repeated testing, and strict and reductive accountability systems. (The fact that these kinds of curricula, tests, and systems are now more and more being mandated should make us even more cautious.) To make this clear, I want to draw on some data from recent research on the effects of these procedures on the structure of teachers' work.

I have argued here and elsewhere that there has been a rapid growth in curricular "systems" in the United States—one that is now spreading to other countries.[25] These curricula have goals, strategies, tests, textbooks, worksheets, appropriate student response, etc., integrated together. In schools where this is taken seriously,[26] what impact has this been having? We have evidence from a number of ethnographic studies of the labor process of teaching to be able to begin to point to what is going on. For example, in one school where the curriculum was heavily based on a sequential list of behaviorally defined competencies and objectives, multiple worksheets on skills which the students were to complete, with pre-tests to measure "readiness" and "skill level" and post-tests to measure "achievement" that were given often and regularly, the intensification of teacher work is quite visible.

In this school, such curricular practice required that teachers spend a large portion of their time evaluating student "mastery" of each of the various objectives and recording the results of these multiple evaluations for later discussions with parents or decisions on whether or not the student could "go on" to another set of skill-based worksheets. The recording and evaluation made it imperative that a significant amount of time be spent on administrative arrangements for giving tests, and then grading them, organizing lessons (which were quite often standardized or pre-packaged), and so on. One also found teachers busy with these tasks before and after school and, very often, during their lunch hour. Teachers began to come in at 7:15 in the morning and leave at 4:30 in the afternoon. Two hours' more work at home each night was not unusual, as well.[27]

Just as I noted in my general discussion of the effects of intensification, here too getting done became the norm. There is so much to do that simply accomplishing what is specified requires nearly all of one's efforts. "The challenge of the work day (or week) was to accomplish the required number of objectives." As one teacher put it, "I just want to get this done. I don't have time to be creative or imaginative."[28] We should not blame the teacher here. In mathematics, for example, teachers typically had to spend nearly half of the allotted time correcting and recording the worksheets the students completed each day.[29] The situation seemed to continually push the workload of these teachers up. Thus, even though they tended to complain at times about the long hours, the intensification, the time spent on technical tasks such as grading and record-keeping, the amount of time spent doing these things grew inexorably.[30]

Few of the teachers were passive in the face of this, and I shall return to this point shortly. Even though the elements of curricular control were effective in structuring major aspects of their practice, teachers often responded in a variety of ways. They subtly changed the pre-specified objectives because they couldn't see their relevance. They tried to resist the intensification as well: first by trying to find some space during the day for doing slower-paced activities; and second by actually calling a halt temporarily to the frequent pre- and post-tests, worksheets and the like and merely having "relaxed discussions with students on topics of their own choosing."[31]

This, of course, is quite contradictory. While these examples document the active role of teachers in attempting to win back some time, to resist the loss of control of their own work, and to slow down the pace at which students and they were to proceed, the way this is done is not necessarily very powerful. In these instances, time was fought for simply to relax, if only for a few minutes. The process of control, the increasing technicization and intensification of the teaching act, the proletarianization of their work—all of this was an absent presence. It was misrecognized as a symbol of their increased *professionalism.*

PROFESSION AND GENDER

We cannot understand why teachers interpreted what was happening to them as the professionalization of their jobs unless we see how the ideology of professionalism works as part of both a class and gender dynamic in education. For example, while reliance on "experts" to create curricular and teaching goals and procedures grew in this kind of situation, a wider range of technical skills had to be mastered by these teachers. Becoming adept at grading all those tests and worksheets quickly, deciding on which specific skill group to put a student in, learning how to "efficiently manage" the many different groups based on the tests, and more, all became important skills. As responsibility for designing one's own curricula and one's own teaching decreased, responsibility over technical and management concerns came to the fore.

Professionalism and increased responsibility tend to go hand in hand here. The situation is more than a little paradoxical. There is so much responsibility placed on teachers for technical decisions that they actually work harder. They feel that since they constantly make decisions based on the outcomes of these multiple pre- and post-tests, the longer hours are evidence of their enlarged professional status. Perhaps a quote will be helpful here.

> One reason the work is harder is we have a lot of responsibility in decision-making. There's no reason not to work hard, because you want to be darn sure that those decisions you made are something that might be helpful . . . So you work hard to be successful at these decisions so you look like a good decision maker.[32]

It is here that the concept of professionalism seemed to have one of its major impacts. Since the teachers thought of themselves as being more professional to the extent that they employed technical criteria and tests, they also basically accepted the longer hours and the intensification of their work that accompanied the program. To do a "good job," you needed to be as "rational" as possible.[33]

We should not scoff at these preceptions on the part of the teachers. First, the very notion of professionalization has been important not only to teachers in general but to women in particular. It has provided a contradictory yet powerful barrier against interference by the state; and just as critically, in the struggle over male dominance, it has been part of a complex attempt to win equal treatment, pay, and control over the day-to-day work of a largely female labor force.[34]

Second, while we need to remember that professionalism as a social goal grew at the same time and was justified by the "project and practice of the market professions during the liberal phase of capitalism,"[35] the strategy of professionalism has historically been used to set up "effective defenses against proletarianization."[36] Given what I said earlier about the strong relationship between the sexual division of labor and proletarianization, it would be not only ahistorical but perhaps even a bit sexist as well wholly to blame teachers for employing a professional strategy.

Hence, the emphasis on increasing professionalism by learning new management skills and so on today and its partial acceptance by elementary school teachers can best be understood not only as an attempt by state bureaucrats to deskill and reskill teachers, but as part of a much larger historical dynamic in which gender politics have played a significant role.

Yet the acceptance of certain aspects of intensification is not only due to the history of how professionalism has worked in class and gender struggles. It is heightened by a number of internal factors as well. For example, in the school to which I referred earlier, while a number of teachers believed that the rigorous specification of objectives and teaching procedures actually helped free them to become more creative, it was clear that subtle pressures existed to meet the priorities established by the specified objectives. Even though in some subject areas they had a choice of how they were to meet the objectives, the objectives themselves usually remained unchallenged. The perceived interests of parents and their establishment of routines helped assure this. Here is one teacher's assessment of how this occurs.

> Occasionally you're looking at the end of the book at what the unit is going to be, these are the goals that you have to obtain, that the children are going to be tested on. That may affect your teaching in some way in that you may by-pass other learning experiences simply to obtain the goal. These goals are going home to parents. It's a terrible thing to do but parents like to see 90's and 100's rather than 60's on skills.[37]

In discussing the use of the skills program, another teacher points out the other element besides parents that was mentioned: "It's got a manual and you follow the manual and the kids know the directions and it gets to be routine."[38]

Coupled with perceived parental pressure and the sheer power of routine is something else: the employment practices surrounding teaching. In many schools, one of the main criteria for the hiring of teachers is their agreement with the overall curricular, pedagogic, and evaluative framework which organizes the day-to-day practice. Such was the case in this study. Beyond this, however, even though some investigators have found that people who tend to react negatively to these pre-packaged, standardized, and systematized curricular forms often leave teaching,[39] given the depressed market for new teachers in many areas that have severe fiscal problems and the conscious decision by some school districts to hire fewer teachers and increase class size, fewer jobs are available right now. The option of leaving or even protesting seems romantic, though current teacher shortages may change this.

GENDERED RESISTANCE

At this point in my argument it would be wise to return to a claim I made earlier. Teachers have not stood by and accepted all this. In fact, our perception that they have been and are passive in the face of these pressures may reflect our own tacit beliefs in the relative passivity of women workers. This would be an unfortunate characterization. Historically, for example, as I shall demonstrate in the following chapter, in England and the United States the picture of women teachers as non-militant and middle-class in orientation is not wholly accurate. There have been periods of exceptional militancy and clear political commitment.[40] However, militancy and political commitment are but one set of ways in which control is contested. It is also fought for on the job itself in subtle and even "unconscious" (one might say "cultural") ways—ways which will be contradictory, as we shall now see. Once again, gender will become of prime importance.

In my own interviews with teachers it has become clear that many of them feel rather uncomfortable with their role as "managers." Many others are less than happy with the emphasis on programs which they often feel "lock us into a rigid system." Here the resistance to rationalization and the loss of historically important forms of self-control of one's labor has very contradictory outcomes, partly as a result of sexual divisions in society. Thus, a teacher using a curricular program in reading and language arts that is very highly structured and test-based states:

> While it's really important for the children to learn these skills, right now it's more important for them to learn to feel good about themselves. That's my role, getting them to feel good. That's more important than tests right now.

Another primary grade teacher, confronted by a rationalized curriculum program where students move from classroom to classroom for "skill groups," put it this way:

> Kids are too young to travel between classrooms all the time. They need someone there that they can always go to, who's close to them. Anyway, subjects are less important than their feelings.

In these quotes, discomfort with the administrative design is certainly evident. There is a clear sense that something is being lost. Yet the discomfort with the process is coded around the traditional distinctions that organize the sexual division of labor both within the family and in the larger society. The *woman's* sphere is that of providing emotional security, caring for feelings, and so on.

Do not misconstrue my points here. Teachers should care for the feelings and emotional security of their students. However, while these teachers rightly fight on a cultural level against what they perceive to be the ill-effects of their loss of control and both the division and the intensification of their labor, they do so at the expense of reinstituting categories that partly reproduce other divisions that have historically grown out of patriarchal relations.[41]

This raises a significant point: much of the recent literature on the role of the school in the reproduction of class, sex, and race domination has directed our attention to the existence of resistances. This realization was not inconsequential and was certainly needed to enable us to go further than the overly deterministic models of explanation that had been employed to unpack what schools do. However, at the same time, this literature has run the risk of romanticizing such resistances. The fact that they exist does not guarantee that they will necessarily be progressive at each and every moment. Only by uncovering the contradictions within and between the dynamics of the labor process *and* gender can we begin to see what effects such resistances may actually have.[42]

LABOR, GENDER, AND TEACHING

I have paid particular attention here to the effects of the restructuring of teachers' work in the school. I have claimed that we simply cannot understand what is happening to teaching and curriculum without placing it in a framework which integrates class (and its accompanying process of proletarianization) and gender together. The impact of deskilling and intensification occurs on a terrain and in an institution that is populated primarily by women teachers and male administrators—a fact that needs to be recognized as being historically articulated with both the social and sexual divisions of labor, knowledge, and power in our society.

Yet, since elementary school teachers are primarily women, we must also look beyond the school to get a fuller comprehension of the impact of these changes and the responses of teachers to them. We need to remember something in this regard: women teachers often work in *two* sites—the school and then the home. Given the modification of patriarchal relations and the intensification of labor in teaching, what impact might this have outside the school? If so much time is spent on technical tasks at school and at home, is it possible that less time may be available for domestic labor in the home? Other people in the family may have to take up the slack, thereby partly challenging the sexual division of household labor. On the other hand, the intensification of teachers' work, and the work overload that may result from it, may have exactly the opposite effect. It may increase the exploitation of unpaid work in the home by merely adding more to do without initially altering conditions in the family. In either case, such conditions will lead to changes, tensions, and conflicts outside of the sphere where women engage in paid work.[43] It is worth thinking very carefully about the effects that working in one site will have on the other. The fact that this dual exploitation exists is quite consequential in another way. It opens up possible new avenues for political intervention by socialist feminists, I believe. By showing the relationship between the home and the job and the intensification growing in both, this may provide for a way of demonstrating the ties between both of these spheres and between class and gender.

Thinking about such issues has actually provided the organizing framework for my analysis. The key to my investigation in this chapter has been reflecting about changes in *how* work is organized over time and, just as significantly, *who* is doing the work. A clearer sense of both of these—how and who—can enable us to see similarities and differences between the world of work in our factories and offices and that of semi-autonomous state employees such as teachers.

What does this mean? Historically the major struggles labor engaged in at the beginning of the use of systematic management concerned resistance to speed-ups.[44] That is, the intensification of production, the pressure to produce more work in a given period, led to all kinds of interesting responses. Craft workers, for example, often simply refused to do more. Pressure was put on co-workers who went too fast (or too slow). Breaks were extended. Tools and machines suddenly developed "problems."

Teachers—given their contradictory class location, their relationship to the history of patriarchal control and the sexual division of labor, and the actual conditions of their work—will find it difficult to respond in the same way. They are usually isolated during their work, and perhaps more so now given the intensification of their labor. Further, machinery and tools in the usual sense of these terms are not visible.[45] And just as importantly, the perception of oneself as professional means that the pressures of intensification and the loss of control will be coded and dealt with in ways that are specific to that workplace and its own history. The ultimate effects will be very contradictory.

In essence, therefore, I am arguing that—while similar labor processes may be working through institutions within industry and the state which have a major impact on women's paid work—these processes will be responded to differently by different classes and class segments. The ideology of professional discretion will lead to a partial acceptance of, say, intensification by teachers on one level, and will generate a different kind of resistance—one specific to the actual work circumstances in which they have historically found themselves. The fact that these changes in the labor process of teaching occur on a terrain that has been a site of patriarchal relations plays a major part here.

My arguments here are not to be construed as some form of "deficit theory." Women have won and will continue to win important victories, as I will demonstrate in the following chapter. Their action on a cultural level, though not overtly politicized, will not always lead to the results I have shown here. Rather, my points concern the inherently *contradictory* nature of teachers' responses. These responses are victories and losses at one and the same time. The important question is how the elements of good sense embodied in these teachers' lived culture can be reorganized in specifically feminist ways—ways that maintain the utter importance of caring and human relationships without at the same time reproducing other elements on that patriarchal terrain.

I do not want to suggest that once you have realized the place of teaching in the sexual division of labor, you have thoroughly understood deskilling and reskilling, intensification and loss of control, or the countervailing pressures of professionalism and proletarianization in teachers' work. Obviously, this is a very complex issue in which the internal histories of bureaucracies, the larger role of the state in a time of economic and ideological crisis,[46] and the local political economy and power relations of each school play a part. What I do want to argue quite strongly, however, is the utter import of gendered labor as a constitutive aspect of the way management and the state have approached teaching and curricular control. Gendered labor is the absent presence behind all of our work. How it became such an absent presence is the topic of the next chapter.

NOTES

1. Erik Olin Wright and Joachim Singelmann, "The Proletarianization of Work in American Capitalism," University of Wisconsin-Madison Institute for Research on Poverty, Discussion Paper No. 647–81, 1981, p. 38.

2. *Ibid.*, p. 43. See also Michael W. Apple, "State, Bureaucracy and Curriculum Control," *Curriculum Inquiry* 11 (Winter 1981), 379–88. For a discussion that rejects part of the argument about proletarianization, see Michael Kelly, *White Collar Proletariat* (Boston and London: Routledge & Kegan Paul, 1980).

3. Deskilling, technical control and proletarianization are both technical and political concepts. They signify a complex historical process in which the control of labor has altered—one in which the skills employees have developed over many years on the job are broken down into atomistic units, redefined, and then appropriated by management to enhance both efficiency and control of the labor process. In the process, workers' control over timing, over defining appropriate ways to do a task, and over criteria that establish acceptable performance are all slowly taken on as the prerogatives of management personnel who are usually divorced from the actual place in which the work is carried out. Deskilling, then, often leads to the atrophy of valuable skills that workers possessed, since there is no longer any "need" for them in the redefined labor process. The loss of control or proletarianization of a job is hence part of a larger dynamic in the separation of conception from execution and the continuing attempts by management in the state and industry to rationalize as many aspects of one's labor as possible. I have discussed this in considerably more detail in Michael W. Apple, *Education and Power* (Boston and London: Routledge & Kegan Paul, 1982). See also Richard Edwards, *Contested Terrain* (New York: Basic Books, 1979), and Michael Burawoy, *Manufacturing Consent* (Chicago: University of Chicago Press, 1979).

4. Erik Olin Wright, "Class and Occupation," *Theory and Society* 9 (No. 2, 1980), 182–3.

5. Apple, *Education and Power*.

6. Wright, "Class and Occupation," 188. Clearly race plays an important part here too. See Michael Reich, *Racial Inequality* (Princeton: Princeton University Press, 1981), and Mario Barrera, *Race and Class in the Southwest: A Theory of Racial Inequality* (Notre Dame: Notre Dame University Press, 1979).

7. Janet Holland, "Women's Occupational Choice: The Impact of Sexual Divisions in Society," Stockholm Institute of Education, Department of Educational Research, Reports on Education and Psychology, 1980, p. 7.

8. *Ibid.*, p. 27.

9. *Ibid.*, p. 45.

10. Gail Kelly and Ann Nihlen, "Schooling and the Reproduction of Patriarchy," in Michael W. Apple (ed.), *Cultural and Economic Reproduction in Education: Essays on Class, Ideology and the State* (Boston and London: Routledge & Kegan Paul, 1982), pp. 167–8. One cannot fully understand the history of the relationship between women and teaching without tracing out the complex connections among the family, domesticity, child care, and the policies of and employment within the state. See especially, Miriam David, *The State, the Family and Education* (Boston and London: Routledge & Kegan Paul, 1980).

11. For an interesting history of the relationship among class, gender and teaching, see June Purvis, "Women and Teaching in the Nineteenth Century," in Roger Dale, Geoff Esland, Ross Fergusson, and Madeleine MacDonald (eds.), *Education and the State, Vol. 2: Politics, Patriarchy and Practice* (Barcombe, Sussex: Falmer Press, 1981), pp. 359–75. I am wary of using a concept such as patriarchy, since its very status is problematic. As Rowbotham notes, "Patriarchy suggests a fatalistic submission which allows no space for the complexities of women's defiance" (quoted in Tricia Davis, "Stand by Your Men? Feminism and Socialism in the Eighties,") in George Bridges and Rosalind Brunt (eds.), *Silver Linings: Some Strategies for the Eighties* (London: Lawrence & Wishart, 1981), p.14. A history of women's day-to-day struggles falsifies any such theory of "fatalistic submission."

12. Jane Barker and Hazel Downing, "Word Processing and the Transformation of the Patriarchal Relations of Control in the Office," in Dale, Esland, Fergusson and MacDonald (eds.), *Education and the State, Vol. 2*, pp. 229–56. See also the discussion of deskilling in Edwards, *Contested Terrain*.

13. For an analysis of how such language has been employed by the state, see Michael W. Apple, "Common Curriculum and State Control," *Discourse* 2 (No. 4, 1982), 1–10, and James Donald, "Green Paper: Noise of a Crisis," *Screen Education* 30 (Spring 1979), 13–49.

14. See, for example, Seymour Sarason, *The Culture of the School and the Problem of Change* (Boston: Allyn & Bacon, 1971).

15. Apple, *Education and Power*, and Susan Porter Benson, "The Clerking Sisterhood: Rationalization and the Work Culture of Sales Women in American Department Stores," *Radical America* 12 (March/April 1978), 41–55.

16. Roger Dale's discussion of contradictions between elements within the state is very interesting in this regard. See Roger Dale, "The State and Education: Some Theoretical Approaches," in *The State and Politics of Education* (Milton Keynes: The Open University Press, E353, Block 1, Part 2, Units 3–4, 1981), and Roger Dale, "Education and the Capitalist State: Contributions and Contradictions," in Apple (ed.), *Cultural and Economic Reproduction in Education*, pp. 127–61.

17. Dale, "The State and Education," p. 13.

18. I have examined this in greater detail in Apple, *Education and Power*. See as well Edwards, *Contested Terrain*, and Daniel Clawson, *Bureaucracy and the Labor Process* (New York: Monthly Review Press, 1980).

19. Magali Larson, "Proletarianization and Educated Labor," *Theory and Society* 9 (No. 2, 1980), 166.

20. *Ibid.*, 167.

21. *Ibid.* Larson points out that these problems related to intensification are often central grievances even among doctors.

22. *Ibid.*, 168.

23. *Ibid.*, 169.

24. *Ibid.*, 167.

25. Apple, *Education and Power*. See also Carol Buswell, "Pedagogic Change and Social Change," *British Journal of Sociology of Education* 1 (No. 3, 1980), 293–306.

26. The question of just how seriously schools take this, the variability of their response, is not unimportant. As Popkewitz, Tabachnick and Wehlage demonstrate in their interesting ethnographic study of school reform, not all schools use materials of this sort alike. See Thomas Popkewitz, B. Robert Tabachnick, and Gary Wehlage, *The Myth of Educational Reform* (Madison: University of Wisconsin Press, 1982).

27. This section of my analysis is based largely on research carried out by Andrew Gitlin. See Andrew Gitlin, "Understanding the Work of Teachers," unpublished Ph.D. dissertation, University of Wisconsin, Madison, 1980.

28. *Ibid.*, 208.

29. *Ibid.*

30. *Ibid.*, 197.

31. *Ibid.*, 237.

32. *Ibid.*, 125.

33. *Ibid.*, 197.

34. This is similar to the use of liberal discourse by popular classes to struggle for person rights against established property rights over the past one hundred years. See Herbert Gintis, "Communication and Politics," *Socialist Review* 10 (March/June 1980), 189–232. The process is partly paradoxical, however. Attempts to professionalize do give women a weapon against some aspects of patriarchal relations; yet, there is a clear connection between being counted as a profession and being populated largely by men. In fact, one of the things that are very visible historically is the relationship between the sexual division of labor and professionalization. There has been a decided tendency for full professional status to be granted only when an activity is "dominated by men—in both management and the ranks." Jeff Hearn, "Notes on Patriarchy: Professionalization and the Semi-Professions," *Sociology* 16 (May 1982), 195.

35. Magali Larson, "Monopolies of Competence and Bourgeois Ideology," in Dale, Esland, Fergusson, and MacDonald (eds.), *Education and the State, Vol. 2*, p. 332.

36. Larson, "Proletarianization and Educated Labor," p. 152. Historically, class as well as gender dynamics have been quite important here, and recent research documents this clearly. As Barry Bergen has shown in his recent study of the growth of the relationship between class and gender in the professionalization of elementary school teaching in England, a large portion of elementary school teachers were both women and of the working class. As he puts it:

Teaching, except at the university level, was not highly regarded by the middle class to begin with, and teaching in the elementary schools was the lowest rung on the teaching ladder. The middle class did not view elementary teaching as a means of upward mobility. But the elementary school teachers seemed to view themselves as having risen above the working class, if not having reached the middle class. . . . Clearly, the varied attempts of elementary teachers to professionalize constitute an attempt to raise their class position from an interstitial one between the working class and middle class to the solidly middle class position of a profession.

See Barry H. Bergen, "Only a Schoolmaster: Gender, Class, and the Effort to Professionalize Elementary Teaching in England, 1870–1910," *History of Education Quarterly* 22 (Spring 1982), 10.

37. Gitlin, "Understanding the Work of Teachers," p. 128.
38. *Ibid.*
39. Martin Lawn and Jenny Ozga, "Teachers: Professionalism, Class and Proletarianization," unpublished paper, The Open University, Milton Keynes, 1981, p. 15 in mimeo.
40. Jenny Ozga, "The Politics of the Teaching Profession," in *The Politics of Schools and Teaching* (Milton Keynes: The Open University Press, E353, Block 6, Units 14–15, 1981), p. 24.
41. We need to be very careful here, of course. Certainly, not all teachers will respond in this way. That some will not points to the partial and important fracturing of dominant gender and class ideologies in ways that signal significant alterations in the consciousness of teachers. Whether these alterations are always progressive is an interesting question. Also, as Connell has shown, such "feminine" approaches are often important counterbalances to masculinist forms of authority in schools. See R. W. Connell, *Teachers' Work* (Boston and London: George Allen & Unwin, 1985).
42. See Henry Giroux, "Theories of Reproduction and Resistance in the New Sociology of Education: A Critical Analysis," *Harvard Educational Review* 53 (August 1983), 257–93, even though he is not specifically interested in gender relations.
43. While I have focused here on the possible impacts in the school and the home on women teachers, a similar analysis needs to be done on men. We need to ask how masculinist ideologies work through male teachers and administrators. Furthermore, what changes, conflicts, and tensions will evolve, say, in the patriarchal authority structures of the home given the intensification of men's labor? I would like to thank Sandra Acker for raising this critically important point. For an analysis of changes in women's labor in the home, see Susan Strasser, *Never Done: A History of American Housework* (New York: Pantheon, 1982).
44. Clawson. *Bureaucracy and the Labor Process*, pp. 152–3.
45. In addition, Connell makes the interesting point that since teachers' work has no identifiable object that it "produces," it can be intensified nearly indefinitely. See Connell, *Teachers' Work*, p. 86.
46. Apple, *Education and Power*, and Manuel Castells, *The Economic Crisis and American Society* (Princeton: Princeton University Press, 1980).

IV

AFTER A CENTURY OF CURRICULUM THOUGHT: CHANGE AND CONTINUITY

OUR PURPOSE IN THIS LAST SECTION of the *Reader* is to sample the contemporary field of curriculum studies. Partly our intent is to introduce a range of topics. Still, focusing on recent scholarship is a tricky business. A challenge that we did not face in summarizing the previous readings is that here in the final section we lack the advantage of hindsight. As scholarship ages, its significance seems to emerge almost like the images in a developing photograph. But with contemporary work we are still guessing. What makes a given line of inquiry a part of the curriculum field? Or does it more properly belong to some other specialization? And if scholarship is included in the broad category of curriculum studies, how central is it to the field? When do particular studies represent the influence of other fields, and when do they represent contributions? What counts as pioneering work, or work that is likely to make a difference in the next generation of curriculum scholarship?

In selecting and organizing the following articles, we have not always had firm or clear answers to these important questions. Rather, we have done our best to steer a general course by acknowledging both change and continuity in the field's contemporary landscape. All of the following articles are conceptually linked (in various ways) to the traditions represented in earlier sections of the *Reader*. This continuity is what gives the readings a family resemblance common to curriculum scholarship per se. At the same time, many of the readings either cross into other fields or signal new directions for previous work. On both counts, we looked for scholarship that did not simply follow the beaten path.

The inseparability of change and continuity is important for practical reasons. If we were concerned only with change such as the field's responsiveness to political headlines, the following scholarship would represent little more than a survey of last season's curricular fashions. Veteran scholars know that today's hot topics in the educational press may well be tomorrow's forgotten curiosities. But if we were to take the other extreme, concerned solely with continuity, our selection would include just those authors who are undisputed "curriculum" scholars and only those readings that focus on developments internal to the field. To do so is to close the field by talking just with those in our particular "discourse." To put this another way, a preoccupation with who we are risks diverting attention from broader educational trends, and it does seem that the field on occasion has been caught unaware as the day-to-day realities of school practice marched over the horizon and out of sight.

We hope our selections avoid both the extremes of faddism and intellectual paralysis. The first two readings in particular illustrate vital connections between the field and current national issues. The first reading is excerpted from the widely known and controversial AAUW report, *How Schools Shortchange Girls*. This report examines issues of gender and equity in education at large. We have reprinted the three chapters of the report that deal specifically with curriculum. A chapter devoted to the *formal curriculum* reviews past research and conceptions of equity as they relate to the explicit messages that schools convey to students. The chapter on the *classroom as curriculum*, which harkens back to Philip W. Jackson's (Part II) emphasis on implicit curricula, argues that the attention given students and the ways in which they are asked to learn usually favor boys over girls. The final chapter in this set is on the *evaded curriculum*, or what has also been referred to as the null curriculum (Eisner, 1979; Flinders et al., 1986). This curriculum includes topics ranging from adolescent sexuality and mental health to emotional expression and gender politics. Perhaps these topics have received increased attention in other professional fields over the past decade, but in education they remain controversial, and still largely evaded.

The second reading, "HIV/AIDS Education: Toward a Collaborative Curriculum," is a chapter from Jonathan Silin's book, *Sex, Death, and the Education of Children*. Most of the chapter is based on the author's work with classroom teachers as they examine how curricula convey both information and cultural myths about HIV/AIDS. In Silin's view, recognizing HIV/AIDS as a social construction is important because the embeddedness of this disease in social norms and cultural beliefs is what creates special challenges for teachers and curriculum developers. These norms and beliefs range from conceptions of childhood to questions of teacher authority. In framing these issues, Silin acknowledges his debt to earlier curriculum thinkers, including John Dewey, the field's critical theorists, and those who have approached curriculum from a phenomenological perspective. Silin also argues that, for better or worse, other past curriculum traditions have significantly influenced contemporary schools practices.

William E. Doll Jr.'s excerpt from his book *A Post-Modern Perspective on Curriculum* illustrates the connections between past and present curriculum thought in another way. Doll argues that our role as scholars is to bring the curriculum field into our post-modern era. On the one hand, the need to update curriculum thought, to move it forward with the times, signals a break from the past, and especially a break from modernism. On the other hand, breaking from tradition is itself something of a tradition in the field. To group Doll with the likes of Bobbitt and Tyler hardly seems appropriate. But regardless of how we categorize this author, Doll's alternative to the Tyler Rationale opens up intriguing questions around the criteria he labels *Richness* (a curriculum's depth of meaning), *Recursion* (the complex structures that support critical reflection), *Relations* (the intersecting of curriculum and cultures), and *Rigor* (one's commitment to exploration).

The fourth reading, Peter Hlebowitsh's "The Burdens of the New Curricularist," contrasts with Doll by attacking reconceptualism, or at least by attacking the abuses of reconceptualism. Hlebowitsh argues that critiques of the field's past have unfairly focused on bureaucratic control and social efficiency. This misrepresentation has led the "new curricularist" to reject the field's traditions out of hand and deny what Hlebowitsh calls the "burdens" of practice, design, unity, and history. Yet the call to shoulder these burdens is not simply a reaction against what seems to some contemporary scholars as endless fault-finding. On the contrary, Hlebowitsh's essay can be viewed as an explicit statement of the change and continuity theme we have already mentioned.

The next article is titled "Voluntary National Tests Would Improve Education." It is a brief article but it serves to introduce the broader trends related to testing, the standards movement, and school accountability. The article's emphasis on low test scores and its focus on college, careers, and the global competition all harken back to *A Nation at Risk*. In other respects, however, this article presages the key notion that testing could be used as a tool of reform. We could argue that the voluntary tests called for in this article do not raise the same level of concerns found in the mandated testing that was soon to follow under *No Child Left Behind*. At the same time, even this early proposal rests on the assumption that curriculum should comply with the design of the test, not the other way around.

For the many benefits claimed by Smith, Stevenson, and Li on behalf of testing, each benefit is flatly denied in the next article by Linda M. McNeil. More than questioning such benefits, McNeil argues that the accountability system in Texas, one of the first states to mandate high-stakes testing, has actually harmed education in significant ways. In particular, she calls attention to the hidden effects of the Texas system on teachers, students, and public debate. Echoing Apple's concerns in the previous section of this volume (Chapter 18), McNeil describes how testing for accountability undermines teacher autonomy and tacitly shifts blame for educational problems away from politicians and onto classroom teachers. McNeil further argues that testing displaces serious learning with what she calls the "noncurriculum" of test preparation. While all educational programs (including test prep programs) teach something, and thus cannot escape having a curriculum of sorts, the intuitive validly of McNeil's label again reminds us that education is also normative; that is, we usually resist using the term "education" to include pernicious or harmful outcomes. Moreover, McNeil contends this noncurriculum is more likely to be adopted by poor schools in a patronizing effort to help "those children," thus increasing educational inequities. Finally, McNeil touches on the political dimension of accountability by suggesting ways in which mandated testing may discourage public debate over the purposes of education, what should be taught, and who should decide.

The next article responds to one of the central rationales given for why we need tougher standards and better accountability in the first place. Since at least the early 1980s, this rationale has been manifested in persistent calls for increased academic rigor. David J. Flinders argues that such calls raise a host of important questions for curriculum scholars. What, for example, do rigorous standards look like in actual classrooms? How do tough academic standards play out in the form of an enacted curriculum? And what consequences does such a curriculum hold for students? Flinders examines these questions using two case narratives of teachers who embrace a "cultural literacy" approach to their work.

Testing is again an issue in one of these cases, but Flinders suggests other ways as well in which enacted curricula may significantly differ from one classroom to another.

Elliot W. Eisner's article develops further the position that we should know more about schools than simply how well their students score on a standardized test. Like other writers in this section of the *Reader*, Eisner situates recent school reforms in a broad context. He then asks us to think more deeply about possible alternatives by imagining a temporary halt to all testing. Without the scores, what questions would we ask to determine the quality of any given school? Some of Eisner's own questions include: What forms of thinking do school experiences invite? Are these experiences connected to life outside of school, and do they encourage multiple forms of literacy? Will these experiences help students form their own purposes, work cooperatively, cultivate their personal talents, and take an active part in assessing their own achievements? Eisner admits that these are difficult questions to answer, but he also contents that such questions are at the heart of coming to value diversity in our schools.

Diversity is addressed in the next two readings as well—the first an article by Stephen J. Thornton on the heteronormativity of curriculum, and the second by Geneva Gay on the importance of multicultural education. Thornton argues that although gay issues are a visible part of public life in contemporary America, they are avoided in schools and especially absent in social studies curricula. Not only can this absence be damning in itself, but it entirely dismisses the question of how sexual orientation should be represented, on what terms, and from whose perspective. Avoiding these questions leaves students in the hands of what Thornton calls "the hidden curriculum everyone sees." This is a curriculum that stigmatizes any deviance from heterosexual experience, which Thornton notes "is surely one of the most successful exercises in social training that schools perform" (this volume).

Gay's article reiterates several of Thornton's ideas in the context of multicultural education. In particular, Gay underscores two important curricular lessons that the field of multicultural education has learned over the past two decades. The first lesson is that multicultural education will be marginalized if approached as an addendum to "core" subjects. It is a mistake, Gay argues, to believe that multicultural education can be achieved by limiting ethnic content to the sidebars of textbooks or to their special-events sections. This misconception is related to Gay's second point—that multicultural education is not so much content as it is a more broadly based conception of human development, one which includes academic excellence. As such, multicultural education cuts across curriculum, policy, instruction, counseling, leadership, and evaluation. Gay's article leaves many questions unanswered, but it also cites a broader range of resources than existed even a decade ago. Finally, Gay's broad conception of multiculturalism underscores the need for interdisciplinary and integrated curriculum.

This emphasis on curriculum integration leads into the next article by David W. Jardine, Annette LaGrange, and Beth Everest. Their concern is that in the rush to make connections among diverse content, which in itself may be a response to deeper and broader cultural fragmentation, educators too readily grasp onto broad concepts and abstract themes. The danger of this thematic approach is what these authors describe as a "random skittering over of topics" and the jarring dislocation of experience. Most teachers will recognize the inadequacy of the type of brainstorming that might follow a question such as, "But how do I get multicultural education into my math lessons?" We use multicultural content as an example because Gay in the previous article also worries about surface responses to curriculum integration. In other ways, Jardine, LaGrange, and Everest echo Eisner's piece.

Although written from different perspectives, both articles advance the argument that schools can do better in promoting the integrity of educational experiences by attending to the particularities of their histories and personal meanings relative to a student's own time and place. Both articles also go on to emphasize that no standard "model" or approach to curriculum development exists to accomplish this end. On the contrary, this deepened sense of integration is not so much a matter of knowledge and values as it is a matter of the ways in which knowledge and values come into play.

The final reading is a chapter on educational aims from Nel Noddings's book, *Happiness and Education*. Noddings surveys the purposes of aims-talk in the work of past educational thinkers and suggests that aims-talk is one of the critical but missing dimensions in contemporary school reform. To underscore the absence of aims-talk in current policy trends, Noddings makes a distinction among educational *objectives*, which typically reference the sequence in which content is taught; *goals*, which reference reasons for teaching particular students a given subject; and *aims*, which refer to who benefits and how. Noddings also argues that while aims are especially important to consider in analyzing present policies, aims more generally do not serve us in mechanical or deterministic ways. Rather, Noddings urges us to consider that aims may be to education what freedom is to democracy. Their relationship is dependent, but not one we can take for granted.

REFERENCES

Eisner, E.W (1979). *The Educational Imagination*. New York: Macmillan.

Flinders, D.J., Noddings, N., and Thornton, S.J. (1986). "The Null Curriculum: Its Theoretical Basis and Practical Implications." *Curriculum Inquiry*, 16, 33–42.

19

How Schools Shortchange Girls: Three Perspectives on Curriculum

AMERICAN ASSOCIATION OF UNIVERSITY WOMEN (AAUW)

THE FORMAL CURRICULUM

The formal curriculum is the central message-giving instrument of the school. It creates images of self and the world for all students. The curriculum can strengthen or decrease student motivation for engagement, effort, growth, and development through the messages it delivers to students about themselves and the world.

Students spend more hours of the day in academic classes than in any other activity. The chief subject areas today are basically the same as they were at the turn of the century, albeit with some changes in name: English (or language arts), history (or social studies), mathematics, science, foreign (or second) language, arts, and physical education. Accreditation of students for further education or employment depends more on grades given for curricular work in these areas than on any other formal measure.

Despite the importance of curriculum, its actual content received scant attention in national reports on education and education restructuring in the late 1980s.[1] These reports found student achievement unsatisfactory, but very few questioned whether curriculum content might in fact be counterproductive to student achievement. The reports suggest that levels of literacy, numeracy, and commitment to life-long learning are not satisfactory for either girls or boys in our society. Improving the situation for girls can also improve it for boys, for when one looks carefully at girls' dilemmas, boys' dilemmas are seen from new perspectives.

Yet in 138 articles on educational reform that appeared in nine prominent educational journals between 1983 and 1987, less than 1 percent of the text addressed sex equity. Only one article discussed curriculum and instruction as they relate to sex equity.[2] A 1990 survey commissioned by the National Education Association revealed that even among programs sponsored by organizations and institutions concerned with equity in education, only three national professional development programs for teachers focused on gender and race in English and social studies curriculum content.[3]

Part four of *How Schools Shortchange Girls: The AAUW Report,* American Association of University Women, Educational Foundation Washington, D.C., 1992. Reprinted by permission.

Research on Curriculum

Since the early 1970s, many studies have surveyed instructional materials for sex bias.[4] Published in 1975, *Dick and Jane As Victims: Sex Stereotyping in Children's Readers* set a pattern for line-by-line examination of the messages about girls and boys delivered by texts, examples, illustrations, and thematic organization of material in everything from basal readers to science textbooks.[5] In 1971 a study of thirteen popular U.S. history textbooks revealed that material on women comprised no more than 1 percent of any text, and that women's lives were trivialized, distorted, or omitted altogether.[6] Studies from the late 1980s reveal that although sexism has decreased in some elementary school texts and basal readers, the problems persist, especially at the secondary school level, in terms of what is considered important enough to study.[7]

A 1989 study of book-length works taught in high school English courses reports that, in a national sample of public, independent, and Catholic schools, the ten books assigned most frequently included only one written by a woman and none by members of minority groups.[8] This research, which used studies from 1963 and 1907 as a base line, concludes that "the lists of most frequently required books and authors are dominated by white males, with little change in overall balance from similar lists 25 or 80 years ago."[9]

During the late 1970s and '80s, experiments with more inclusive school curricula were aided by the rapid development of scholarly work and courses in black studies, ethnic studies, and women's studies in colleges and universities. Publications of the Council on Interracial Books for Children (founded in 1966), The Feminist Press (founded in 1970), and the federally funded Women's Educational Equity Program (started in 1974) inspired many teachers to develop more inclusive reading lists and assignments that draw on students' lives.

What effects did the revised curricula have on students? A 1980 review of research on how books influence children cited twenty-three studies that demonstrated that books do transmit values to young readers, that multicultural readings produce markedly more favorable attitudes toward nondominant groups than do all-white curricula, that academic achievement for all students was positively correlated with use of nonsexist and multicultural curriculum materials, and that sex-role stereotyping was reduced in those students whose curriculum portrayed females and males in nonstereotypical roles.[10]

During the 1980s, federal support for research and action on sex equity and race equity dropped sharply.[11] But many individual teachers, librarians, authors, and local or state school authorities continued a variety of efforts to lessen stereotyping and omission, or expand and democratize the curriculum.[12]

Virtually all textbook publishers now have guidelines for nonsexist language. Unfortunately, not all insist that authors follow them.[13] Change in textbooks is observable but not striking. Research on high school social studies texts reveals that while women are more often included, they are likely to be the usual "famous women," or women in protest movements. Rarely is there dual and balanced treatment of women and men, and seldom are women's perspectives and cultures presented on their own terms.[14]

Researchers at a 1990 conference reported that even texts designed to fit within the current California guidelines on gender and race equity for textbook adoption showed subtle language bias, neglect of scholarship on women, omission of women as developers of history and initiators of events, and absence of women from accounts of technological developments.[15] An informal survey of twenty U.S. history textbooks compiled each year from

1984 to 1989 found a gradual but steady shift away from an overwhelming emphasis on laws, wars, and control over territory and public policy, toward an emphasis on people's daily lives in many kinds of circumstances.[16]

The books, however, continued to maintain the abstract, disengaged tone that was characteristic of the earlier texts. The recommended assignments still relied heavily on debate techniques in which students were asked to develop an argument defending a single point of view. Few assignments offered students an opportunity to reflect on a genuine variety of perspectives or to consider feelings as well as actions.[17]

Conceptualizations of Equity in the Curriculum

Side by side with research on gender and the curriculum came various ways of conceptualizing and categorizing what is meant by gender and race equity in curriculum content. Recognizing elements of bias was an important first step. Building on earlier efforts, including work by Martha Matthews and Shirley McCune at the National Foundation for the Improvement of Education, leaders of workshops sponsored by the National Council of Teachers of Foreign Languages in 1984 listed six common forms of sex bias in instructional materials: *exclusion* of girls, *stereotyping* of members of both sexes, *subordination or degradation* of girls, *isolation* of materials on women, *superficiality* of attention to contemporary issues or social problems, and *cultural inaccuracy*, through which most of the people active in a culture are excluded from view.[18] The Coalition of Women in German has monitored textbooks using this checklist for several years and reports significant changes in texts.[19]

In 1990, after a review of more than 100 sex- and race-equity programs identified further markers of bias in the classroom, the National Education Association developed a checklist specifying eleven kinds of sex bias. The "overt and subtle behaviors" it listed include: double standards for males and females, condescension, tokenism, denial of achieved status or authority, backlash against women who succeed in improving their status, and divide-and-conquer strategies that praise individuals as better than others in their ethnic or gender group.[20]

Unfortunately, checklists on bias, prejudice, and discrimination can sometimes hurt the very groups they are meant to help by assigning them the status of "victims." In a provocative essay, "Curriculum As Window and Mirror," Emily Style compares the curriculum to an architectural structure that schools build around students.[21] Ideally, the curriculum provides each student with both windows out onto the experiences of others and mirrors of her or his own reality and validity. But for most students, the present curriculum provides many windows and few mirrors.

Teachers themselves may recall few mirrors. For the last eleven years, teachers joining a large faculty-development project have been asked, "What did you study about women in high school?" More than half initially respond, "Nothing." Some recall a heroine, one or two historical figures, a few goddesses or saints. Marie Curie is the only female scientist who has been mentioned in ten years of this survey.[22] Many women as well as men are surprised at their answers, and surprised to realize how little they themselves are teaching about women and girls. Questions about cultural diversity draw similar responses. Virtually all teachers polled recall feeling a distance between their own lives and what was portrayed in the formal curriculum.

Curriculum researcher Gretchen Wilbur states that gender-fair curriculum has six attributes. It acknowledges and affirms *variation*, i.e., similarities and differences among and within groups of people. It is *inclusive*, allowing both females and males to find and identify positively with messages about themselves. It is *accurate*, presenting information that is data-based, verifiable, and able to withstand critical analysis. It is *affirmative*, acknowledging and valuing the worth of individuals and groups. It is *representative*, balancing multiple perspectives. And, finally, it is *integrated*, weaving together the experiences, needs, and interests of both males and females.[23]

Wilbur maintains that so far no major curriculum-reform efforts have used explicitly gender-fair approaches. For example, the National Council of Teachers of Mathematics has developed new mathematics standards that shift the emphasis of curriculum from computational skills to mastery of concepts and processes.[24] The new standards advocate (1) conceptual orientation, (2) active involvement physically and mentally, (3) thinking, reasoning, and problem solving, (4) application, (5) broad range of content, and (6) use of calculators.[25] Wilbur states that, if implemented effectively, this approach will fulfill three out of the six criteria for gender-fair content: variation, accuracy, and representation. However, there is no assurance that the curriculum will be inclusive, affirming, or integrated.

Currently, science-curriculum-reform efforts under Project 2061 of the American Association for the Advancement of Science describe equity as the central organizing principle; however, the materials produced to date send contradictory messages. For example, while acknowledging that scientific discoveries have been made around the world, the new science materials refer specifically to only European scientific history and the usual "great men." So far, women are no more visible in Project 2061 than in standard science-curriculum materials.[26]

Wilbur categorizes many attempts to design gender-fair courses as *pullout* curricula, which target a "problem" population (for example, pregnant teenagers or persons with disabilities), or *fragmented* curricula, which add units on "women's issues" to the main curriculum. Such approaches, she maintains, fall short of genuinely gender-fair integration of women into central course content.

These and other kinds of corrective programs have been noted by other educators. James Banks identifies four ways in which ethnic content has been integrated into the curriculum since the 1960s. He describes these ways, or "levels," as follows.

Level 1: The Contributions Approach	Focuses on heroes, holidays, and discrete cultural elements.
Level 2: The Additive Approach	Content, concepts, themes, and perspectives are added to the curriculum without changing its structure.
Level 3: The Transformation Approach	The structure of the curriculum is changed to enable students to view concepts, issues, events, and themes from the perspectives of diverse ethnic and cultural groups.
Level 4: The Social Action Approach	Students make decisions on important social issues and take actions to help solve them.[27]

In another typology, Peggy McIntosh identifies five interactive phases of curricular and personal change that she observed in educators trying to teach more inclusively than they were themselves taught.[28] The following analysis, which uses history as an example, applies to all subject areas. McIntosh describes Phase I as "Womanless and All-White History." Phase II is "Exceptional Women and Persons of Color in History," but only considered from the conventional perspective of, for instance, military, political, or publicly acknowledged leaders. Phase III she terms the "Issues" Curriculum," treating "Women and People of Color as Problems, Anomalies, Absences, or Victims in History." Phases I, II, and III have a vertical axis of "either/or thinking" that views winning and losing as the only alternatives. An important conceptual and emotional shift occurs in Phase IV, which she labels" "Women's Lives or the Lives of People of Color *As* History." In Phase IV we see, for the first time, the cyclical nature of daily life, the making and mending of the social fabric, which was projected onto "lower-caste" people. Phase IV features lateral and plural thinking, sees "vertical" thinking as simply one version of thinking, and encourages all students to "make textbooks of their lives."[29] This phase, when interactively explored with the other phases, makes possible the eventual reconstruction of Phase V, "History Redefined and Reconstructed to Include Us All."

Many school subjects, as presently taught, fall within the general descriptions of Phases I and II. In the upper grades especially, the curriculum narrows and definitions of knowing take on gender-specific and culture-specific qualities associated with Anglo-European male values.[30] For example, current events and civics curricula, which take up topics from the news media, tend to focus, like their sources, on news as controversy and conflict. Much of the daily texture of life is ignored in most current-events classes.[31]

Debate clubs, usually located at the boundary of the formal curriculum as an extracurricular activity, take for granted the adversarial, win/lose orientation of debate. "The definition of the citizen in debate clubs and current events classes relates more to what psychologist Carol Gilligan names "the ethos of justice" (negotiating rights and responsibilities) than to "the ethos of care" (working relationally to make and keep human connections and avoid damage).[32]

Over the last forty years, most educators have assumed that the existing subject areas of the curriculum serve a useful purpose. They are in such universal use that consideration of alternatives is difficult. They are viewed as providing a rational educational grounding, especially in preparation for standardized tests such as College Board or Regents' Exams in individual subject areas. Increasingly, however, educational organizations, colleges, and testing agencies themselves are acknowledging the importance of students' gaining the ability not only to describe concepts but to apply them in new situations. Traditional discipline-based courses, while providing factual information, may not be the best way to do this.

Changing the curriculum in any substantial way is bound to result in some initial resistance. A recent study commissioned by the National Education Association identified several key barriers to gender equity in the curriculum. The report cited students' reluctance to be singled out as having cultural or gender experience that does not fit the assumed norms; parents' suspicions about unfamiliar curricula; teachers' lack of training on multicultural and gender-neutral goals and techniques; unwillingness to commit funds for teachers to participate in curriculum-change efforts.[33]

School systems often lack in-service funds and energy to provide new opportunities for teachers. Tracy Kidder's noted study of a year in the life of a fourth-grade teacher, *Among Schoolchildren*, notes that the teacher uses twenty-year-old curriculum guides.[34]

Arthur Applebee, author of the noted *Study of Book-Length Works Taught in High School English Courses*, says that twenty years of consciousness raising and resource development have not changed the basic curriculum because teachers have not had the time and support to familiarize themselves with new materials. He recommends preservice course work in schools of education, in-service workshops, and departmental discussion groups to give teachers enough familiarity with alternative materials so that they will be comfortable in finding their own ways to introduce new works into their classes.[35] The restructuring of schools should acknowledge that curricular design and revision are central—not peripheral— to teachers' work with students.

The Multicultural Debate

The most important impediment to gender-fair and multicultural curricula may be inherited views of what education is and whom it should serve. For example, when it became clear that New York's schools were not serving the population well, New York Commissioner of Education Thomas Sobol created a committee for the review and development of Social Studies curricula in the schools. The committee's report is a clear commitment to curricular principles of democracy, diversity, economic and social justice, globalism, ecological balance, ethics and values, and the individual and society.[36] It recommends that curriculum and teaching methods be more inclusive and respectful of diversity. The report has created a furor in the New York media, reflecting the larger debate going on throughout the country. Critics have called Ethnic Studies and Women's Studies "political," as if a curriculum that leaves women out altogether is not also "political." Multicultural work has been termed "divisive" without recognizing that an exclusively white male curriculum is divisive when it ignores the contributions others make to society. Critics who insist that students must focus on our "common heritage" appear to overlook the experiences of Native Americans as well as the immigrant history of the rest of the population, which makes diversity one of the key elements of the "common" heritage of the United States.

In a democracy, schools must address the educational needs of all students. Each student should find herself or himself reflected in the curriculum. When this happens, students learn and grow.

Girls, Self-Esteem, and the Curriculum

Researchers have puzzled over the drop in girls' self-esteem as they go through school, even though they do as well as boys on many standardized measures and get better grades. Teacher trainer Cathy Nelson attributes this drop in self-esteem to the negative messages delivered to girls by school curricula.[37] Students sit in classes that, day in and day out, deliver the message that women's lives count for less than men's. Historian Linda Kerbez suggests a plausible connection between falling self-esteem and curricular omission and bias. "Lowered self-esteem is a perfectly reasonable conclusion if one has been subtly instructed that what people like oneself have done in the world has not been important and is not worth studying."[38] There is no social science research to document cause and effect in this matter, but educators must take more responsibility for understanding that the curriculum is the central message-giving instrument of the school.

THE CLASSROOM AS CURRICULUM

Students can learn as much from what they experience in school as they can from the formal content of classroom assignments. Classroom interactions, both with the teacher and other students, are critical components of education. These interactions shape a school. They determine in large measure whether or not a school becomes a community: a place where girls and boys can learn to value themselves and others, where both the rights and the responsibilities of citizens are fostered.

Teacher-Student Interactions

Whether one looks at preschool classrooms or university lecture halls, at female teachers or male teachers, research spanning the past twenty years consistently reveals that males receive more teacher attention than do females.[1] In preschool classrooms boys receive more instructional time, more hugs, and more teacher attention.[2] The pattern persists through elementary school and high school. One reason is that boys demand more attention. Researchers David and Myra Sadker have studied these patterns for many years. They report that boys in one study of elementary and middle school students called out answers eight times more often than girls did. When boys called out, the typical teacher reaction was to listen to the comment. When girls called out, they were usually corrected with comments such as, "Please raise your hand if you want to speak."[3]

It is not only the attention demanded by male students that explains their greater involvement in teacher-student exchanges. Studies have found that even when boys do not volunteer, the teacher is more likely to solicit their responses.[4]

The issue is broader than the inequitable distribution of teacher *contacts* with male and female students; it also includes the inequitable *content* of teacher comments. Teacher remarks can be vague and superficial or precise and penetrating. Helpful teacher comments provide students with insights into the strengths and weaknesses of their answers. Careful and comprehensive teacher reactions not only affect student learning, they can also influence student self-esteem.[5]

The Sadkers conducted a three-year study of more than 100 fourth-, sixth- and eighth-grade classrooms. They identified four types of teacher comments: praise, acceptance, remediation, and criticism.

They found that while males received more of all four types of teacher comments, the difference favoring boys was greatest in the more useful teacher reactions of praise, criticism, and remediation. When teachers took the time and made the effort to specifically evaluate a student's performance, the student receiving the comment was more likely to be male.[6] These findings are echoed in other investigations, indicating that boys receive more precise teacher comments than females in terms of both scholarship and conduct.[7]

The differences in teacher evaluations of male and female students have been cited by some researchers as a cause of "learned helplessness," or lack of academic perseverance, in females. Initially investigated in animal experiments, "learned helplessness" refers to a lack of perseverance, a debilitating loss of self-confidence.[8] This concept has been used to explain why girls sometimes abandon while boys persistently pursue academic challenges for which both groups are equally qualified.[9]

One school of thought links learned helplessness with attribution theory. While girls are more likely to attribute their success to luck, boys are more likely to attribute their success to ability. As a result of these different causal attributions, boys are more likely to feel mastery and control over academic challenges, while girls are more likely to feel powerless in academic situations.[10]

Studies also reveal that competent females have higher expectations of failure and lower self-confidence when encountering new academic situations than do males with similar abilities.[11] The result is that female students are more likely to abandon academic tasks.[12]

However, research also indicates that the concepts of learned helplessness and other motivation constructs are complex. Psychologist Jacquelynne Eccles and her colleagues have found that there is a high degree of variation within each individual in terms of motivational constructs as one goes across subject areas. New evidence indicates that it is too soon to state a definitive connection between a specific teacher behavior and a particular student outcome.[13] Further research on the effects of teacher behavior and student performance and motivation is needed.

The majority of studies on teacher-student interaction do not differentiate among subject areas. However, there is some indication that the teaching of certain subjects may encourage gender-biased teacher behavior while others may foster more equitable interactions. Sex differences in attributing success to luck versus effort are more likely in subject areas where teacher responses are less frequent and where single precise student responses are less common.[14]

Two recent studies find teacher-student interactions in science classes particularly biased in favor of boys.[15] Some mathematics classes have less biased patterns of interaction overall when compared to science classes, but there is evidence that despite the more equitable overall pattern, a few male students in each mathematics class receive particular attention to the exclusion of all other students, male and female.[16]

Research on teacher-student interaction patterns has rarely looked at the interaction of gender with race, ethnicity, and/or social class. The limited data available indicate that while males receive more teacher attention than females, white boys receive more attention than boys from various racial and ethnic minority groups.[17]

Evidence also suggests that the attention minority students receive from teachers may be different in nature from that given to white children. In elementary school, black boys tend to have fewer interactions overall with teachers than other students and yet they are the recipients of four to ten times the amount of qualified praise ("That's good, but . . .") as other students.[18] Black boys tend to be perceived less favorably by their teachers and seen as less able than other students.[19] The data are more complex for girls. Black girls have less interaction with teachers than white girls, but they attempt to initiate interaction much more often than white girls or than boys of either race. Research indicates that teachers may unconsciously rebuff these black girls, who eventually turn to peers for interaction, often becoming the class enforcer or go-between for other students.[20] Black females also receive less reinforcement from teachers than do other students, although their academic performance is often better than boys."[21]

In fact, when black girls do as well as white boys in school, teachers attribute their success to hard work but assume that the white boys are not working up to their full potential.[22] This, coupled with the evidence that blacks are more often reinforced for their social behavior while whites are likely to be reinforced for their academic accomplishments, may contribute to low academic self-esteem in black girls.[23] Researchers have found that black females value their academic achievements less than black males in spite of their better performance.[24] Another study found that black boys have a higher science self-concept than black girls although there were no differences in achievement.[25]

The Design of Classroom Activities

Research studies reveal a tendency beginning at the preschool level for schools to choose classroom activities that will appeal to boys' interests and to select presentation formats in which boys excel or are encouraged more than are girls.[26] For example, when researchers looked at lecture versus laboratory classes, they found that in lecture classes teachers asked males academically related questions about 80 percent more often than they questioned females; the patterns were mixed in laboratory classes.[27] However, in science courses, lecture classes remain more common than laboratory classes.

Research indicates that if pupils begin working on an activity with little introduction from the teacher, everyone has access to the same experience. Discussion that follows after all students have completed an activity encourages more participation by girls.[28] In an extensive multistate study, researchers found that in geometry classes where the structure was changed so that students read the book and did problems *first* and *then* had classroom discussion of the topic, girls outperformed boys in two of five tests and scored equally in the other three. Girls in the experimental class reversed the general trend of boys' dominance on applications, coordinates, and proof taking, while they remained on par with boys on visualizations in three dimensions and transformations. In traditional classes where topics were introduced by lecture first and then students read the book and did the problems, small gender differences favoring boys remained.[29]

Successful Teaching Strategies

There are a number of teaching strategies that can promote more gender-equitable learning environments. Research indicates that science teachers who are successful in encouraging girls share several strategies.[30] These included using more than one textbook, eliminating sexist language, and showing fairness in their treatment and expectations of both girls and boys.

Other research indicates that classrooms where there are no gender differences in math are "girl friendly," with less social comparison and competition and an atmosphere students find warmer and fairer.[31]

In their 1986 study, *Women's Ways of Knowing*, Belenky, Clinchy, Goldberger, and Tarule point out that for many girls and women, successful learning takes place in an atmosphere that enables students to empathetically enter into the subject they are studying, an approach the authors term "connected knowing." The authors suggest that an acceptance of each individual's personal experiences and perspectives facilitates students' learning. They argue for classrooms that emphasize collaboration and provide space for exploring diversity of opinion.[32]

Few classrooms foster "connected learning," nor are the majority of classrooms designed to encourage cooperative behaviors and collaborative efforts. The need to evaluate, rank, and judge students can undermine collaborative approaches. One recent study that sampled third-, fifth-, and seventh-grade students found that successful students reported fewer cooperative attitudes than did unsuccessful students. In this study the effects of gender varied as a function of grade level. Third-grade girls were more cooperative than their male peers, but by fifth grade the gender difference had disappeared.[33] Other studies do not report this grade level-gender interaction, but rather indicate that girls tend to be more cooperative than boys but that cooperative attitudes decline for all students as they mature.[34]

Some educators view the arrival of new classroom organizational structures as a harbinger of more effective and more equitable learning environments. "Cooperative learning" has been viewed as one of these potentially more successful educational strategies.

Cooperative learning is designed to eliminate the negative effects of classroom competition while promoting a cooperative spirit and increasing heterogeneous and cross-race relationships. Smaller cooperative work groups are designed to promote group cohesion and interdependence, and mobilize these positive feelings to achieve academic objectives.[35] Progress and academic performance are evaluated on a group as well as an individual basis; the group must work together efficiently or all its members will pay a price.[36] A number of positive results have been attributed to cooperative learning groups, including increasing cross-race friendships, boosting academic achievement, mainstreaming students with disabilities, and developing mutual student concerns.[37]

However, positive cross-sex relationships may be more difficult to achieve than cross-race friendships or positive relationships among students with and without disabilities. First, as reported earlier in this report, there is a high degree of sex-segregation and same-sex friendships in elementary and middle school years.[38] Researchers have found that the majority of elementary students preferred single-sex work groups.[39] Second, different communication patterns of males and females can be an obstacle to effective cross-gender relationships. Females are more indirect in speech, relying often on questioning, while more direct males are more likely to make declarative statements or even to interrupt.[40] Research indicates that boys in small groups are more likely to receive requested help from girls; girls' requests, on the other hand, are more likely to be ignored by the boys.[41] In fact, the male sex may be seen as a status position within the group. As a result, male students may choose to show their social dominance by not readily talking with females.[42]

Not only are the challenges to cross-gender cooperation significant, but cooperative learning as currently implemented may not be powerful enough to overcome these obstacles. Some research indicates that the infrequent use of small, unstructured work groups is not effective in reducing gender stereotypes, and, in fact, increases stereotyping. Groups often provide boys with leadership opportunities that increase their self-esteem. Females are often seen as followers and are less likely to want to work in mixed-sex groups in the future.[43] Another study indicates a decrease in female achievement when females are placed in mixed-sex groups.[44] Other research on cooperative education programs have reported more positive results.[45] However, it is clear that merely providing an occasional group learning experience is not the answer to sex and gender differences in classrooms.

Problems in Student Interactions

The ways students treat each other during school hours is an aspect of the informal learning process, with significant negative implications for girls. There is mounting evidence that boys do not treat girls well. Reports of student sexual harassment—the unwelcome verbal or physical conduct of a sexual nature imposed by one individual on another—among junior high school and high school peers are increasing. In the majority of cases a boy is harassing a girl.[46]

Incidents of sexual harassment reveal as much about power and authority as they do about sexuality; the person being harassed usually is less powerful than the person doing the harassing. Sexual harassment is prohibited under Title IX, yet sex-biased peer interactions appear to be permitted in schools, if not always approved. Rather than viewing sexual harassment as serious misconduct, school authorities too often treat it as a joke.

When boys line up to "rate" girls as they enter a room, when boys treat girls so badly that they are reluctant to enroll in courses where they may be the only female, when boys feel it is good fun to embarrass girls to the point of tears, it is no joke. Yet these types of behaviors are often viewed by school personnel as harmless instances of "boys being boys."

The clear message to both girls and boys is that girls are not worthy of respect and that appropriate behavior for boys includes exerting power over girls—or over other, weaker boys. Being accused of being in any way like a woman is one of the worst insults a boy can receive. As one researcher recently observed:

> "It is just before dismissal time and a group of very active fourth-graders are having trouble standing calmly in line as they wait to go to their bus. Suddenly one of the boys grabs another's hat, runs to the end of the line, and involves a number of his buddies in a game of keep-away. The boy whose hat was taken leaps from his place in line, trying to intercept it from the others, who, as they toss it back and forth out of his reach, taunt him by yelling, "'You woman! You're a woman!'" When the teacher on bus duty notices, she tells the boys that they all have warnings for not waiting in line properly. The boys resume an orderly stance but continue to mutter names—'Woman!' 'Am not.' 'Yes, you are.'—under their breath."

Margaret Stubbs, October 1990

Harassment related to sexual orientation or sexual preference has received even less attention as an equity issue than heterosexual sexual harassment.[47] Yet, examples of name calling that imply homophobia, such as "sissy," "queer," "gay," "lesbo," are common among students at all levels of schooling. The fourth-grade boys who teased a peer by calling him a "woman" were not only giving voice to the sex-role stereotype that women are weaker than and therefore inferior to men; they were also challenging their peer's "masculinity" by ascribing feminine characteristics to him in a derogatory manner. Such attacks often prevent girls, and sometimes boys, from participating in activities and courses that are traditionally viewed as appropriate for the opposite sex.

When schools ignore sexist, racist, homophobic, and violent interactions between students, they are giving tacit approval to such behaviors. Environments where students do not feel accepted are not environments where effective learning can take place.

Implications

Teachers are not always aware of the ways in which they interact with students. Videotaping actual classrooms so that teachers can see themselves in action can help them to develop their own strategies for fostering gender-equitable education. The use of equitable teaching strategies should be one of the criteria by which teaching performance is evaluated.

Research studies indicate that girls often learn and perform better in same-sex work groups than they do in mixed-sex groupings. Additional research is needed, however, to better understand the specific dynamics of these interactions, particularly the circumstances under which single-sex groupings are most beneficial. Single-sex classes are illegal under Title IX, but usually single-sex work groups within coed classes are not. Teachers should be encouraged to "try out" many different classroom groupings, not only in mathematics and science classes but across a wide range of subject matter. It is critical that they carefully observe the impact of various groupings and write up and report their findings.

THE EVADED CURRICULUM

The evaded curriculum is the term coined in this report for matters central to the lives of students and teachers but touched upon only briefly, if at all, in most schools. These matters include the functioning of bodies, the expression and valuing of feelings and the dynamics of power. In both formal course work and in the informal exchanges among teachers and students, serious consideration of these areas is avoided. When avoidance is not possible—as in the case of required health or sex-education courses—the material is often presented in a cursory fashion. Students are offered a set of facts devoid of references to the complex personal and moral dilemmas they face in understanding and making decisions about critical facets of their lives.

Youth is traditionally seen as a time of healthy bodies and carefree minds, but as numerous studies, reports, and television documentaries have outlined recently, young people in the United States are falling prey to what are being called the "new morbidities." These new morbidities are not necessarily caused by viruses or bacteria but rather by societal conditions that can lead young people into eating disorders, substance abuse, early sexual activity, unintended pregnancy, sexually transmitted diseases (including AIDS), and suicide.

Not only are many young people engaging in risky behaviors, frequently with lifetime consequences, but they are taking part in constellations of behaviors that are interrelated.[1] Young people who drink, for example, are far more likely than others to engage in unprotected sex or be involved in car accidents. Girls who are doing badly in school are five times as likely as others to become teen parents.[2] It is estimated that about one-quarter of all adolescents engage in multiple problem behaviors, often with devastating consequences.[3]

While the exact demographic makeup of the highest risk groups is not known, data on separate risk behaviors indicate that there are more young males than females at high risk. When the different patterns of risk behavior are considered, however, it becomes clear that in some areas girls are at higher risk than their male classmates.

The health and well-being of young people are related to their ability to complete school.[4] It is obvious that girls who use drugs or liquor, suffer from depression, become pregnant, or give birth as teenagers cannot take full advantage of the educational programs presented them.

Substance Use

The initial use of harmful substances is occurring at younger ages than ever before. A recent survey showed that among the 1987 high school class, significant numbers of students first tried alcohol and drugs during elementary and middle school. Two out of three students using cigarettes began smoking before the ninth grade, and one out of four first used marijuana before the ninth grade. One out of twenty students who used cocaine used it before entering ninth grade.[5]

Differences between male and female patterns of reported drug use have declined over the past two decades to the point where researchers no longer consider the sex of an adolescent a good predictor of drug use.[6] One report states that "girls are more like boys in use of substances during adolescence than at any time later in life."[7] There are some sex differences in use patterns, however. Girls are more likely to use stimulants and over-the-counter weight-reduction pills, while boys are slightly more likely to report higher levels of illicit-drug use and episodes of binge drinking.[8] White high school students are more than twice as likely as black students to smoke cigarettes, and more white females are frequent smokers than students from any other sex/race group.[9]

Sexual Activity/Contraceptive Use

Initiation of sexual activity is also occurring at younger ages. Recent reports state that at least 28 percent of adolescents are sexually active by their fourteenth birthday; the average

age at the initiation of sexual activity for this group is 12.[10] A recent survey from the Alan Guttmacher Institute indicates that 38 percent of girls between the ages of fifteen and seventeen are sexually active—a 15 percent increase since 1973.[11] There has been a dramatic increase in the numbers of sexually active teenage girls who are white or from higher-income families, reducing previous racial and income differences.[12]

Contraceptive use for adolescents remains erratic, and age is a significant factor, with younger adolescents using contraception far less frequently. Reasons adolescents give for not using contraception include (1) inadequate knowledge (both boys and girls state that they are not at risk of becoming involved in a pregnancy if they have unprotected sex), (2) lack of access to birth control, and (3) not liking to plan to have sex.[13]

Before age fifteen, only 31 percent of sexually active girls report using contraceptives. By age fifteen, only 58 percent report contraceptive use; but by age nineteen, 91 percent report that they use contraceptives.[14] Meanwhile, there is some preliminary evidence that condom use is increasing; among seventeen- to nineteen-year-old males in metropolitan areas, reports of condom use at last intercourse more than doubled in the last decade—from 21 percent in 1979 to 58 percent in 1988.[15] Because of increased condom use, the proportion of teens using contraception at first intercourse rose from half to two-thirds between 1982 and 1988.[16] Unprotected sexual intercourse can result in too-early childbearing, discussed in detail earlier in this report. It can also result in sexually transmitted diseases (STDs).

Sexually Transmitted Diseases

Syphilis rates are equal for boys and girls, but more adolescent females than males contract gonorrhea.[17]

More than 1 million teens each year suffer from chlamydia infections, the most common STD among adolescents. Researchers speculate that teenage girls suffer high rates of STDs because the female reproductive system is particularly vulnerable during the early teen years.[18]

Nearly 715 teenagers age thirteen to nineteen have diagnosed cases of AIDS.[19] The number with HIV infection, which normally precedes AIDS, is much higher. The HIV infection rate for teenage girls is comparable to, and in some cases higher than, that for boys. While among adults, male AIDS cases are nine times more prevalent than female cases, the pattern of HIV infection among adolescents is very different. A 1989 study in the District of Columbia reports the HIV infection rate at 4.7 per 1,000 for girls, almost three times the 1.7 rate for boys.[20]

Other researchers who have been following the incidence of AIDS nationally state that teenage girls between thirteen and nineteen represent 24.9 percent of reported cases among females.[21] Women make up the fastest-growing group of persons with AIDS in the United States. The Centers for Disease Control (CDS) acknowledges that the number of reported cases is probably underestimated by 40 percent and the undercounting of women is probably more severe than for other groups because many of their symptoms are not listed in the CDC surveillance definition.[22]

Furthermore, there are differences in how AIDS is transmitted between men and women. Many more women (32.7 percent) than men (2.3 percent) become infected through a heterosexual contact; more women than men also contact AIDS through intravenous drug use.[23]

Body Image/Eating Disorders

Girls are much less satisfied with their bodies than are boys and report eating disorders at far higher rates. For example, more girls than boys report food bingeing and chronic dieting. They are also more likely to report vomiting to control their weight.[24] Severe cases of bulimia (binge eating followed by forced vomiting) and anorexia nervosa (the refusal to maintain an adequate body weight) can cause death.

Depression

An important longitudinal research study recently noted evidence of increasingly early onset and high prevalence of depression in late adolescence, with slightly more girls than boys scoring in the high range of depressive symptomology. One of the most striking findings of the study is that severely depressed girls had higher rates of substance abuse than did similarly depressed boys. Significant gender differences were found in school performance measures among the most depressed students. Grade point averages were lower for girls, and 40 percent more girls failed a grade than boys.[25]

Suicide

Adolescent girls are four to five times more likely than boys to attempt suicide (although boys are more likely to die because they choose more lethal methods, for example guns rather than sleeping pills).

A recent survey of eighth- and tenth-graders found girls are twice as likely as boys to report feeling sad and hopeless. This is consistent with clinical literature, which shows that females have higher rates of depression than males, both during adolescence and adulthood.[26]

Cohesive families, neighborhoods with adequate resources, caring adults, and quality schools all help protect teens.[27] But because the dangers they face result from a complex web of interactive social conditions and behaviors, there can be no single solution. For any program to succeed in reducing risks to teens, policymakers at every level must recognize that the needs and circumstances of girls and young women often differ from those of boys and young men.

The Functioning of Healthy Bodies

In spite of reports indicating strong public support for sex education in the schools and an increase in the number of sex-education programs offered, sex education is neither widespread nor comprehensive.[28] Few schools include sex education in the early grades, and most middle and junior high schools offer short programs of ten hours or less. It has been estimated that fewer than 10 percent of all students take comprehensive sex-education courses, i.e., courses of more than forty hours or courses designed as components within a K-12 developmental-health or sex-education program.[29]

For most teachers, knowledge of human sexuality is largely a matter of personal history rather than informed study.[30] Such knowledge is often based on traditional male-defined views of human sexuality, including unexamined gender-role-stereotyped beliefs about sexual behavior. Knowledge about sexual development is usually limited, regardless of whether the teacher is male or female.

The content of sex-education classes varies from locale to locale, in part because program planners must address local sensitivities.[31] One of the few carefully controlled field studies on sexuality- and contraceptive-education programs recently compared the impact of a special sex-education class on thirteen- to nineteen-year-old males and females.[32] The findings indicate that publicly funded sexuality- and contraceptive-education programs as brief as eight to twelve hours appear to help participants increase their knowledge, initiate effective contraceptive use, and improve the consistent use of effective contraceptive methods by both girls and boys.

The experimental intervention appears to have been most helpful for males with prior sexual experience, improving the consistency of their use of effective methods of contraception. Females without prior sexual experience seemed to respond better to traditional sex-education programs; researchers hypothesize that the girls may have been uncomfortable with the structured, interactive, and confrontational aspects of the experimental program. The study also found that prior experience with sex education was an important predictor of contraceptive efficiency, suggesting that formal sexuality education may be an incremental learning process whose efforts may not be evident on short-term follow-up.

The absence of adequate instruction and discussion about menstruation and contraception is only a piece of the problem. The alarming increases in STDs and HIV infection among adolescents, the increase in childbearing among young teens and the increase in eating disorders make the lack of comprehensive courses on sexuality, health, and the human body unacceptable. An understanding of one's body is central to an understanding of self. The association of sexuality and health instruction exclusively with danger and disease belies the human experience of the body as a source of pleasure, joy, and comfort. Schools must take a broader, more comprehensive approach to education about growth and sexuality. An awareness that relationships with others and the development of intimacy involve both the body and the mind should be critical components of these courses.

The Expression and Valuing of Feelings

By insisting [on a dichotomy] between feelings and emotions on the one hand and logic and rationality on the other, schools [shortchange] all students. Classrooms must become places where girls and boys can express feelings and discuss personal experiences. The lessons we learn best are those that answer our own questions. Students must have an opportunity to explore the world as they see it and pose problem that they consider important. From Sylvia Ashton Warner to AAUW teacher awardee Judy Logan, good teachers have always known this and have reflected it in their teaching.[33] The schools must find ways to facilitate these processes.

When this is done, issues that may not always be considered "appropriate" will undoubtedly arise. They should. Child abuse is a brutal fact of too many young lives. Children must have a "safe place" to acknowledge their pain and vulnerability and receive help and support. While girls and boys are more or less equally subjected to most forms of physical and emotional abuse, girls confront sexual abuse at four times the rate of boys.

We need to help all children, particularly girls, to know and believe that their bodies are their own to control and use as they feel appropriate—and not objects to be appropriated by others.[34] This, of course, is particularly difficult in a culture that uses the female body to advertise everything from toilet cleanser to truck tires and where the approved female roles remain service-oriented. The so-called "womanly" values of caring for and connecting with others are not ones that women wish to lose, but they are values that must be buttressed by a sense of self and a faith in one's own competence.

In July 1991, *Newsweek* ran a story titled "Girls Who Go Too Far," about the newly aggressive pursuit of boyfriends by some young teens.[35] The comments of the girls themselves illustrate their dilemma in having grown up to believe that a man is an essential part of every woman's life, that only male attention can give them a sense of themselves, and that the culturally accepted way to achieve a goal is to resort to aggressive, even violent, behavior.

Rather than highlighting aggressive behavior among girls, we must address the degree to which violence against women is an increasingly accepted aspect of our culture. School curricula must help girls to understand the extent to which their lives are constrained by fear of rape, the possibility of battering, and the availability of pornography. Boys must be helped to understand that violence damages both the victim and the perpetrator, and that violence against women is not in a somehow-more-acceptable category than other violent acts. The energies and passions so routinely expressed in violence toward others in our culture must be rechanneled and redirected if our society is to fulfill its promise.

A strong line of feminist research and thinking, including the work of Jane Rowan Martin, Jean Baker Miller, Carol Gilligan, Nel Noddings, and Mary Belenky and her colleagues, addresses the strengths girls and women can bring to communities through the sense of connection with and concern for others that is more often encouraged and "permitted" in their lives than it is in boys'.[36] Others, such as Alfie Kohn, have written extensively about the need for schools that can help students learn and grow as part of a "prosocial" community.[37] A democracy cannot survive without citizens capable of seeing beyond immediate self-interest to the needs of the larger group.

When asked to describe their ideal school, one group of young women responded:

> 'School would be fun. Our teachers would be excited and lively, not bored. They would act caring and take time to understand how students feel. . . . Boys would treat us with respect. . . . If they run by and grab your tits, they would get into trouble'.[38]

Care, concern, and respect—simple things, but obviously not the norm in many of our nation's classrooms. These young women are not naive. Their full statement recognizes the need to pay teachers well and includes a commitment to "learn by listening and consuming everything" as well as a discussion of parental roles.[39] What they envision is needed by their male classmates and their teachers as well; it is what we as a nation must provide.

Gender and Power

Data presented earlier in this report reveal the extent to which girls and boys are treated differently in school classrooms and corridors. These data themselves should be a topic of discussion. They indicate power differentials that are perhaps the most evaded of all topics in our schools. Students are all too aware of "gender politics." In a recent survey, students in Michigan were asked, "Are there any policies, practices, including the behavior of teachers in classrooms, that have the effect of treating students differently based on their sex?" One hundred percent of the middle school and 82 percent of the high school students responding said "yes."[40]

Gender politics is a subject that many in our schools may prefer to ignore, but if we do not begin to discuss more openly the ways in which ascribed power, whether on the basis of race, sex, class, sexual orientation, or religion, affects individual lives, we will not be truly preparing our students for citizenship in a democracy.

NOTES
The Formal Curriculum

1. We analyze these reports in Part One. None examines curriculum content in depth. Recently, however, the leaders of more than thirty-three national subject-matter groups met to form an organization devoted to putting curricular issues at the top of the education-reform agenda. This effort promises to call attention to the central position of curriculum in schooling. "Alliance Formed to Push Curriculum to Front of Reform Agenda," *Education Week*, September 4, 1991, p. 14.

2. M. Sadker, D. Sadker, and S. Steindam, "Gender Equity and Education Reform," *Educational Leadership* 46, no. 6 (1989):44–47. See also M. Tetreault and P. Schmuck, "Equity, Education Reform, and Gender," *Issues in Education* 3, no. 1 (198):45–67.

3. K. Bogart, *Solutions That Work: Identification and Elimination of Barriers to the Participation of Female and Minority Students in Academic Educational Programs*, 3 vols. and User's Manual (Washington, D.C.: National Education Association, forthcoming, 1992). The three ongoing national faculty-development programs that focus on creation of gender-fair curriculum in K-12 classes in humanities and social studies are the National Women's History Project, Windsor, CA; the Harvard Graduate School of Education, Summer Institutes on "American History: The Female Experience"; and the multidisciplinary National SEED Project (Seeking Educational Equity and Diversity) of the Wellesley College Center for Research on Women. The Educational Materials and Service Center of Edmonds, WA, and the GESA Program (Gender Expectations and Student Achievement) of the Graymill Foundation, Earlham, IA, offer equity training that bears indirectly on course content.

4. For general reviews of curriculum research, see P. Arlow and C. Froschl, "Textbook Analysis," in F. Howe, ed., *High School Feminist Studies* (Old Westbury, NY: The Feminist Press, 1976), pp. xi-xxviii; K. Scott and C. Schau, "Sex Equity and Sex Bias in Instructional Materials," and P. Blackwell and L. Russo, "Sex Equity Strategies in the Content Areas," in S. Klein, ed., *Handbook for Achieving Sex Equity Through Education* (Baltimore, MD: Johns Hopkins University Press, 1985), pp. 218–60; M. Hulme, "Mirror, Mirror on the Wall: Biased Reflections in Textbooks and Instructional Materials," in A. Carelli, ed., *Sex Equity in Education: Readings and Strategies* (Springfield, IL: Charles C. Thomas, 1988), pp. 187–208.

5. *Dick and Jane As Victims: Sex Stereotyping in Children's Readers* (Princeton, NJ: Women on Words and Images, 1975); *Help Wanted: Sexism in Career Education Materials* (Princeton, NJ: Women on Words and Images, 1976) and *Sexism in Foreign Language Texts* (Princeton, NJ: Women on Words and Images, 1976). See also L. Weitzman and D. Rizzo, *Biased Textbooks and Images of Males and Females in Elementary School Textbooks* (Washington, D.C.: Resource Center on Sex Roles in Education, 1976); G. Britton and M. Lumpkin, *A Consumer's Guide to Sex, Race, and Career Bias in Public School Textbooks* (Corvallis, OR: Britton Associates, 1977).

6. J. Trecker, "Women in U.S. History High School Textbooks," *Social Education* 35, no. 3 (1971):249–60, 338.

7. O. Davis et al. "A Review of U.S. History Textbooks," *The Education Digest* 52, no. 3 (November 1986):50–53; M. Hitchcock and G. Tompkins, "Basal Readers: Are They Still Sexist?" *The Reading Teacher* 41, no. 3 (December 1987):288–92; M. Tetreault, "Integrating Women's History: The Case of United States History High School Textbooks," *The History Teacher* 19 (February 1986):211–62; M. Tetreault, "The Journey from Male-Defined to Gender-Balanced Education," *Theory into Practice* 25, no. 4 (Autumn 1986):227–34; A. Nilsen, "Three Decades of Sexism in School Science Materials," *School Library Journal* 34, no. 1 (September 1987):117–22; E. Hall, "One Week for Women? The Structure of Inclusion of Gender Issues in Introductory Textbooks," *Teaching Sociology* 16, no. 4 (October 1988):431–42; P. Purcell and L. Stewart, "Dick and Jane in 1989," *Sex Roles* 22, nos. 3 and 4 (February 1990):177–85.

8. A. Applebee, *A Study of Book-Length Works Taught in High School English Courses* (Albany, NY: Center for the Learning and Teaching of Literature, State University of New York School of Education, 1989).

9. Ibid., p. 18.

10. P. Campbell and J. Wirtenberg, "How Books Influence Children: What the Research Shows," *Interracial Books for Children Bulletin* 11, no. 6 (1980):3–6.

11. At its highest level of support in 1980, the Office of Education spent only 2 percent of its budget on sex equity. Subsequently, however, the Reagan administration attempted unsuccessfully to reduce to "zero budget" the two largest programs supporting race and sex equity, the Title IV programs of the Civil

Rights Act and the Women's Educational Equity Act. The sense that race equity and sex equity programs figured in a federal agenda diminished. This disinvestment is reflected by the absence of sex, gender, and cultural awareness in most of the national reports of the late 1980s. See K. Levy, *What's Left of Federal Funding for Sex Equity in Education and Social Science Research?* (Tempe, AZ: Arizona State University Publications Office, 1985).

12. Initiatives have included classroom innovations by thousands of individual teachers, conferences, and summer institutes for teachers at the University of Arizona, University of New Hampshire, Dana Hall School, and Ohio State University. The National Coalition for Sex Equity in Education (NCSEE) developed an active network of equity professionals. Further efforts have also included the forming of women's caucuses in professional organizations; workshops and materials from the National Women's History Project; dissemination of syllabi and bibliographies; new journals including *Feminist Teacher*; special focus sections of journals, for example, *English Journal 77*, no. 6 (October 1988), 78, no. 6 (October 1989); inservice activities sponsored by local school boards and districts; and aid from ten federal Equity Assistance Centers. Despite decreased funding, the Women's Education Equity Act Program continues to fund projects and to support the dissemination of materials via the WEEA Publishing Center at the Educational Development Center in Newton, MA.

13. Scott and Schau, "Sex Equity and Sex Bias," p. 226. See also the discussion by B. Wright in "The Feminist Transformation of Foreign Language Teaching," in M. Burkhard and E. Waldstein, eds., *Women in German Yearbook 1* (Lanham, MD: University Press of America, 1985), pp. 95–97. Wright lists thirteen publishing houses that issued guidelines between 1972 and 1981 on avoiding or eliminating sex stereotypes. She discusses problems of noncompliance, as well as the limits of strategies for elimination of simple sex stereotyping in the face of larger problems such as overwhelmingly masculine and/or elite perspectives in texts as a whole.

14. M. Tetreault, "Integrating Women's History: The Case of U.S. History High School Textbooks," *The History Teacher* 19 (February 1986):211–62; "Women in the Curriculum," *Comment on Conferences and Research on Women* (February 1986):1–2; "Rethinking Women, Gender, and the Social Studies," *Social Education* 51 (March 1987):171–78.

15. Newsletter of the Special Interest Group on Gender and Social Justice, National Council for Social Studies, December 1990.

16. Surveys were taken in the Andrew W. Mellon, Geraldine Rockefeller Dodge, Kentucky and National SEED Project Seminars for College and School Teachers, sponsored by the Wellesley College Center for Research on Women. Twenty U.S. History textbooks were analyzed each year with regard to the representation of women as authors/editors and subjects in text and illustrations and the representation of domains of life outside of war, law, policy, government, and management of public affairs.

17. Homework assignments and study questions given in textbooks most frequently depend on the type of knowing which the authors of *Women's Ways of Knowing* identify as "separated," in which the mode is detached or distant from the subject. Girls and women, in a study of students in six schools and colleges, preferred a mode of knowing that the investigators named "connected," which involves empathetic identification with the subject. The investigators call for more "connected teaching," in which the capacity for identification is seen as an aspect of knowing and of learning about course content. M. Belenky et al. *Women's Ways of Knowing* (New York: Basic Books, 1986), pp. 100—30, 214–29.

18. See B. Wright, "What's in a Noun? A Feminist Perspective on Foreign Language Instruction," *Women's Studies Quarterly* 12, no. 3 (Fall 1984):2–6; B. Schmitz, "Guidelines for Reviewing Foreign Language Textbooks for Sex Bias," *Women's Studies Quarterly* 12, no. 3 (Fall 1984):7–9.

19. L. Pinkle, "Language Learning from a Feminist Perspective: Selected College-Level Grammar Textbooks," *Women's Studies Quarterly* 12, no. 3 (Fall 1984):10–13. Since 1985, *The Women in German Yearbook* (Lanham, MD: University Press of America) has published periodic reviews of research on instructional materials for German courses, including high school texts. The most recent review was published in the Spring 1991 issue: "Frauen/Unterricht: Feminist Reviews of Teaching Materials," L. French, K. Von Ankum, and M. Webster, eds.

20. Bogart, *Solutions That Work*, vol. 3, pp. 107–108.

21. E. Style, "Curriculum As Window and Mirror," in *Listening for All Voices: Gender Balancing the School Curriculum* (Summit, NJ: Oak Knoll School, 1988), pp. 6–12.

22. Surveys were taken in the Andrew W. Mellon, Geraldine Rockefeller Dodge, Kentucky, and National SEED Project Seminars for college and school teachers, sponsored by the Wellesley College Center for Research on Women.

23. G. Wilbur, "Gender-fair Curriculum," research report prepared for Wellesley College Center for Research on Women, August, 1991.

24. National Council of Teachers of Mathematics, *Curriculum and Evaluation Standards for School Mathematics* (Reston, VA: National Council of Teachers of Mathematics, 1989).

25. Ibid., p. 17.

26. F. Rutherford and A. Ahlgren, *Science for All Americans* (New York: Oxford University Press, 1989), pp. 204–14.

27. J. Banks, "Integrating the Curriculum with Ethnic Content: Approaches and Guidelines," in J. Banks and C. Banks, eds., *Multicultural Education: Issues and Perspectives* (Boston, MA: Allyn and Bacon, 1989), pp. 192–207.

28. P. McIntosh, *Interactive Phases of Curricular Re-Vision: A Feminist Perspective*, Working Paper No. 124 (Wellesley, MA: Wellesley College Center for Research on Women, 1983). For further typologies in phase theory, see M. Schuster and S. Van Dyne, eds., *Women's Place in the Academy: Transforming the Liberal Arts* (Totawa, NJ. Rowman and Allanheld, 1985); and M. Tetreault, "Feminist Phase Theory: An Experience-Derived Evaluation Model," *Journal of Higher Education* 56 (July-August 1985); and "Integrating Content about Women and Gender into the Curriculum," in Banks and Banks, eds., *Multicultural Education*, pp. 124–44. See also *Comment on Conferences and Research on Women* 15, no. 2, Claremont, CA (February 1986): 1–4.

29. E. Style, *Multicultural Education and Me: The Philosophy and the Process, Putting Product in Its Place* (Madison, WI: Teacher Corps Associates, University of Wisconsin, 1982), p. 11.

30. "Stages of Curriculum Transformation," in M. Schuster and S. Van Dyne, eds., *Women's Place in the Academy: Transforming the Liberal Arts Curriculum* (Totawa, NJ: Rowman & Allanheld Publishers, 1985), pp. 13–29; M. Tetreault, "Women in U.S. History—Beyond a Patriarchal Perspective," *Interracial Books for Children Bulletin* 11 (1980):F-10; McIntosh, *Interactive Phases of Curricular Re-Vision*. See also M. Belenky et al. *Women's Ways of Knowing* (New York: Basic Books, Inc., 1986); C. Gilligan, *In a Different Voice* (Cambridge, MA: Harvard University Press, 1982); E. Minnich, *Transforming Knowledge* (Philadelphia, PA: Temple University Press; 1990).

31. P. McIntosh, *Interactive Phases of Curricular and Personal Re-Vision With Regard to Race*, Working Paper No. 219 (Wellesley, MA: Wellesley College Center for Research on Women, 1990), p. 6.

32. Gilligan, *In a Different Voice*.

33. Bogart, *Solutions That Work*, vol. 1, pp. 97–98.

34. T. Kidder, *Among Schoolchildren* (New York: Avon Books, 1989), p. 27.

35. A. Applebee, *A Study of Book-Length Works*, p. 18. For an example of a product that came out of a school-based departmental discussion, see *New Voices for the English Classroom* C. Peter, ed. (Providence, RI: Lincoln School, 1986). For similar strategies, see E. Style, *Multicultural Education and Me*, and the school-based, teacher-led seminars established through the National SEED Project on Inclusive Curriculum, Wellesley College Center for Research on Women.

36. State of New York, Education Department, *One Nation, Many Peoples: A Declaration of Cultural Interdependence, The Report of the New York State Social Studies Review and Development Committee, June 1991*, pp. 18–126. See also memos of July 12 and 15 from Commissioner T. Sobol to the Board of Regents.

37. C. Nelson, "Gender and the Social Studies: Training Preservice Secondary Social Studies Teachers" (Ph.D. diss., University of Minnesota, 1990), pp. 8, 38–39.

38. J. Kerber, "'Opinionative Assurance': The Challenge of Women's History," address to the Organization of History Teachers, American Historical Association, New York, NY, 28 December 1990, p. 11.

The Classroom as Curriculum

1. See for example, J. Brophy and T. Good, *Teacher-Student Relationships: Causes and Consequences* (New York: Holt, Rinehart, and Winston, 1974); M. Jones, "Gender Bias in Classroom Interactions," *Contemporary Education* 60 (Summer 1989):216–22; M. Lockheed, *Final Report: A Study of Sex Equity in Classroom Interaction* (Washington, D.C.: National Institute of Education, 1984); M. Lockheed and A.

Harris, *Classroom Interaction and Opportunities for Cross-Sex Peer Learning in Science*, paper presented at the Annual Meeting of the American Educational Research Association, New York, April 1989; M. Sadker and D. Sadker, "Sexism in the Classroom: From Grade School to Graduate School," *Phi Delta Kappan* 68 (1986):512; R. Spaulding, *Achievement, Creativity and Self-Concept Correlates of Teacher-Pupil Transactions in Elementary School* Cooperative Research Project No. 1352 (Washington, D.C.: U.S. Department of Health Education and Welfare, 1963).

2. L. Serbin et al. "A Comparison of Teacher Responses to the Pre-Academic and Problem Behavior of Boys and Girls," *Child Development* 44 (1973):796–804; M. Ebbeck, "Equity for Boys and Girls: Some Important Issues," *Early Child Development and Care* 18 (1984):119–31.

3. D. Sadker, M. Sadker, and D. Thomas, "Sex Equity and Special Education," *The Pointer* 26 (1981):33–38.

4. D. Sadker and M. Sadker, "Is the OK Classroom OK?," *Phi Delta Kappan* 55 (1985):358–67.

5. J. Brophy, "Teacher Praise: A Functional Analysis," *Review of Educational Research* 51 (1981):5–32; A. Gardner, C. Mason, and M. Matyas, "Equity, Excellence and 'Just Plain Good Teaching!'" *The American Biology Teacher* 51 (1989):72–77.

6. M. Sadker and D. Sadker, *Year 3: Final Report, Promoting Effectiveness in Classroom Instruction* (Washington, D.C.: National Institute of Education, 1984).

7. D. Baker, "Sex Differences in Classroom Interactions in Secondary Science," *Journal of Classroom Interaction* 22 (1986):212–18; J. Becker, "Differential Treatment of Females and Males in Mathematics Classes," *Journal for Research in Mathematics Education* 12 (1981):40–53; L. Berk and N. Lewis, "Sex Role and Social Behavior in Four School Environments," *Elementary School Journal* 3 (1977):205–21; L. Morse and H. Handley, "Listening to Adolescents: Gender Differences in Science Classroom Interaction," in *Gender Influences in Classroom Interaction*, L. Wilkerson and C. Marrett, eds., (Orlando, FL: Academic Press, 1985), pp. 37–56.

8. M. Seligman and S. Maier, "Failure to Escape Traumatic Shock," *Journal of Experimental Psychology* 74 (1967):1–9.

9. C. Dweck and N. Repucci, "Learned Helplessness and Reinforcement Responsibility in Children," *Journal of Personality and Social Psychology* 25 (1973):109–16; C. Dweck and T. Goetz, "Attributions and Learned Helplessness," in *New Directions in Attributions Research*, J. Harvey, W. Ickes, and R. Kidd, eds. (Hillsdale, NJ: Erlbaum, 1978).

10. See for example, K. Deaux, "Sex; A Perspective on the Attribution Process," in *New Directions in Attribution Research*; C. Dweck and E. Bush, "Sex Differences in Learned Helplessness: I. Differential Debilitation with Peer and Adult Evaluators," *Developmental Psychology* 12 (1976):147–56; C. Dweck, T. Goetz, and N. Strauss, "Sex Differences in Learned Helplessness: IV. An Experimental and Naturalistic Study of Failure Generalization and Its Mediators," *Journal of Personality and Social Psychology* 38 (1980):441–52; L. Reyes, *Mathematics Classroom Processes*, paper presented at the Fifth International Congress on Mathematical Education, Adelaide, Australia, August 1984; P. Wolleat et al. "Sex Differences in High School Students' Causal Attributions of Performance in Mathematics," *Journal for Research in Mathematics Education* 11 (1980):356–66; D. Phillips, "The Illusion of Incompetence among Academically Competent Children," *Child Development* 55 (1984): 2000–16; E. Fennema et al. "Teachers' Attributions and Belief about Girls, Boys, and Mathematics," *Educational Studies in Mathematics* 21 (1990):55–69.

11. E. Maccoby and C. Jacklin, *The Psychology of Sex Differences* (Stanford, CA: Stanford University Press, 1974); E. Lenney, "Women's Self-Confidence in Achievement Settings," *Psychological Bulletin* 84 (1977):1–13; J. Parsons and D. Ruble, "The Development of Achievement-Related Expectancies," *Child Development* 48 (1977):1075–79; Dweck, Goetz, and Strauss, "Sex Differences in Learned Helplessness IV"; J. Goetz, "Children's Sex Role Knowledge and Behavior. An Ethnographic Study of First Graders in the Rural South," *Theory and Research in Social Education* 8 (1981):31–54.

12. W. Shepard and D. Hess, "Attitudes in Four Age Groups Toward Sex Role Division in Adult Occupations and Activities," *Journal of Vocational Behavior* 6 (1975):27–39; C. Dweck and E. Elliot, "Achievement Motivation," in *Handbook of Child Psychology*, vol. 4, P. Mussen and E. Hetherington, eds. (New York: Wiley, 1983); R. Felson, "The Effect of Self-Appraisals of Ability on Academic Performance," *Journal of Personality and Social Psychology* 47 (1984):944–52; M. Stewart and C. Corbin, "Feedback Dependence among Low Confidence Preadolescent Boys and Girls," *Research Quarterly for Exercise and Sport* 59 (1988):160–64.

13. J. Eccles-Parsons et al. "Sex Differences in Attributions and Learned Helplessness," *Sex Roles* 8 (1982):421–32; J. Eccles-Parsons, C. Kaczala, and J. Meece, "Socialization of Achievement Attitudes

and Beliefs: Classroom Influences," *Child Development* 53 (1982):322–39; J. Eccles, "Expectancies, Values and Academic Behaviors," in *Achievement and Achievement Motives*, J. Spence, ed. (San Francisco, CA: W.H. Freeman and Co., 1983); J. Eccles, *Understanding Motivation: Achievement Beliefs, Gender-Roles and Changing Educational Environments*, address before American Psychological Association, New York, 1987.

14. B. Licht, S. Stader, and C. Swenson, "Children's Achievement Related Beliefs: Effects of Academic Area, Sex, and Achievement Level," *Journal of Educational Research* 82 (1989):253–60.

15. J. Kahle, "Why Girls Don't Know," in *What Research Says to the Science Teacher—the Process of Knowing*, M. Rowe, ed. (Washington; DC: National Science Testing Association, 1990), pp. 55–67; V. Lee, "Sexism in Single-Sex and Co-educational Secondary School Classrooms," paper presented at the annual meeting of the American Sociological Association, Cincinnati, OH, August 8, 1991.

16. J. Eccles, "Bringing Young Women to Math and Science," in *Gender and Thought: Psychological Perspectives*, M. Crawford and M. Gentry, eds. (New York: Springer-Verlag, 1989), pp. 36–58; Licht et al., "Children's Achievement Related Beliefs."

17. Sadker and Sadker, *Year 3*; L. Grant, "Race-Gender Status, Classroom Interaction and Children's Socialization in Elementary School," in *Gender Influences in Classroom Interaction*, L. Wilkinson and C. Marrett, eds. (Orlando, FL: Academic Press, 1985), pp. 57–75.

18. Grant, "Race-Gender Status," p. 66.

19. C. Cornbleth and W. Korth, "Teacher Perceptions and Teacher-Student Interaction in Integrated Classrooms," *Journal of Experimental Education* 48 (Summer 1980):259–63; B. Hare, *Black Girls: A Comparative Analysis of Self-Perception and Achievement by Race, Sex and Socioeconomic Background*, Report No. 271 (Baltimore, MD: John Hopkins University, Center for Social Organization of Schools, [1979]).

20. S. Damico and E. Scott, "Behavior Differences Between Black and White Females in Desegregated Schools," *Equity and Excellence* 23 (1987):63–66; Grant, "Race-Gender Status." See also J. Irvine, "Teacher-Student Interactions: Effects of Student Race, Sex, and Grade Level," *Journal of Educational Psychology* 78 (1986):14–21.

21. Damico and Scott, "Behavior Differences"; Hare, "Black Girls: A Comparative Analysis."

22. Damico and Scott, "Behavior Differences;" L. Grant, "Black Females 'Place' in Integrated Classrooms," *Sociology of Education* 57 (1984):98–111.

23. Damico and Scott, "Behavior Differences."

24. D. Scott-Jones and M. Clark, "The School Experience of Black Girls: The Interaction of Gender, Race and Socioeconomic Status," *Phi Delta Kappan* 67 (March 1986):20–526.

25. V. Washington and J. Newman, "Setting Our Own Agenda: Exploring the Meaning of Gender Disparities Among Blacks in Higher Education," *Journal of Negro Education* 60 (1991):19–35.

26. E. Fennema and P. Peterson, "Effective Teaching for Girls and Boys: The Same or Different?" in *Talks to Teachers*, D. Berliner and B. Rosenshine, eds. (New York: Random House, 1987), pp. 111–25; J. Stallings, "School Classroom and Home Influences on Women's Decisions to Enroll in Advanced Mathematics Courses," in *Women and Mathematics: Balancing the Equation*, S. Chipman, L. Brush, and D. Wilson, eds. (Hillsdale, NJ: Erlbaum, 1985), pp. 199–224; S. Greenberg, "Educational Equity in Early Education Environments," in *Handbook for Achieving Sex Equity Through Education*, S. Klein, ed. (Baltimore, MD: John Hopkins University Press, 1985), pp. 457–69.

27. D. Baker, "Sex Differences in Classroom Interactions in Secondary Science," *Journal of Classroom Interaction* 22 (1986):212–18.

28. D. Jorde and A. Lea, "The Primary Science Project in Norway," in *Proceedings of Growth GSAT Conference*, J. Kahle, J. Daniels, and J. Harding, eds. (West Lafayette, IN: Purdue University, 1987), pp. 66–72.

29. P. Flores, "How Dick and Jane Perform Differently in Geometry: Test Results on Reasoning, Visualization and Affective Factors," paper presented at American Educational Research Association Meeting, Boston, MA, April 1990.

30. J. Kahle, *Factors Affecting the Retention of Girls in Science Courses, and Careers: Case Studies of Selected Secondary Schools* (Reston, VA: The National Association of Biology Teachers, October 1983).

31. Eccles, "Bringing Young Women to Math and Science."

32. M. Belenky et al. *Women's Ways of Knowing—The Development of Self, Body, and Mind* (New York: Basic Books, Inc., 1986).

33. G. Engelhard and J. Monsaas, "Academic Performance, Gender and the Cooperative Attitudes of Third, Fifth and Seventh Graders," *Journal of Research and Development in Education* 22 (1989):13–17.

34. A. Ahlgren and D. Johnson, "Sex Differences in Cooperative and Competitive Attitudes from 2nd Through the 12th Grades," *Development Psychology* 15 (1979):45–49; B. Herndon and M. Carpenter, "Sex Differences in Cooperative and Competitive Attitudes in a Northeastern School," *Psychological Reports* 50 (1982):768–70; L. Owens and R. Straton, "The Development of Co-operative Competitive and Individualized Learning Preference Scale for Students," *Journal of Educational Psychology* 50 (1980):147–61.

35. S. Sharon et al. eds., *Cooperation in Education* (Provo, UT: Brigham Young University Press, 1980); S. Bossert, *Task Structure and Social Relationships* (Cambridge, MA: Harvard University Press, 1979); W. Shrum, N. Cheek, and S. Hunter, "Friendship in the School: Gender and Racial Homophily," *Sociology of Education* 61 (1988):227–39.

36. E. Aronson, *The Jigsaw Classroom* (Beverly Hills, CA: Sage, 1978); D. DeVries and K. Edwards, "Student Teams and Learning Games: Their Effects on Cross-Race and Cross-Sex Interaction," *Journal of Educational Psychology* 66 (1974):741–49; P. Okebukola, "Cooperative Learning and Students' Attitude to Laboratory Work," *Social Science and Mathematics* 86 (1986):582–90; R. Slavin, "How Student Learning Teams Can Integrate the Desegregated Classroom," *Integrated Education* 15 (1977):56–58.

37. N. Blaney et al. "Interdependence in the Classroom: A Field Study," *Journal of Educational Psychology* 69 (1977):121–28; D. Devries and K. Edwards, "Student Teams and Learning Games: Their Effects on Cross-Race and Cross-Sex Interaction," *Journal of Educational Psychology* 66 (1974):741–49; Sharon et al., *Cooperation in Education*; R. Slavin, "Cooperative Learning," *Review of Educational Research* 50 (1980):315–42; R. Slavin, "Cooperative Learning and Desegregation," in W. Hawley, ed., *Effective School Desegregation* (Berkeley, CA: Sage, 1981); R. Weigle, P. Wiser, and S. Cook, "The Impact of Cooperative Learning Experiences on Cross-Ethnic Relations and Attitude," *Journal of Social Issues* 3 (1975):219–44.

38. M. Hallinan, *The Evolution of Children's Friendship Cliques* (ERIC Document Reproduction Service no. ED 161556, 1977); R. Best, *We've All Got Scars: What Boys and Girls Learn in Elementary School* (Bloomington, IN: University Press, 1983); J. Eccles-Parsons, "Sex Differences in Mathematics Participation," in M. Steinkamp and M. Maehr, eds., *Women in Science* (Greenwich, CT: JAI Press, 1984); M. Hallinan and N. Tumma, "Classroom Effects on Change in Children," *Sociology of Education* 51 (1978):170–282.

39. M. Lockheed, K. Finklestein, and A. Harris, *Curriculum and Research for Equity: Model Data Package* (Princeton, NJ: Educational Testing Service, 1979).

40. B. Eakins and R. Eakins, "Sex Roles, Interruptions, and Silences in Conversation," in B. Thorne and N. Henley, eds., *Sex Differences in Human Communication* (Boston, MA: Houghton Mifflin, 1978); N. Henley and B. Thorne, "Women Speak and Men Speak: Sex Differences and Sexism in Communications, Verbal and Nonverbal," in A. Sargent, ed., *Beyond Sex Roles* (St. Paul, MN: West Publishing Company, 1977); R. Lakoff, *Languages and Women's Place* (New York: Harper Colophone Books, 1976); D. Tannen, *You Just Don't Understand: Women and Men in Conversation* (New York: William Morrow, 1990).

41. L. Wilkinson, J. Lindow, and C. Chiang, "Sex Differences and Sex Segregation in Students' Small-Group Communication," in L. Wilkinson and C. Marret, eds., *Gender Influences in Classroom Interaction* (Orlando, FL: Academic Press, 1985), pp. 185–207.

42. J. Berger, T. Conner, and M. Fisek, eds., *Expectation States Theory: A Theoretical Research Program* (Cambridge, MA: Winthrop, 1974); M. Lockheed and A. Harris, "Cross-Sex Collaborative Learning in Elementary Classrooms," *American Educational Research Journal,* 21 (1984):275–94.

43. Lockheed and Harris, "Cross-Sex Collaborative Learning."

44. C. Weisfeld et al. "The Spelling Bee: A Naturalistic Study of Female Inhibitions in Mixed-Sex Competitions," *Adolescence* 18 (1983):695–708.

45. For example, M. Lockheed and A. Harris, "Classroom Interaction and Opportunity for Cross-Sex Peer Learning in Science," *Journal of Early Adolescence* (1982):135–43.

46. S. Strauss, "Sexual Harassment in the School; Legal Implications for Principals," *National Association of Secondary School Principles Bulletin* (1988):93–97; N. Stein, "Survey on Sexual Harassment," *Vocational Options in Creating Equity,* VI (Boston, MA: Department of Education, 1990), p. 1.

47. D. Grayson, "Emerging Equity Issues Related to Homosexuality," *Peabody Journal of Education* 64 (1989):132–45.

The Evaded Curriculum

1. R. Jessor, "Risk Behavior in Adolescence: A Psychosocial Framework for Understanding and Action," paper prepared for Cornell University Medical College Conference "Adolescents at Risk: Medical and Social Perspectives," Cornell University, February 1991; J. Dryfoos, *Youth at Risk: Prevalence and Prevention* (Oxford: Oxford University Press, 1990).

2. *Preventing Adolescent Pregnancy: What Schools Can Do* (Washington, D.C.: Children's Defense Fund, 1986).

3. Dryfoos, *Youth at Risk*, p. 107.

4. J. Earle and V. Roach, "Female Dropouts: A New Perspective," in *Women's Educational Equity Act Publishing Center Digest* (Newton, MA: Education Development Center, 1988); M. Fine, *Framing Dropouts* (Albany, NY: State University of New York Press, 1991).

5. J. Gans and D. Blyth, *America's Adolescents: How Healthy Are They?* (Chicago, IL: American Medical Association, 1990), p. 28.

6. H. Adger, "Problems of Alcohol and Other Drug Use and Abuse in Adolescence," paper prepared for Cornell University Medical College Conference "Adolescents at Risk: Medical and Social Perspectives," Cornell University, February 1991.

7. *Facts and Reflections on Girls and Substance Use* (New York: Girls Clubs of America, Inc., 1988), p. 9.

8. Adger, "Problems of Alcohol."

9. U.S. Centers for Disease Control, Youth Risk Behavior Survey, quoted in Ellen Flax, "White Students Twice as Likely as Blacks to Smoke, Study Finds," *Education Week* 11 (September 1991):10.

10. D. Scott-Jones and A. White, "Correlates of Sexual Activity in Early Adolescence," *Journal of Early Adolescence* 10 (May 1990):221–38; Dryfoos, *Youth at Risk*, chart p. 67.

11. D. Forrest and S. Singh, "The Sexual and Reproductive Behavior of American Women," *Family Planning Perspectives* 22 (1990):208, Table 4.

12. C. Irwin and M. Shafer, "Adolescent Sexuality: The Problem of a Negative Outcome of a Normative Behavior," paper prepared for the Cornell University Medical College Conference "Adolescents at Risk: Medical and Social Perspectives," Cornell University, February 1991.

13. M. Sullivan, *The Male Role in Teenage Pregnancy and Parenting: New Directions for Public Policy* (New York: Vera Institute of Justice, 1990), p. 21.

14. Irwin and Shafer, "Adolescent Sexuality."

15. Children's Defense Fund, unpublished paper, Washington, D.C., 1991.

16. K. Moore, *Facts at a Glance* (Washington, D.C.: Child Trends, 1988). See also K. Moore, "Trends in Teenage Childbearing in the U.S.: 1970–1988" (Los Alamitos, CA: TEC Networks, March 1991).

17. Irwin and Shafer, "Adolescent Sexuality."

18. Ibid.

19. Quoted over the phone by the National AIDS Clearing House from U.S. Centers for Disease Control, *U.S. AIDS Cases Reported in July 1991*, 1991.

20. L. D'Angelo et al. "HIV Infection in Adolescents: Can We Predict Who Is at Risk?" poster presentation at the Fifth International Conference on AIDS, June 1989.

21. M. Wolfe, "Women and HIV/AIDS Education," paper prepared for the NEA Health Information Network, Atlanta, 1991.

22. Ibid.

23. Ibid.

24. *The State of Adolescent Health in Minnesota*, Minnesota Youth Health Survey (Minneapolis: Adolescent Health Database Project, February 1989).

25. H. Reinherz, A. Frost, and B. Pakiz, *Changing Faces: Correlates of Depressive Symptoms in Late Adolescence* (Boston: Simmons College School of Social Work, 1990).

26. Gans and Blyth, *America's Adolescents*, p. 11.

27. D. Hawkins, "Risk Focussed Prevention," speech to the Coordinating Council on Juvenile Justice and Delinquency Prevention, 1990; Jessor, "Risk Behavior"; J. Gibbs, *Not Schools Alone* (Sacramento, CA: California Department of Education, 1990); E. Werner, "Vulnerability and Resiliency: The Children of Kauai," paper presented at a conference on Vulnerability and Resiliency in Children and Families, Baltimore, March 1991.

28. U.S. National Research Council, Panel on Adolescent Pregnancy and Childbearing, C. Hayes, ed., *Risking the Future: Adolescent Sexuality, Pregnancy, and Childbearing* (Washington, D.C.: National Academy, 1987).

29. Hayes, *Risking the Future*; D. Kirby, *Sexuality Education: An Evaluation of Programs and Their Effects* (Santa Cruz: Network Publications, 1984); J. Leo, "Sex and Schools," *Time* (November 1986):54–60.

30. M. Stubbs, *Sex Education and Sex Stereotypes: Theory and Practice*, Working Paper No. 198 (Wellesley, MA: Wellesley College Center for Research on Women, ERIC Document Service No. 306–655, 1989), p. 7.

31. Ibid., p. 8; M. Rotheram-Borus et al. "Reducing HIV Sexual Risk Behaviors among Runaway Adolescents," *Journal of the American Medical Association* 266 (4 September 1991): 1237–41.

32. M. Eisen, G. Zellman, and A. McAlister, "Evaluating the Impact of a Theory-Based Sexuality and Contraceptive Education Program," *Family Planning Perspectives* 22 (November/December 1990):261–71; M. Rotheram-Borus et al. "Reducing HIV Sexual Risk Behaviors."

33. S. Ashton-Warner, *Teacher* (New York: Simon and Schuster, 1963); J. Logan, *Teaching Stories*, paper presented at the American Association of University Women Fellowship, Washington, D.C., 1991.

34. For some disabled girls and women, issues surrounding control and ownership of their own bodies are particularly problematic. For a full discussion of many of these issues see M. Fine and A. Asch, eds., *Women with Disabilities: Essays In Psychology, Culture, and Politics* (Philadelphia, PA: Temple University Press, 1988).

35. Emily Yoffe; "Girls Who Go Too Far," *Newsweek*, 22 July 1991, pp. 58–59.

36. J. Martin, *Reclaiming a Conversation: The Ideal of the Educated Woman* (New Haven, CT: Yale University Press, 1985); J. Miller, *Toward a New Psychology of Women* (Boston, MA: Beacon Press, 1976); C. Gilligan, N. Lyons, and T. Hammer, eds., *Making Connections: The Relational Worlds of Adolescent Girls at the Emma Willard School* (Troy, NY: Emma Willard School, 1989); C. Gilligan et al., eds., *Mapping the Moral Domain: A Contribution of Women's Thinking to Psychological Theory and Education* (Cambridge, MA: Harvard University Press, 1988); N. Noddings and P. Shore, *Awakening the Inner Eye: Intuition in Education* (New York: Teachers College Press, 1984); N. Noddings, *Caring: A Feminine Approach to Ethics and Moral Education* (Berkeley, CA: University of California Press, 1984); C. Witherell and N. Noddings, *Stories Lives Tell: Narrative and Dialogue in Education* (New York: Teachers College Press, 1991); M. Belenkey et al., *Women's Ways of Knowing: The Development of Self, Voice, and Mind* (New York: Basic Books, 1986); see also P. Elbow, *Writing without Teachers* (London: Oxford University Press, 1973).

37. A. Kohn, "Caring Kids: The Role of the School," *Phi Delta Kappan* 72 (March 1991):496–506; A. Kohn, "Responding to Others: The Child Development Project," *The Brighter Side of Human Nature* (New York: Basic Books, 1990).

38. As quoted in *In Their Own Voices: Young Women Talk about Dropping Out*, Project on Equal Education Rights (New York: National Organization for Women Legal Defense and Education Fund, 1988), p. 12.

39. Ibid.

40. State of Michigan, Department of Education, Office of Sex Equity in Education, "The Influence of Gender Role Socialization on Student Perceptions," June 1990.

20

HIV/AIDS Education: Toward a Collaborative Curriculum

Jonathan Silin

AIDS radically calls into question the pleasures and dangers of teaching.

—Cindy Patton, *Inventing AIDS*

AIDS MAKES NO SENSE. However, the continuing proliferation of HIV/AIDS curricula speaks to our very real desire to claim epistemological rationality and epidemiological certainty in a world plagued by a new and as yet incurable disease. In defining HIV/AIDS as a biomedical event that can be addressed only by those trained in science and health education, we attempt to make it safe, contained within a specific discipline, so that it will not contaminate other areas of study. When the topic of HIV/AIDS is sanitized, teachers and students are protected from the truly unhealthy aspects of society that might otherwise be revealed; the status quo is ensured.

But diseases are constituted through dynamic interactions of biomedical, economic, psychosocial, and political factors. The existential realities of otherness, the politics of distancing, and our search for certainty suggest key elements in the social construction of HIV/AIDS. Understanding the meanings of a given illness involves far more than simply identifying a causal agent and a medical remedy. Just as efforts at prevention cannot be limited to the presentation of risk-reduction strategies, in the hope that exposure to a few facts and rehearsal of skills will lead to lasting changes in behavior, so coming to terms with the social ramifications of HIV/AIDS cannot be achieved through a limited focus on scientific knowledge. Effective prevention involves individual struggles with the meaning of sex and drugs, and a successful societal response calls for recognition of the multiple factors shaping the disease process.

HIV/AIDS presents a complex set of challenges for the curriculum maker. At first, school administrators perceived HIV/AIDS primarily as a policy problem requiring the attention of legal and public health experts to assess the feasibility of excluding students and staff with HIV. But as the crisis over the presence of people with HIV/AIDS in the schools abated, and awareness that HIV/AIDS was not confined to marginal risk groups grew, educators turned toward their pedagogical function. The process was hastened as more and more states mandated K–12 AIDS education.

Early curricular materials reflected simplified interpretations of the disease; they focused on prevention for adolescents and claimed to offer only "facts." But the assertion of objectivity is in itself a form of bias, carrying the implication that it is possible to separate fact from value, object from subject, the word from the world. It is this mindset that was exemplified by a New York City public school official who, in response to a film made to be shown in the city high schools, remarked, "There was a segment that was too long, simply to the effect that you should be nice to homosexuals. The attitude was not a problem, but this is not an attitude film. This is supposed to be an *educational* film" (*CDC AIDS Weekly*, 1986, p. 9). In the scene referred to, a heterosexual man recounts his first reactions to learning that his brother is gay and has AIDS.

If we acknowledge that attitudes and values play a role in shaping individual behaviors and the allocation of material resources in society, it is hard to understand how exclusion of these very factors can lead to a serious discussion of the problem at hand. The denial of subjectivity within the curriculum only falsifies experience and alienates students from their own possibilities. This is not to say that subjectively held opinions must be accepted uncritically but rather that they can become the text for examining the social determination of "private" ideas. Students can learn to question the sources of their knowledge and its reliability and to identify alternative reference points. HIV/AIDS provides an opportunity to practice the critical thinking skills valued so highly by educators today. It is an issue that most graphically illustrates the paradoxes and contradictions of our society.

In this chapter I seek to understand the fundamental inadequacies of our past efforts to talk with children about HIV/AIDS and to create new possibilities for such dialogues. Beginning with younger children and moving on to adolescents, I draw on my work with teachers, administrators, children, and parents in many public and private schools across New York State. These schools were located in a diverse cross-section of racial, ethnic, religious, and economic communities and reflected very different commitments to HIV/AIDS education.

LISTENING TO YOUNG CHILDREN

As an early childhood educator, I was trained to listen to and observe young children. Raised and educated in a Deweyan tradition, I understand curriculum as a negotiated process, an outgrowth of the interests of the child and the community. While teachers come to the classroom with an agenda based on knowledge of the community, their art rests in helping children move outward from more narrowly based concerns toward the world of larger ideas. At its best, education enables children to see the way that the concepts and skills offered by their teachers, and eventually encoded in the formal disciplines, amplify their powers of understanding and control. The role of teachers is to help their students make sense of the world. Imposing predetermined, formal curriculum on children without reference to their lived experience can leave them alienated from the possibilities of school-based learning.

When I was a doctoral student, encounters with Marxist and critical theorists made me conscious of the manner in which schooling functions to maintain and reproduce unequal distributions of economic and cultural capital (Apple, 1979; Bowles & Gintis, 1976). Recognizing that the most mundane classroom activities, such as recess, might be described as moments of ideological hegemony, I also began to think about the internal contradictions within any system that allow for reflection and transformation. But it is the phenomenologically oriented educationists (Barritt, Beekman, Bleeker, & Mulderij, 1985; van Manen, 1990) who are most mindful of the limitations of scientistically imposed frames of reference and of the need to ground our work in the world of childhood. They urge us to return to the children themselves to uncover what it is that seems to matter, to grasp how they make sense of experience. To accept such a challenge is to abandon the safety of science that allows us to know children from the privileged position of distanced adults. It is to risk the uncertainty of an engagement that threatens the boundaries between knower and known.

When called on to assist schools with curriculum formulation, I began by asking teachers what the children were saying about AIDS. This obviously reflected my commitment as a progressive educator as well as my experiences learning from people with HIV infection. The teachers' responses clearly indicated that HIV/AIDS had entered their classrooms through the voices of their students, regardless of age or formal instruction. Ironically, many of these opportunities occurred in elementary classrooms—that is, precisely those classrooms in which the prospect of HIV/AIDS education seemed most daunting. Sometimes these voices had been heard at unexpected moments, sometimes on more predictable occasions. Almost always, teachers had felt unprepared to take advantage of the moment to begin a dialogue that could lead to more structured learning.

Interestingly, teachers often had to work hard even to remember these incidents. Emblematic of this forgetfulness were the responses of teachers in a seminar I conducted in a semirural community on eastern Long Island. My inquiry as to what they had observed about their students' knowledge of HIV/AIDS was greeted with a painfully long silence. I began to wonder if I had arrived in the only area in New York State that had not been touched by the disease. Then a first-grade teacher tentatively raised her hand. She described the pandemonium that had broken out in her classroom that very morning when the principal announced, over the school intercom, that AIDS would be the subject of the afternoon staff meeting. Children started accusing each other of having AIDS and warning the teacher not to attend the meeting for fear she might contract HIV from the guest speaker. Given permission by the principal's announcement, the children had released their suppressed concerns. And then a third-grade teacher confirmed that for the past several months AIDS had been the reigning epithet on the playground during recess. It was the label of choice when a group of children wanted to ostracize someone. Games of tag were predicated on avoiding a child who was supposedly HIV-infected.

To these children the mere mention of AIDS provoked excited responses. Whether motivated by specific fears and anxieties, or simply the emotional resonance of the word in our culture, their behaviors accurately mimicked the responses of the majority of adults. To know in more detail what AIDS means to children would require the kind of probing by teachers that leads to a negotiated curriculum, a curriculum in which dialogue is respected and teachers learn with and from their students. For the moment, however, it should be noted that isolation and fear of contagion are being played out without interruption. Educators must recognize their complicity in discrimination by permitting children to use HIV/AIDS, if only in their games, as a means to exclude someone from the social arena. Like gender, race, ethnicity, and disability, HIV/AIDS is an issue of equity.

But children also reveal their awareness of HIV/AIDS in moments that are less incendiary and more focused. In an urban setting, for example, a teacher reported her consternation on a recent class trip upon hearing one child anxiously admonish a friend not to sit down in the subway for fear of contracting AIDS from the seat. The teacher admitted that it was only her concern for the children's safety in the moving train that prompted her to contradict this advice, which had been delivered in the most serious tone. A colleague at the same meeting described overhearing one little boy warning another not to pick up a stick in the park. The warning was based on the child's knowledge that people who use drugs frequented the area at night and his belief that they are the source of HIV infection.

There are few formal studies of young children's knowledge. Farquhar (1990b) documents the practical difficulties in conducting research when we would prefer to protect children than provoke their curiosity. Although Schvaneveldt, Lindauer, and Young (1990) indicate that preschool children know very little about HIV/AIDS, this should not be taken as an indication that they know nothing at all or that AIDS education is irrelevant to their lives. As the anecdotes reported here suggest, HIV/AIDS can be a specter that haunts their movement in the world. For young children, and for many adults as well, fear needs to be replaced by understanding, misinformation by facts. HIV is part of daily life and should be treated as such in schools. To be meaningful, HIV/AIDS information should not be delayed till fourth-grade science curriculum or sixth-grade health class, where it may seem too abstract, removed from students' lived experience. Containing HIV/AIDS within the confines of the highly rational curriculum may offer adults a sense of protection but only at the price of placing their students at increased risk. If we avoid engaging with children about HIV/AIDS, even to counter false information about transmission, we foster the belief that HIV/AIDS is a mystery, a taboo subject that teachers cannot or will not address.

What teachers think about childhood also influences how or even if they will approach HIV/AIDS with their students. For some, children inhabit a very different world from adults. Despite what they may be exposed to at home, on the street, or in the media, they require educational settings where the flow of information is carefully controlled. In contrast, others suggest that what happens to children outside of school should become the object of classroom study. The school is a safe place to make sense of complex and confusing realities. Teachers who believe in this approach are more likely to provide opportunities for critical social issues to become part of the curriculum. For example, I observed a teacher of 6- and 7-year-olds open a class meeting with the simple questions, "What do people use drugs for?" Information and misinformation poured forth from the children. They debated the ethical implications of the use of steroids by Olympic athletes (a subject very much in the news at the time), tried to understand how people actually snort cocaine (believing that it is placed on the outside of the nose), and struggled with why people do things to themselves that they know are harmful. The children saw drugs, rather than infected blood, as the source of HIV infection, and they clearly equated AIDS with death. They proved themselves to be curious, knowledgeable, and capable of thoughtful reflection. Their mistakes were surprisingly rational, the questions they raised worthy of any adult's attention.

In other classrooms the subject of HIV/AIDS may come up in a more oblique manner. A second-grade teacher reported, for example, that her AIDS curriculum began with the failure of two baby rabbits to thrive. Sitting near the cage with a small group of concerned children, one girl began to wonder out loud if perhaps they might have AIDS. The teacher told the children that, while she did not know very much about HIV/AIDS, she did not think it was a disease of animals. Picking up on their concern, the teacher sought more information from the health teacher, whom she also recruited to talk directly with the children. In the kindergarten classroom down the hall, the children had built a block city with a large hospital at its center. In questioning them one day about the ambulance speeding toward its entrance, the teacher was informed that it was carrying a person with AIDS who was very, very sick and going to die. For her, this was the moment to explore what the children really knew about AIDS, part of a larger commitment to understand her students and to bring greater definition to their worlds.

Farquhar (1990b), observing 8- and 10-year-olds, confirms that children's HIV/AIDS knowledge is variable in the extreme. Researchers using developmental frameworks suggest that knowledge is primarily age-dependent. However, Farquhar offers two insights that broaden our appreciation of children's social learning. First, students' emergent understanding of HIV/AIDS is closely associated with knowledge of related topics like sexual behavior or drug use. For example, an 8-year-old's belief that you could "catch AIDS . . . when you go to bed in the same bed" is not surprising given that the child describes "sex" as going to bed with somebody. Similarly, the statement by another child that "smoking causes AIDS" should be understood in the context of her knowledge that cigarettes contain nicotine, nicotine is a drug, and drugs are somehow implicated in HIV transmission. Second, Farquhar notes that many beliefs reflect the myths and stereotypes held by adults and promoted by the media. As they struggle to construct their own meaning, children's knowledge often mirrors that of the adults who surround them.

Even while those committed to conserving the past try to limit the role of the school, the majority are asking it to address an increasingly broad social agenda. Under pressure to do more and to do it better, in a world that offers fewer and fewer support systems for children, there is always the danger of reductionism. Schools reduce complicated social problems to simplified fragments of information, adopt pedagogic strategies that focus on measurable, behavioral outcomes, and define the child as a "learner," as the sum of his or her cognitive competencies. Many teachers see the curriculum in place as the biggest obstacle to effective education, for they recognize that issues such as HIV/AIDS cannot be segmented into discrete, 40-minute units.

THE CURRICULUM IN PLACE

Attending to children suggests the informal ways that HIV/AIDS enters the school and the daily openings teachers have for beginning a dialogue that can lead to a more formal learning plan. Unfortunately, most teachers learn about HIV/AIDS through the demands of a highly rationalized curriculum and without time for reflection. It is not surprising that they react with anger and frustration. Teachers need to be supported as curriculum makers who can respond to their students' immediate concerns while cognizant of the larger bodies of knowledge with which they may be connected. This approach is not compatible with the top-down imposition of lesson plans that are far removed from the children's lived experiences.

The New York State *AIDS Instructional Guide* (New York State Education Department, 1987) is one example of the technocratic mindset that undermines the role of teachers as decision makers. Although designed to be a "guide" and carefully labeled as such, it is worth considering in detail, since many districts adopted it *in toto* as the curriculum in order to save time and avoid controversy. This is an interesting political document, with its community review panels to assure decency, its denial of the sexual realties of teenagers' lives, and its careful attention to parents' right to withdraw their children from lessons dealing with HIV prevention. To educators, however, this guide may appear as a far more curious pedagogical document because of the way that it parcels out information across the grades.

The *AIDS Instructional Guide* presents a total of 37 lesson plans clustered by grade levels. The K–3 lessons deal with health in general. They barely mention HIV/AIDS at all, though teachers are told that some children may fear contracting the disease and that their questions should be addressed "honestly and simply." Somewhat less than half of the grade 4–6 lessons deal with HIV/AIDS. They describe communicable diseases, the immune system, how HIV is not transmitted, and how to prevent AIDS by abstaining from drug use. Only in the grade 7–8 lessons, a majority of which directly address HIV/AIDS, is there discussion of the sexual transmission of HIV and the possibility of prevention through sexual abstinence. Then, in a country where the median age of first intercourse is 16, and where a third of males and 20% of females have intercourse by 15—and of those currently sexually active, less than half report using condoms—teachers are instructed to emphasize the 13 ways that abstinence makes us free (*Chronic Disease and Health . . .*, 1990).

On the grade 9–12 level, the social and economic consequences of HIV/AIDS are confined to a single lesson featuring a debate on mandatory HIV-antibody testing. Although certain lessons are geared to elicit sympathy for people with HIV/AIDS and thus attempt to curb potential discrimination, never does the guide address the homophobia, racism, and addictophobia underlying much of the HIV/AIDS hysteria that the curriculum is ostensibly trying to dispel. This superficial approach to "humanizing" the disease belies the extensive introductory comments about the importance of pluralism and democratic values. It also denies the fundamental reality of HIV infection in our country—that it has disproportionately affected groups of people who have been marginalized and subjected to various forms of physical and psychological violence (Fraser, 1989). Convincing students to listen to any messages about HIV/AIDS and to understand personal vulnerability cannot be accomplished without interrupting the "us-versus-them" mentality that pervades our social thinking.

There are two assumptions underlying this curriculum guide that bear careful scrutiny. The first is that children's minds are compartmentalized, able to deal with HIV/AIDS information in a logical, sequential order. It assumes, for example, that children can discuss how HIV is *not* transmitted while holding in abeyance for several lessons and/or years how it is transmitted—and how to prevent its spread. No attempt is made to assess what knowledge children come to school with or the kinds of questions their personal experiences may have generated. The child is read as a *tabula rasa* with respect to HIV/AIDS. The New York State Planners appear to have been attending more to the logical order in which they wanted to present a specific body of information than to the psychological order that may reflect children's questions and interests. It seems only fair to ask for the voices of the children in the curriculum—the voices heard on the playground, on the subway, and in the block area. But who is listening? Who has the time?

The second assumption is that HIV/AIDS is a medical phenomenon to be located within the confines of the health curriculum. If we accept that there are economic, political, and social as well as biomedical strands in the Gordian knot that is HIV/AIDS, then an effective educational response does not reside in the province of the health teacher alone. A successful response is a collaborative one involving teachers from all the disciplines, administrators, and parents. In order for students to understand the disease, they must understand the cultural context in which it is occurring. For it is this context that defines how individuals and society at large respond to people with HIV and assign resources to prevention, research, and care.

From this perspective it is easy to see how HIV/AIDS lends itself as a subject for current events and social studies classes. HIV/AIDS raises many questions about access to health care and its costs, the ethics of confidentiality, diseases of poverty, availability of new drugs, and conduct of scientific research. Sloane and Sloane (1990) report on the integration of HIV/AIDS in a class on the history of the United States since 1877, which already includes discussion of the living conditions of North American cities in the late nineteenth century and the incredible toll of epidemic diseases, such as yellow fever, scarlet fever, influenza, and consumption. Here the modern-day epidemic can help students understand the fears and responses of earlier generations and offer the opportunity to clarify the differences between airborne diseases and HIV/AIDS.

There is also a growing body of novels, plays, and poetry emerging in response to this disease, and they provide further opportunities to introduce HIV/AIDS into language arts and English classes (Klein, 1989; Murphy & Poirier, 1993; Nelson, 1992; Pastore, 1992; Preston, 1989). More and more artists and musicians are also turning their attention to the issue, as well might our students in their own work (Klusacek & Morrison, 1992; J. Miller, 1992). The curriculum should reflect the richness of all these imaginative reconstructions, as they offer alternative routes to understanding the impact of HIV/AIDS (Brunner, 1992; Engler, 1988).

In effect, I want to argue that students would be best served if the assumptions underlying the curriculum in place were inverted. First, rather than creating elaborate instructional guides based on a formal ordering of facts, it would be far more helpful to ground the curriculum in the issues that children themselves find challenging, a principle upheld by progressive educators from Dewey to Friere. Second, our very definition of the disease needs to be reexamined in such a way as to permit its multiple ramifications to emerge across the disciplines. This is not to deny the importance of messages about prevention but to underscore the less visible interconnectedness of our social institutions. Successful prevention efforts at all age levels do not seek to abstract and control specific behaviors but rather to help people examine sexual and drug-using practices in the context of their total lives.

THE TEACHER'S PERSPECTIVE

My own research on pedagogical authority in early childhood (Silin, 1982) revealed that teachers think of themselves as objective professionals acting in the best interests of children. By legitimating this self-definition in their knowledge of child development, teachers could speak authoritatively about other people's children while suggesting a space for family prerogatives with respect to the inculcation of values. Interviews with primary school teachers illustrate the commitment to keeping personal attitudes and beliefs out of the classroom (Farquhar, 1990a). One teacher commented:

> It would be very wrong of me to put my personal interpretation, the standards I use for living my life, to tell them "this is how you should live." . . . It is not the place of the school to criticize in that way, or the teacher to criticize or to imply that one way is right and another way is wrong. (p. 12)

Teachers want to believe that the primary school is simply a purveyor of objective knowledge, that "we present a neutral sort of attitude to facts" (p. 12).

My work on HIV/AIDS curricula with teachers, however, suggests that personal values, prejudices, and preconceptions play a critical role in determining what information they do and do not provide. When people first began to take the facts about HIV transmission seriously, they had to explore previously unrecognized moments of vulnerability in their own lives. The middle-aged woman whose husband had just been through major surgery needed to calculate the odds that he might have received a unit of infected blood; the young male teacher needed to assess his resistance to carrying a condom on his weekend date; and the mother of a grown daughter who shared an apartment with two gay men needed to come to terms with her anxieties about casual contact as a source of HIV infection. Although everyone is better informed today than in 1985, when I began working with teachers on HIV/AIDS curricula, immersion in this issue inevitably leads to rethinking potential risk. When this does not happen, the lack of personal relevance can in some cases lead to a lack of interest. As one of Farquhar's (1990a) interviewees commented:

> This is a big turn-off. It's a big bore for me, because I know I've got nothing to worry about. I've led a monogamous life, I know I'm clear, and I'll always be clear, and I'm not going to come into touch with it. I'm not going to get caught up in drugs, I'm not going to go injecting myself. The blood contamination is the only one that could get me. (p. 12)

In a sense HIV/AIDS happens all at once. Coming to learn about HIV/AIDS in the context of their professional lives, most teachers recognize that this disease has meanings that extend far beyond the clinic office or hospital room, meanings that will seep into conversations with their own children, affect attitudes toward friends and family, and change lifelong behaviors. It has meaning that even challenge their sense of safety in the workplace. This is the all-at-onceness of HIV/AIDS, a disease that not only destroys an individual's immune system but also breaks down the artificial barriers that we construct between professional and personal lives.

Successful preservice and inservice education depends on the provision of adequate time for teachers to express their feelings about HIV/AIDS and their reactions to talking with children about HIV-related issues (Basch, 1989; Sanders & Farquhar, 1991). For only after these feelings have been acknowledged and discussed can teachers attend to the task at hand. In describing the introduction of an anti-bias curriculum, for example, Derman-Sparks and the A.B.C. Task Force (1989) provide a model for staff development about HIV/AIDS. They emphasize group consciousness-raising for teachers as the first step in creating new curricula on social issues. This process is one that respects the teacher as an adult learner, providing an opportunity to understand the subject matter in more than a superficial manner. A reading of the anti-bias curriculum also suggests that teachers who have placed equity issues high on their own agendas will have less difficulty integrating HIV/AIDS into the ongoing curriculum; these teachers have already created environments in which human differences are discussed and valued. HIV/AIDS education must proceed out of a meaningful context, so students can recognize the familiar and understandable as well as the new and unexpected in this issue.

Institutional Constraints

Talk of staff development, consciousness-raising groups, and adults as learners is not to deny the real constraints under which teachers work. Ironically, the press for school reform initiated by the publication of *A Nation at Risk* in 1984 has resulted in increased demands for required courses, quantitative measurement, and universal standards. The introduction of HIV/AIDS education has meant that teachers must squeeze an additional topic into their already overcrowded, overorganized days. It becomes another requirement that impinges on what little discretionary time remains to them. Even as leaders of industry and labor are calling for greater teacher autonomy to increase school effectiveness, and experiments in teacher-based school governance proliferate, state mandates for HIV/AIDS education allocate few resources for staff development (Kenney, Guardado, & Brown, 1989). If teachers are to engage in the decision-making activities that would define them as professionals, then they must be given the opportunity to develop the knowledge appropriate to such responsibilities (Wirth, 1989).

Thus for teachers, the introduction of HIV/AIDS into the curriculum has also meant preoccupation with negotiating school bureaucracies and calculating the risks of fomenting change. In most school districts where I have worked, teachers are in agreement about institutionally imposed limitations on what may be said. However, they are often in disagreement as to what their individual responses should be. Three solutions to this dilemma are common.

The first solution accepts the limits but recognizes that there are ways to work around them. The second solution, more cynical and despairing, resists any participation in what are perceived to be duplicitous practices. For teachers advocating the first solution, compromise is essential in order to get critical information to their students. For teachers adopting the second solution, however, the main compromise—that they may respond to questions as raised by students but not initiate certain "hot" topics—is unacceptable. Placing teachers in a position where they rely on student questions, and then refer students back to their parents or to after-school counseling sessions, can undermine the teacher's authority. Unfortunately, the legitimate anger expressed over the moral bind in which they are placed is too often projected onto the subject of HIV/AIDS itself rather than directed at creating a changed educational context.

A third solution to institutionally imposed limits is premised on the teacher's sense of privacy and control when the classroom door is closed; these teachers feel that they are free to say what they want when they are alone with students. Grumet (1988), exploring the experiences of women teachers as well as the histories of women writers and artists, suggests the self-defeating nature of this strategy. Describing the importance of private spaces for the development of ideas, she also points to the incipient dangers of isolation and privatization that can result when the doors to these rooms are never opened. The potential for community change can be fostered or thwarted by our willingness to make public that which has been nurtured in private.

But the institutions in which we live and work are often far more permeable than we imagine (Sarason, 1982). If teachers are to be successful change agents—and HIV/AIDS always involves change—then professional education programs must prepare them for their extra-classroom roles. Knowledge of institutional power structures, budget making, and community relations is as appropriate for the classroom teacher as for the administrator. All school personnel need to understand that institutions are often less monolithic and more heterogeneous when looked at closely with specific ends in view. Internal contradictions provide openings for change. Frequently it is our own perception of hegemony that is the biggest block to creating effective local strategies. Finally, while for some adults the reluctance to talk with children about HIV/AIDS reflects their own lack of knowledge, for others it is part of a consciously held belief system about the nature of childhood. For example, Robin Alexander (1984), in a study of British primary and junior schools, found teachers committed to the idea of childhood as a time of innocence. Although the "primary ideology" recognizes that children are capable of unacceptable behavior, it also deems them free of any malicious intent. Ideas about original sin once promoted by religious reformers have been abandoned, replaced by images of moral purity. In an observational study of three schools, R. King (1978) confirms teachers' determination to protect young children from harsh and corrupting realities of the adult world. In America, California kindergarten teachers have opposed any discussion of HIV/AIDS in their classrooms because they want to protect children from any unpleasant and, in their view, irrelevant subjects.

When *Young Children*, the Journal of the National Association for the Education of Young Children (NAEYC), published its first HIV/AIDS article, entitled "What We Should and Should Not Tell Our Children About AIDS," it emphasized that the role of the teacher was to soothe the potentially frightened child and avoid presenting unnecessary information (Skeen & Hudson, 1987). Two years later an article on substance abuse prevention in the same journal reinforced a similar philosophy. Misleadingly titled "Drug Abuse Prevention Begins in Early Childhood (And is much more than a matter of instructing young children about drugs!)," it deals solely with the need for parent education and calls for an analysis of parenting styles that promote positive self-images among young children (Oyemade & Washington, 1989). There is little recognition in either article that children may be all too aware of the social problems that exist in their communities. While teachers are constantly reminded to structure environments that are psychologically supportive of personal growth, never is it suggested that they take the lead in providing information about HIV/AIDS or drugs. Nor are they encouraged to help students sort through the multiple meanings they may have already assigned to them. The message is that as long as we follow developmentally appropriate practices, little must change in the way we think about children's lives.

PREPARING CLASSROOM TEACHERS TO TALK ABOUT HIV/AIDS

To accept that children live in a world where they come to learn about HIV/AIDS, drugs, poverty, and homelessness at a far earlier age than most of us would prefer does not mean we are participating in the denial of childhood. But it does mean we need to create classrooms in which children feel comfortable exploring these issues. Teacher educators can foster this process in two critical ways. First, they can highlight for their students the tension between what we have learned about the social construction of childhood, the embeddedness of our ideas in specific historical contexts, and what we may believe to be optimal conditions for children's growth (James & Prout, 1990a). Wanting the newcomer to feel at home in the world, we each struggle with the degree to which we see childhood as a separate life period requiring specialized protections and professionalized care, and the degree to which we see it as a time for full participation in the ongoing life of the community. The work of those who look at how the social environment is changing the experience of childhood—from the growth of electronic information sources, parental pressure for achievement, and the increasing isolation of children in age-segregated institutions, to the pervasive violence in young people's lives—would be especially helpful with this project (Elkind, 1981b; Garbarino, 1992; Polakow, 1982; Postman, 1982).

Second, given the stressful lives of contemporary children, it is important for teacher educators to emphasize their competencies as well as their developmental deficiencies, a theme I pursue at greater length in Chapter 4. Here I would mention the use of the anthropological or sociological lens (Felsman, 1989; Glauser, 1990) to focus on the strengths and healthy adaptation rather than weaknesses or pathology of children living in difficult circumstances. I also refer to our increasing knowledge of young children's narrative skills, their use of and understanding of abstract concepts, binary oppositions, metaphor, and humor (Egan, 1988; Sutton-Smith, 1988). Like Robert Coles (1989), we need to listen to the moral energy coursing through the stories of older children living in poverty, as they question and reflect upon their experiences. These stories can tell us how children resist despair, claim dignity in dehumanizing situations, and create redemptive moments out of sorrow.

A Question of Authority

Preparing classroom teachers to integrate HIV/AIDS into the curriculum is a complex process not just because it raises personal concerns for individuals or because it may force them to address new subjects such as sex and death. It is complex because it provokes inquiry into basic philosophical issues about the nature of pedagogy, the meaning of childhood, and the role of the teacher as change agent. An incident in the spring of 1986 crystallized for me the underlying theme of this inquiry and much of the teacher discourse on HIV/AIDS. At that time I was asked to talk to a group of angry parents and teachers who were attempting to exclude a 5-year-old girl with AIDS from their school. Within a few minutes of my opening remarks about the severity of the HIV/AIDS problem in the community, I was interrupted by an angry, bearded man in his mid-30s who announced himself to be a teacher, a historian of science, and a parent in the school. Citing the newness of the disease and the constant flow of information from the medical world, he began to question the credentials of the panelists—a physician, a public health official, a school administrator, a parent leader, and myself—one by one. At that moment of attack, rather than becoming defensive as many of the others did, I began to relax. As a former teacher, I recognized a familiar issue emerging, the issue of authority. This irate father was challenging not only the specific information we offered but, more significantly, our fundamental right to influence his children. The shadow of the school–family struggle for the child was lengthening to include HIV/AIDS.

Although this scene took place at the height of HIV/AIDS hysteria, it exemplifies a critical and ongoing theme in the HIV/AIDS discourse: the challenge that the disease poses to traditional concepts of authority. For many, authority implies certainty, the right to guide others based on full knowledge of the outcomes of the recommended actions. But HIV/AIDS is not about absolutes. It is defined by a series of changing practices, bodies of knowledge, and contexts. AIDS educators and policy makers are skilled at juxtaposing theoretical possibilities against actual probabilities, an unsatisfying dialectic for those who feel personally threatened and seek safety through guarantees. Yet physicians and other officials who assert certainty lose credibility as well. For in their attempt to reassure, they fail to acknowledge the reality of indeterminacy, an acknowledgment that would allow them to form a sympathetic alliance with an anxious audience. The ethical and practical implications of HIV/AIDS test our tolerance for uncertainty as well as our commitment to live the democratic principles that speak to inclusive rather than exclusive modes of behavior.

While the father described in this incident was particularly direct in his attempt to discredit our authority, or perhaps more accurately, even the possibility of the existence of authoritative knowledge about HIV/AIDS, he was raising the same question that emerged in countless sessions with teachers at that time. Teachers were faced with a dual quandary. They saw themselves as possibly in danger, not only because they were acceding to policies based on calculated risks, but also because they were being asked to initiate HIV/AIDS instruction without feeling confident about the information they would be transmitting. Obviously, HIV/AIDS also meant talking about sex, drugs, and death, often taboo subjects that are not easily packaged into highly rationalized lessons. Without certainty, lacking definitive research or a legitimated history to support current assertions, teachers wondered what stance to adopt with regard to the subject. They wondered how not to place their own authority in jeopardy with students. When teachers believe their ability to influence students rests in the control of information, the lack of that control can lead to a lethal silence.

Teachers now recognize that their failure to respond to many teachable moments reflects a lack of confidence in their own HIV/AIDS knowledge. A subtle but more positive shift in attitudes has occurred when professionals refer to their ignorance rather than to lack of scientific proof. The reservations are less about the validity of scientific knowledge than about their familiarity with it. Yet there is something fundamentally askew when teachers are unwilling to admit to students that they do not know the answers to their questions and use this as a rationale for pretending that the subject does not exist. While the obvious remedy to this situation is to provide all teachers with a good basic education about HIV/AIDS so that they feel competent, a long-range response must also be pursued by encouraging teachers and those who work with them to examine the sources of their authority. For HIV/AIDS is not the only difficult issue teachers face in the classroom where the willingness to model the role of learner takes precedence over the traditional role of knower.

Collaboration in Health and Education

The high degree of control and standardization in American public schools that undermines the initiative of teachers has been amply documented by historians and sociologists of education (Apple, 1982; Tyack, 1974). Frequently denied the choices that would express their pedagogic expertise, teachers are reluctant to take on subjects like sex, illness, and death that leave them in undefined territory where previous understandings of authority may seem less relevant. In such territory, student-teacher distinctions based on the ownership of knowledge may break down in the face of the greater commonalities that we all share regardless of age.

The breakdown of hierarchical authority that may ensure when certainty becomes doubtful has been actively sought by people with HIV/AIDS and their advocates and is a development educators might watch carefully. As individuals confront radical care and treatment decisions, the authority of institutions and private practitioners has come under increasing scrutiny. People with HIV/AIDS often have more information about new drugs or treatments than their health care provider; at other times, the provider may have to acknowledge that little is known about how a drug works or even if it is effective. A collaborative model of health care in which the patient is a full participant seems only appropriate given these circumstances. Such a collaborative model has implications for all professionals who may have once defined their right to practice by the exclusive control of a particular body of knowledge and skills.

As more and more people with HIV/AIDS strive to become involved in the decisions affecting their care, they set an agenda for themselves that does not sound so very different from one that good teachers may set for their students—or indeed that teachers as a group may have for their own development. This is an agenda of increasing independence, autonomy, and self-reliance. Illich (1976), in a book written just prior to the emergence of HIV/AIDS, makes an illuminating distinction between medical and health care, associating the former with the highly rationalized scientific management of illness offered by experts in institutional settings, and the latter with the sociopolitical process that enables people to make life-affirming choices on a daily basis. To Illich, medical care is only a part of a larger set of contextual issues that facilitate or inhibit health. This is not to deny the critical role of technology and professional care but to question how reliance on them affects our sense of dignity and agency.

It would seem that teachers express a similar set of concerns, not only when they question the ultimate meanings of the technocratic curriculum but also when they assess the administrative structures that frustrate their ability to decide how and what they will teach. For the belief in expert control undermines teachers who are asked only to implement curricula designed by others, undermines students forced to learn in classrooms in which they are not active participants, and undermines sick people made passive observers of the healing process (Rosenberg, 1987). Collaboration, in education as in health care, may appear risky because it means that experts relinquish some of their control. But it is also a recognition that not all knowledge is about control. While there needs to be space for mastery, there also needs to be a role for understanding and acceptance, for emancipation and liberation.

IS THERE SAFETY IN SAFER SEX?
The interests of early childhood and elementary classroom teachers in becoming knowledgeable and establishing a rationale for HIV/AIDS education with younger children are different from those of teachers working with adolescents. In junior and senior high schools, health teachers are trained to talk about sex and sexuality, though permitted to do so with varying degrees of freedom. It is now assumed that HIV/AIDS education is relevant to all students who are potentially sexually active. This has not always been the case.

It is understandable that adults were at first reluctant to admit the presence of a complex, wily virus such as HIV in a chameleon-like population that itself often appears to have no other goal than to test the limits of human possibility. During the earliest years of the epidemic, this reluctance to view teenagers as vulnerable to HIV infection was reinforced by the dominant risk-group vocabulary, which suggested that the virus would be contained within specific populations. The social and political marginalization of gay men and injection drug users allowed many to discount their experiences. Today, although there continues to be widespread denial of the existence of gay-identified youth in our classrooms (Rofes, 1989), there is a greater acceptance of the fact that any teenager may experiment with behaviors or accede to peer pressure in such a way as to place him- or herself at risk for contracting HIV. Indeed, it is these very attributes that are most frequently cited as the reasons for making HIV education so daunting.

Whether motivated by irrational fear or realistic assessment of the problem, a strong national consensus exists in favor of HIV/AIDS education for young people (Center for Population Options, 1989). Although compliance may be inconsistent and resistance from the religious right fierce (Gallagher, 1993), over half of the states have mandated HIV/AIDS education in their schools and most others strongly recommend it. Only 13 states have established complete programs including published curricula, training or certification requirements, and inservice education for staff (Kenney et al. 1989). The absence of resources for staff development is especially notable given recent calls for greater teacher autonomy to increase school effectiveness and the adoption of experiments in teacher-based school governance. In many of the nation's largest school districts, education about HIV has begun to take precedence over education about sexuality. While the majority of schools address both topics, the transitional and often confusing nature of the moment is evidenced by the number of sites that offer HIV/AIDS education but not sexuality education, and others where the situation is reversed.

HIV-related curricula tend to have a strong prevention focus. Not surprisingly, the prevention method of choice is clearly abstinence. Of the 27 state-approved curricula, only 8 address abstinence and strategies appropriate for sexually active students in a balanced manner and provide comprehensive information about the epidemic. Indeed, the subject of safer sex is one of the least likely to be discussed with students. While teachers blame their own discomfort with this topic on parental and administrative constraints, lack of appropriate materials, and the embarrassment with which students approach discussions of sexuality, they report little difficulty teaching abstinence and sexual decision making (Kerr, Allensworth, & Gayle, 1989). This suggests that the latter topic is not so much about learning to make choices from a world of possibilities as about deciding to say "no" to sex, based on a predetermined set of behavioral rules. That decision making has become a code phrase for a "just say no" message is underlined by teachers' responses to survey questions. There is almost universal commitment to programs that enable students to examine and develop their own values; yet three-quarters of the same teachers believe that students should be explicitly taught not to have sex (Forrest & Silverman, 1989). The values clarification discussion becomes the critical vehicle for persuading students to own the adult perspective.

Despite media and school-based efforts, teenagers remain woefully ignorant about HIV and ill disposed toward people with AIDS (Brooks-Gunn, Boyer, & Hein, 1988; Hingson & Strunin, 1989). This is of increased concern for African-American and Latino communities whose youth represent 34% and 18% respectively of adolescents with AIDS but who, in comparison with their white peers, are less knowledgeable about HIV and the effectiveness of condoms for prevention (DiClemente, Boyer, & Morales, 1988). Overall, AIDS is the sixth leading cause of death among those aged 15 to 24 (*Chronic Disease and Health . . .*, 1990). While adolescents are only 2% of total AIDS cases, for the past six years the number of cases among 13- to 19-year-olds has doubled every 14 months, the same rate of expansion seen among gay males in the first years of the epidemic. Other studies indicate that 7% of homeless and runaway youth and 1% of all teenagers in high-incidence cities like New York and Miami may have already contracted HIV (Society for Adolescent Medicine, 1994). Most disturbingly, over one-fifth of people with AIDS are in their 20s. Because the average latency period between initial infection with HIV and the onset of CDC-defined AIDS is 10 years or more, it can be inferred that many of these people contracted the virus as teenagers.

State-approved HIV/AIDS curricula usually give priority to information about healthful lifestyles, communicable diseases, and HIV transmission and prevention. But many pose constraints to the discussion of subjects that might be interpreted as facilitating sex-ual activity—contraception, safer sex, and sexuality—even though studies indicate that sex education leads not to more sex but to more responsible sex, including the postpone-ment of first intercourse, safer practices, and fewer unwanted pregnancies (Altman, 1993a).

Unfortunately, evidence also suggests a lack of practical efficacy in our efforts; only 8% of males and 2% of females reported condom use after exposure to AIDS education. Among homosexual/bisexual males, those who reported using condoms increased from 2% to 19% after AIDS education (Bell, 1991). Studies (New York City Board of Education, 1990) conducted two years after implementation of specific curricula point to little or no change in actual knowledge. When asked, students report that they learn about HIV/AIDS primarily from the media and interpersonal sources—for example, friends and parents ("What High School Students Want . . .," 1990). Schools are listed third, and teachers are described as ill informed, reluctant to talk about disease and sexual activity, and uninter-ested in HIV/AIDS education. Students themselves request more extensive and intensive education, beginning earlier, and including presentations by people with HIV/AIDS, tar-geted information about prevention, condom availability, and discussion of the psychoso-cial impact of the disease.

The Life-Skills Approach

In order to create more effective programs, some curriculum makers (Basch, 1989; Keeling, 1989) have focused on what they perceive as a critical gap between information and/or self-perception and behavioral change. Mickler (1993), studying AIDS-preventive behavior among college adolescents, found that knowledge of AIDS was not predictive or strongly related to safer sex practices. Others (Koopman, Rotheram-Borus, Henderson, Bradley, & Hunter, 1990), working with adolescent runaways and self-identified gay males, reported that both groups had moderately positive beliefs about their self-efficacy and self-control in sexual situations. Yet in focus groups they were unable to role-play safer be-haviors, such as asking about their partners' sexual history or asking their partners to use a condom. More significantly, although three-quarters had engaged in sexual activity in the previous three months, with a mean of 2.7 partners, all reported infrequent condom use.

Increasingly, HIV/sexuality education curricula emphasize an ill-defined cluster of be-haviors variously labeled as coping, problem solving, or life skills. Depending on the com-mitment of the particular curriculum, it is claimed that these skills will enable teenagers to remain abstinent until marriage, delay intercourse until an unspecified time in the future, or negotiate safer sex practices as necessary. Through active participation in role-playing, brainstorming sessions, and games, students are taught resistance or refusal skills so that they will not succumb to pressures from peers. These skills are often reduced to a set of sharp retorts that permit students to say "no" to sexual activity without losing face among their friends. In some instances a few lessons are added to more traditional, direct-instruction curricula, while in others, information is interwoven into a consistently inter-active format (Brick, 1989).

But as progressive educators have asserted since the last century (Dewey, 1900/1956), students learn most effectively when in the midst of meaningful activities. Programs that abstract social skills provide neither the motivation nor intentionality required for sub-stantive learning. A curriculum that attempts, in a few brief lessons, to teach students how to make critical decisions cannot make up for years of education that have denied them the right to become autonomous, self-determining learners. Friday afternoon "magic circles" to build self-esteem or Monday morning rehearsals of refusal skills divert our attention from the realities of contemporary children, who too seldom have the opportunity to make meaningful choices, follow through on them, and reflect on their consequences.

Skill-based approaches are built on the understanding that the lack of a positive self-image is the biggest factor preventing teenagers from making healthy decisions. Nationally distributed curricula such as "Project Charlie" (Charest, Gwinn, Reinisch, Terrien, & Strawbridge, 1987) and "Growing Healthy" (National Center for Health Education, 1985) are being described as panaceas to a wide variety of problems, including high school dropout rates, lowered academic performance, widespread alcohol and substance abuse, and teenage pregnancy. As in similar programs designed to improve adult productivity in the workplace, the focus on changes in self-perception and interpersonal skills masks material barriers to real equity and autonomy (Steinberg, 1990; L. Williams, 1990). Self-esteem has become a popular buzzword for efforts to promote better psychological adjustment to the political status quo.

The seemingly humanistic techniques of self-empowerment models often become a means to reproduce a hegemonic ideology, instantiating subtle but powerful forms of social control (Young, 1990). This occurs, for example, when the press to insure safer sex, whether condom use for gay men or abstinence for teenagers, impels facilitators to assume responsibility *for* group members rather than *toward* them. The most sympathetic educators may fail to exercise pedagogical tact when confronting HIV/AIDS. Programs are coercive to the degree that they compromise the participants' abilities to draw their own conclusions from experiences that take place within a context that specifically proclaims the importance of individual choice. Experiential learning becomes a means to an end rather than an open exploration of possibility, including the potential rejection of safer sex practices.

Both individual behavior change and self-empowerment models are based on the instrumentalist assumption that behavior can be isolated, analyzed, and understood apart from the socioeconomic context in which it occurs—an assumption that negates the necessity of addressing issues of the differential distribution of economic and cultural capital. Brandt (1987) comments:

> These assumptions with which we still live regarding health-related behavior rest upon an essentially naive, simplistic view of human nature. If anything has become clear in the course of the twentieth century it is that behavior is subject to complex forces, internal psychologies, and external pressures all not subject to immediate modifications, or, arguably, to modifications at all. (p. 202)

The historical record not only documents the past failure of narrow approaches to the control of sexually transmitted diseases but also the degree to which they are constructed upon a set of moralistic judgments about the nature of sexual activity (Fee & Fox, 1988).

In a democratic society that is respectful of pluralism and accepting of different rates and ways of learning, the public health goal of zero transmission, 100% risk reduction, is not only counterproductive but politically unacceptable (Bell, 1991). Compromise is inevitable in societies where absolute control over citizens' (mis) behaviors is given up in the interests of the responsible exercise of individual freedom. It is as inappropriate to employ coercive measures as it is to gauge the success of HIV/AIDS education by gross measures of behavioral change.

The Collective-Action Approach

While much is to be learned from the cognitive social learning theory (e.g., active engagement of students, multiple levels of learning, and variable strategies) underlying skill-based programs (Flora & Thoresen, 1988), its limitations are highlighted by a triphasic map of health education including individual behavioral change, self-empowerment, and collective action models (French & Adams, 1986; Homans & Aggleton, 1988). The underlying assumption of the first two approaches, also referred to as direct-instruction or experientially based programs, is that increased information about HIV risk behaviors reduces infections (Eckland, 1989). The linear reasoning embedded in these approaches, along with questions of long-term effectiveness and ethics, is exposed when they are juxtaposed against a collective-action model of health education. In addition to addressing the need for information and communicative skills, the collective-action approach encourages organizing to transform the social and political forces that shape and give meaning to individual behavior.

When the connection between health status and poverty, employment, income, and social class is fully recognized, then socioeconomic factors appear to have greater significance for health than do individual behaviors ("Demand side," 1993; Hubbard, 1993). These factors are best addressed through collective action in the political process. While this position is consistent with radical definitions of health and illness (Illich, 1976), it threatens the official governmental position on disease causation, as summarized by the Presidential Commission on the Human Immunodeficiency Virus Epidemic (1988), which is that "the heaviest burden of illness in the technically advanced countries today is related to individual behavior, especially the long-term patterns of behavior often referred to as 'life-style'" (p. 89). Paradoxically, it is this attempt to define critical social issues as private and personal rather than as public and political that heightens the very bigotry that the Presidential Commission seeks to dispel.

In fact, safer sex organizing began as a grass roots political movement within the gay community (Patton, 1990). Its greatest successes occurred in the first years of the epidemic prior to the professionalization and bureaucratization of HIV prevention. Some continue to understand that health education, community building, and political resistance are inextricably linked. Cranston (1992), for example, proposes HIV/AIDS education among gay and lesbian youth based on Paulo Freire's concept of the community of conscience. Consistent with a collective action model, this is HIV prevention that leads to political engagement because it values and fosters respect for gay histories, identities, and futures. Others (Gasch, Poulson, Fullilove, & Fullilove, 1991) understand the disproportional impact of HIV/AIDS on African-American populations as part of a more generalized pattern of excessive risk and mortality. They stress the role of the social and material environment in conditioning health-related behaviors. Poor African-American communities are best served by developing an analysis that will enable their members to work toward means connecting individual behavior to larger social changes.

Assessing the impact of a curriculum requires an exploration of the knowledge assumptions on which it is based. This assessment is critical to dispelling the myths about sexual identity and behavior that prevent effective HIV/AIDS education. Limiting the terrain of HIV/AIDS education to that of a "solvable" social question involving risk-reduction strategies has led to correspondingly limited answers focusing on either behavioral or attitudinal changes (Diorio, 1985). Valued knowledge is construed in the former case as the sum of facts and skills and in the latter as the ability to understand the intentions of others through improved communication abilities. However, HIV/AIDS is not only a question of individual behaviors and social norms. It is also a question of material conditions and resources, and structural inequities based on race, class, gender and sexual identities.

SEX, HIV, AND THE PERMEABLE CURRICULUM

AIDS is a disease of contradictions. It is a disease that is not a disease, a biological reality that has had a greater impact on sociopolitical practices than on medical care, an illness of hiddenness that has led to irreversible changes in public discourse. Unfortunately, HIV infection has also become a disease of adolescence, a period characterized in our society by its own unique logic—moments of sudden growth and regression, of open search and certain definition, of personal power and extreme susceptibility to the influence of others. An additional conundrum now presents itself: Safer sex alone will not make us safe from the effects of HIV.

The complexity of HIV/AIDS mandates a multifaceted approach. Reconceptualizing HIV/AIDS education means abandoning the instrumentalist assumptions of information- and skill-based programs that have led many to theorize the problem of HIV/AIDS education as one of bridging a gap between knowledge and behavior. Preventing the transmission of HIV involves not only learning about condoms, spermicides, and negotiating sex; it also means developing tools of political analysis, a commitment to social change, and an ethic of caring and responsibility. In short, we must shift our attention from HIV prevention narrowly defined as a means of behavioral control to a broader focus that would more accurately reflect our students' life worlds. HIV/AIDS education should further the goal of preparing students to become active participants in a democratic society. But what are the elements of such an approach?

First, HIV/AIDS education needs to begin with the youngest children and permeate the curriculum in order to break down the taboos with which it is associated and to make the subject a more comfortable one for discussion (Quackenbush & Villarreal, 1988). Our efforts should be informed by an appreciation of the development levels and experiential bases of different groups of students. We must ask whether the curriculum ensures equal access to HIV/AIDS information for all students. Access means that students not only have the opportunity to hear information but that it is presented in a language and style easily understood by specific target groups (Nettles & Scott-Jones, 1989). At the same time, as with other subject areas, we must be concerned with unwarranted differences in curriculum predicated on the race, class, gender, or sexual orientation of our students (Apple & Weiss, 1983; Willis, 1977).

Effective sexuality education itself, education that empowers students by building their sense of entitlement and decreasing their vulnerability, is based on our willingness to listen to and work with experiences students bring with them. This requires giving up presuppositions about the nature of sexuality and the outcomes of our efforts in favor of a sociohistorical appreciation of the ways in which sexual meanings are constructed and changed (D'Emilio & Freedman, 1988; Rubin, 1984). Safer sex can be less about the limitations imposed by HIV and the inculcation of specific behaviors and more about exploring multiple zones of bodily pleasures and the transformation of culturally determined constraints (Patton, 1985). In a time of HIV/AIDS, a discursive analysis becomes essential to re-imagining sexual practices in life-affirming, sex-positive ways.

Our goal should be to replace isolated lessons calculated to build self-esteem and social skills with an ongoing discourse of desire that problematizes violence and victimization (Fine, 1988). If the experiences of our students are valorized, they will be better able to understand the sources of pleasure and danger in their own lives. This process begins when students find a safe place in which to tell their stories. To accept these narratives is not only to foster respect for individual differences but also to reveal their distance from officially given versions of human sexuality, a distance that is clearly identified by recent studies of the high school curriculum (Trudell, 1992; Ward & Taylor, 1992). At the same time it is impossible to ignore externally imposed constraints to liberation, for even the best-intended pedagogic efforts may have little impact without increased life options for poorer students and easy access to birth control materials, health clinics, and substance-abuse treatment for everyone.

The permeable curriculum requires balancing our concerns about individual responsibility for transmitting HIV with an analysis of the changing social context in which it thrives. At a personal level, the curriculum causes students to reflect on their own behaviors as they affect the transmission of HIV and the lives of those who already carry the virus. At a social level, the curriculum provokes critical consciousness, fostering responsive and responsible citizens. Students should be asking questions about the societal responses to HIV/AIDS and learning to see themselves as citizens who can make decisions that will give direction to that response in the future. They need access to all kinds of citizens, especially those living with HIV, who model active responses to the disease (Navarre, 1987).

And what does the permeable curriculum say about people with HIV infection—gays, injection drug users, and others? Fear-based appeals have never been successful in preventing the spread of sexually transmitted diseases (Mickler, 1993). Greater familiarity with HIV, not less, is needed in order to break down the distancing mechanisms that allow us to feel that we can remain untouched. Images of diversity remind us that people with HIV/AIDS are a part of all our lives. Although some have real anxiety about what they perceive as a disintegration of culture and an erosion of values in the modern world, HIV/AIDS is not an appropriate metaphor for these concerns. The permeable curriculum is about caring for others and inclusion, not about isolation and exclusion.

Just as effective sexuality education is based on an entire school experience that encourages decision making, problem solving, and self-worth, successful HIV/AIDS education is built on a continuing appreciation of equity and pluralism in society. It cannot be assumed that an absence of negative comment signifies a lack of bias or commitment to social justice (Croteau & Morgan, 1989; Vance, 1984). Educators must take an active role in bringing the full spectrum of human differences to the classroom, acknowledging the ways that these have become sources of conflict and domination as well as the ways that they enrich and form the basis of participatory democracy. A curriculum that is permeable to the impact of students, one through which they can learn the skills of responsible citizenship, lays the groundwork for all AIDS education. For the history of HIV constantly reminds us not only of individual suffering and pain but also of the power and creativity that reside in a collective response.

Although HIV/AIDS may challenge our prior ideas about pedagogical authority, it also offers us an opportunity to examine new models that more accurately reflect who we understand ourselves to be and what we would like our students to become. From HIV/AIDS we learn about the limits of science and the importance of human vision, the frailty of the body and the strength of the spirit, the need to nurture the imagination even as we direct our attention to rational cognitive structures. In the end, the HIV/AIDS curriculum can be more about life than about death, more about health than about illness, more about the body politic than the body physical.

REFERENCES

Alexander, R. J. (1984). *Primary teaching.* London: Holt, Rinehart & Winston.

Altman, L. (1993a, June 15). Conference ends with little hope for AIDS cure. *The New York Times*, p. C1, 3.

Apple, M. W. (1979). *Ideology and curriculum.* London: Routledge & Kegan Paul.

Apple, M. W. (Ed.). (1982). *Cultural and economic reproduction in education.* Boston: Routledge & Kegan Paul.

Apple, M. W., & Weiss, L. (Eds.). (1983). *Ideology and practice in schooling.* Philadelphia: Temple University Press.

Barritt, L., Beekman, T., Bleeker, H., & Mulderij, K. (1985). *Researching educational practice.* Grand Forks: University of North Dakota Press.

Basch, C. E. (1989). Preventing AIDS through education: Concepts, strategies, and research priorities. *Journal of School Health, 59*, 296–300.

Bell, N. Z. (1991). Ethical issues in AIDS education. In F. G. Reimer (Ed.), *AIDS and ethics* (pp. 128–154). New York: Columbia University Press.

Bowles, S., & Gintis, H. (1976). *Schooling in capitalist America.* New York: Basic Books.

Brandt, A. M. (1987). *No magic bullet: A social history of venereal disease in the United States since 1800.* New York: Oxford University Press.

Brick, P. (1989). *Teaching safer sex.* Hackensack, NJ: Planned Parenthood of Bergen County.

Brooks-Gunn, J., Boyer, C. B., & Heim, K. (1988). Preventing HIV infection and AIDS in children and adolescents: Behavioral research and intervention strategies. *American Psychologist, 43*, 958–965.

Brunner, D. D. (1992). Discussing sexuality in the language arts classroom: Alternative meaning making and meaning making as an alternative. In J. T. Sears (Ed.), *Sexuality and the curriculum* (pp. 226–242). New York: Teachers College Press.

CDC AIDS Weekly. (December 15, 1986). p. 9.

Center for Population Options (1989). *Adolescents, AIDS and HIV: A community wide responsibility.* [Available from Center for Population Options, 1012 14th Street, N. W., Washington, D.C.]

Charest, P., Gwinn, T., Reinisch, N., Terrien, J., & Strawbridge, C. (1987). *Project Charlie.* [Available from Storefront/Youth Action, 4570 West 77th Street, Edina, MN 55435.]

Chronic disease and health promotion reprints from the mmwr: 1990 youth risk behavior surveillance system. (1990). [Available from U.S. Department of Health and Human Services, Centers for Disease Control, Atlanta, GA 30333.]

Coles, R. (1989). Moral energy in the lives of impoverished children. In T. F. Duggan & R. Coles (Eds.), *The child in our times: Studies in the development of resiliency* (pp. 45–55). New York: Brunner/Mazel.

Cranston, K. (1992). HIV education for gay, lesbian, and bisexual youth: Personal risk, personal power, and the community of conscience. In K. Harbeck (Ed.), *Coming out of the classroom closet* (pp. 247–259). New York: Haworth.

Croteau, J. M., & Morgan, S. (1989). Combating homophobia in AIDS education. *Journal of Counseling & Development, 68*, 86–91.

The demand side of the health care crisis. (1993). *Harvard Magazine, 95*(4), 30–32.

D'Emilio, J., & Freedman, E. B. (1988). *Intimate matters: A history of sexuality in America.* New York: Harper & Row.

Derman-Sparks, L., & the A.B.C. Task Force (1989). *Anti-bias curriculum: Tools for empowering young children.* Washington, D.C.: National Association for the Education of Young Children.

Dewey, J. (1956). *The child and the curriculum/The school and society.* Chicago: University of Chicago Press. (Original works published 1902 and 1900).

DiClemente, R. J., Boyer, C. B., & Morales, E. D. (1988). Minorities and AIDS: Knowledge, attitudes and misconceptions among black and Latino adolescents. *American Journal of Public Health, 78,* 55–57.

Dioro, J. (1985). Contraception, copulation, domination, and the theoretical barrennes of sex education literature. *Educational Theory, 35,* 239–255.

Eckland, J. D. (1989). Policy choices for AIDS education in the public schools. *Education Evaluation and Policy Analysis, 11,* 377–387.

Egan, K. (1988). Education and the mental life of young children. In L. Williams & D. Fromberg (Eds.), *The proceedings of "Defining the field of early childhood education: An invitational symposium"* (pp. 41–77). New York: Teachers College, Columbia University.

Elkind, D. (1981b). *The hurried child: Growing up too fast, too soon.* Reading, MA: Addison-Wesley.

Engler, R. K. (1988, October). *Safe sex and dangerous poems: AIDS, literature and the gay and lesbian community college student.* Paper presented at the Annual National Literature Conference, Chicago.

Farquhar, C. (1990a). *Answering children's questions about HIV/AIDS in the primary school: Are teachers prepared?* Unpublished manuscript, University of London, Institute of Education, Thomas Coram Research Unit, London.

Farquhar, C. (1990b). *What do primary school children know about AIDS?* (Working Paper No. 1). London: University of London, Institute of Education, Thomas Coram Research Unit.

Fee, E., & Fox, D. M. (1988). *AIDS: The burdens of history.* Berkeley: University of California Press.

Felsman, J. K. (1989). Risk and resiliency in childhood: The lives of street children. In T. F. Duggan & R. Coles (Eds.), *The child in our times: Studies in the development of resiliency* (pp. 56–80). New York: Brunner/Mazel.

Fine, M. (1988). Sexuality, schooling, and adolescent females: The missing discourse of desire. *Harvard Educational Review, 58*(1), 29–53.

Flora, J. A., & Thoresen, C. E. (1988). Reducing the risk of AIDS in adolescents. *American Psychologist, 43,* 965–971.

Forrest, J. D., & Silverman, J. (1989). What public school teachers teach about preventing pregnancy, AIDS and sexually transmitted diseases. *Family Planning Perspectives, 21*(2), 65–72.

Fraser, K. (1989). *Someone at school has AIDS.* Alexandria, VA: National Association of State Boards of Education.

French, J., & Adams, L. (1986). From analysis to synthesis. *Health Education Journal, 45*(2), 71–74.

Gallagher, J. (1993, June 15). Why Johnny can't be safe. *The Advocate, 631,* 46–47.

Garbarino, T. (1992). *Children in danger.* San Francisco: Jossey-Bass.

Gasch, H., Poulson, M., Fullilove, R., & Fullilove, M. (1991). Shaping AIDS education and prevention programs for African Americans amidst community decline. *Journal of Negro Education, 60*(1), 85–96.

Glauser, B. (1990). Street children: Deconstructing a construct. In A. James & A. Prout (Eds.), *Constructing and reconstructing childhood* (pp. 138–156). New York: Falmer Press.

Grumet, M. (1988). *Bitter milk.* Amherst: University of Massachusetts Press.

Hingson, R., & Strunin, L. (1989). *Summary of results: Boston schools baseline surveys, spring 1988, 1989.* Unpublished manuscript, Boston University, School of Public Health.

Homans, H., & Aggleton, P. (1988). Health education, HIV infection and AIDS. In P. Aggleton & H. Homans (Eds.), Social aspects of AIDS (pp. 154–176). London: Falmer Press.

Hubbard, R. (1993, Spring). Viewpoint. *The AIDS Report* [The Harvard AIDS Institute], pp. 13–14.

Illich, I. (1976). *Medical nemesis: The expropriation of health.* New York: Pantheon.

James, A., & Prout, A. (1990a). *Constructing and reconstructing childhood: Contemporary issues in the sociological study of childhood.* New York: Falmer.

Keeling, R. P. (Ed.). (1989). *AIDS on the college campus.* Rockville, MD: American College Health Association.

Kenney, A. M., Guardado, S., & Brown, L. (1989). Sex education and AIDS education in the schools: What states and large school districts are doing. *Family Planning Perspectives, 21*(2), 56–64.

Kerr, D. L., Allensworth, D. D., & Gayle, J. A. (1989). The ASHA national HIV education needs assessment of health and education professionals. *Journal of School Health, 59,* 301–305.

King, R. (1978). *All things bright and beautiful: A sociological study of infants' classrooms.* Chichester: Wiley.

Klein, M. (1989). *Poets for life: Seventy-six poets respond to AIDS.* New York: Crown.

Klusacek, A., & Morrison, K. (1992). *Leap in the dark: AIDS, art & contemporary cultures.* Montreal: Véhicule Press.

Koopman, C., Rotheram-Borus, M., Henderson, R., Bradley, J., & Hunter, J. (1990). Assessment of knowledge of AIDS and beliefs about prevention among adolescents. *AIDS Education and Prevention, 2*(1), 58–70.

Mickler, S. E. (1993). Perceptions of vulnerability: Impact on AIDS-preventive behavior among college adolescents. *AIDS Education and Prevention, 5*(1), 43–53.

Miller, J. (Ed.). (1992). *Fluid exchanges: Artists and critics in the AIDS crisis.* Toronto: University of Toronto Press.

Murphy, T. F., & Poirier, S. (Eds.). (1993). *Writing AIDS: Gay literature, language and analysis.* New York: Columbia University Press.

National Center for Health Education. (1985). *Growing healthy.* (Available from the National Center for Health Education, 30 East 29th Street, New York, NY 10016.)

Navarre, M. (1987). Fighting the victim label. *October, 43,* 143–147.

Nelson, E. S. (1992). *AIDS: The literary response.* New York: Twayne Publishers.

Nettles, S. M., & Scott-Jones, D. (1989). The role of sexuality and sex equity in the education of minority adolescents. *Peabody Journal of Education, 64*(4), 183–198.

New York State Education Department (1987). *AIDS Instructional Guide.* Albany, NY: Author.

Oyemade, U. J., & Washington, V. (1989). Drug abuse prevention begins in early childhood. *Young Children, 44*(5), 6–12.

Pastore, J. (1992). *Confronting AIDS through literature.* Champaign: University of Illinois Press.

Patton, C. (1985). *Sex and germs: The politics of AIDS.* Boston: South End Press.

Patton, C. (1990). *Inventing AIDS.* New York: Routledge.

Polakow, V. (1982). *The erosion of childhood.* Chicago: University of Chicago Press.

Postman, N. (1982). *The disappearance of childhood.* New York: Delacorte.

Presidential Commission on the Human Immunodeficiency Virus Epidemic. (1988). *Report of the Presidential Commission on the Human Immunodeficiency Virus Epidemic.* Washington, D.C.: U.S. Government Printing Office.

Preston, J. (1989). *Dispatches.* Boston: Alyson Press.

Quackenbush, M., Villarreal, S. (1988). *"Does AIDS hurt?" Educating young children about AIDS.* Santa Cruz, CA: Network Publications.

Rofes, E. (1989). Opening up the classroom closet: Responding to the educational needs of gay and lesbian youth. *Harvard Educational Review, 59*(4), 444–452.

Rosenberg, C. E. (1987). *The care of strangers: The rise of America's hospital system.* New York: Basic Books.

Rubin, G. (1984). Thinking sex: Notes for a radical theory of the politics of sexuality. In C. S. Vance (Ed.), *Pleasure and danger: Exploring female sexuality* (pp. 267–320). Boston: Routledge & Kegan Paul.

Sarason, S. B. (1982). *The culture of the school and the problem of change.* Boston: Allyn & Bacon.

Schvaneveldt, J. D., Lindauer, S., & Young, M. H. (1990). Children's understanding of AIDS: A developmental viewpoint. *Family Relations, 38,* 330–335.

Silin, J. (1982). *Protection and control: Early childhood teachers talk about authority.* Unpublished doctoral dissertation, Teachers College, Columbia University, New York.

Skeen, P., & Hudson, D. (1987). What we should and should not tell our children about AIDS. *Young Children, 42*(4), 65–71.

Sloane, D. C., & Sloane, B. C. (1990). AIDS in schools: A comprehensive initiative. *McGill Journal of Education, 25*(2), 205–227.

Society for Adolescent Medicine. (1994). HIV infection and AIDS in adolescents: A position paper for the Society for Adolescent Medicine. *Journal of Adolescent Health, 15*(5), 427–434.

Steinberg, C. (1990, February 18). How "magic circles" build self-esteem. *The New York Times,* sec. 12, p. 1.

Sutton-Smith, B. (1988). Radicalizing childhood: The multivocal mind. In L. Williams & D. Fromberg (Eds.), *The proceedings of "Defining the field of early childhood education: An invitational symposium"* (pp. 77–153). New York: Teachers College, Columbia University.

Trudell, B. K. (1992). Inside a ninth-grade sexuality classroom: The process of knowledge construction. In J. T. Sears (Ed.), *Sexuality and the curriculum* (pp. 203–226). New York: Teachers College Press.

Tyack, D. (1974). *The one best system.* Cambridge, MA: Harvard University Press.

Vance, C. S. (1984). Pleasure and danger: Toward a politics of sexuality. In C. S. Vance (Ed.), *Pleasure and danger: Exploring female sexuality* (pp. 1–27). Boston: Routledge & Kegan Paul.

van Manen, M. (1990. *Researching lived experience: Human science for an action sensitive pedagogy.* Albany: State University of New York Press.

Ward, J. V., & Taylor, J. M. (1992). Sexuality education for immigrant and minority students: Developing culturally appropriate curriculum. In J. T. Sears (Ed.), *Sexuality and the curriculum* (pp. 183–203). New York: Teachers College Press.

What high school students want from an HIV education program and how it can be delivered effectively: A report to the Bureau of School Health Education Services, New York State Education Department. (1990). (Available from MAGI Educational Services, Inc., Larchmont, NY)

Williams, L. (1990, March 28) Using self-esteem to fix society's ills. *The New York Times*, pp. C1, 10.

Willis, P. (1977). Learning to labour. Westmead, UK: Saxon House.

Wirth, A. G. (1989). The violation of people at work in schools. *Teachers College Record, 90*(4), 535–549.

Young, R. (1990). *A critical theory of education.* New York: Teachers College Press.

21

The Four R's—an Alternative to the Tyler Rationale

WILLIAM E. DOLL JR.

THE THREE R'S OF "READIN','RITIN', and 'Rithmetic" were late nineteenth- and early twentieth-century creations, geared to the needs of a developing industrial society. Reading was the functional reading of sales slips and bills of lading, combined with the inspirational stories of Horatio Alger and the moral aphorisms of McGuffey. Writing was literally penmanship, with the Palmer method introducing a ledger-oriented style in the first grade. Such cursive training had to begin early, for by the fifth grade half of those who had entered as first graders had left. Arithmetic, not mathematics, was essentially column addition and subtraction, with algorithmic multiplication and division coming in the later elementary years. Again, the emphasis was on store clerk functionalism, keeping the sales slips and ledgers accurate and neat. Problem solving was introduced as early as the second grade, but it was heavily, if not exclusively, associated with buying in an urban store.

Born in the early 1930s, I had my early elementary school training in these three R's. My word-lists for reading and spelling prepared me for the urban, industrial society my parents and I inhabited. The Palmer method was begun in the first grade, with an itinerant teacher brought in weekly to instruct us in the big O's and C's so distinctive of its style—flowing but clear. From Miss Wiley, Miss James, and Miss Thatcher—the maiden ladies who taught grades one, two, and three—I learned to keep my ten's column digits out of my hundred's column or my unit's column, and *always* beginning with the right column to "bring down" a single digit and to "carry" into the next column any digits left over. Miss Newcomb in the fourth grade made a small modification to this "consonant" method—namely, that with decimals it was the decimal points which needed to form a vertical, unbroken phalanx. Zeros were added to the right of the decimal point to keep the right column, the hundredths (often considered as pennies), in line.

Mr. Bartlett, our corner grocer, was not as good as my triumvirate of maiden teachers at keeping his columns straight. Further, he began his addition with the left, not the right

From William E. Doll Jr. *A Post-Modern Perspective on Curriculum.* New York: Teachers College Press, 1993: pp. 174–183. Reprinted by permission.

column. When questioned he stated that he wished to make no mistakes with the dollars or dimes and this method assured him greater accuracy with those important columns. Worse, he grouped digits together either in his head or with small notations in combinations equal to ten. This method intrigued me. I passed on my newfound wisdom to Miss Thatcher (married women were not allowed to teach school). She, however, dismissed Mr. Bartlett's methods as heresy. In retrospect, I think Mr. Bartlett was more industrially oriented than Miss Thatcher and maybe even a better pedagogue. In dealing with my own elementary school classes, I have found that much columnar addition—at least of any practical type—has a better "feel" when it is done left to right, thus allowing intuition and estimation to come into play. Further, doing simple columnar work by grouping numerals into combinations of ten not only produces more accurate and quicker answers but also encourages structural and situational thinking—for example, doing 101–49 as 102–50, or maybe as 100–50 with two added on. Such "chaotic ordering" has been a hallmark of my students' *modus operandi* for many years now—before I read Whitehead or heard of postmodernism; it has generally served them well (Doll, 1977, 1989a).

At first glance one does not see a connection between the Tyler rationale and the three R's. However, a pre-set functionalism underlies both. While Tyler's frame expands and broadens industrial functionalism beyond the sales slips and ledgers of the three R's, the assumption of pre-set goals still exists. In this frame, *goals* do not emerge—as Cvitanovi? suggests they should—by "playing with" experiences; rather, goals are predetermined as are the *experiences* and *methods* for developing those experiences. All are firmly in place before any interaction with students occurs. *Evaluations* are designed to correlate the experiences only with the pre-set goals, not to explore what the students generate personally after reflecting on the experiences. In fact, as was pointed out earlier in the chapter, framing evaluation in terms of generation, reflection, transformation is virtually oxymoronic from a modernist perspective.

So what would serve as criteria for a curriculum designed to foster a post-modern view? What criteria might we use to evaluate the quality of a post-modern curriculum—a curriculum generated not predefined, indeterminate yet bounded, exploring the "fascinating imaginative realm born of God's laughter," and made up of an ever-increasing network of "local universalities?" I suggest the four R's of Richness, Recursion, Relations and Rigor might serve this purpose.

Richness. This term refers to a curriculum's depth, to its layers of meaning, to its multiple possibilities or interpretations. In order for students and teachers to transform and be transformed, a curriculum needs to have the "right amount" of *indeterminacy, anomaly, inefficiency, chaos, disequilibrium, dissipation, lived experience*—to use words and phrases already described. Just what is the "right amount" for the curriculum to be provocatively generative without losing form or shape cannot be laid out in advance. This issue is one to be continually negotiated among students, teachers, and texts (the latter having long histories and basic assumptions that cannot be neglected). But the issue of the curriculum needing disturbing qualities is not to be negotiated; these qualities form the problematics of life itself and are the essence of a rich and transforming curriculum. Another way to state this is to say that the *problematics, perturbations, possibilities* inherent in a curriculum are what give the curriculum not only its richness but also its sense of being, its *dasein*.

The main academic disciplines taught in schools have their own historical contexts, fundamental concepts, and final vocabularies. Hence, each will interpret richness in its own way. Language—including reading, writing, literature, and oral communication—

develops its richness by focusing heavily (but not exclusively) on the interpretation of metaphors, myths, narratives. Saying this places language within a hermeneutic frame; it is to see language as integrated with culture, as one of the determinants of culture.

Mathematics—a subject in which computational arithmetic plays but a small part—takes its form of richness from "playing with patterns." Obviously, this can be done *par excellence* with computers—tools that any mathematically rich curriculum should possess—but computers are not a *sine qua non*. Patterns may be seen, developed; played with in simple number combinations (as with the Fibonnaci series) or with geometry of both a Euclidean and fractal sort. Breaking a square into right triangles is an example of the former; the Sierpinski triangle is an example of the latter. At all levels, from kindergarten through graduate school, mathematics can be dealt with meaningfully as "playing with patterns."

Science—including the biological and the physical—can be seen as intuiting, developing, probing, "proving" hypotheses concerning the world in which we live. This moves science beyond the collection of "facts"—with the assumption these facts are objective bits of reality—into the realm of manipulating, creating, working with facts or information in an imaginative and (thermo)dynamic manner. This view of science is obviously more Whiteheadian than Newtonian, more oriented toward Prigogine than Laplace. The social sciences—those multiple disciplines of anthropology, economics, history, psychology, and sociology—take their concept of richness from dialoguing about, or negotiating passages between, various (often competing) interpretations of societal issues. Here, probably more than in any other discipline, assumptions are questioned. It is these assumed givens that form the foundations of society's mores, norms, standards; and in a democratic society it is imperative these givens be open to dialogue.

Obviously these disciplines, their languages, and histories are not mutually exclusive. The concept of developing richness through dialogue, interpretations, hypothesis generation and proving, and pattern playing can apply to all we do in curriculum. Again, such ideas sound strange to those imbued with a modernist perspective, which helps explain why we need to transcend this perspective to a post-modernist one.

Recursion. From recur, to happen again,[1] recursion usually is associated with the mathematical operation of iteration. In iteration a formula is "run" over and over, with the output of one equation being the input for the next. In $y = 3x + 1$, a y of 4 (if the $x = 1$) becomes the next x, and the new y of 13 becomes the next x, and so on. In such iterations, there is both stability and change; the formula stays the same, the variables change (in an orderly but often nonpredictable manner). As was explained in Chapter Four, some interesting complex patterns develop with particular formulae and particular x, y variables.

However, when Bruner (1986) states that "any formal theory of mind is helpless without recursion" (p. 97)—and asserts the importance of recursion for epistemology and pedagogy—he refers less to mathematics and more to the human capacity of having thoughts loop back on themselves. Such looping, thoughts on thoughts, distinguishes human consciousness; it is the way we make meaning. As Bruner says:

> Much of the process of education consists of being able to distance oneself in some way from what one knows by being able to reflect on one's own knowledge. (p. 127)

This is also the way one produces a sense of self, through reflective interaction with the environment, with others, with a culture. As I pointed out in Chapter Six, such "recursive reflection" lies at the heart of a transformative curriculum; it is *the process* which Dewey, Piaget, Whitehead all advocate. In the 1960s Bruner made a beginning at defining a recursive curriculum with his "spiral curriculum" (1960) and his elementary school social studies program, "Man: A Course of Study" (1966). However, in our then-modernist mode both of these were misseen, attaining only popular approval and notoriety. Their power never became evident; the former got lost in the question of calculus for first graders, the latter in the issue of Bruner's patriotism.

In a curriculum that honors, values, uses recursion, there is no fixed beginning or ending. As Dewey has pointed out, every ending is a new beginning, every beginning emerges from a prior ending. Curriculum segments, parts, sequences are arbitrary chunks that, instead of being seen as isolated units, are seen as opportunities for reflection. In such a frame, every test, paper, journal entry can be seen not merely as the completion of one project but also as the beginning of another—to explore, discuss, inquire into both ourselves as meaning makers and into the text in question. This curriculum will, of course, be open not closed; like post-modernism itself, it is Janus-faced, eclectic, interpretive.

Recursion and repetition differ in that neither one, in any way, reflects the other. Repetition, a strong element in the modernist mode, is designed to improve set performance. Its frame is closed. Recursion aims at developing competence—the ability to organize, combine, inquire, use something heuristically. Its frame is open. The functional difference between repetition and recursion lies in the role reflection plays in each. In repetition, reflection plays a negative role; it breaks the process. There is a certain automaticity to repetition that keeps the same process going—over and over and over, as in flash card arithmetic drills or in ball machine tennis drills. In recursion, reflection plays a positive role; for thoughts to leap back on themselves, as in Dewey's secondary experience reflecting back on primary experience, or in Piaget's reflexive intelligence reflecting back on practical intelligence, it is necessary, as Bruner has said, to step back from one's doings, to "distance oneself in some way" from one's own thoughts.[2] Thus, in recursion it is a necessity to have others— peers, teachers—look at, critique, respond to what one has done. Dialogue becomes the *sine qua non* of recursion: Without reflection—engendered by dialogue—recursion becomes shallow not transformative; it is not reflective recursion, it is only repetition.

Relations. The concept of relations is important to a post-modern, transformative curriculum in two ways: in a *pedagogical* way and in a *cultural* way. The former might, naturally, be called pedagogical relations, referring to those within the curriculum—the matrix or network which gives it richness. The latter might, just as naturally, be called cultural relations, referring to those cultural or cosmological relations which lie outside the curriculum but form a large matrix within which the curriculum is embedded. Both relations are important; each complements the other.

In focusing on *pedagogical relations*, one focuses on the connections within a curriculum's structure which give the curriculum its depth as this is developed by recursion. Here the twin processes of doing and reflecting-on-doing are important, and through these processes the curriculum becomes richer with the passage of time. As Prigogine is fond of saying, time in a Newtonian frame is *reversible and unimportant;* in the dissipative structure frames he studies, it is *irreversible and important* (1988; with Stengers, 1984, Ch. 7). If the universe is already set, time does no more than give one the chance to "see" more of that universe. "Mastery learning" assumes this frame—the student is to take the time necessary to master the material presented to a certain, predetermined level of repetitious proficiency (Torshen, 1977). In a universe of and in process, time takes on a different, qualitative dimension; it acquires a transformative aspect, since development of one sort or another is always occurring. Conditions, situations, relations are always changing; the present does not recreate the past (though it is certainly influenced by the past) nor does the present determine the future (though it is an influencer). So, too, the curriculum frame operating at the beginning of the course is unavoidably different from the curriculum frame operating at the end of the course. The issue is not difference but degree or quality of difference—whether the difference is a difference that makes a difference.

Recognizing the contingency of relations, and hoping that these relations will be positively and communally developed during the course of a semester, I organize my undergraduate and graduate university courses to enhance this development. Among the devices I use, one is to provide a syllabus that lists common readings for only two-thirds of the course; for the last third various groups choose their readings from a selected list. Class time is devoted not to summarizing these various readings but to interconnecting them to both the common readings and to each other. The quality of discussion improves as the semester *develops;* so, too, papers written early in the semester improve dramatically when rewritten and reframed after utilizing the insights gained. Sometimes the change is transformative.

In junior high classes, where I have often used a set text, I build time-oriented relationships by asking students to reframe the material presented, to choose from or reframe chapter questions, and to deal with the textual material on both a "what-if" (imaginary) basis and a "relate-it-to-yourself" (real) basis. In dealing with elementary school grades, I follow the same general procedures but use far more manipulative materials, story telling, projects, and dramatic presentations. The textbook, throughout all this, is seen as something to revise, not as something to follow. It is the base from which transformation occurs. Curriculum in a post-modern frame needs to be created (self-organized) by the classroom community, not by textbook authors.

It should be obvious in all these personal anecdotes that, in building a curriculum matrix with a rich set of relationships, I have been strongly influenced by Whitehead's (1929/1967a) dictum to "not teach too many subjects" but to "teach thoroughly" what I do teach, and to let the main ideas "be thrown into every combination possible" (p. 2).

The concept of *cultural relations* grows out of a hermeneutic cosmology—one which emphasizes narration and dialogue as key vehicles in interpretation. Narration brings forward the concepts of history (through story), language (through oral telling), and place (through a story's locality). Dialogue interrelates these three to provide us with a sense of culture that is local in origin but global in interconnections. Thus, all our interpretations relate to local culture and interconnect with other cultures and their interpretations via a global matrix. Discourse (narration and dialogue) operates, then, within such a double-tiered cultural frame; it does this far more so than within the foundationalist, abstract, and privileged frame modernism posited. Discourse now becomes what Jim Cheney (1989) calls "contextualist" (p. 123)—bound always by the localness of ourselves, our histories, our language, our place, but also expanding into an ever-broadening global and ecological network. It is this double-tiered or dual-focused nature that makes cultural relations so complex.

Recognizing the contextualist nature of discourse helps us realize that the constructs of those participating frame all conversations, all acts of teaching. As teachers we cannot, do not, transmit information directly; rather, we perform the teaching act when we help others negotiate passages between their constructs and ours, between ours and others'. This is why Dewey says teaching is an interactive process with learning a *by-product* of that interaction.

Modernism has not adopted such an interrelational view; it has taken as one of its hallmarks movement beyond the local and contextual to the universal and abstract. Instead of the narrational, it has aimed for, indeed created, the *meta*narrational, the *grand écrit* Lyotard attacks. Teachers, fitting unconsciously into this paradigm—as we all do—have unwittingly carried on their discourses with students by speaking *ex cathedra*. Too often, teacher explanations have resounded with the authority of God; too rarely have meaningful, interactive, participating dialogues been held.

C.A. Bowers (1987; with Flinders, 1990) has tied the concept of cultural relationships to the ecological crises we face today. In doing this he draws our attention to modernism's overly strong sense of individualism. Individualism has tended to pit humanity against nature (civilization is defined as society improving on nature) and to believe that progress occurs through competition, not cooperation. This is one of modernism's myths founded on beliefs like Bacon's that we should *subject Nature to the hand of man*. This statement would be abhorrent, even sacrilegious, to pre-modern or tribal cultures such as the North American Indian.

But this belief in competition and the virtue of controlling the natural is part of our present day pedagogy and cosmology. Bowers, Griffin, and Oliver (also Lydon, 1992) are among the few curricularists who encourage us to rethink our concept of relations, who see that *cultural relationships* extend beyond our personal selves to include the ecosystem—indeed the cosmos in which we live. Only now, in the past decade or so, are we beginning to develop a cosmic and interrelational consciousness. The challenge of such recognition is twofold: on the one hand, to honor the localness of our perceptions and, on the other hand, to realize that our local perspectives integrate into a larger cultural, ecological, cosmic matrix. Our progress and our existence—as individuals, as communities, as a race, as a species, as a life form—depend on our ability to bring these two perspectives into complementary harmony.

Rigor. In some ways the most important of the four criteria, rigor keeps a transformative curriculum from falling into either "rampant relativism" or sentimental solipsism. In presenting transformation as an alternative to our current measurement frame, it is easy to see transformation as no more than anti-measurement or nonmeasurement. Here, transformation becomes not a true alternative but yet another variation on the very thing it tries to replace. This certainly happened in the progressive and open education movements. Dewey wrestled with the problem in the progressive education movement and wrote "Need for a Philosophy of Education" to explain why progressive education needed to be more than anti-traditional, why progressive education had to have its own foundation and frame. In contrasting his view of progressive education—developmental and transformative—with either the received progressive view (which he considered too romantic) or the established traditional view (which he considered too rigid), he said:

> This alternative is not just a middle course or compromise between the two procedures. It is something radically different from either. Existing likes and powers are to be treated as possibilities. (1934/1964c, p. 8)

In such a transformative frame, with its emphasis on indeterminacy, shifting relationships, and spontaneous self-organization, rigor wears a very different set of clothes than it did in the modernist frame. Rigor began, at least in the scholastic sense, with the Jesuits' Q.E.D.—"Quod Est Demonstratum" (Thus it is demonstrated)—from the deductive power of their Aristotlean-based logic. Descartes objected to this logic, replacing it with his own "clear and distinct" ideas—those which no reasonable person could doubt, those he received from God, but also ones he "saw" with his mind's eye. Rigor thus moved from Aristotlean-Euclidean logic to deeply felt perceptions and conceptions. The English empiricists wanted to move rigor yet again, away from subjective states, no matter how personally appealing, to the objective and observable. Here rigor entered a world that could be measured and manipulated. Our present twentieth-century concept of rigor has elements of all these strains—scholastic logic, scientific observation, and mathematical precision.

To think of rigor without these qualities is to call for a virtual redefinition of the concept. Rigor in a post-modern frame requires just this. It draws on qualities foreign to a modernist frame—interpretation and indeterminacy, to mention but two. In dealing with indeterminacy, one can never be certain one "has it right"—not even to the 95th or 99th percentile of probability. One must continually be exploring, looking for new combinations, interpretations, patterns. This is why, in his scientific methodology, Dewey (1933/1971) listed the fourth stage as "the mental elaboration of an idea" (p. 107), "developing the relations of ideas to one another" (p. 113), and "playing with concepts" (p. 182). Here we find echoes and presagings of statements made by Whitehead, Kuhn, Bruner—not to close too early or finally on the rightness of an idea, to throw all ideas into various combinations. Here rigor means purposely looking for different alternatives, relations, connections. Michel Serres does this well, as shown in his wolf and sheep essay, drawing together LaFontaine's fable and Descartes' right method (see Chapter One).

In dealing with interpretation rigorously, one needs to be aware that all valuations depend on (often hidden) assumptions. As frames differ so do the problems, procedures, and valued results. Rigor here means the conscious attempt to ferret out these assumptions, ones we or others hold dear, as well as negotiating passages between these assumptions, so the dialogue may be meaningful and transformative. As Iser points out, dialogue between reader and text is a two-way process, each has a voice, and in this dialogue there is a combining of determinacy and indeterminacy. Indeterminacy here does not mean arbitrariness; rather, it "allows [for] a spectrum of actualization" (1978, p. 24)—better yet, it allows for a range of possibilities from which actualizations appear. Which actualization does appear for development depends on the interaction process itself, on mixing indeterminacy with determinacy.

So, too, rigor may be defined in terms of mixing—indeterminacy with interpretation. The quality of interpretation, its own richness, depends on how fully and well we develop the various alternatives indeterminacy presents. In this new frame for rigor—combining the complexity of indeterminacy with the hermeneutics of interpretation—it seems necessary to establish a community, one critical yet supportive. Such a community is, I believe, what Dewey thought a school should be.

NOTES

1. It is interesting to note that *recursion* (as well as *recur*) is derived from the Latin *recurrere* (to run back). In this way recursion is allied with *currere* (to run), the root word for curriculum.

2. As I've said already, it is this distancing of oneself from one's actions and thoughts that is missing in Schön's concept of reflection.

REFERENCES

Bowers, C.A. (1987). *Elements of a post-liberal theory of education.* New York: Teachers College Press.

Bowers, C.A., & Flinders, D. J.(1980). *Responsive teaching.* New York: Teachers College Press.

Bruner, J. (1960). *The process of education.* Cambridge, MA: Harvard University Press.

———.(1986). *Actual minds, possible worlds.* Cambridge, MA: Harvard University Press.

Cheney, J. (1989). Post-Modern environmental ethics: Ethics as bioregional narrative. *Environmental Ethics, 11* (Summer), 117–134.

Dewey, J. (1964c). Need for a philosophy of education. In R. D. Archambault (Ed.), *John Dewey on education: Selected writings* (pp. 3–14). New York: Random House. (Original work published 1934)

———. (1971). *How we think.* Chicago: Henry Regnery. (Original work published 1933)

Doll, W. E., Jr. (1977). The role of contrast in the development of competence. In Alex Molner & John Zahorik (Eds.), *Curriculum theory* (pp.50–63). Washington, D.C.: Association for Supervision and Curriculum Development.

———. (1989a). Complexity in the classroom. *Educational Leadership, 47,* 65–70.

Iser, W. (1978). *The act of reading.* Baltimore: Johns Hopkins University Press.

Lydon, A. (1992). Cosmology and curriculum. Unpublished dissertation, Louisiana State University.

Prigogine, I. (1988). The rediscovery of time. In Richard F. Kitchener (Ed.), *The world view of contemporary physics: Does it need a new metaphysics?* (pp. 125–143). Albany: SUNY Press.

Prigogine, I., & Stengers, I. (1984). *Order out of chaos: Man's new dialogue with nature.* New York: Bantam Books.

Torshen, K. (1977). *The mastery approach to competency-based education.* New York: Academic Press.

Whitehead, A. N. (1967a). *The aims of education.* New York: Free Press. (Original work published 1929)

22

The Burdens of the New Curricularist

PETER HLEBOWITSH

CURRICULARISTS HAVE LONG PLAYED A SIGNIFICANT ROLE in the historical struggle to give coherence and identity to the American school experience. Historically speaking, their methods have usually been practical and institutional in orientation, dedicated to offering curriculum development frameworks centered on using the school for the maintenance and improvement of the public interest. Progressive curricularists, especially those working out of experimentalist views of Dewey, provided unique insight into the process of curriculum development by insisting that school practice make itself accountable to three fundamental factors: the nature of the learner, the values and aims of the society, and the wider organization of knowledge or subject matter. Not surprisingly, practical proposals for school improvement flowed freely from these progressive curricularists. William Kilpatrick, for instance, articulated the Project Method, Jesse Newlon tested "life situations" curricula in the Denver schools, Ralph Tyler formulated his famous Rationale in the context of the Eight Year Study, Harold Rugg wrote a series of provocative social studies texts, and laboratory schools across the nation, often led by directors schooled in curriculum development, tested the practical vigor of various new ideas.

The times, however, have changed, and a good share of the contemporary curriculum community now perceives the historical effort to build the field around the act of curriculum development as a wanting and misguided project. In a recently published "synoptic" text that assumes the responsibility of covering the full dimensions of the curriculum field, Pinar and others (1995) have written the epitaph for curriculum development. Believing that the historical growth of curriculum development was tied to an administrative need to impose unreasonable control and authority on teachers and children, Pinar and others (1995) have proclaimed the act of curriculum development to be no longer relevant to the work of the curriculum scholar.

The significance of Pinar's proclamation is tied to the fact that he is claiming to represent the field in a text that ostensibly encourages the understanding of the curriculum

Reprinted by permission of Blackwell Publishers from *Curriculum Inquiry*, Vol. 29., No. 3, 1999, pp. 343–354.

from multitudinous "discourses." The young student's introduction to the field of curriculum in the book not only includes being reminded that curriculum development is dead, but also that the history of the curriculum field is rooted in the traditions of social efficiency and the act of destructive social control.

Many scholars see such criticism as credible and acknowledge the need for the curriculum field to move in a new direction. Of course, there are many ways to examine the field of curriculum and it is not always easy to find categories that accommodate various curriculum perspectives. Nevertheless, it is fair to say that a new curricularist has indeed emerged. Pinar has described a reconceptualist movement in the field, a new assemblage of thinkers interested in reconceiving the work of the curricularist. One could even describe the new curricularist in postmodern terms, as a scholar informed by a theoretical position that resonates with studies in hermeneutics, poststructuralism, feminism, aesthetics, racial theory, and among others, politics. More sensitive to race and gender issues than his historical counterpart, the new curricularist is on a mission to put the old curriculum tradition to rest and to make it clear that a new project is at hand.

Although variations obviously exist among all curricularists, the fact that a reconceptualization in the field has been declared and that few scholars have disputed its validity is itself some certification of a new broad perspective in the field.

In this article, I would like to raise a few issues about the potential effects of this new perspective. There are, like it or not, several important functions and purposes to the work of the curricularist embedded in the traditions and the historical development of the field. They are the responsibilities given to those who claim to represent and advance the field by those who have built the field. They include responsibilities related to the development of school practice and school design, the securing of unity in the field, and the honest interpretation of historical knowledge. I call these the burdens of the new curricularist because they are the overlooked inherited ideals of the field.

THE BURDEN OF PRACTICE

During the 1970s, various curriculum scholars declared the field of curriculum studies to be moribund. The reasoning behind this declaration had everything to do with a perceived crisis in the theoretical anchor of the field (Schwab 1970). Theory in the context of the curriculum was not believed to be very theoretical; it had encroached on practice in a way that made the two virtually indistinguishable, leading to axiomatic statements about how to teach and how to organize a curriculum. Theory, in this sense, had lost its soul, giving priority to prescriptive judgments instead of reflective and deliberative ones.

The problem with theory was probably best embodied in the manner in which the educational research community separated the concepts of curriculum and instruction. This theoretical separation allowed many educational researchers to sanction classroom actions that openly separated the question of "what" was taught from the question of "how" it was taught. Thus, ideas such as "time on task" and instructional (Madeline Hunterlike) models of teaching dominated the discussion. Teachers were reminded, for instance, that "time on task" was important, irrespective of the task's nature, and were told that particular types of methodologies and models were pivotal to good teaching, no matter *what* one attempted to teach with them. Similarly, the teacher effectiveness literature, which gained so much popularity during the 1980s, told us that "effective" teachers, among other things, were expected to focus clearly on academic goals, present information clearly, cover subject matter extensively, monitor student progress and provide quick and well-targeted feedback. It had nothing to say, however, about the nature of what the teacher was organizing, monitoring, or targeting. The separation between curriculum and instruction led to a simplified instructional and mechanical teaching orientation. To many curriculum theorists, this situation constituted a clear practical crisis.

Some of the reaction to this crisis, however, embraced theory as something separate from practice and as something that was no longer directly folded into the actions of class-room teachers. And this is where the reconceptualist themes of Pinar and others arrived on the scene. Theory, in their eyes, became a construct of dissent or protest, no longer looking for practical application as much as looking to provide critical commentary that might inform the emergent judgments of people working in emergent situations. The idea of breaking the organic relation between theory and practice produced a new level of curriculum discourse. Practice was now largely an individualistic affair, and individual's personalized argument for action. The idea of curriculum development was declared out-of-date, disparaged as a managerial mechanism that destroyed the experiential variance of the school.

In the past, of course, it would have been quite unreasonable to argue that theory should separate itself from practice. To the new curricularist, however, such a separation is essential. The result has led to the open rejection of what one might call conventional design considerations (objectives, evaluative mechanisms, and so forth). Such design factors, as the argument goes, always carry a privileging dimension that serves some groups and individuals, while simultaneously harming others. Because design leads to an identifiable program of knowledge and skills to be learned, and identifiable objectives as well as identifiable evaluation techniques, it cannot sanction the full complement of cultural, linguistic, political, racial, gender, and life style differences that might prevail in the student population. Thus, design fails to honor the chaos in the complexity of schooling; it fails to honor the significance of place, and it limits the possibilities for autonomous and emergent judgments.

According to the new curricularist, the great sin of those who argued for the power of curriculum design was that they placed the heavy hand of control into the lives of individuals by supporting measures of procedural imposition. Needless to say, behavioristic traditions have partially prevailed in the schools over the past several decades, but not without a struggle and certainly not with the support of the entire curriculum development community. Even Tyler, it should be recalled, was a critic of behavioristic influences in the curriculum. And in a decentralized system that offers most of its veteran teachers tenure protections, American teachers have more freedom and choice than is typically appreciated.

Still, to the new curricularists, the act of control by its very existence seems to mean that people and their experiences will be harmed. There is no appreciation for or acknowledgment of the important role that control plays in a free democracy. The view is not dissimilar to believing that a traffic light at a busy cross-section is an imposition on the driver, who, to be truly free and creative, should be able to motor about the streets at his or her own will. The red light, of course, regulates the freedom of the driver, frees him from the paralytic conditions that would surely prevail if everyone were free to drive according to their felt passions. The position articulated by the new curricularist promotes a malevolent interpretation of control in the context of curriculum development. Here control could only lead to stunted experiences.

Such a negative view of control manifests openly when the question of curriculum objectives is raised. Perkinson (1993), for instance, has written a lengthy essay about the uselessness of objectives in the curriculum, stating that their presence in the curriculum implies a transmissive attitude toward knowledge. Perkinson believes that the act of teaching and learning has to be injected with a critical perspective that is irreducible to any preset goals. He believes that teachers should simply help children with their skill development in a free, critical, and supportive environment.

> Teachers should abandon goals. Teachers should have no predetermined expected outcomes for students, no preset standards, no expected kinds of student performance. Instead of having a goal, teachers should adopt an agenda. Then the teacher's task becomes one of helping students get better in some skill, or area, or domain. (Perkinson 1993, p. 28)

Pinar's work has followed along the same course. Pinar (1992) has specifically written about the need to unhinge theory from practice, to distance theory from popular factory and corporate models of education and to underscore the relativity of teaching. The idea behind Pinar's work is to provide a theory that is unencumbered by practice in a way that helps it to release more creative and critical perspectives on teaching. Part of the response from Pinar is in reaction to his particularized historical view of curriculum development, which he sees as essentially administrative and procedural in orientation.

But the question facing curriculum theorists and curriculum developers interested in schooling is one that always comes down to a schedule of time and place and to a sense of what knowledge and experiences are most worthwhile. This is a reality that cannot be ignored. Few in the context of the school would likely see much worth in any recommendation that advises the school to abandon all goals, all standards, and all preset notions on how to proceed. To even consider such a possibility will simply result in giving greater power to players less informed by the curriculum literature, such as testing services, politicians, state departments of education, and commercial industries. For curricularists to repudiate the development of some sense of standards, objectives, and performance expectations will only mean that someone else will assume the responsibility.

Where the public interest and the school converge, the curriculum must prevail with an intervention. This requires some sense of what is to be done, when it is to be done, and how it is to be done. These do not necessarily need to be overtly technical or prescriptive interventions, but they do have to actualize a fundamental framework that makes a case for what is best for schooling in a democracy. The centrality of practical and deliberate judgments in the curriculum are underscored by the institutional character of the curriculum (Reid 1994). This has been the received view of the field since its inception. Dewey clearly understood this when he observed that "the conception of education as a social process and function has no definite meaning until we define the kind of society we have in mind." Although the nature of learning is always fluid and cannot be completely understood before-hand, it is still framed with a directive purpose.

As one of the leading voices of the new curriculum perspective, Pinar (1992) seems to not worry about such matters. He is passionate about supporting local conditions and he puts his faith in the informed and emergent condition. He also draws a line in the sand against universal applications in the curriculum. In effect, he says that curriculum theorists should not have a program to offer because they cannot have a program to offer. The curriculum is not preordained or ever fashioned with objectives, but is brought to life by a self-affirming and emancipated educator whose thinking is freed from the mechanical functions of curriculum practice.

Over the years, many educational scholars have been judged not by any particular improvement that they might have suggested but by their dissenting voice, by their ability to argue for a change without stipulating how the change might proceed. The work of the new curricularists could perhaps be viewed in such a light. But, in the end, such voices will ultimately be judged in the educational situation. What actually occurs in the classroom in the name of postmodernism or in the name of reconceptualism cannot escape notice or debate. When one proclaims a theoretical position advocating, say, "counterhegemonic" or "emancipatory" practices in the school, one immediately has to ask how such practices will be conducted? What will they be? What hidden effects might result from their application? Will there be sinister things happening in the name of such high-minded rhetoric? The practicality of theory can never be forsaken if one is going to expect theory to have manifest effects in practice. This is another way of saying that the separation of curriculum theory from curriculum development is practically impossible because, in the words of Ralph Tyler, it results in denying the essential purpose of the theory. This is the burden of practice.

THE BURDEN OF DESIGN

In 1994, Jean Anyon engaged in a critical appraisal of the problems that have resulted from leftist influences in educational studies. Sympathetic to leftist causes, Anyon nevertheless found that there is still a need to erect "socially useful theory" that "produces a dialogue between concepts of one's goals or vision, and people's current activities and problems" (p. 118). She further explained that such theory must be capable of enactment. To my mind, the enactment of socially useful theory points directly to a curriculum development strategy. Theory that is socially useful works within social and political realities and is carried out for the purpose of testing its power in practice. Theory that produces a discussion about the relation between vision (goals) and activities, is one that must influence practical action; it must point to a sense of *how to proceed*.

The distancing of theory from practice makes theory deliberately less socially useful and less conscious of its implementational feasibility. Social and political realities might very well provide a drag on theory, but that is precisely the point. The living actualities of the school situation and of the larger societal or community culture have to be considered to make theory workable. Even if one wanted to change these realities, such an effort would have to proceed practically and deliberately.

Curriculum scholars have always had their feet planted in both the theoretical and the practical. Dewey was a theoretical giant with very practical ideas about the educative process, the thinking process, and the nature of conduct in a democracy. The early progressive tradition in curriculum, which was launched as a theoretical counter against traditional humanism, provided a wealth of practical insight drawn from experimental schools. Besides Dewey's laboratory school, there were the experimental schools described in the 26th Yearbook of the National Society for the Study of Education (1927), the descriptive accounts provided by Rugg and Shumaker (1928), and by Dewey and his daughter, Evelyn (1915), the Lincoln School teacher units published by the Bureau of Publications at Teachers College, and the school work of Parker, Newlon, Horn, Washburne, Caswell, Tyler, and many others. The vestiges of these early efforts are not reducible to the kinds of administrative/social efficiency traditions that many curriculum scholars seem only to see. Whole language instruction, cooperative learning, teacher-made units, interdisciplinary reform, teacher participation in curriculum development, teacher release time, general education, experimental schooling, civic learning, and the general perspective of placing the act of teaching and schooling in the context of the nature of the learner and the values of the society (to name only a very short list), are all, in some way, attributable to these early initiatives. The crisis of theory that concerns the new curricularist has not, at least in the history of the curriculum, been one that has led exclusively to a hyper-specified curriculum enacted by procedural compulsions.

In Tyler's tradition, the construction of objectives and other design considerations was part of a theoretical framework that had to be accountable to *the nature of the learner, to the values of the society and to the wider world of organized knowledge.* The curriculum was free to pursue various philosophical pleasures within these limits. This is one reason why we are still discussing the viability of the Rationale some five decades after its original publication. Although many critics of the Rationale have been quick to point to the so-called prescriptive features of Tyler's idea, Kliebard (1970), whose criticism of the Rationale is best known, has argued that the Rationale did not provide *enough* guidance for curriculum making. But if Tyler lacked guidance, what do we make of many of today's new thinkers?

The guiding curriculum development features favored by Tyler provided a guard or counterbalance against overtly ideological views of schooling and education. The new curricularists have instead created the conditions for understanding the curriculum as a phenomenon that largely arises out of personalized or overtly ideologized desires. This is, in some ways, befuddling because there is absolutely no design framework protecting against the very imperialism and overt ideologizing that the new curricularist apparently fears in the work of others. But it could very well be that the enthusiasm with which the new curricularists embrace the rejection of design has everything to do with the promotion of a political agenda that is more easily advanced without the encumbrance of a literature that speaks to the nature of the learner and to the expression of a common social mandate.

The issue of a public mandate is particularly important in this respect. The desire to honor the significance of place in the curriculum, an important theme in the work of the new curriculum perspective, is highly problematic when done without consideration of a broader public mandate. Admittedly, the American school curriculum has functioned historically in a governance structure that has supported localized traditions and that has kept the school close to the hands of the people. This was the ideal originally embraced by the Puritans. But in an increasingly complex and pluralistic society, the public school also has to provide children with an enlargening and amalgamating experience that purposefully goes beyond (or even challenges) local traditions. The desire to advance the moral dimensions of the curriculum by calling for a community-based vision only makes sense if it is accompanied by the wider purpose of building common political communities across parochial (community) lines. Although communities are clearly important (largely because they represent common interests, common histories, and a common discourse), they are not always benevolent places. To take an extreme example, the significance of place in a community dominated by White Supremacists, or by certain religious extremists (or by any group or community socializing its youth with one clear ethnic, political, or religious stamp), will require the challenging of place. The schools in such communities need a broader conception of experience rooted perhaps in constitutional principles and in an exposure to a variance of values and attitudes and knowledge that might otherwise not be gained by the students. Such a function precisely underscores the importance of design. Design structures the larger experience. It tells us which knowledge is most worthwhile and which community traditions may or may not be worthy. This is the burden of design.

THE BURDEN OF UNITY

The process of proclaiming a reconceptualization in the curriculum field has drawn a line between those who walk with Tyler and those who have walked away from Tyler. It has helped to create a field that is now largely in schism (Hlebowitsh 1997). Many of us who have worked out of an experimentalist-progressive line continue to be labeled as traditionalists who are caught up in the task of designing oppressive environments for youth (Slattery 1995). The labeling has even extended into portraying the work of progressive curricularists as the exercise of heterosexual male dominion over the classroom work of predominantly female teachers (Pinar 1999). Such views are not only manifestly unfair, but they also are fundamentally unscholarly, because they misunderstand the historical development of the field and ultimately create serious wedges in the field. Although there is a new awakening of diversity in curriculum studies, it has come at the cost of the field's sense of itself and of its capacity to build upon its own heritage and to consolidate its historical gains. Questions that gave the field some coherence, such as what knowledge is most worthwhile, what learning and teaching patterns are most appropriate, and what evaluative mechanisms can best capture the effects of the curriculum experience, no longer hold sway. The more difficult issue of paradigmatic development in the field seems practically hopeless. The curriculum community, in fact, resists talk of paradigms or the less threatening idea of a consensual framework, mostly out of fear of committing the instrumentalist's sin of design.

Achieving a sense of unity has always been an issue in the field. In 1926, Harold Rugg put together several forums dedicated to discussing central questions pertinent to the field. Participation in the forums was inclusive; luminaries such as George Counts, W. W. Charters, Ernest Horn, Franklin Bobbitt, Jesse Newlon, William Bagley, Stuart Courtis, and William Kilpatrick were all involved. The by-products of these inquiries and discussions were published in the NSSE 26th Yearbook, a work that helped to acknowledge fundamental differences in the field and that searched for new bases of professional commonality and community. It was among the few curriculum documents that cataloged and reviewed the theoretical divergencies of its day and that brought forward the major thinkers of the time for a discussion aimed at cultivating a sense of understanding and unity. One could debate the worth of the composite statement of unity on the foundations of curriculum-making forged in the yearbook, as others have, but few would question the worth of trying to find some reorientation and balance in the field, one that strikes the chord of conversation and community.

But the questions asked by Rugg focussed on curriculum-making and on various design differences in progressive experimental schools. The diversity of the field was foundationally anchored, vested in a common commitment to the institution of public schooling and to the belief in testing new curriculum frameworks. The problem of unity today is much more difficult and much more dangerous, because there is essentially no center of gravity. We cannot even agree on the kinds of questions to ask, or even agree that curriculum theory should be tied into school practice. How can we, then, see ourselves as a field?

This is the condition inherited and partly generated by the new curricularist. If the field is going to hold together, it has to have a sense of itself; it has to be sure that the rising generation of scholars will be socialized into some common understandings. Where are the common forces in a field wracked by pronouncements that have declared one vital historical line of inquiry dead? How can the common causes of the field be reawakened when the very ground that provided stability is viewed as contaminated? How can a postmodern theory of protest stand for anything when it actively seeks deconstruction? This is the burden of unity.

THE BURDEN OF HISTORY

Another burden that weighs on the new curricularist is related to historical interpretation. A challenge has been posed to the new curricularist over the preferred portrayal of Tyler and other "traditional" scholars in the field (Hlebowitsh 1993). Complaints about the overreaching effects of the social efficiency doctrine in the schools are important, but such criticisms were well-established long ago. In fact, arguably the best criticism ever written of social efficiency, particularly against the work of Franklin Bobbitt, was authored by Boyd Bode (1927), in his classic *Modern Educational Theories*. Unfortunately, many scholars fail to understand that the progressive-experimentalist tradition in the field of curriculum grew out of a theoretical foundation forged by Dewey, a tradition that included Tyler. What seems to prevail today is a social efficiency interpretation of Tyler and of the general evolutionary line of curriculum studies.

This is as problematic as it is significant because the proclamation of a reconceptualization of the field has still not made a very convincing case against the very traditions against which it claims to be working. I have argued elsewhere that the Tyler rationale is not a behavioristic construct that has taken its genes from the atomized curriculum that Franklin Bobbitt supported in earlier years (Hlebowitsh 1992, 1995). The rationale itself is a progressive document that grows out of Dewey's work on reflective thinking and the educative process. I also have argued that the position taken on the idea of social control by many theorists has been constructed in an unbalanced manner that fails to reflect some early progressive efforts to put children in control of their lives as opposed to putting them under control (Hlebowitsh 1993).

If the very traditions against which the reconceptualists have protested have themselves been misunderstood, then the reconceptualization itself is suspect. If one's antidote to x is y, what happens to the argument when one discovers that x is not x? If the so-called traditionalists were actually progressive-liberals who took their framework from the early work of Dewey and if the history of the curriculum field does not fit into the argument of malevolent social control, then it very well might be time to reconceptualize the entire effort at reconceptualization, or, as my colleague, William Wraga, once observed, to restore the field. We can start the process by reconsidering the idea of design and by trying to learn from both the mistakes and the strengths of the historical struggle to pose an American curriculum. This is the burden of history.

CONCLUSION

If the new curricularists want to move the theoretical focus of the field away from the public school and the historical/institutional regard for *civitas*, in favor of more symbolic and individualistic theoretical expressions, does any responsibility toward school practice necessarily remain? At a time when we expect the school to address concerns that some families have relinquished and to craft experiences that assist with the socialization of children in an increasingly pluralistic democracy, how can anyone be comfortable with a theoretical emphasis that contains no sharp sense of how to proceed with schooling in a democracy?

The progressive branch of the curriculum field has always viewed schooling as operating within a miniature unit of democracy that was *deliberately and consciously* conceived to produce a comprehensive and enlargening social experience, where children learned about their differences and their commonalities, where vocational pursuits coexisted with academic ones, and where the ideals of tolerance and social mutuality were met by the needs for dissent and critical mindedness.

The new curricularist, however, has abandoned this historical conviction and has left us with an embrace of alternativeness and the power of place, a theoretical position that differs little from the free market principles of conservative politics and capitalism. As the public school agenda continues to be ravaged by privatization arguments and by the appetites of various special interests, how does the reconceptualist commitment to variety separate from the call of the marketplace?

To be the bearer of the field, the new curricularists have to have an answer. This means that they have to find a way to transcend their own proclivity toward criticism and protest, and frame a useful theory of conduct that could endure their own style of criticism. The slashing and burning of a field are always done in the interest of cultivating more fertile soil. But the burden is to grow a crop, to construct a practical theory of action that represents an enlightened school pathway for all American youth.

I have argued that the new curriculum scholar has several key questions to answer before declaring any reconceptualization. The effect on the field will be fatal if the new curricularists do not deal with the relativism toward the school curriculum that they have helped to bring forward. This means that some discussion must prevail over questions of design and practice. At the same time, the preferred historical interpretation used by the new curricularist has to be reexamined. Has there been misjudgment in the historical belief that curriculum history is rooted unremediably in the most malevolent forms of social control and social efficiency? If so, quite a bit of reformulation is in order. These questions of practice, design, and history, in the end, will determine whether the house will stand. These are the burdens of the new curricularist.

REFERENCES

Anyon, J. 1994. The retreat of marxism and socialist feminism: Postmodern and poststructural theories in education. *Curriculum Inquiry* 24(2): 115–134.

Bode, B. 1927. *Modern educational theories*. New York: Macmillan Publishing Co.

Dewey, J., and Dewey, E. 1915. *Schools of tomorrow*. New York: E.P. Dutton and Co.

Hlebowitsh, P. S. 1992. Amid behavioral and behavioristic objectives: Reappraising appraisals of the Tyler Rationale. *Journal of Curriculum Studies* 24(6): 533–547.

Hlebowitsh, P. S. 1993. *Radical curriculum theory reconsidered*. New York: Teachers College Press.

Hlebowitsh, P. S. 1995. Interpretations of the Tyler Rationale: A reply to Kliebard. *Journal of Curriculum Studies* 27(1): 89–94.

Hlebowitsh, P. S. 1997. The search for the curriculum field. *Journal of Curriculum Studies* 29(5): 507–511.

Kliebard, H. 1970. The Tyler Rationale. *School Review* 78(2): 259–272.

National Society for the Study of Education. 1927. *Curriculum-making: Past and present*. Twenty-Sixth Yearbook. Part I. Bloomington, IL: Public School Publishing Co.

Perkinson, H. J. 1993. *Teachers without goals, students without purposes*. New York: McGraw-Hill.

Pinar, W. F. 1992. Dreamt into existence by others: Curriculum theory and school reform. *Theory into Practice* 31(3): 228–235.

Pinar, W. F. 1999. Response: Gracious submission. *Educational Researcher* 28(1): 14.

Pinar, W. F., Reynolds, W. M., Slattery, P., and Taubman, P. M. 1995. *Understanding curriculum.* New York: Peter Lang.

Reid, W. 1994. *Curriculum planning as deliberation.* (Rapport No. 11) Universitetet I Oslo, Oslo, Norway.

Rugg, H., and Shumaker, A. 1928. *The child-centered school.* New York: Word Book Co.

Schwab, J. J. 1970. *The practical: The language for curriculum.* Washington, D.C.: National Education Association.

Slattery, P. 1995. *Curriculum development in the postmodern era.* Hamden, CT: Garland Press.

23

Voluntary National Tests Would Improve Education

Marshall S. Smith, David L. Stevenson, and Christine P. Li

VOLUNTARY NATIONAL EXAMS IN READING AND MATHEMATICS WOULD MOBILIZE AMERICANS TO INCREASE STUDENT ACHIEVEMENT

At Crestview Elementary School, 4th grader Ashley reads voraciously and independently about fishing in the Yurok culture, while 8th grader Ricky devises and solves algebraic equations. At Del Mar Elementary School, Melanie struggles to make sense of her social studies textbook, while Scott multiplies four-digit numbers in his 8th grade mathematics class. Why are Ashley and Ricky developing more advanced academic skills than Melanie and Scott? Why do schools hold such different expectations for what students can learn? To help ensure that *all* of America's children have the opportunity to achieve academic success in reading and mathematics, President Clinton has proposed the development of voluntary national tests in 4th grade reading and 8th grade mathematics.

WHY 4th GRADE READING AND 8th GRADE MATHEMATICS?

Reading independently by the 4th grade is the gateway to learning in all subjects. By 4th grade, teachers usually stop teaching reading and expect students to have made the transition from learning to read to reading to learn. As a poor reader, Melanie will likely experience school difficulties without intensive interventions. She may have difficulty comprehending mathematics story problems, analyzing literature, and interpreting historical documents in the higher grades. She is more likely to be identified as learning disabled, receive lower grades, and not graduate from high school (Velluntino, Scanlon, and Spearing 1995; Natriello, McDill, and Pallas 1990; McMillan, Kaufman, and Klein 1997). Melanie is not alone. Forty percent of 4th grade students read below the basic level on the National Assessment of Educational Progress (NAEP) and have trouble understanding the overall meaning of what they read (Campbell, Donahue, Reese, and Phillips 1994).

Learning some algebra and geometry by the end of 8th grade is the gateway to taking challenging mathematics courses in high school and college (Stevenson, Schiller, and

Reprinted by permission from *Educational Leadership*, Vol. 55, No. 6, March 1998, pp. 42–44.

Schneider 1994). Having learned some algebra and geometry by the end of the 8th grade, Ricky will enter high school prepared to study demanding mathematics. Upon entering college, he will be able to choose from a multitude of careers, particularly in rapidly growing industries such as information technology. Even if Ricky does not attend college, his higher math skills will yield benefits. Richard Murnane and Frank Levy have demonstrated that male high school graduates with higher math skills who do not go to college earn more than those with lower math skills (Murnane and Levy 1996).[1] However, many of our students do not have the same opportunities as Ricky. Only 25 percent of 8th grade students and fewer than 15 percent of low-income students take algebra by the end of 8th grade (National Center for Education Statistics 1996).

VOLUNTARY NATIONAL TESTS WOULD DIFFER FROM OTHER TESTS

The idea behind the proposed voluntary national tests is not simply to have another test, but to improve the chances that all children will receive high quality instruction in reading and mathematics. Unique features of the voluntary national tests would enable parents and teachers to use the tests as tools to improve education from the grassroots level.

Public and independent. An independent, bipartisan board, the National Assessment Governing Board (NAGB), would develop the tests with extensive public involvement. The tests would be based on the highly respected NAEP frameworks, which NAGB also oversees, and which were developed through a broad-based consensus process. Under the guidance of NAGB, teachers, principals, business and community leaders, parents, and reading and math specialists would create the test items. Throughout this process, NAGB would hold public hearings. The tests would be free of racial, cultural, or gender bias and would make accommodations for disadvantaged, limited English proficient, and disabled students. In addition, the National Academy of Sciences would conduct three studies related to the tests. It would study the quality and fairness of the test items, make recommendations for practices and safeguards in the use of the test results, and determine if an equivalency scale could be developed to link commercially available standardized tests and state assessments to NAEP.

Unlike NAEP, which is not an individual test and is given to a sample of students, the voluntary national tests would be given to individual students and yield individual student scores. The tests are strictly voluntary. The federal government would not withhold funding from a state or local education agency based on its participation, nor would the federal government receive individual test results. Under the current schedule, the pilot test would be conducted in March 1999, and the first field test would follow in March 2000. The first voluntary national tests would be administered in March 2001, and the government would offer a new version of the tests on an annual basis.

Tied to challenging external standards. The voluntary national tests would measure student performance against challenging external standards of what students know and can do. The tests would be explicitly linked to NAEP performance levels and, in mathematics, also to the performance scale for the Third International Mathematics and Science Study (TIMSS).

The NAEP performance standards are challenging. In cases where states set performance standards, their standards are generally below the NAEP standards. A recent Southern Regional Education Board study revealed that in some states, more than 80 percent of the students are proficient on state assessments, but only 20 percent or fewer are proficient based on NAEP standards (Musick 1996).

The results of a standards assessment based on national and international benchmarks would be powerful tools for local change. With a clear picture of the performance of their children, communities could better invest their time, money, and energy in schools. Teachers could target students' needs and use test results for self-evaluations. Administrators could support the professional development their schools and teachers need. Parents could choose to become more involved in their children's education.

Public release of the tests. Within two weeks of the test administration in March, the test items, answers, and explanatory information would be widely distributed via the Internet and other avenues. In May, teachers would receive individual students' answers to every test item, along with explanatory information.

Before the end of the school year, teachers and parents would know how their students' performance measures against high academic standards, *and* they would have the tools to help improve their performance. Teachers and parents would have a clear explanation of what the NAEP standards are and detailed examples of proficient performance based on those standards. Teachers and parents could address individual student needs. Educators could evaluate their current teaching materials and instructional methods and make plans to help their students during the same school year. Principals and teachers could review the test results to evaluate the effectiveness of their instructional programs, to plan their summer professional development, and to mobilize school communities to improve performance.

Rich supplemental information. The annual public release of the tests would include rich supplemental information that clearly explains the performance standards and the content area of each item. For mathematics, the content areas include numbers and operations, geometry, and estimation. Parents and teachers would receive examples of student work for each item, as well as examples of the work needed to meet different levels of performance. Teachers would have access to instructional strategies, research-based curriculum materials, and a sample test a year before the first administration of the tests.

Through the Internet and other means, parents and teachers would have immediate access to test results and elaborative information. In fact, the power of technology would give parents and teachers innumerable opportunities to improve student performance in reading and mathematics. For example, through a Web site for the voluntary national tests, parents and teachers would be able to request technical assistance, join networks, access sample lesson plans, view reading lists recommended by the American Library Association and the International Reading Association, and learn about programs that provide assistance in improving students' reading and mathematics skills.

Helping teachers teach challenging content. The tests would provide educators with tools to teach challenging content. The rich supplemental information would give teachers a clear understanding of the content areas in reading and mathematics. Each year the tests are offered, the content areas would remain the same, but the items would be different. The tests would *not* be designed to encourage teachers to have students memorize items or master testing "tricks." With consistent content areas, but new test items each year, the tests would encourage teachers to teach students demanding content.

National focus. The voluntary national tests would center the nation's attention on improving reading and mathematics education. The president and others would talk about the tests every week for the next two years. This national focus would help mobilize local communities to improve the quality of instruction in schools. Business and community organizations could form school partnerships, and community members could participate in campaigns to improve reading and mathematics. The Department of Education, with many partners, is already involved in such campaigns. The America Reads Challenge includes a corps of trained reading tutors, reading specialists, and tutor coordinators; parental support; and early intervention for our most disadvantaged children. The Department of Education and the National Science Foundation have developed an action plan to build public understanding of challenging mathematics, to help equip teachers with the skills and knowledge to teach challenging mathematics, and to assist communities in efforts to implement high-quality curriculums and instructional materials.

The voluntary national tests would challenge students to achieve high academic standards at key points in their school careers. By ensuring that every 4th grader can read independently and every 8th grader can solve challenging mathematics problems, the tests would create a foundation for their school careers. If we do not help them establish this foundation, students from schools like Crestview and Del Mar will be unequally prepared to enter the demanding workplace of the 21st century. Students like Melanie will continue to struggle to read, and those like Scott will continue to do rote computation. The voluntary national tests would give parents and teachers powerful tools to help *all* America's children excel academically, compete in a global economy, and become responsible citizens in our democratic society. The voluntary national tests alone would not change American education. But they could help mobilize local efforts for improvement in two of the most essential basics of American education: reading and mathematics.

NOTE

1. For further discussion, see United States Department of Education Planning and Evaluation Service. (October 20, 1997). "Mathematics Equals Opportunity." White paper prepared for U.S. Secretary of Education Richard W. Riley.

REFERENCES

Campbell, J. R., P. L. Donahue, C. M. Reese, and G. W. Phillips. (1994). *NAEP 1994 Reading Report Card for the Nation and the States.* Washington, D.C.: U.S. Government Printing Office.

McMillan, M., P. Kaufman, and S. Klein. (1997). *Dropout Rates in the United States 1995.* Washington, D.C.: U.S. Government Printing Office.

Murnane, R. J., and F. Levy. (1996). *Teaching the New Basic Skills.* New York: Free Press.

Musick, M. D. (1996). *Setting Education Standards High Enough.* Atlanta: Southern Regional Education Board.

National Center for Education Statistics. (1996). *NAEP Facts: Eighth-Grade Algebra Course-Taking and Mathematics Proficiency.* Washington, D.C.: U.S. Government Printing Office.

Natriello, G., E. L. McDill, and A. M. Pallas. (1990). *Schooling Disadvantaged Children: Racing Against Catastrophe.* New York: Teachers College Press.

Stevenson, D. L., K. Schiller, and B. Schneider. (1994). "Sequences of Opportunities for Learning." *Sociology of Education* 67: 187–198.

Velluntino, F. R., D. M. Scanlon, and D. Spearing. (1995). "Semantic and Phonological Coding in Poor and Normal Readers." *Journal of Experimental Child Psychology,* 59: 76–123.

24

Creating New Inequalities: Contradictions of Reform

Linda M. McNeil

The enduring legacy of Ross Perot's school reforms in Texas is not merely the strengthening of bureaucratic controls at the expense of teaching and learning. It is also the legitimating of a language of accountability as the governing principle in public schools. Incipient in the Perot reforms was the shifting of control over public schooling away from "the public" and away from the profession—and toward business-controlled management accountability systems. These systems use children's scores on standardized tests to measure the quality of the performance of teachers and principals, and they even use a school's aggregate student scores as data for the comparative "ratings" of schools.

There have been several iterations of state testing and test-driven curricula implemented since the reforms first begun under the Perot legislation in Texas in the mid-1980s. The current Texas Assessment of Academic Skills (TAAS) is rarely referred to by its full name. It is known by its advocates in the state government and among the state's business leaders as "the Texas Accountability System," the reform that has "shaped up" schools. It is touted as the system that holds "teachers and principals accountable." In many schools, tenure for principals has been replaced by "performance contracts," with "performance" measured by a single indicator—the aggregation of student TAAS scores in the school. Publicity about the "Texas Accountability System," centered on rising test scores, has generated copycat legislation in a number of states, where standardized testing of students is increasingly being used as the central mechanism for decisions about student learning, teacher and administrator practice, and even whole-school quality.[1]

Teachers know well that most reforms have a short life and that "this too shall pass." The specific rules and prescriptions enacted under the Perot reforms did, indeed, pass. But the institutionalizing of a shift in the locus of control over curriculum, teaching, and assessment, which began with the legislated reforms of the 1980s, has more than persisted.

As a result, a very narrow set of numerical indicators (student scores on statewide tests) has become the *only* language of currency in education policy in the state. Principals

Reprinted by permission of Phi Delta Kappa International, from *Phi Delta Kappan*, vol. 81, No 10, 2000, pp. 729–734.

report that there can be little discussion of children's development, of cultural relevance, of children's contributions to classroom knowledge and interactions, or of those engaging sidebar experiences at the margins of the official curriculum where children often do their best learning. According to urban principals, many have supervisors who tell them quite pointedly, "Don't talk to me about anything else until the TAAS scores start to go up."

Teachers also report that the margins—those spaces where even in highly prescriptive school settings they have always been able to "really teach"—are shrinking as the account-ability system becomes increasingly stringent, with teacher and principal pay tied to stu-dent scores. Under the Perot reforms, teachers were still sometimes able to juggle the official, prescribed, and tested curriculum with what they wanted their students to learn.[2] Even if they had to teach two contradictory lessons in order to ensure that students en-countered the "real" information (as well as the test-based facts), many teachers managed to do so in order that their students did not lose out on a chance for a real education. Under TAAS, there are fewer and fewer opportunities for authentic teaching.

A continued legacy, then, of the Perot reforms is that the testing of students increasingly drives curriculum and compromises both teaching and the role of students in learning. This prescriptive teaching creates a new form of discrimination as teaching to the frag-mented and narrow information on the test comes to substitute for a substantive curricu-lum in the schools of poor and minority youths. Disaggregating school-level scores by children's race appears to be an attempt to promote equity, but the high stakes attached to the scores have made many schools replace the regular curriculum in minority students' classrooms with test-prep materials that have virtually no value beyond practicing for the tests. The scores go up in these classrooms, but academic quality goes down. The result is a growing inequality between the content and quality of education provided to white, middle-class children and that provided to those in poor and minority schools.

MANDATING A NONCURRICULUM

In minority schools, in the urban school district where I conducted case studies, and in many schools across Texas, substantial class time is spent practicing bubbling in answers and learning to recognize "distractor" (obviously wrong) answers. Students are drilled on such strategies as the pep rally cheer "Three in a row? No, No, No!" (If you have answered "b" three times in a row, you know that at least one of those answers is likely to be wrong, because the maker of a test would not be likely to construct three questions in a row with the same answer indicator.) The basis for such advice comes from the publishers of test-prep materials, many of whom send consultants into schools—for a substantial price—to help plan pep rallies and to "train" teachers to use the TAAS-prep kits.

Under the Perot-era system of test-driven curricula, the observed teachers retained some discretion over how to "teach" to the test-based curriculum. They could teach the numbered curricular content items (as the district directed them to do). They could ignore the official, numbered curriculum and hope that their students would do well on the tests by virtue of having learned from the lessons the teacher had developed. Or they could try to juggle the two—an important option when they saw that the test-based curriculum for-mat so trivialized and fragmented course content that the "knowledge" represented was too far removed from the curriculum the teachers wanted their students to learn. The test-ing, by having students select among provided responses, negated the teachers' desires they come to understandings, or that they connect course content with their prior knowledge.

Teachers, even those who know their subjects and their students well, have much less latitude when their principals purchase TAAS-prep materials to be used in lieu of the regular curriculum. The decision to use such materials forces teachers to set aside their own best knowledge of their subject in order to drill their students on information whose primary (often sole) usefulness is its likely inclusion on the test. A particular example reveals not only how test prep diminishes the role of the teacher, but also how it distances course content from the cultures of the students.

One teacher, a graduate of an Ivy League university with a master's degree from a second selective college, had spent considerable time and personal money assembling a rich collection of historical and literary works of importance in Latino culture. Her building of this classroom resource collection for her high school students was extremely important given the school's lack of a library. Her students responded to her initiative with a real enthusiasm to study and learn. Upon returning from lunch one day, she was dismayed to see that the books for her week's lessons had been set aside. In the center of her desk was a stack of test-prep booklets with a note saying, "Use these instead of your regular curriculum until after the TAAS." The TAAS test date was three months away. (The prep materials were covered with military camouflage designs, calling for "war against the TAAS." The company's consultants came to the school in camouflage gear to do a TAAS pep rally for the students and faculty.)

This teacher reported that her principal, a person dedicated to these students and to their need to pass the TAAS in order to graduate, had used almost the entire year's instructional budget to purchase these expensive materials. The cost was merely one problem. Inside the practice booklets for the "reading" test were single-page activities, with brief nonsense paragraphs, followed by TAAS-type multiple-choice questions. This teacher's students, who had been analyzing the poetry of Gary Soto and exploring the initiation theme in *Bless Me, Ultima*, had to set aside this intellectual work to spend more than half of every class period working through the TAAS-prep booklet. This is not an isolated horror story. It is a case all too representative of the displacement of curriculum in the name of raising building-level test scores in minority schools.

The imposition throughout the entire school of TAAS-prep as a substitute curriculum recast the role of teachers, making them into people who need outside consultants to tell them ways to raise test scores (and to "pep them up"). That these commercial materials were imposed precluded resistance on the teachers' part. It also made it difficult for teachers to make accommodations at the margins, to try to hold onto the more substantive curriculum and cultural connections essential to real learning.

When their students' learning is represented by the narrow indicators of a test like the TAAS, teachers lose the capacity to bring into the discussion of the school program their knowledge of what children are learning. Test scores generated by centralized testing systems like the TAAS—and by test-prep materials aimed at producing better scores—are not reliable indicators of learning. It is here where the effects on low-performing students, particularly minority students, begin to skew the possibilities for their access to a richer education.

At the school whose principal had purchased the high-priced test-prep materials and at other Latino schools where TAAS-prep is replacing the curriculum, teachers report that, even though many more students are passing TAAS "reading" tests, few of their students are actual readers. Few of them can use reading for assignments in other classes; few choose to read or to share books with their friends. In schools where TAAS reading scores are going up, by whatever means, there is little or no will to address this gap. First, so much publicity surrounds the rising scores—and the principals' job security and superintendents' bonuses are contingent on that rise—that the problem of nonreaders is swept under the rug. Second, with the problem hidden, there can be no leverage to add the necessary resources, change the teaching, or invite discussions about the sources of the problem. In fact, the opposite occurs: the rise in scores is used to justify even more TAAS-prep, even more pep rallies, even more substituting of test-based programs for a serious curriculum.

Advocates of TAAS sometimes argue that being able to pass the reading skills section of TAAS is better than not being able to read at all. However, teachers are reporting that the kind of test prep frequently done to raise test scores may actually hamper students' ability to learn to read for meaning. In fact, high school students report that in the test-prep drills and on the TAAS reading section, they frequently mark answers without reading the sample of text: they merely match key words in the answer choice with key words in the text. And elementary teachers note that so many months of "reading" the practice samples and answering multiple-choice questions on them undermines their students' ability to read sustained passages of several pages. The reading samples are material the students are *meant to forget* the minute they mark their answers; at all grade levels this read-and-forget activity is using up the school year with a noncurriculum.

That this is happening chiefly in African American and Latino schools means that the gap between what these children learn and what the children in non-test-prep—usually middle-class and white—schools learn is widening even more dramatically. The subjects not yet tested (science, arts, social studies) are also affected as teachers in historically low-performing schools (minority, poor) are increasingly required to stop teaching those subjects in order to use class time to drill for TAAS math or reading—not to teach reading, but to drill for reading or grammar sections of the TAAS. As Angela Valenzuela has noted, under this system there is a growing, cumulative deficit separating minority students from the education being provided their more privileged peers.[3]

What is happening to and with students under the test-prep system—and what is happening to their access to curriculum content—is completely absent from consideration under an accounting system that uses only one set of indicators on which to base administrative, economic, and instructional decisions in schools.

Equally serious in its consequences is the legacy of institutionalizing the externalized authority over schools. During the years of desegregation, there were public discussions of the purposes of education, the role of the school in the community, and the issue of who should be educated and who should govern access to and provision for education. There were even debates over what constituted a public language with which to discuss public education—the languages of equity, of academic quality, and of community values all intersected and mutually informed the highly contested decisions regarding means to break the power of segregation. When education is governed by an "accountability system," these public languages are displaced by an expert technical language. When educational practice and policy are subsumed under a narrow set of indicators, then the only vocabulary for discussing those practices and policies and their effects on various groups of students is the vocabulary of the indicators—in this case, scores on a single set of tests.

Behind the test scores and the technical policy debates, however, is the growing reality that the Texas system of educational accountability is harming children, teaching, and the content of public schooling. Even more significant for the long run, this system of testing is restratifying education by race and class.

THE NEW DISCRIMINATION

The educational losses that a centralized, standardized system of testing creates for minority students are many. What such youngsters are taught, how they are taught, how their learning is assessed and represented in school records, what is omitted from their education—all these factors are hidden in the system of testing and in the accounting system that reports its results. The narrowing of the curriculum in test-prep schools is creating a new kind of discrimination—one based not on a blatant stratification of access to knowledge through tracking, but one that uses the appearance of sameness to mask persistent inequalities.

This masking shows up first in the words of well-meaning people who restratify expectations by a focus on "basics." The myth that standardization produces sameness—and therefore equity—is based on the notion that standardization "brings up the bottom." The idea is that everyone should get the fundamentals. First, students have to "get the basics" before they can get to the "creative" or "interesting" part of the curriculum. According to this myth, any good teacher or good school will "go beyond the basics" to provide a creative, interesting education.

There is increasing evidence that this focus on "basics" is being applied to minority children, who are viewed as "other people's children."[4] If "those children" are somehow different from "our children" (who are getting the regular curriculum), then they should be grateful for an education that provides them for the first time with the basics. But evidence from classrooms points out several flaws in the constructing of curriculum around the needs of "those students" for the basics.

First, students learn the "basics" when they undertake purposeful instructional activities, when they have models of thinking to emulate, and when they can see how new skills can be applied at the next level. The teachers in the schools in which I conducted case studies (heirs to Dewey and others) engaged students' minds so that they could learn both the "basics" and the ideas and knowledge that cannot be sequenced in a linear fashion because they are part of an organic whole. Yet officials' pride in the TAAS system stems largely from the notion that, "for the first time, those students are getting the same education that *our* students have been getting." The sameness is false, because the resources provided to the schools of minority children and to the academic tracks in which they are frequently placed are dramatically inferior to those provided to the schools and tracks of white, middle-class children. The apparent "sameness" of the test masks these persistent disparities in the conditions of learning that the children face.

That the political climate is becoming more accepting of this patronizing characterization of minority children was made graphically clear at an event in which Latino students would be demonstrating their learning. A white corporate executive had sponsored the implementation of several packaged curricula in Latino schools in a poor neighborhood. Each of the programs was expensive, including classroom materials, consultants to train the teachers to use the materials, tests to evaluate the students' mastery of the content, and so on. The curricular programs, in math and reading, were aimed at the "basics."

The Latino children, dressed in their Sunday best, filed in by grade level to demonstrate their skills in basic math operations. The children's parents and teachers were seated in the large hall. Between the performances by groups of children, the corporate executive would talk about the program. After one group of children had exhibited their skills in adding, he looked over the heads of the Latino parents to the white corporate and community leaders standing around the room and said, "Isn't this great? Now, this may not be the math you would want for *your* children, but for *these* children—isn't this just great?" His remarks were met with smiles and nods.

The pervasiveness of TAAS-prep as a substitute for the curriculum in poor and minority schools is legitimated by the tacit (and mistaken) understanding that for such children repetitive practice in test-drill workbooks may be better than what they had before and is useful in raising their test scores.

Data are beginning to emerge that document the exact opposite. In a compelling study to be released this year, Walter Haney has analyzed graduation rates of cohorts of high school students from 1978 to the present. Using official data from the Texas Education Agency, Haney tracked ninth-grade cohorts to graduation. In 1978, more than 60% of black students and almost 60% of Latinos graduated—15% below the average graduation rate for whites. By 1990, after four years of the Perot-era standardization reforms, graduation rates for blacks, Latinos, and whites had all dropped. By 1990, according to Haney, *fewer than 50% of all black and Latino* ninth-graders made it to graduation. (The graduation rate for whites was more than 70%.) The gap between minorities and whites was widening. By 1999, Haney's data show that the white graduation rate had regained its 1978 level (around 75%). The graduation rate for Latinos and blacks, however, remained below 50%.[5]

Standardization may, through intensive test-practice drills, "raise scores." But standardization has not enhanced children's learning. To those who would say that the graduation rate is dropping because the TAAS is "raising the bar," one must answer that to increase cut-off scores and make no investment in equalizing educational resources is no reform. It is a creative new form of discrimination.

MASKING INEQUITIES

The TAAS system of testing restratifies access to knowledge in schools. It further harms the education of poor and minority youths by masking historical and persistent inequities. When the precursor to TAAS was implemented in the 1980s, two rationales were given. First, it would provide an "objective measurement" of the curriculum. Second, according to a central office administrator, it would ensure that "Algebra I at [a poor, minority high school] is the same as Algebra I at [a suburban, middle- to upper-middle-class, mostly white high school]." The imposition of the test-based curriculum, however, carried with it no new resources for the historically under-resourced schools. Sameness, without massive investments at the under-resourced schools, is achieved by "leveling down" from the top, if at all. It is a poor proxy for equity.

The TAAS system of test-driven accountability masks the inequities that have for decades built unequal structures of schooling in Texas. The investments in expensive systems of testing, test design, test contracts and subcontracts, training of teachers and administrators to implement the tests, test security, realignment of curricula with tests, and the production of test-prep materials serve a political function in centralizing control over education and linking public education to private commerce.[6] But these expenditures do nothing to reverse the serious inequities that have widened over time across the state. In fact, investments in the "accountability system" are cynically seen to obviate the need for new investments in the schools. Even more cynical is the inverting of investments related to accountability *not* to equalize resources but to reward those whose scores go up: the investment comes as a reward for compliance, not as a means to ensure educational improvement.

Meanwhile, scarce resources at the school and district levels are being invested in those materials and activities that will raise scores, not in curricula of lasting intellectual or practical value to students. Experience over the past five years—the period in which principals have traded tenure for TAAS-based performance contracts—shows that it is the historically under-resourced schools, those serving the greatest numbers of poor and minority students, that have shifted their already scarce resources into the purchase of test-prep materials.

Jean Anyon writes compellingly in *Ghetto Schooling* about the pauperization of central city Newark—the dwindling of neighborhood resources in all areas of funding and public goods—as whites left those parts of the city.[7] The poverty of the people and the institutions that remained was a result of this pauperization by alliances of more powerful political and economic interests. In much the same way, the stratifying of academic resources in the name of compliance with an accountability system is pauperizing many urban schools, which only serves to compound their academic insufficiencies, since they are already academically weak and there is little public will to address their lack of resources.

ACCOUNTABLE TO WHOM?

Accountability implies responsibility to a higher authority: being held to account for or being obligated to account to. Within the urban district I have studied and in the state of Texas, during the Perot reforms and at present, accountability has been invoked to locate the problems of schooling at the level of the lowest employees, the teachers. The use of the word itself distracts from the historical inequities in funding, staff allocation, investment in materials, and social support from the broader community. By implying a hierarchy and a culpability at the bottom of the system, such calls for accountability empower those who use the term. The presumption is that those who are calling for accountability feel that they are in control and that others (located beneath them) must answer to them. A common feint is to claim that "the public demands accountability"—though, when the public has tried to demand accountability in education, it has traditionally tried to make the top of the education structure responsive to its particular school and community.

The current accountability system bases assessment of schools and school personnel on children's test scores. A system of education that reduces student learning to scores on a single state test—and uses those scores for such high-stakes decisions as grade promotion and high school graduation—rules out the possibility of discussing student learning in terms of cognitive and intellectual development, in terms of growth, in terms of social awareness and social conscience, in terms of social and emotional development. It is as if the "whole child" has become a stick figure. Upper-level administrators who tell principals not to speak about their students or their programs except in terms of TAAS scores are participating in the de-legitimating of students as young human beings.

Furthermore, the reduction of students to test scores has two contradictory but equally depersonalizing effects. First, the individual scores ignore the social and collaborative aspects of learning. Second, in the reporting of scores, children are subsumed into depersonalized, often meaningless, aggregates. A 75% passing rate at a school this year may appear to be an improvement over a 66% passing rate at the same school last year, but in an urban setting there is no assurance that even half of the children are the same in two successive years.

The accountability system likewise depersonalizes teachers, flattening any representation of their particular practice into the aggregate pass rates for their schools. The role of principal has been severely limited; principals now have greater authority to allocate resources for activities aimed at raising test scores but less discretionary power to undertake other kinds of work in their schools or to have that work recognized.

The use of a language of accountability also takes the discussion of public schooling away from the normal language of families and communities. Parents feel that they have to master a jargon to understand how their children are doing; teachers feel mystified by the mathematical formulas that can turn known weak schools into "exemplary" ones. Parents report feeling confused by their children's TAAS report sheets.

Finally, "accountability" is a closed system that allows no critique. The only questions about the system that generate a response are those having to do with technical aspects: At what point should children whose first language is not English have to take the reading portion of TAAS in English? Are the test questions valid? Are they culturally biased? Is the cut-off score for graduation set too high or too low? Questions about technical tinkering are tolerated. And to all such questions, there is one basic answer: more controls. If there is lax security, the test materials must be more tightly controlled. If scores are going up, then test prep must be working. If scores are slipping, then more test prep must be needed. There is no acknowledgment among district or state officials that the real problem is not cheating by altering answer sheets. Instead, the real problem inherent in such an accountability system is that it severely undermines teaching and learning, while masking problems within the school.

The educational costs of standardization, then, include not only the direct impact on teaching and learning, but also the high costs of compliance when compliance silences professional expertise and marginalizes parental and public discourse.

If the language of accountability comes to dominate public school policy, it will eliminate the means by which the public—parents and teachers and other citizens of a community—can challenge the system of accountability. We have already seen the harmful effects of such a system on curriculum and teaching. We have seen its tendencies to create new forms of discrimination as its control mechanisms reward those administrators who shift resources into the means of compliance rather than toward improving the quality of education—a pervasive pattern in minority schools with a history of low scores on standardized tests.

More than two decades ago in *Legislated Learning*, Arthur Wise warned that attempts to legislate learning and to legislate teaching frequently have "perverse effects."[8] He was speaking of the kinds of effects that have been documented in the poor and minority schools described here in their responses to the TAAS. And the effects within schools and school systems may not be nearly so "perverse" as the effects within our system of democracy, because these attempts to legislate and control learning reduce the public's possibilities for retaining democratic governance of schools once the controls are in place. One reason for this—mentioned above—is that an accountability-based control system, because it is a closed system, structures out possibilities for external criticism.

Throughout the history of public schooling America, maintaining our democracy has been cited as the fundamental justification for public support of schools. Education is essential for effective citizenship, for playing an active role in the economic, cultural, and political life of the nation. Democracy has been both the real reason for extending an education to all children and—at times—the cover story that masked our failure to provide such an education equitably. Even when the education we provided was inequitable, it carried such democratic slogans as "separate but equal." Given our democratic heritage, the ways in which the language of accountability is displacing democratic discourse need to be carefully examined.

The current accountability system has been implemented slowly and in stages. First came state tests that held almost no consequence for students; then came state tests that held moderate consequences for students (scores were recorded in their records but not used for high-stakes decisions). Now the system uses students' scores for the evaluation of teachers, principals, schools, and even districts. Students who have been in school only during the past 10 years (the life span of the TAAS) know nothing different. Teacher who have taught for fewer than 10 years and who have not come in from another state assume outcomes testing to be a sad but "inevitable" feature of schooling. The incremental normalizing of an accountability system and the casual use of its language in conversations about education can silence criticism and stifle the potential to pose counter models and to envision alternative possibilities. That is the insidious power of the language of accountability: to sound just enough like common sense not to be recognized as a language meant to reinforce unequal power relations.

It is only by understanding the differential effects of accountability systems on varied groups of students, on teachers, on parents, and on communities that we can know whether they serve our children and our goals for public education well. And it is only by going inside schools and inside classrooms that we can begin to build that understanding at a deeply informed level.

These highly rationalized and technical systems of schooling are being touted as very beneficial for their states and districts—after all, test scores are rising. When we examine such systems more closely, however, we may find that these benefits prove to be short-lived and as artificial and inflated as the test scores produced by months of test preparation. And we may also find that the costs of these systems are being borne by the weakest participants in our education systems—the children. The slogans of "reform" can be truly seductive. As researchers and as citizens we need to look behind those slogans and see what effects our fancy systems are having on the children.

NOTES

1. Jay Heubert and Robert Hauser, eds., *High Stakes: Testing for Tracking, Promotion, and Graduation* (Washington, D.C.: National Research Council, 1998).
2. Linda M. McNeil, *Contradictions of School Reform: Educational Costs of Standardized Testing* (New York: Routledge, 2000), chap. 6.
3. Linda M. McNeil and Angela Valenzuela, "Harmful Effects of the TAAS System of Testing in Texas: Beneath the Accountability Rhetoric," in Mindy Komhaber, Gary Orfield, and Michal Kurlaendar, eds., *Raising Standards or Raising Barriers? Inequality and High-Stakes Testing in Public Education* (New York: Century Foundation, forthcoming).
4. Lisa Delpit, *Other People's Children: Cultural Conflict in the Classroom* (New York: New Press, 1995).

5. Walter Haney, "Study of Texas Education Agency Statistics on Cohorts of Texas High School Students, 1978–1998," unpublished paper, Center for the Study of Testing, Evaluation, and Educational Policy, Boston College, 1999.

6. Walter Haney, George Madaus, and Robert Lyons, *The Fractured Marketplace of Standardized Testing* (Boston: Kluwer Academic Publishers, 1993).

7. Jean Anyon, *Ghetto Schooling: A Political Economy of Urban Educational Reform* (New York: Teachers College Press, 1997).

8. Arthur Wise, *Legislated Learning: The Bureaucratization of the American Classroom* (Berkeley: University of California Press, 1979).

25

Teaching for Cultural Literacy: A Curriculum Study

David J. Flinders

For many public secondary schools, the past decade has brought increased graduation requirements and a renewed emphasis on academic standards. Jennings writes that "today more high school students are taking more academic subjects involving more rigorous coursework than ever before."[1]

A more academic curriculum, however, is not in and of itself cause for optimism; nor does it resolve issues. On the contrary, this trend only opens the door to a new set of questions. What does academically "rigorous" coursework look like in actual classrooms? How are the potential benefits of an academic curriculum brought to fruition? Or to put this question another way, Under what conditions will more academic content translate into a better education for students?

To inform these questions, curriculum research must not only examine lesson content per se but also the enactment of content and its consequent meanings for those directly involved. The study reported below represents an effort to move research in this direction. The report itself is divided into three sections. The first section introduces the study by describing its aims and methodological framework. The second section presents two case narratives. In focusing on the enactment of academic content, these narratives provide concrete examples of what one research participant described as "teaching for cultural literacy."[2] The final section compares the two cases in order to illustrate the forms of conceptual analysis used in this type of research.

TOWARD A METHODOLOGY FRAMEWORK

The study described below was designed to examine those complexities and vicissitudes of classroom life that others have called the enacted curriculum. Snyder, Bolin, and Zumwalt define the enacted curriculum as "educational experiences jointly created by student and teacher."[3] They argue that enactment is an important concept because it represents a shift in basic assumptions about the types of activities that teachers perform. From an

Reprinted by permission of Association for Supervision and Curriculum Development, from *Journal of Curriculum and Supervision*, Vol. II, No. 4, 1996. pp. 351–366.

enactment perspective, teachers do more than simply deliver information or adapt it to the needs of a particular class. Transactional processes go on as well. Teachers and students interact to interpret ideas, construct understandings, make meaning. The implications of this view are particularly significant for those interested in the aesthetic foundations of education. By placing the use of lesson content within the broader category of how people create meaning, enactment brings into focus the similarities between teaching and other forms of creative work.

Outside of education, the quintessential examples of creative work come from the arts, a domain that suggests several points of comparison. First, teachers are like artists in that they actively mediate and shape the messages they convey. Second, both of these professional arenas are ones in which skill, form, and style count for those who are engaged in such work or who seek to understand it. And third, much like the products of art, those of teaching are often anticipated but not entirely predictable. Adjustments, accommodations, corrections, and so forth are made "in process" as the work itself unfolds.

The importance of this analogy is that it forms the underlying rationale for a compatible methodological framework. That framework is borrowed from educational criticism, a form of qualitative inquiry developed by Elliot W. Eisner.[4] Educational criticism takes its lead from the work of critics in fields such as literature, drama, film, music, and the visual arts. Using this approach to study curriculum enactment takes advantage of the conceptual tools that have been developed by those who, like art critics, seek to elucidate the processes and products of human invention. According to Eisner, educational critics pursue this type of disclosure by using four dimensions of inquiry: (1) description, (2) interpretation, (3) evaluation, and (4) thematics.

Briefly stated, the descriptive dimension of criticism relates to the particulars that are observed in a school or classroom. These particulars might include, for example, the behavior of teachers and students, their activities and patterns of interaction, their ways of speaking to one another, or the settings in which events unfold. The primary aim of criticism, however, is not to state meanings but to express them.[5] For this reason, critics must attend to both what they say and how they say it. In other words, the descriptive side of their work involves not only the use of literal language but also the management of impressions and a sensitivity to style. Voice, tone, metaphor, symbolism, and other linguistic forms play a legitimate, sometimes central, role in rendering the type of vivid descriptions on which the veracity of this approach depends.

The interpretive dimension of criticism places greater emphasis on expository traditions than what is typically implied in descriptive work alone. The difference is that while the aims of description focus on re-presenting the qualities one has observed, the aims of interpretation focus on why those qualities are the way they are. Eisner makes this distinction in suggesting that interpretation provides an "account for" what description provides an "account of."[6] This difference, however, is only a difference in emphasis; it means neither that these two dimensions are entirely separate nor that interpretation seeks to provide definitive explanations. Instead, the contribution of interpretation is that it asks researchers to make explicit their suppositions about what is going on in the particular classrooms described.

The evaluative dimension of criticism is normative in the sense that critics are among those expected to shed light on the qualities that constitute excellence within a given domain. As such, this dimension of criticism raises yet a different set of questions—

questions that focus explicitly on matters of significance, value, or merit. What do descriptions or interpretations of practice mean in terms of our conceptions of educational purpose? Are the results of a study good news or bad news, and why?

Such questions are important in the context of classroom research for two reasons. First, teaching itself is a normative enterprise; it seeks to foster something that the teacher considers worth fostering.[7] Second, normative issues pervade all forms of social research; they are present even when they remain (as they often do) one of the implicit aspects of how the research is carried out.

The fourth dimension of criticism, its thematic dimension, is focused on the recurrent messages, principles, or salient ideas that people are able to take away from the particulars of a given study. By comparing attributes and images, the critic/researcher seeks to extract the lessons that can be learned from individual cases. Just as every significant work of art contains a message that reaches beyond itself, every case in case study research is a case of something; it speaks not just to the particulars at hand but also to the categories to which those particulars belong. This is the main reason classrooms are studied to begin with—not for their own sake, but to learn about classroom life, its meanings, forms of organization, and so forth. The substantive products of that learning constitute the themes of one's work.

FIELDWORK AND DATA SOURCES

The study's initial fieldwork was conducted in seven classrooms selected to represent a range of grade levels and subject areas. All of the classrooms were in public schools serving lower- to upper-middle-class suburban communities. The classroom teachers were first interviewed to collect information about their background. Then, over the next five months, I observed a total of more than 120 lessons, taking field notes and collecting documents such as sample text materials, worksheets, and class handouts. These field notes were summarized and the documents reviewed at the end of each weekly observation period.

One purpose of the fieldwork was to look for variations in content use between and within each classroom.[8] The two classrooms that offered the greatest contrast with respect to enactment were of special interest because they happened to be taught by two teachers who shared a similar content orientation. More specifically, both teachers justified their lesson content as inherently worth learning, this being one of the key assumptions of what was referred to earlier as a cultural literacy approach. In addition, their classroom lessons were the most subject-centered among those observed.

The two classrooms stood at opposite poles, but not so much in their underlying approach as in their ways of enacting that approach. Because the study's aim was to examine differences at this level of practice, initial observations were followed up by videotaping a series of 10 lessons in what at that point had become the two target classrooms. The videotapes were subsequently reviewed at least a dozen times to create draft descriptions of each lesson. Finally, lessons from each classroom were selected to represent both the forms of enactment and the quality of the curriculum as suggested by the information gathered as a whole. The narratives below are based on the draft descriptions of these lessons together with information drawn from the original interviews and field notes.

CASE NARRATIVE #1: THE ICARUS POEMS

Ann Halstead teaches junior and senior English classes at Forester High School.[9] She takes much of her lesson content straight from the two literature anthologies assigned for her courses. These textbooks offer the standard fare of American and British writers, including Shakespeare, Blake, Wordsworth, Coleridge, Dickens, Melville, Clemens, and Joyce. Authors of such standing cast a long shadow in Halstead's classroom, giving her curriculum its strong academic bent. However, this teacher also mixes in a generous portion of less canonized material—poetry and fiction from *The New Yorker* magazine, nonfiction from *The Atlantic Monthly*, back-page editorials, or anything else that qualifies in Halstead's view as an illustration of well-crafted writing. One recent assignment, for example, was based on a short story she read to the class from a seat-pocket airline magazine.

Halstead is younger than most of her colleagues, having taught high school English since finishing college only eight years ago. She dresses casually in canvas sneakers, designer jeans, and sweaters. Her first-period students are juniors, also casually but well dressed. On Tuesday, they come into the classroom and sit facing Halstead's desk in front of the chalkboard. The lesson for this day will focus on three short poems that retell the story of Icarus and his ill-fated flight on homemade wings. Halstead passes out mimeographed copies of the first poem, reads it aloud to her students, and then begins the discussion:

Halstead: This first poem is by Anne Sexton, a contemporary poet. And I'm not sure where this first appeared, but the title's there at the top, "To a Friend Whose Work Has Come to Triumph." What kind of poem is it?

Student: A sonnet.

Halstead: What kind of sonnet? [No response.] O.K., what's the only kind of sonnet we've studied?

Student: Shakespearian.

Halstead: Good. Now, how does knowing that help us understand the poem? Let's take the couplets first . . .

The sonnet form is reviewed point by point, the students struggling to recover what they had learned about Shakespearian sonnets from lessons several months earlier. Halstead then quickly brings the discussion back to the particular example at hand.

Halstead: Look at these first lines again. Can you hear how vivid they are? How does Sexton lodge, or how is she able to lodge such strong images in our minds?

Student: The punctuation.

Halstead: Right, the rhythm here is like the pumping of wings. What else?

Student: Alliteration in the third line. The line sort of takes off.

Halstead: O.K. Sexton is making her sounds work with her meanings. Anything else?

Student: Doggerel.

Halstead: Yes. Where's the doggerel?

Student: In the last line: "While his sensible daddy goes straight into town." It's ironic.

Halstead: O.K. She takes advantage of that couplet, but it's not just the rhyme. What else is she using?

Student: Rhythm.

Halstead: That's right. The line's too regular, too pat. "While his sensible daddy goes straight into town." What does it remind you of?

Student: Jack and Jill.

Student: Dr. Seuss.

Halstead nods enthusiastically, delighted with their examples. The discussion then turns to the poem's theme. The students are quick to recognize that the message of this poem celebrates the courage of youth, striving to great heights, and the need to take risks. As one student summarizes: "It's like the Nike ad: 'Just do it.'"

The second poem is by Alastair Reid. Again, Halstead distributes copies and then reads the poem aloud. The risk-taking theme is expressed in this poem as well. However, Reid recounts the story from the point of view of Daedalus, the father. His dilemma soon becomes a focus for Halstead and her students. On the one hand, Daedalus has a responsibility to protect his son from harm. On the other hand, he does not want to squelch the boy's freedom or, one could say, "clip his wings." Many students now are sitting more to the front of their chairs than they were before. Talk of freedom and control seems to have a special draw. The students are quick to compare family rules, what their own parents allow and disallow. Halstead is patient with their discussion, but she also keeps driving at the words on the printed page and what those words mean:

Student: The word *grounded* in line seven has a real negative meaning. When you're grounded you can't go anywhere. You're stuck home; you're stuck down. You're not free.

Halstead: O.K. That's good. And yet what other meanings does *grounded* have?

Student: Having your feet on the ground?

Halstead: And if you have a firm grounding in something?

Student: You know what it's about; you're connected with it.

Halstead: So the word can be used in at least a double sense. What does that ambiguity have to do with Daedalus's view? Remember, he's the parent.

Student: He doesn't know what's right. He can see both sides. That's the point of the poem.

Halstead: So Reid's changing the simple morality of this story to something more human. What other words are ambiguous here?

The questions continue for another 10 minutes; then the class moves on to the third poem. Halstead reads the poem aloud, this time from her copy of the text as the students follow along in their books. The poem, by W. H. Auden, uses the Icarus tale to illustrate human tragedy writ large. In so doing, Auden laments the impetuosity of youth with the same force that Sexton has used to exalt it. Halstead, however, shifts the focus of discussion yet again, this time away from theme and back to form. Unlike the first two poems, the last is written in free verse. Halstead calls the students' attention to line length and how shape combines with sound to emphasize a particular image or idea. "Auden," she comments, "is using different techniques than the other two. He blocks out the ideas visually as well as through his words. Let's look at the first few lines again . . ."

Three short poems, exhibits of a sort, expositions that are read, probed, compared, pulled apart, and pieced back together—all in a matter of 50 minutes. During the lesson Halstead and her first-period students have traversed the aspirations of youth, the prudence of age, and the failings of both. Picked up along the way are various poetic standards of form and technique: the sonnet, rhyme, rhythm, couplets, imagery, alliteration, doggerel, word connotation, free verse.

Through the remainder of the school year, Halstead and her students will move on to new lessons and new challenges. Yet, they take something with them as well, achievements that range from improved academic skills to broadened assumptions about the meanings of academic content itself.

CASE NARRATIVE #2: CONSTITUTIONAL AMENDMENTS

Aaron Stewart is a social studies teacher with 14 years of classroom experience. He arrives at Edison Middle School each day dressed in jeans and an open-necked shirt. His current teaching schedule includes an 8th grade civics class, a course for which Stewart does not use a textbook. Instead, he uses primary source documents that are supplemented by an eclectic array of worksheets, multiple-page handouts, and a pamphlet series titled *Youth and the Law*.

His civics class is now in the middle of a unit on the Constitution. Each student has been given a copy of the Constitution, together with Stewart's own mimeographed notes summarizing each article and each amendment. "I want these kids to read the Constitution," Stewart tells me, "because it's something everyone should be familiar with. It's how our system works, and that's about as basic to citizenship as you can get."

Today the students' desks are arranged in their usual U-shaped configuration facing the front of the classroom. Stewart has written on the front chalkboard:

Preamble: We (who) to do what—EJ—IDT—PCD—PGW and SBL—to O & P, do ordain and E, this C—USA.

As the 28 students settle into their chairs before class, Stewart asks them to copy these lines into their notes. His list of abbreviations is a type of shorthand to help the students memorize the Constitution's preamble. Stewart waits for the students to finish writing, then begins class.

Stewart: We'll pick up where we left off yesterday. I want to run through as many of the amendments as we can today. The quiz on these will be Thursday, unless you need more time. I'm sure you'll want at least one day to review your notes. This one [the quiz] is four pages, 82 questions; so it covers a lot. Just getting through the amendments will take a couple more days. Today we pick up where? Amendment 22. [A student comes in late and takes a seat.] Jack, we're just starting. Amendment 22 limits the president to two terms of office. When was it passed?

Student: In the 50s?

Stewart: That's right, 1951, what must seem like the dark ages to you kids. What's 21?

Student: Prohibition.

Stewart: No, prohibition is 18. Twenty-one repeals 18. Why was it repealed? I guess too many important men made money importing whiskey from Canada. Let's go on to 20. This one sets the term of office for the president so he has a little bit more time. Who knows what a lame duck is? [no response] How should I explain this? If I were told I'm not going to be hired next year . . .

Student: [jokingly] You'd be a lame teacher?

Stewart: [also smiling] That's a lame *duck* teacher, thank you. Let's go on to 19. What is suffrage? I have suffrage; you don't have suffrage. You have to suffer a few more years before you get suffrage.

Student: I don't know what to write in my notes.

Stewart: You have to think. What questions would I ask? The 19th grants suffrage to women. When was it passed?

Student: During a war.

Stewart: During a war?

Student: World War II?

Stewart: No, before that, 1920. Everybody get that? O.K., we're going to skip 16, 17, and 18. They're explained in your notes. Instead, we'll look at amendments 13, 14, and 15. Sometimes these are called the "black" amendments, but they don't actually use that word. Fourteen defines what a citizen is and says that all citizens have a right to due process and equal protection. Amendment 15 guarantees the right to vote. Underline that first sentence in 15: "The right of citizens of the United States to vote shall not be denied or abridged by the United States or any state on account of race, color, or previous condition of servitude."

Student: But that's not *always* true, is it?

Stewart: Oh, yes it is. If someone won't let you vote because of your race, you can take 'em all the way to the Supreme Court.

The class discussion of each amendment continues through the Bill of Rights. Stewart keeps the lesson moving at a brisk pace by posing questions and interjecting brief comments. An undercurrent of light banter between Stewart and his students animates their work. Frequently Stewart urges the students to attend to their basic study skills. "Keep your notes organized chronologically," he tells the class. "Underline all dates," "Look for the key words as you read," and "Make separate note cards for each amendment."

By midweek the class has covered 23 amendments and several articles. The students are then given the next two days to review their notes before the unit quiz. On these review days, Stewart pairs the students off to study in teams. Each student moves to face his or her partner, and together they take turns asking each other seemingly random questions: Which amendment describes the electoral college? What year was it passed? Which amendment defines who can be a citizen? What is suffrage? Which amendment prohibits slavery? What rights are guaranteed in the First Amendment? Which amendment protects against unreasonable search or seizure?

The nature of this review activity is largely drill and practice, but its routine appears to keep most of the students engaged with the material. Their back-and-forth exchanges are focused on the content at hand, and a businesslike atmosphere prevails. Stewart rarely needs to admonish students for being off-task.

On the day of the quiz, the students come in visibly tense. Several of the students joke with Stewart to provide some comic relief. Two boys parody their distress by singing in a low, off-key lament, "Nobody knows the trouble I've seen . . ." The student desks are moved into four straight rows to make full use of the classroom space, and the students sit facing the chalkboard. As Stewart passes out copies of the quiz, one student asks in jest: "Why did they write the Constitution anyway, Mr. Stewart? Just so we'd have something to study in your class?" Regardless of their real or imagined dismay, the students score well on the quiz. They have learned, by this measure, much of the content that Stewart intended them to learn.

DISCUSSION

What to make of these two narratives? Schofield notes that together with the growth of qualitative research comparisons across case studies also have become more common.[10] Moreover, Halstead's and Stewart's lessons are neither highly exceptional nor out of place within the range of expectations for what goes on in secondary school classrooms. How, then, do these classrooms compare? In what ways do they strike a familiar chord? These questions are addressed below using the four dimensions of educational criticism mentioned earlier (description, interpretation, evaluation, and thematics). The aim is to show how these dimensions can bring into focus the types of differences that shape the enactment of classroom lessons.

Description

The descriptive dimension of the study names the particulars of content. This dimension is mentioned only briefly at this point because it is largely represented by the narratives themselves. A series of actual lessons are presented. Halstead's lesson focuses on three short poems that retell the Icarus myth. The lesson is not only about these particular poems, but also about poetic forms and techniques such as the sonnet, free verse, rhyme, alliteration, irony, and doggerel. Stewart's lessons focus on a review of the Constitutional amendments. Content here includes such topics as Prohibition, presidential term limits, suffrage, voting rights, and equal protection.

These comments are not meant to imply that either narrative should be taken as a purely descriptive account. Description in this context inevitably overlaps with the interpretive aspects of classroom research. Yet, as far as lesson content is concerned, these narratives focus principally on what has been called "the surface curriculum" of topics, facts, and ideas to which students are exposed simply by virtue of being in the classroom at a particular time.[11] The narratives do not speak for themselves precisely because the curricular meanings that count most in comparing Halstead's and Stewart's classrooms are those meanings that reside below the surface of their lesson content.

Interpretation and Evaluation

Interpretation is the first step beyond this surface-level content and into questions of meaning. From an enactment perspective, this dimension of the study pertains directly to how content ideas are understood within the context of instruction.

Two examples from Halstead's lesson illustrate one of the strategies through which such classroom meanings are brought into play. The first example is how students respond when Halstead talks about the rhythm of a line in the Sexton poem as being "too pat, too regular." The students acknowledge this point by framing it in terms of their own vernacular, nonacademic experience—that is, the stories of Dr. Seuss and the nursery rhyme of Jack and Jill. For a children's book author and a nursery rhyme to be invoked in the context of "serious" poetry is no small matter. That invocation symbolizes the grasp of an idea and thus the manner of curriculum enactment.

The second example is the topic of risk taking, the main theme of the same poem. This topic concerns Sexton's meaning rather than her use of a technique. Yet, as in the first example, the students are quick to connect the content at hand with a point of reference as common and as ordinary as the Nike advertising slogan, "Just do it." Again, the juxtaposition of academic and nonacademic domains is significant because it represents a form of enactment that confirms the accessibility of poetic meaning based on the students' experience outside of the classroom.

These two examples demonstrate connections being made between lesson content and the students' prior knowledge. Another type of content meaning in Halstead's lesson is emphasized by connections between those topics that focus on poetic technique (e.g., rhythm, alliteration, doggerel) and those that focus on an idea (e.g., risk taking, freedom, groundedness). These connections take place at several points during the lesson, Halstead herself making them explicit with comments such as, "Sexton is making her sounds work with her meanings," and "Auden . . . blocks out the ideas visually as well as through his words." The message is that techniques and ideas work hand-in-hand, two dimensions of the text that must be understood in terms of their relationship or as parts of a larger whole. Moreover, this message is widely applicable to other poems, other literary genres, and to a variety of nonlinguistic forms of expression as well.

It is more difficult in Stewart's case to cite similar examples, either of the connections between academic and nonacademic domains or of recurrent messages that transcend his specific content. Some topics are explained by using contemporary examples. Lame duck presidency is likened to Stewart hypothetically not having his contract renewed, and suffrage is related to the students' future right to vote. However, these examples are passed over rather quickly as the class is driven, in Stewart's words, to "run through" as many amendments as possible during a given class period. Moreover, Stewart elicits examples from his students less often, usually providing his own instead. And finally, explanations of content tend to remain academic (i.e., subject-centered). When one student implies violations of the 15th amendment (the right to vote regardless of race), Stewart responds within the context of constitutional procedure: "If someone won't let you vote," he replies, ". . . you can take 'em all the way to the Supreme Court."

It would be a mistake to assume that the differences noted here are solely a function of the particular topics or ideas addressed in each class. Nothing inherent in Stewart's content is preventing the type of connections or enactment strategies that are more readily found in Halstead's lesson. Some of the amendment topics (e.g., race, the right to vote, equal protection) may be easily imagined as being relevant to a broad range of contemporary issues. But consider a seemingly more difficult example, that of presidential term limits. At first glance, this topic might appear to be nothing more than a technical point in the mechanics of government. Does such content have any immediate connection with the day-to-day lives of middle school students? One answer could be pursued by reflecting on the possible reasons for imposing term limits. The question then becomes, Why limit anyone's term of office? Should "term limits" be applied to teachers? Because most schools are organized in such a way that students move on each year to new teachers, the effect is the same. Thus students would have some experience from which to discuss the advantages or disadvantages of a similar, although often taken-for-granted, practice.

Focusing on how connections are (or could be) developed offers only the beginnings of an interpretive analysis. Even this first step, however, suggests another dimension of the study. By drawing out the type of connections made or absent in each of the two classrooms, an evaluative stance is implied with respect to the particulars of enactment in each case.

As it turns out in this study, the narratives can be viewed as offering both good news and bad news for the proponents of a cultural literacy approach. The good news is that Halstead's lesson illustrates how a highly academic curriculum can be enacted in ways that avoid some of the disadvantages typically assumed by those who argue that an academic curriculum is elitist as well as irrelevant to much of a student's lived experience. These arguments were not borne out in Halstead's classroom. Many if not most of her students found relevance in the poetic retellings of the Icarus myth, and doing so in their own vernacular undercut the elitism that might have otherwise been a problem. In addition, their efforts to make academic content accessible were achieved through a logic suggested within the arguments of a cultural literacy approach itself. The advocates of this approach have long held that academic subject matter represents widely shared concerns, the very type of concerns explored by Halstead and her students as together they probed the Icarus poems for understandings of risk taking, freedom, responsibility, and the follies of human pride.

The bad news for advocates of cultural literacy is that academic content is only a necessary rather than sufficient condition for realizing the most significant aspirations of this approach. Stewart's lessons tend to illustrate this point. From an academic perspective, his content is just as strong as Halstead's content. The Constitution is not only a primary source document, but also specifically recommended as subject matter in Mortimer Adler's *Paideia Proposal*.[12] It is, in the words of E.D. Hirsch Jr. and his collaborators, "What every American needs to know."[13] Moreover, the students seem to have learned this material. That they scored well on the unit quiz is hardly a trivial matter. Also, when asked by their study partners, most students were able to recite the Constitution's preamble word for word.

Stewart deserves credit for this because in several ways he is skilled at teaching content. He frequently reviews topics, summarizes the material, and provides opportunities for his students to work together. Unlike Halstead and her students, however, Stewart and his class place little emphasis on connecting content with ideas relevant beyond the immediate context of classroom learning. Their work unfolds on the assumption that the amendments are like a string of small islands, a curricular archipelago that in this case takes the form of a chronological list. The students visit each amendment, one after the other, stopping just long enough to learn its name and its position on the list. Enactment is by the numbers: What is the 15th amendment? The 14th? The 13th? The 12th?

This sequential form of enactment is supported by its over-arching point of reference: the unit quiz. Moreover, the students are reasonably interested in exactly what they will be tested on. They explicitly ask Stewart what they should write down in their class notes, and Stewart encourages them to anticipate the types of information they will need. One student's joke that the Constitution was written so that future generations of school children would have something to study is symptomatic of learning conceived in this way. The joke symbolizes the degree to which schooling comes to be recognized as an end in and of itself. More than a little irony is involved in this particular example because one answer to the student's question ("Why did they write the Constitution anyway, Mr. Stewart?") is rather eloquently stated in the very content—the preamble to the Constitution—that the students have so dutifully memorized.

Thematics

The notion that a study offers good news and bad news (indeed, the word *news* itself) points to the fourth dimension of educational criticism. This dimension, known as thematics, involves the development of ideas or concepts that are able to serve as themes. The purpose of a theme is to connect the particulars observed with whatever significance those particulars reveal. For the study at hand, one might ask whether the two narratives contribute in any way to informed understandings of educational practice. And more specifically, what, if anything, do Halstead's and Stewart's lessons reveal about either the forms or functions of curriculum enactment?

Although a number of possible themes could be developed from the case narratives reported here, I will focus on only one in particular. This is that by enacting an academic curriculum, teachers and students also enact cultural patterns of belief concerning the value and utilities of academic content. The relatively self-contained enactment patterns in Stewart's classroom, what might be called learning for the sake of a test, communicate commonly recognized assumptions about the nature of academic study as it is more broadly understood. The assumptions in this case are reflected in the pejorative uses and connotations of the word "academic." This term is often used as an adjective (e.g., an "academic question" or an "academic exercise") to mean that the noun it modifies may be dismissed as unrelated to matters of any practical consequence.

Counterpoint to this way of thinking is the success that Halstead and many of her students share in integrating their academic work with other realms of experience. Their ability to interpret poetry on the basis of a Nike advertisement or to see their own parents in the visage of Daedalus, represents pedagogical moves that imply assumptions quite different than those suggested by learning for the sake of a test. In Halstead's classroom, academic content may be an unfamiliar window for some, but it is still a window that looks out onto one's own backyard. The poems comment on matters not so distant, as it turns out, from making one's way in the world. In the long run, either sense of what "academic" means is likely to be one of the most enduring lessons that students learn.

SUMMARY AND CONCLUDING COMMENT

In the wake of recent trends, questions surrounding the use of academic content deserve to be cast in brighter light. The study reported in this article uses the concept of curriculum enactment for this purpose. Enactment not only calls attention to the classroom-level uses of content; it also positions this level of use within the context of how people create meaning. The study's methodological framework, in turn, draws on the four dimensions of educational criticism. The descriptive dimension, represented in the two case narratives, serves to recount the particulars observed during the course of a lesson; the interpretive dimension focuses on how these particulars are understood; the evaluative dimension poses questions of merit; and the thematic dimension looks to the qualities or concepts that the study means to illustrate.

With respect to Halstead's and Stewart's lessons, the use of academic content is of special interest on several counts. First, their classrooms should remind the advocates and opponents of cultural literacy that variations within this approach make a substantial difference in what lesson content comes to mean for the students and teachers involved. Second, Halstead's particular modes of enacting academic content might encourage researchers to further examine actual teaching that successfully connects lesson content with seemingly unrelated sources of student knowledge. Third, these connections between content and experience represent "acts of meaning,"[14] which thus become what researchers must address if they are to provide informed accounts of the enacted curriculum.

This last point may be the most significant because it brings those who are interested in lesson content back to the type of arenas in which educational criticism offers some guidance. The methods of this approach have a long history in the arts and humanities, fields where criticism has served to affirm that the processes and products of human invention are neither enigmatic nor beyond the scope of disciplined inquiry. The enactment of lesson content presents analogous conceptions of practice. Much like a literary text or dramatic performance, enactment is an expression of meanings created as the work itself unfolds. While enactment can and should be approached in other ways as well, few alternatives offer traditions so well focused on the ability to create messages and share meanings.

NOTES

1. John F. Jennings, ed., *National Issues in Education* (Bloomington, IN: Phi Delta Kappa International, 1995), p. vii.
2. The hallmark of a cultural literacy approach is its emphasis on content, especially content drawn from a literary, classical, or liberal arts tradition. See, for example, E. D. Hirsch Jr., *Cultural Literacy: What*

Every American Needs to Know (Boston: Houghton Mifflin, 1987); Mortimer J. Adler, *The Paideia Proposal: An Educational Manifesto* (New York: Macmillan, 1982).

3. Jon Synder, Frances Bolin, and Karen Zumwalt, "Curriculum Implementation," in *The Handbook of Research on Curriculum*, ed. Philip W. Jackson (New York: Macmillan, 1992), p. 418.

4. Elliot W. Eisner, *The Educational Imagination: On the Design and Evaluation of School Programs*, 3rd ed. (New York: Macmillan, 1994).

5. The distinction between statement and expression of meaning is from John Dewey, *Art as Experience* (New York: Perigee, 1934).

6. Elliot W. Eisner, *The Enlightened Eye* (New York: Macmillan, 1991), p. 95.

7. See, for example, R. S. Peters, *Authority, Responsibility, and Education* (London: George Allen and Unwin, 1960).

8. This is a technique suggested by Michael Q. Patton, *How to Use Qualitative Methods in Evaluation* (Newbury Park, CA: Sage, 1987).

9. Pseudonyms are used for all individual and place names to protect anonymity.

10. Janet Ward Schofield, "Increasing the Generalizability of Qualitative Research," in *Qualitative Inquiry in Education: The Continuing Debate*, ed. Elliot W. Eisner and Alan Peshkin (New York: Teachers College Press, 1990), pp. 201–242.

11. See Anne Bussis, Edward Chittenden, and Marianne Amerel, *Beyond Surface Curriculum: An Interview Study of Teachers' Understandings* (Boulder, CO: Westview Press, 1976).

12. Mortimer J. Adler, *The Paideia Proposal: An Educational Manifesto* (New York: Macmillan, 1982).

13. E. D. Hirsch Jr., *Cultural Literacy: What Every American Needs to Know* (Boston: Houghton Mifflin, 1987).

14. Jerome Bruner, *Acts of Meaning* (Cambridge, MA: Harvard University Press, 1990).

26

What Does It Mean to Say a School is Doing Well?

Elliot W. Eisner

Driven by discontent with the performance of our schools, we are, once again, in the midst of education reform, as we were in 1983 with *A Nation at Risk*, in 1987 with America 2000, and a few years later with Goals 2000. Each of these reform efforts was intended to rationalize the practice and performance of our schools. Each was designed to work out and install a system of measurable goals and evaluation practices that would ensure that our nation would be first in science and mathematics by the year 2000, that all our children would come to school ready to learn, and that each school would be drug-free, safe, and nonviolent.[1]

The formulation of standards and the measurement of performance were intended to tidy up a messy system and to make teachers and school administrators truly accountable. The aim was then, and is today, to systematize and standardize so that the public will know which schools are performing well and which are not. There were to be then, and there are today, payments and penalties for performance.

America is one of the few nations in which responsibility for schools is not under the aegis of a national ministry of education. Although we have a federal agency, the U.S. Department of Education, the 10th Amendment to the U.S. Constitution indicates that those responsibilities that the Constitution does not assign explicitly to the federal government belong to the states (or to the people). And since the Constitution makes no mention of education, it is a responsibility of the states.

As a result, we have 50 departments of education, one for each state, overseeing some 16,000 school districts that serve 52 million students in more than 100,000 schools. In addition, each school district has latitude for shaping education policy. Given the complexity of the way education is organized in the U.S., it is understandable that from one perspective the view looks pretty messy and not altogether rational. Furthermore, more than a few believe that we have a national problem in American education and that national problems

Reprinted by permission of Phi Delta Kappa International, From *Phi Delta Kappan*, Vol. 82, No. 5, 2001, pp 367–372.

require national solutions. The use of highly rationalized procedures for improving schools is a part of the solution.

I mention the concept of rationalization because I am trying to describe the ethos being created in our schools. I am trying to reveal a world view that shapes our conception of education and the direction we take for making our schools better.

Rationalization as a concept has a number of features. First, it depends on a clear specification of intended outcomes.[2] That is what standards and rubrics are supposed to do. We are supposed to know what the outcomes of educational practice are to be, and rubrics are to exemplify those outcomes. Standards are more general statements intended to proclaim our values. One argument for the use of standards and rubrics is that they are necessary if we are to function rationally. As the saying goes, if you don't know where you're headed, you will not know where you have arrived. In fact, it's more than knowing where you're headed; it's also knowing the precise destination. Thus the specification of intended outcomes has become one of the primary practices in the process of rationalizing school reform efforts. Holding people accountable for the results is another.

Second, rationalization typically uses measurement as a means through which the quality of a product or performance is assessed and represented. Measurement, of course, is *one* way to describe the world. Measurement has to do with determining matters of magnitude, and it deals with matters of magnitude through the specification of units. In the United States, the unit for weight is pounds. In Sweden or the Netherlands, it is kilograms. It's kilometers in Europe; it's miles in the United States. It really doesn't matter what unit you use, as long as everyone agrees what the unit is.[3]

Quantification is believed to be a way to increase objectivity, secure rigor, and advance precision in assessment. For describing some features of the world, including the educational world, it is indispensable. But it is not good for everything, and the limitations of quantification are increasingly being recognized. For example, although initial discussions about standards emphasized the need for them to be *measurable*, as standards have become increasingly general and ideological, measurability has become less salient.

Third, the rationalization of practice is predicated on the ability to control and predict. We assume that we can know the specific effects of our interventions, an assumption that is questionable.

Fourth, rationalization downplays interactions. Interactions take into account not simply the conditions that are to be introduced in classrooms or schools but also the kinds of personal qualities, expectations, orientations, ideas, and temperaments that interact with those conditions. Philosophical constructivists have pointed out that what something means comes both from the features of the phenomenon to be addressed and from the way those features are interpreted or experienced by individuals.[4] Such idiosyncratic considerations always complicate assessment. They complicate efforts to rationalize education as well. Prediction is not easy when what the outcome is going to be is a function not only of what is introduced in the situation but also of what a student makes of what has been introduced.

Fifth, rationalization promotes comparison, and comparison requires what is called "commensurability." Commensurability is possible only if you know what the programs were in which the youngsters participated in the schools being compared. If youngsters are in schools that have different curricula or that allocate differing amounts of time to different areas of the curriculum, comparing the outcomes of those schools without taking into account their differences is extremely questionable. Making comparisons between the math performance of youngsters in Japan and those in the United States without taking into account cultural differences, different allocations of time for instruction, or different approaches to teaching makes it impossible to account for differences in student performance or to consider the side effects or opportunity costs associated with different programs in different cultures. The same principle holds in comparing student performance across school districts in the U.S.

Sixth, rationalization relies upon extrinsic incentives to motivate action; that's what vouchers are intended to do. Schools are likened to businesses, and the survival of the fittest is the principle that determines which ones survive. If schools don't produce effective results on tests, they go out of business.

In California and in some other parts of the country, principals and superintendents are often paid a bonus if their students perform well on standardized tests: payment by results. And, of course, such a reward system has consequences for a school's priorities. Are test scores the criteria that we want to use to reward professional performance?

The features that I have just described are a legacy of the Enlightenment. We believe our rational abilities can be used to discover the regularities of the universe and, once we've found them, to implement, as my colleague David Tyack titled his book, "the one best system."[5] We have a faith in our ability to discover what the U.S. Department of Education once described as "what works." The result is an approach to reform that leaves little room for surprise, for imagination, for improvisation, or for the cultivation of productive idiosyncrasy. Our reform efforts are closer in spirit to the ideas of René Descartes and August Compte than to those of William Blake. They are efforts that use league tables to compare schools and that regard test scores as valid proxies for the quality of education our children receive.[6] And they constitute an approach to reform that has given us three major educationally feckless reform efforts in the past 20 years. Are we going to have another?

What are the consequences of the approach to reform that we have taken and what should we pay attention to in order to tell when a school is doing well? First, one of the consequences of our approach to reform is that the curriculum gets narrowed as school district policies make it clear that what is to be tested is what is to be taught. Tests come to define our priorities. And now we have legitimated those priorities by talking about "core subjects." The introduction of the concept of core subjects explicitly marginalizes subjects that are not part of the core. One of the areas that we marginalize is the arts, an area that when well taught offers substantial benefits to students. Our idea of core subjects is related to our assessment practices and the tests we use to determine whether or not schools are doing well.

Because those of us in education take test scores seriously, the public is reinforced in its view that test scores are good proxies for the quality of education a school provides. Yet what test scores predict best are other test scores. If we are going to use proxies that have predictive validity, we need proxies that predict performances that matter outside the context of school. The function of schooling is not to enable students to do better in school. The function of schooling is to enable students to do better in life. What students learn in school ought to exceed in relevance the limits of the school's program.

As we focus on standards, rubrics, and measurement, the deeper problems of schooling go unattended. What are some of the deeper problems of schooling? One has to do with the quality of conversation in classrooms. We need to provide opportunities for youngsters and adolescents to engage in challenging kinds of conversation, and we need to help them learn how to do so. Such conversation is all too rare in schools. I use "conversation" seriously, for challenging conversation is an intellectual affair. It has to do with thinking about what people have said and responding reflectively, analytically, and imaginatively to that process. The practice of conversation is almost a lost art. We turn to talk shows to experience what we cannot do very well or very often.

The deeper problems of schooling have to do with teacher isolation and the fact that teachers don't often have access to other people who know what they're doing when they teach and who can help them do it better.[7] Although there are many issues that need attention in schooling, we search for the silver bullet and believe that, if we get our standards straight and our rubrics right and make our tests tough enough, we will have an improved school system. I am not so sure.

The message that we send to students is that what really matters in their education are their test scores. As a result, students in high-stakes testing programs find ways to cut corners—and so do some teachers. We read increasingly often not only about students who are cheating but also about teachers who are unfairly helping students get higher scores on the tests.[8] It's a pressure that undermines the kind of experience that students ought to have in schools.

Perhaps the major consequence of the approach we have taken to rationalize our schools is that it ineluctably colors the school climate. It promotes an orientation to practice that emphasizes extrinsically defined attainment targets that have a specified quantitative value. This, in turn, leads students to want to know just what it is they need to do to earn a particular grade. Even at Stanford, I sometimes get requests from graduate students who want to know precisely, or as precisely as I can put it, what they need to do in order to get an A in the class.

Now from one angle such a request sounds reasonable. After all, it is a means/ends approach to educational planning. Students are, it can be said, rationally planning their education. But such planning has very little to do with intellectual life, where risk-taking, exploration, uncertainty, and speculation are what it's about. And if you create a culture of schooling in which a narrow means/ends orientation is promoted, that culture can undermine the development of intellectual dispositions. By intellectual dispositions I mean a curiosity and interest in engaging and challenging ideas.

What the field has not provided is an efficient alternative to the testing procedures we now use. And for good reason. The good reason is that there are no efficient alternatives. Educationally useful evaluation takes time, it's labor intensive and complex, and it's subtle, particularly if evaluation is used not simply to score children or adults but to provide information to improve the process of teaching and learning.

The price one pays for providing many ways for students to demonstrate what has been learned is a reduction of commensurability. Commensurability decreases when attention to individuality increases. John Dewey commented about comparisons in a book that he wrote in 1934 when he was 76 years old. The book is *Art as Experience*. He observed that nothing is more odious than comparisons in the arts.[9] What he was getting at was that attention to or appreciation of an art form requires attention to and appreciation of its distinctive features. It was individuality that Dewey was emphasizing, and it is the description of individuality we would do well to think about in our assessment practices. We should be trying to discover where a youngster is, where his or her strengths are, where additional work is warranted. Commensurability is possible when everybody is on the same track, when there are common assessment practices, and when there is a common curriculum. But when students work on different kinds of problems, and when there is concern with the development of an individual's thumbprint, so to speak, commensurability is an inappropriate aim.

What have been the consequences of the rationalized approach to education reform that we have embraced? Only this: in our desire to improve our schools, education has become a casualty. That is, in the process of rationalization, education—always a delicate, complex, and subtle process having to do with both cultural transmission and self-actualization—has become a commodity. Education has evolved from a form of human development serving personal and civic needs into a product our nation produces to compete in a global economy. Schools have become places to mass produce this product.

Let us assume that we impose a moratorium on standardized testing for a five-year period. What might we pay attention to in schools in order to say that a school is doing well? If it is not higher test scores that we are looking for, what is it? Let me suggest the kind of data we might seek by raising some questions that might guide our search.

What kinds of problems and activities do students engage in? What kind of thinking do these activities invite? Are students encouraged to wonder and to raise questions about what they have studied? Perhaps we should be less concerned with whether they can answer our questions than with whether they can ask their own. The most significant intellectual achievement is not so much in problem solving, but in question posing. What if we took that idea seriously and concluded units of study by looking for the sorts of questions that youngsters are able to raise as a result of being immersed in a domain of study? What would that practice teach youngsters about inquiry?

What is the intellectual significance of the ideas that youngsters encounter? (I have a maxim that I work with: If it's not worth teaching, it's not worth teaching well.) Are the ideas they encounter important? Are they ideas that have legs? Do they go someplace?

Are students introduced to multiple perspectives? Are they asked to provide multiple perspectives on an issue or a set of ideas? The implications of such an expectation for curriculum development are extraordinary. To develop such an ability and habit of mind, we would need to invent activities that encourage students to practice, refine, and develop certain modes of thought. Taking multiple perspectives is just one such mode.

In 1950 the American psychologist J.P. Guilford developed what he called "the structure of intellect," in which 130 different kinds of cognitive processes were identified.[10] What if we used that kind of structure to promote various forms of thinking? My point is that the activities in which youngsters participate in classes are the means through which their thinking is promoted. When youngsters have no reason to raise questions, the processes that enable them to learn how to discover intellectual problems go undeveloped.

The ability to raise telling questions is not an automatic consequence of maturation. Do you know what's the biggest problem that Stanford students have in the course of their doctoral work? It is not getting good grades in courses; they all get good grades in courses. Their biggest obstacle is in framing a dissertation problem. We can do something about that before students get to the doctoral level. In a school that is doing well, opportunities for the kind of thinking that yields good questions would be promoted.

What connections are students helped to make between what they study in class and the world outside of school? A major aim of education has to do with what psychologists refer to as "transfer of learning." Can students apply what they have learned or what they have learned how to learn? Can they engage in the kind of learning they will need in order to deal with problems and issues outside of the classroom? If what students are learning is simply used as a means to increase their scores on the next test, we may win the battle and lose the war. In such a context, school learning becomes a hurdle to jump over. We need to determine whether students can use what they have learned. But even being able to use what has been learned is no indication that it will be used. There is a difference between what a student can do and what a student will do.

The really important dependent variables in education are not located in classrooms. Nor are they located in schools. The really important dependent variables are located outside schools. Our assessment practices haven't even begun to scratch that surface. It's what students do with what they learn when they can do what they want to do that is the real measure of educational achievement.

What opportunities do youngsters have to become literate in the use of different representational forms? By representational forms, I mean the various symbol systems through which humans shape experience and give it meaning.[11] Different forms of human meaning are expressed in different forms of representation. The kinds of meaning one secures from poetry are not the kinds of meaning one secures from propositional signs. The kinds of meanings expressed in music are not the meanings experienced in the visual arts. To be able to secure any of those meanings, you have to know how to "read" them. Seeing is a reading. Hearing is a reading. They are processes of interpreting and *construing* meaning from the material encountered; reading text is not only a process of decoding, it is also a process of encoding. We *make* sense of what we read.

What opportunities do students have to formulate their own purposes and to design ways to achieve them? Can a school provide the conditions for youngsters, as they mature, to have increased opportunity to set their own goals and to design ways to realize them? Plato once defined a slave as someone who executes the purposes of another. I would say that, in a free democratic state, at least a part of the role of education is to help youngsters learn how to define their own purposes.

What opportunities do students have to work cooperatively to address problems that they believe to be important? Can we design schools so that we create communities of learners who know how to work with one another? Can we design schools and classrooms in which cooperating with others is part of what it means to be a student?

Do students have the opportunity to serve the community in ways that are not limited to their own personal interests? Can we define a part of the school's role as establishing or helping students establish projects in which they do something beyond their own self-interest? I want to know that in order to know how well a school is doing.

To what extent are students given the opportunity to work in depth in domains that relate to their aptitudes? Is personal talent cultivated? Can we arrange the time for youngsters to work together on the basis of interest rather than on the basis of age grading? Youngsters who are interested in ceramics might work in depth in ceramics; those interested in science might work in depth in science. To make these possibilities a reality, we would need, of course, to address the practical problems of allocating time and responsibility. But without a conception of what is important, we will never even ask questions about allocating time. A vision of what is educationally important must come first.

Do students participate in the assessment of their own work? If so, how? It is important for teachers to understand what students themselves think of their own work. Can we design assessment practices in which students can help us?

To what degree are students genuinely engaged in what they do in school? Do they find satisfaction in the intellectual journey? How many students come to school early and how many would like to stay late? The motives for such choices have to do with the "locus of satisfactions." Satisfactions generate reasons for doing something. Basically, there are three reasons for doing anything. One reason for doing something is that you like what it feels like and you like who you are when you do it. Sex, play, and art fall into this category. They are intrinsically satisfying activities.

A second reason for doing something is not because you like doing it, but because you like the results of having done it. You might like a clean kitchen, but you might not enjoy cleaning your kitchen. The process is not a source of enjoyment, but the outcome is.

A third reason for doing something is not because you like the process or even the outcome, but because you like the rewards. You like the grades you earn. You like the paycheck you receive. That's what Hannah Arendt described as labor.[12] There is too much labor in our schools—and not enough work. Work is effort from which you derive satisfaction. We ought to be paying attention to the joy of the journey. This is easy to say but difficult and challenging to do. Nevertheless, we ought to keep our minds focused on it as a goal.

Are teachers given the time to observe and work with one another? To what degree is professional discourse an important aspect of what being a teacher means in the school? Is the school a resource, a center for the teacher's own development? Is the school a center for teacher education?

The center for teacher education is not the university; it is the school in which the teacher works. Professional growth should be promoted during the 25 years that a teacher works in a school—not just during the year and a half that he or she spends in a teacher education program. Can we create schools that take the professional development of teachers seriously? And what would they look like? Schools will not be better for students than they are for the professionals who work in them.

All of us who teach develop repertoires. We all have routines. We all get by. We get by without serious problems, but getting by is not good enough. We need to get better. And to get better, we have to think about school in ways that address teachers' real needs. And when I say, "addressing teachers' real needs," I don't mean sending them out every 6,000 miles to get "inserviced" by a stranger.

Are parents helped to understand what their child has accomplished in class? Do they come to understand the educational import of what is going on? Very often children's artwork is displayed in the school, with the only information provided being the student's name, the grade, and the teacher's name, all in the lower right-hand corner. Then the best student work is posted more formally. What we do, in effect, is use a gallery model of exhibition. We take the best work, and we display it. What we need to create is an educationally interpretive exhibition that explains to viewers what problems the youngsters were addressing and how they resolved them.[13] This can be done by looking at prior work and comparing it with present work—that is, by looking at what students have accomplished over time. I am talking about interpretation. I am talking about getting people to focus not so much on what the grade is, but on what process led to the outcome.

What is my point? All my arguments have had to do with creating an educationally informed community. We need to ask better questions.

Can we widen what parents and others believe to be important in judging the quality of our schools? Can we widen and diversity what they think matters? Can those of us who teach think about public education not only as the education of the public in the schools (i.e., our students), but also as the education of the public outside of our schools (i.e., parents and community members)? Can a more substantial and complex understanding of what constitutes good schooling contribute to better, more enlightened support for our schools?

Can a more informed conception of what constitutes quality in education lead to greater equity for students and ultimately for the culture? Educational equity is much more than just allowing students to cross the threshold of the school. It has to do with what students find after they do so. We ought to be providing environments that enable each youngster in our schools to find a place in the educational sun. But when we narrow the program so that there is only a limited array of areas in which assessment occurs and performance is honored, youngsters whose aptitudes and interests lie elsewhere are going to be marginalized in our schools. The more we diversify those opportunities, the more equity we are going to have because we are going to provide wider opportunities for youngsters to find what it is that they are good at.

And that leads me to the observation that, in our push for attaining standards, we have tended to focus on outcomes that are standard for all youngsters. We want youngsters to arrive at the same place at about the same time. I would argue that really good schools increase variance in student performance. Really good schools increase the variance *and* raise the mean. The reason I say that is because, when youngsters can play to their strengths, those whose aptitudes are in, say, mathematics are going to go faster and further in that area than youngsters whose aptitudes are in some other field. But in those other fields, those youngsters would go faster and further than those whose aptitudes are in math. Merely by conceiving of a system of educational organization that regards productive variance as something to be valued and pursued, we undermine the expectation that everybody should be moving in lockstep through a series of 10-month years in a standardized system and coming out at pretty much the same place by age 18.

Part of our press toward standardization has to do with what is inherent in our age-graded school system. Age-graded systems work on the assumption that children remain more alike than different over time and that we should be teaching within the general expectations for any particular grade. Yet, if you examine reading performance, for example, the average range of reading ability in an ordinary classroom approximates the grade level. Thus at the second grade, there is a two-year spread; at the third grade, a three-year range; at the fourth grade, a four-year range. Consider how various the picture would be if performance in four or five different fields of study were examined. Children become more different as they get older, and we ought to be promoting those differences and at the same time working to escalate the mean.

Does more enlightened grasp of what matters in schools put us in a better position to improve them? I hope so. What I have argued here is intended to divert our focus away from what we normally use to make judgments about the quality of schools and redirect it instead toward the processes, conditions, and culture that are closer to the heart of education. I am unabashedly endorsing the promotion of improvisation, surprise, and diversity of outcomes as educational virtues that we ought to try to realize through our teaching.

The point of the questions I have raised is to provide something better than the blinkered vision of school quality that now gets front-page coverage in our newspapers. Perhaps this vision serves best those in positions of privilege. Perhaps our society needs losers so it can have winners. Whatever the case, I believe that those of us who wish to exercise leadership in education must do more than simply accept the inadequate criteria that are now used to determine how well our schools are doing.

We need a fresh and humane vision of what schools might become because what our schools become has everything to do with what our children and our culture will become. I have suggested some of the features and some of the questions that I believe matter educationally. We need reform efforts that are better than those we now have. The vision of education implicit in what I have described here is just a beginning.

NOTES

1. The document that most directly expresses this view is National Commission on Excellence in Education, *A Nation at Risk: The Imperative for Educational Reform* (Washington, D.C.: U.S. Government Printing Office, 1983).

2. Donald Schon describes the process of rationalization of behavior as "technical rationality." See Donald Schon, *The Reflective Practitioner: How Professionals Think in Action* (New York: Basic Books, 1983). Nor is this the first time technically rational approaches to planning and assessment have dominated schooling. The efficiency movement in American schools—from about 1913 to about 1930—is one example. The behavioral objectives and accountability movements of the 1960s and 1970s are two more.

3. For a discussion of issues pertaining to the quantification and use of standards, see Elliot W. Eisner, "Standards for American Schools: Help or Hindrance?," *Phi Delta Kappan,* June 1995, pp. 758–64.

4. One of the foremost philosophical constructivists is John Dewey. The concept of interaction was a central notion in his philosophy of mind and in his conception of the educational process. For a succinct view of his ideas pertaining to education, see John Dewey, *Experience and Education* (New York: Macmillan, 1938).

5. David Tyack, *The One Best System* (Cambridge, Mass.: Harvard University Press, 1974).

6. League tables not only affect the priorities of the school, they are a major influence on real estate values. The value of houses is influenced significantly by perceptions of the quality of the schools in a neighborhood, and test scores are the indices used to determine such quality.

7. For a full discussion of the processes of observation and disclosure as they pertain to teaching and its improvement, see my book *The Enlightened Eye: Qualitative Inquiry and the Enhancement of Educational Practice* (New York: Macmillan, 1991).

8. For an insightful and lucid discussion of the pressures secondary school students experience in the high-stakes environment that we have created in schools, see Denise Pope, "Doing School" (Doctoral dissertation, Stanford University, 1998).

9. John Dewey, *Art as Experience* (New York: Minton, Balch and Company, 1934), especially chap. 13.

10. J.P. Guilford, *The Nature of Human Intelligence* (New York: McGraw-Hill, 1967).

11. Elliot W. Eisner, "Forms of Understanding and the Future of Educational Research," *Educational Researcher,* October 1993, pp. 5–11. Also see my book *Cognition and Curriculum Reconsidered* (New York: Teachers College Press, 1994).

12. Hannah Arendt, *The Human Condition* (Chicago: University of Chicago Press, 1958).

13. For a discussion and illustration of what I call educationally interpretive exhibitions, see Elliot W. Eisner et al. *The Educationally Interpretive Exhibition: Rethinking the Display of Student Art* (Reston, Va.: National Art Education Association, 1997).

27

Silence on Gays and Lesbians in Social Studies Curriculum

Stephen J. Thornton

IMAGINE, AS WAS ONCE THE CASE, that today's social studies curriculum measured all else against a standard of being male, Protestant, and Anglo-Saxon.[1] Women, African Americans, Catholic and Eastern Orthodox Christians, Jews, and Muslims, not to mention other religious, ethnic, and racial groups, would react with righteous outrage. With justification, we can claim that today's social studies curriculum has become more inclusive of a range of groups and perspectives within and beyond the United States.

Although still imperfect, the contemporary K-12 social studies curriculum has moved away from the tacit equating of "American" with, for example, Protestant, or Christian for that matter. At least one major exception to this legitimation of diversity persists: it is still tacitly assumed that everyone is heterosexual until proven otherwise. Despite striking growth in social, political, legal, and media presence of gays in American life, especially in the past decade,[2] few social studies materials appear to have substantive treatment of gay history and issues. Indeed, many of these materials fail to even mention such words as homosexual, straight, or gay. It is as if the millions of gay inhabitants of the United States, past and present, did not exist. Although scholarship studied in colleges is now sometimes rich with gay material, Americans who do not attend college—and the least educated are precisely those who are most inclined to be prejudiced against gay people[3]—are unlikely to hear of such scholarship.

The belief that the archetypal human is straight is called *heteronormativity*. It belies an inclusive curriculum. Moreover, it encourages stereotypes. As James Banks has warned, using a "mainstream" benchmark against which group differences are measured promotes "a kind of 'we-they' attitude among mainstream students and teachers."[4] Banks's observation about multiethnic education seems equally applicable to the study of homosexuals: "Ethnic content should be used to help students learn that all human beings have common needs and characteristics, although the ways in which these traits are manifested frequently differ cross-culturally."[5]

Reprinted by permission of the National Council for the Social Studies, From *Social Education*, vol. 67, No. 4, 2003, pp. 226–230.

Heteronormativity goes basically unchallenged in teaching materials for K-12 social studies. Unless children are raised in a limited number of locales or have teachers who go beyond what the textbook provides, they may graduate from high school being none the wiser that heteronormativity paints an inaccurate picture of social life and perpetuates intolerance, sometimes with tangibly destructive consequences such as harassment and physical violence.[6]

CURRICULAR LIMITATIONS OF CURRENT INCLUSION

The social studies curriculum, because it must make some attempt at describing the world as it is, has always dealt with "difference." The debate, as Margaret Smith Crocco shows, has centered on what the differences are and how they have been dealt with.[7] The common failure even to mention the existence of lesbians and gay men (let alone bisexual and transgender persons) clearly clashes with gay matters today being a visible part of the public landscape in most of America. Thus, a first step that social studies educators need to take is frank acknowledgment that differences in sexual orientation (and other taboo subjects such as religion) exist in America.[8] To put it another way, educators must answer the question, Does everybody count as human?[9]

One current and widely used U.S. history high school textbook is illustrative of the current failures. In its treatment of postwar African American novelists, James Baldwin is described as writing about "patterns of discrimination" directed toward blacks. This point is placed as a precursor to the struggle against racial injustice in the civil rights era.

The text is silent, however, about Baldwin's being both African American and homosexual. He wrote eloquently of "patterns of discrimination" directed toward gay men. For example, in *Giovanni's Room* and in *Another Country*, which were written in the same postwar and civil rights period of American history, Baldwin explores how young gay men fled prejudice in family and community in the United States for the relative anonymity of Paris.[10]

This silence on homosexual expatriate writers stands in stark contrast to the treatment of heterosexual expatriate writers. U.S. history textbooks routinely discuss the "lost generation" of the 1920s, the group of literary artists such as Hemingway and Scott Fitzgerald who, disillusioned with American materialism, traveled to Paris searching for meaning. Their fictional characters and the motives of these characters are frequently canonized in high school history textbooks, while Baldwin's fictional gay characters and the motives of his characters go unmentioned.

The same silences that characterize the American history curriculum appear in global history and geography. Take the subject of human rights. There has been a great deal of attention, especially since September 11, 2001, to the oppression of Afghan women by the harsh, extremist brand of Islam embraced by the Taliban. Properly, this denial of basic human rights to women has widely stood condemned both in the West and in the Islamic world. But no such condemnation of systematic persecution of gay men (or allegedly gay men) in parts of the Islamic world, such as recently in Egypt, appears in the curriculum although, as with Afghan women, the persecution rests on these men simply for being who they are.

Social studies courses most directly devoted to citizenship, such as government and civics, routinely extol the freedoms Americans enjoy because they are Americans. That such freedoms still extend only to some people and not to others, however, is likely to go unmentioned in textbooks. For example unlike important allies such as the United Kingdom, of whose armed forces in Afghanistan and the Persian Gulf we have heard so much recently, U.S. armed forces legally discriminate against lesbians and gay men. Although American youngsters will certainly study American freedoms in social studies courses, they may never be told or question that other closely associated nations also extend freedoms to gays that are denied them in the United States. American history and government texts justifiably vaunt our belief in self-evident rights dating back to at least 1776; they omit that some of these rights are selectively available depending on a person's sexual orientation.

The limitations of the current curriculum, however, run deeper than exclusion from history and other courses. Although acknowledgment of the humanity of gay people and democratic tolerance for them should be fundamental, these aims fail to strike at the heart of heteronormativity. While it is generally acknowledged that the social studies should prepare young people for citizenship, gay people are vulnerable to the way freedom to participate fully in the affairs of the state is defined. At present, as Nel Noddings writes, it seems that "to improve their status, the vulnerable must either become more like the privileged or accept some charitable form of the respect taken for granted by those acknowledged as full citizens."[11] In other words, even if gay people were identified as gay people in the curriculum, this begs the questions of what should be said about them and from what perspectives.

THE HIDDEN CURRICULUM EVERYBODY SEES

The hidden curriculum of schools rigidly patrols the boundaries of sex role behavior. Homophobia is common in American schools.[12] Although unmentioned in the publicly announced curriculum, all young people learn that sex role deviance, actual or perceived, exacts a heavy price. It is surely one of the most successful exercises in social training that schools perform. Moreover, this unannounced curriculum functions in practically all schools regardless of racial and ethnic composition, social class, and so forth. Indeed, young people who are themselves oppressed by poverty, crime, or racial mistreatment frequently become oppressors of peers perceived to be gay.[13]

Whether by choice or neglect, school professionals are implicated in patrolling sex role boundaries.[14] In corridors and classrooms, for example, few if any taunts are more common than "fag," and embedded in history textbooks are messages about what it means to behave in a "masculine" fashion.[15] In other parts of school grounds such as parking lots, bathrooms, and locker rooms, where youngsters are frequently unsupervised by adults who know them, sex role deviations sometimes meet with physical violence.

There seems to be a variety of motives for how teachers respond to all of this. Some teachers may be afraid of being labeled "gay" if they correct students for bigoted behavior. Disturbingly, some teachers appear to agree with condemnations of perceived departures from "normal" sex roles; girls must be "feminine" and boys must not be "effeminate." They may ignore, and sometimes even encourage, harassment of students perceived to be gay. Administrators and teachers may counsel harassed students to avoid "flaunting" their allegedly deviant behavior, in effect, blaming the victim.[16]

What is clear is that administrators and teachers are not being neutral or impartial when they ignore this hidden curriculum. Silence, far from neutral, implicitly condones continuation of the persecution. Studies have long shown that depression and suicide are far more common among youngsters who are gay than among their straight peers.[17] School professionals—classroom teachers, administrators, counselors, and librarians— are frequently the only responsible adults to whom these at-risk children can turn for both needed support and equal educational opportunities.

TOWARD MORE INCLUSIVE CURRICULUM

It is too easy for educators to feel absolved of responsibility because authorities have frequently omitted gay people and gay issues from curriculum documents and materials. Moreover, censorship of gay material is commonplace. Ominously, these forms of neglect exist alongside a persistent countermovement. Every step forward for the well-being of gay students and a curriculum more inclusive of lesbian and gay experience has been doggedly challenged by anti-gay groups.[18]

Teachers have choices. All teachers are curricular-instructional gatekeepers—they largely decide the day-to-day curriculum and activities students experience.[19] How teachers enact curriculum, even with today's constraints such as standards and high-stakes tests, still matters both practically and ethically. Opportunities to incorporate at least some gay material into the standard curriculum exist; in many instances, all that is required is the will to call attention to aspects of standard subject matter that heretofore went unmentioned.

Quite a few inclusion opportunities in mainstay secondary school courses such as U.S. history, world history, and geography present themselves. No U.S. history survey textbook that I have seen, for instance, omits Jane Addams. She is rightly portrayed as one of the nation's greatest social and educational thinkers and activists, not to mention her formidable work for world peace. Addams never married. She chose to spend her adult life among a community of women and had a long-time special relationship with one woman.[20] This may raise ample opportunities for properly directed class discussion: What did it mean that a considerable number of educated women of Addams's means and generation chose to forsake marriage and pursue careers beyond domesticity? Were they models for gender equity for later generations of women's rights and equity advocates?

Note, we have not directly addressed Addams's sexual orientation. (The evidence, in any case, seems inconclusive.) Perhaps more important than a rush or need to judge, however, is to ask if this woman's accomplishments would be diminished or enhanced by such knowledge. Or a primary educational objective could be to understand how Addams, who rejected some gender conventions for her day, helped shape her times and her legacy for today. Her significance, in this scheme, incorporates the complexities and controversial aspects of her life as well as speaking to different but nonetheless related questions today.

Other topics such as the ancient world in global history courses provide different pathways to incorporate the gay experience. Again, let me underscore that we are still working with standard material in the curriculum. No new instructional materials are required. Specialist knowledge, while as desirable as ever, is unessential.

Take the topic of Alexander the Great. One high school world history textbook I examined, for example, shows how, through his military genius and statesmanship, Alexander built a "multicultural" empire. Although adjectives such as "multicultural" (and "gay" for that matter) are anachronistic here, the point for today's readers seems plain enough: Alexander was a leader, probably before his time, in building what we might call today an inclusive society.

Here we might pause to challenge how inclusive (or "multicultural") this textbook treatment is. No mention is made of Alexander's homosexuality. Teachers, however, could readily place Alexander's homosexuality in its cultural and temporal context. In those terms, his sexual orientation was relatively unremarkable. Sensitively approached, such a perspective may lead students to rethink stereotypes of both warriors and homosexuals.

Classical Greece provides numerous opportunities to explore beyond the information given. Textbooks routinely feature photographs of idealized male images such as Greek athletes and actors. Why did the Greeks so prize the male form? What does it reveal about their culture? How does it relate to today's notions of athleticism and the arts? How is the ideal of male community perpetuated by today's college campus fraternities?

Of course, gay materials may also be an instructional focus rather than ancillary to the main part of a lesson or unit. In U.S. history courses, a unit on the civil rights struggle of the 1950s and 1960s is standard. These days a wide range of groups in addition to African Americans are often featured in this unit, such as Latinos, women, Native Americans, and so forth. But seldom does this extend to gay people. Such a unit could be made more genuinely inclusive if it also included a lesson devoted to a turning point in civil rights for gay people, such as the 1969 Stonewall riots in Greenwich Village, New York City.

Although much more the exception than the rule, teachers in some parts of the country have designed instructional sequences on gay topics longer than a lesson or two. One civics teacher, for example, as part of a nine-week unit on "Tolerance and Diversity," included a two-week mini-unit on "Homophobia Prevention." He has written of the experience and materials he used.[21]

Current events instruction is also a ready site for dealing with gay material. By way of illustration, recently published secondary school American history textbooks are silent on the "history" of former U.S. President Bill Clinton's "don't ask, don't tell" policy for gays in the military. Teachers, however, could still treat this rights topic in the classroom because the media report on it with some regularity. A good issue for critical thinking might be why the number of persons discharged from the armed forces for their homosexuality has continued to rise in the decade since the supposed implementation of the policy.[22]

CONCLUSION

Even concerned and willing educators face some significant obstacles to incorporating gay material in the curriculum. Many veteran teachers may never have studied gay material during their preservice teacher education programs, either in academic or professional courses. As noted, this situation has changed somewhat in the academy today in courses in history, the social sciences, and literature. In teacher education, too, the situation has altered. "Student sexual diversity guidelines for teachers" now appear in some teacher education textbooks, for instance.[23] Furthermore, explicit training for and sensitivity to inclusion is now common in teacher education programs in diverse regions of the nation. We probably shouldn't expect, however, in-service workshops devoted to gay subject matter to arise everywhere in the nation any time soon. But nearly everywhere the legal realities of protecting the rights of gay students, if nothing else, may compel some staff development.[24]

Heteronormativity is also a concern because many students in our schools now have parents who are gay or lesbian. These children have the same rights to an equal education as do their peers whose parents are heterosexual. About ten years ago, however, a storm of controversy erupted in New York City when it was suggested that the children's book *Heather Has Two Mommies* even be allowed as an option to be included on a several-hundred-page list of curriculum ideas on diversity from which teachers might choose.[25]

Although it is now most noticeable in large cities, many schoolchildren across the nation have lesbian or gay parents. Yet only "traditional" families tend to be included in the curriculum. Despite *Heather's* apparent sensitivity to appropriate treatment for the intended age group, this failed to prevent its being removed from the list of suggested (not mandated) books. However, at least some more encouraging reports of teachers addressing the issue of nontraditional families have appeared more recently. For example, one New York City teacher reported on positive outcomes from teaching a novel to middle school students that concerned a boy coming to terms with his father's being gay.[26]

If we are to be inclusive in the social studies curriculum, then the kinds of changes I have sketched here are vital first steps. The alternative, if many educators perpetuate heteronormativity, is that most young people will continue to learn about homosexuality through a popular prejudiced lens.

NOTES

1. Frances FitzGerald, *America Revised: History Schoolbooks in the Twentieth Century* (New York: Vintage, 1980).

2. Suzanna Danuta Walters, *All the Rage: The Story of Gay Visibility in America* (Chicago: University of Chicago Press, 2001).

3. Patricia G. Avery, "Teaching Tolerance: What Research Tells Us," *Social Education* 66, no. 5 (2002): 270–275.

4. James A. Banks, *Multiethnic Education* (Boston: Allyn and Bacon, 1988), 177.

5. Ibid., 175.

6. Human Rights Watch, *Hatred in the Hallways: Violence and Discrimination against Lesbian, Gay, Bisexual, and Transgender Students in U.S. Schools* (New York: Human Rights Watch, 2001).

7. Margaret Smith Crocco, "Dealing with Difference in the Social Studies: A Historical Perspective" *International Journal of Social Education* (in press).

8. Rahima Wade, "Diversity Taboos: Religion and Sexual Orientation in the Social Studies," *Social Studies and the Young Learner* 7, no. 4 (1995): 19–22.

9. Stephen J. Thornton, "Does Everybody Count as Human?" *Theory and Research in Social Education* 30, no. 2 (2002): 178–189.

10. See James Baldwin, Giovanni's Room (New York: Modern Library, 2001) and Another Country (New York: Dial Press, 1962).

11. Nel Noddings, "Caring, Social Policy, and Homelessness," *Theoretical Medicine* 23 (2002): 441.

12. For an analysis of this state of affairs, see Margaret Smith Crocco, "The Missing Discourse about Gender and Sexuality in the Social Studies," *Theory into Practice* 40, no. 1 (2001): 65–71 and "Homophobic Hallways: Is Anyone Listening?" *Theory and Research in Social Education* 30, no. 2 (2002): 217–232.

13. Kevin C. Franck, "Rethinking Homophobia: Interrogating Heteronormativity in an Urban School," *Theory and Research in Social Education* 30, no. 2 (2002): 274–286.

14. Human Rights Watch, op. cit.

15. Jeffrey J. Kuzmic, "Textbooks, Knowledge, and Masculinity: Examining Patriarchy from Within," in *Masculinities at School*, ed. Nancy Lesko (Thousand Oaks, CA: Sage, 2000).

16. Perry A. Zirkel, "Courtside: Gay Days," *Phi Delta Kappan* 84, no. 5 (2003): 412–413.

17. Human Rights Watch, op. cit., 75.

18. See, for example, People for the American Way, "Right Wing Watch: Back to School with the Religious Right," www.pfaw.org/pfaw/general/default.aspx?oid=3652, accessed February 4, 2003.

19. For elaboration of this point, see Stephen J. Thornton, "From Content to Subject Matter," *The Social Studies* 92, no. 6 (2001): 237–242 and "Teacher as Curricular-Instructional Gatekeeper in Social Studies," Handbook of Research on Social Studies Teaching and Learning, ed. James P. Shaver (New York: Macmillan, 1991).

20. Jean Bethke Elshtain, *Jane Addams and the Dream of American Democracy: A Life* (New York: Basic Books, 2002).

21. Brian K. Marchman, "Teaching about Homophobia in a High School Civics Course," *Theory and Research in Social Education* 30, no. 2 (2002): 302–305.

22. David Harris has developed a scoring rubric for classroom discussions of controversial issues, in which he uses this issue as the running example. See David Harris, "Classroom Assessment of Civic Discourse," in *Education for Democracy: Contexts, Curricula, and Assessments*, ed. Walter C. Parker (Greenwich, CT: Information Age, 2002).

23. See, for example, Myra Pollack Sadker and David Miller Sadker, *Teachers, Schools, and Society* (Boston: McGraw Hill, 2000).

24. Zirkel, op. cit.

25. Leslea Newman and Diana Souza, *Heather Has Two Mommies* (Boston: Alyson Publications, 1989).

26. Greg Hamilton, "Reading 'Jack,'" *English Education* 30, no. 1 (1998): 24–39.

28

The Importance of Multicultural Education

Geneva Gay

Multiculturalism in U.S. schools and society is taking on new dimensions of complexity and practicality as demographics, social conditions, and political circumstances change. Domestic diversity and unprecedented immigration have created a vibrant mixture of cultural, ethnic, linguistic, and experiential plurality.

Effectively managing such diversity in U.S. society and schools is at once a very old and a very new challenge. Benjamin Barber (1992) eloquently makes the point that:

> America has always been a tale of peoples trying to be a People, a tale of diversity and plurality in search of unity. Cleavages among [diverse groups] . . . have irked and divided Americans from the start, making unity a civic imperative as well as an elusive challenge. (p. 41)

Accomplishing this end is becoming increasingly important as the 21st century unfolds. People coming from Asia, the Middle East, Latin America, Eastern Europe, and Africa differ greatly from earlier generations of immigrants who came primarily from western and northern Europe. These unfamiliar groups, cultures, traditions, and languages can produce anxieties, hostilities, prejudices, and racist behaviors among those who do not understand the newcomers or who perceive them as threats to their safety and security. These issues have profound implications for developing instructional programs and practices at all levels of education that respond positively and constructively to diversity.

A hundred years ago, W. E. B. Du Bois (1994) proposed that the problem of the 20th century was conflict and controversy among racial groups, particularly between African and European Americans. He concluded that:

> Between these two worlds [black and white], despite much physical contact and daily intermingling, there is almost no community of intellectual life or point of transference where the

Reprinted by permission from *Educational Leadership*, Vol. 61, No. 4, December 2003/January 2004, pp. 30–35.

thoughts and feelings of one race can come into direct contact and sympathy with the thoughts and feelings of the other.

Although much has changed since Du Bois's declarations, too much has not changed nearly enough. Of course, the color line has become more complex and diverse, and legal barriers against racial intermingling have been dismantled. People from different ethnic, racial, and cultural groups live in close physical proximity. But coexistence does not mean that people create genuine communities in which they know, relate to, and care deeply about one another. The lack of a genuine community of diversity is particularly evident in school curriculums that still do not regularly and systematically include important information and deep study about a wide range of diverse ethnic groups. As disparities in educational opportunities and outcomes among ethnic groups continue to grow, the resulting achievement gap has reached crisis proportions.

Multicultural education is integral to improving the academic success of students of color and preparing all youths for democratic citizenship in a pluralistic society. Students need to understand how multicultural issues shape the social, political, economic, and cultural fabric of the United States as well as how such issues fundamentally influence their personal lives.

CONCEPTIONS OF MULTICULTURAL EDUCATION

Even though some theorists (Banks & Banks, 2002) have argued that multicultural education is a necessary ingredient of quality education, in actual practice, educators most often perceive it either as an addendum prompted by some crisis or as a luxury. Multicultural education has not yet become a central part of the curriculum regularly offered to all students; instead, educators have relegated it primarily to social studies, language arts, and the fine arts and have generally targeted instruction for students of color.

These attitudes distort multicultural education and make it susceptible to sporadic and superficial implementation, if any. Textbooks provide a compelling illustration of such an attitude: The little multicultural content that they offer is often presented in sidebars and special-events sections (Loewen, 1995).

Another obstacle to implementing multicultural education lies with teachers themselves. Many are unconvinced of its worth or its value in developing academic skills and building unified national community. Even those teachers who are more accepting of multicultural education are nevertheless skeptical about the feasibility of its implementation. "I would do it if I could," they say, "but I don't know how." "Preparing students to meet standards takes up all my time," others point out. "School curriculums are already overburdened. What do I take out to make room for multicultural education?"

A fallacy underlies these conceptions and the instructional behaviors that they generate: the perception of multicultural education as separate content that educators must append to existing curriculums as separate lessons, units, or courses. Quite the contrary is true. Multicultural education is more than content; it includes policy, learning climate, instructional delivery, leadership, and evaluation (see Banks, 1994; Bennett, 2003; Grant & Gomez, 2000). In its comprehensive form, it must be an integral part of everything that happens in the education enterprise, whether it is assessing the academic competencies of students or teaching math, reading, writing, science, social studies, or computer science.

Making explicit connections between multicultural education and subject- and skill-based curriculum and instruction is imperative.

It is not pragmatic for K-12 educators to think of multicultural education as a discrete entity, separated from the commonly accepted components of teaching and learning. These conceptions may be fine for higher education, where specialization is the rule. But in K-12 schools, where the education process focuses on teaching eclectic bodies of knowledge and skills, teachers need to use multicultural education to promote such highly valued outcomes as human development, education equality, academic excellence, and democratic citizenship (see Banks & Banks, 2001; Nieto, 2000).

To translate these theoretical conceptions into practice, educators must systematically weave multicultural education into the central core of curriculum, instruction, school leadership, policymaking, counseling, classroom climate, and performance assessment. Teachers should use multicultural content, perspectives, and experiences to teach reading, math, science, and social studies.

For example, teachers could demonstrate mathematical concepts, such as less than/greater than, percentages, ratios, and probabilities using ethnic demographics. Younger children could consider the ethnic and racial distributions in their own classrooms, discussing which group's representation is greater than, less than, or equal to another's. Older students could collect statistics about ethnic distributions on a larger scale and use them to make more sophisticated calculations, such as converting numbers to percentages and displaying ethnic demographics on graphs.

Students need to apply such major academic skills as data analysis, problem solving, comprehension, inquiry, and effective communication as they study multicultural issues and events. For instance, students should not simply memorize facts about major events involving ethnic groups, such as civil rights movements, social justice efforts, and cultural accomplishments. Instead, educators should teach students how to think critically and analytically about these events, propose alternative solutions to social problems, and demonstrate understanding through such forms of communication as poetry, personal correspondence, debate, editorials, and photo essays.

Irvine and Armento (2001) provide specific examples for incorporating multicultural education into planning language arts, math, science, and social studies lessons for elementary and middle school students and connecting these lessons to general curriculum standards. One set of lessons demonstrates how to use Navajo rugs to explain the geometric concepts of perimeter and area and to teach students how to calculate the areas of squares, rectangles, triangles, and parallelograms.

These suggestions indicate that teachers need to use systematic decision-making approaches to accomplish multicultural curriculum integration. In practice, this means developing intentional and orderly processes for including multicultural content. The decision-making process might involve the following steps:

Creating learning goals and objectives that incorporate multicultural aspects, such as "Developing students' ability to write persuasively about social justice concerns."
Using a frequency matrix to ensure that the teacher includes a wide variety of ethnic groups in a wide variety of ways in curriculum materials and instructional activities.
Introducing different ethnic groups and their contributions on a rotating basis.

Including several examples from different ethnic experiences to explain subject matter concepts, facts, and skills.

Showing how multicultural content, goals, and activities intersect with subject-specific curricular standards.

Virtually all aspects of multicultural education are interdisciplinary. As such, they cannot be adequately understood through a single discipline. For example, teaching students about the causes, expressions, and consequences of racism and how to combat racism requires the application of information and techniques from such disciplines as history, economics, sociology, psychology, mathematics, literature, science, art, politics, music, and health care. Theoretical scholarship already affirms this interdisciplinary need; now, teachers need to model good curricular and instructional practice in elementary and secondary classrooms. Putting this principle into practice will elevate multicultural education from impulse, disciplinary isolation, and simplistic and haphazard guesswork to a level of significance, complexity, and connectedness across disciplines.

MULTICULTURALISM AND CURRICULUM DEVELOPMENT

How can teachers establish linkages between multicultural education and the disciplines and subject matter content taught in schools? One approach is to filter multicultural education through two categories of curriculum development: *reality/representation* and *relevance*.

Reality/Representation

A persistent concern of curriculum development in all subjects is helping students understand the *realities* of the social condition and how they came to be as well as adequately representing those realities. Historically, curriculum designers have been more exclusive than inclusive of the wide range of ethnic and cultural diversity that exists within society. In the haste to promote harmony and avoid controversy and conflict, they gloss over social problems and the realities of ethnic and racial identities, romanticize racial relations, and ignore the challenges of poverty and urban living in favor of middle-class and suburban experiences. The reality is distorted and the representations incomplete (Loewen, 1995).

An inescapable reality is that diverse ethnic, racial, and cultural groups and individuals have made contributions to every area of human endeavor and to all aspects of U.S. history, life, and culture. When students study food resources in the United States, for example, they often learn about production and distribution by large-scale agribusiness and processing corporations. The curriculum virtually overlooks the contributions of the many ethnically diverse people involved in planting and harvesting vegetables and fruits (with the Mexican and Mexican American farm labor unionization movement a possible exception). School curriculums that incorporate comprehensive multicultural education do not perpetuate these exclusions. Instead, they teach students the reality—how large corporations and the food industry are directly connected to the migrant workers who harvest vegetables and pick fruits. If we are going to tell the true story of the United States, multicultural education must be a central feature of telling it.

School curriculums need to reverse these trends by also including equitable *representations* of diversity. For example, the study of American literature, art, and music should include contributions of males and females from different ethnic groups in all genres and in different expressive styles. Thus, the study of jazz will examine various forms and techniques produced not just by African Americans but also by Asian, European, and Latino Americans.

Moreover, educators should represent ethnically diverse individuals and groups in all strata of human accomplishment instead of typecasting particular groups as dependent and helpless victims who make limited contributions of significance. Even under the most oppressive conditions, diverse groups in the United States have been creative, activist, and productive on broad scales. The way in which Japanese Americans handled their internment during World War II provides an excellent example. Although schools must not overlook or minimize the atrocities this group endured, students should also learn how interned Japanese Americans led dignified lives under the most undignified circumstances and elevated their humanity above the circumstances. The curriculum should include both issues.

Relevance

Many ethnically diverse students do not find schooling exciting or inviting; they often feel unwelcome, insignificant, and alienated. Too much of what is taught has no immediate value to these students. It does not reflect who they are. Yet most educators will agree that learning is more interesting and easier to accomplish when it has personal meaning for students.

Students from different ethnic groups are more likely to be interested and engaged in learning situations that occur in familiar and friendly frameworks than in those occurring in strange and hostile ones. A key factor in establishing educational relevance for these students is cultural similarity and responsiveness (see Bruner, 1996; Hollins, 1996; Wlodkowski & Ginsberg, 1995). For example, immigrant Vietnamese, Jamaican, and Mexican students who were members of majority populations in their home countries initially may have difficulty understanding what it means to be members of minority groups in the United States. Students who come from education environments that encourage active participatory learning will not be intellectually stimulated by passive instruction that involves lecturing and completing worksheets. Many students of color are bombarded with irrelevant learning experiences, which dampen their academic interest, engagement, and achievement. Multicultural education mediates these situations by teaching content about the cultures and contributions of many ethnic groups and by using a variety of teaching techniques that are culturally responsive to different ethnic learning styles.

Using a variety of strategies may seem a tall order in a classroom that includes students from many different ethnic groups. Research indicates, however, that several ethnic groups share some learning style attributes (Shade, 1989). Teachers need to understand the distinguishing characteristics of different learning styles and use the instructional techniques best suited to each style. In this scenario, teachers would provide alternative teaching techniques for clusters of students instead of for individual students. In any given lesson, the teacher might offer three or four ways for students to learn, helping to equalize learning advantages and disadvantages among the different ethnic groups in the classroom.

Scholars are producing powerful descriptions of culturally relevant teaching for multiethnic students and its effects on achievement. Lipka and Mohatt (1998) describe how a group of teachers, working closely with Native Alaskan (Yup'ik) elders, made school structure, climate, curriculum, and instruction more reflective of and meaningful to students from the community. For 10 years, the teachers translated, adapted, and embedded Yup'ik cultural knowledge in math, literacy, and science curriculums. The elders served as resources and quality-control monitors of traditional knowledge, and they provided the inspiration and moral strength for the teachers to persist in their efforts to center the schooling of Yup'ik students around the students' own cultural orientations. In math, for instance, the teachers now habitually make connections among the Yup'ik numeration system, body measurements, simple and complex computations, geometry, pattern designs, and tessellations.

Similar attributes apply to the work of such scholars as Moses and Cobb (2001), Lee (1993), and Boykin and Bailey (2000), who are studying the effects of culturally relevant curriculum and instruction on the school performance of African American students.

Moses and his colleagues are making higher-order math knowledge accessible to African American middle school students by teaching this material through the students' own cultural orientations and experiences. To teach algebra, they emphasize the experiences and familiar environments of urban and rural low-income students, many of whom are at high risk for academic failure. A key feature of their approach is making students conscious of how algebraic principles and formulas operate in their daily lives and getting students to understand how to explain these connections in nonalgebraic language before converting this knowledge into the technical notations and calculations of algebra. Students previously considered by some teachers as incapable of learning algebra are performing at high levels—better, in fact, than many of their advantaged peers.

Evidence increasingly indicates that multicultural education makes schooling more relevant and effective for Latino American, Native American, Asian American, and Native Hawaiian students as well (see McCarty, 2002; Moll, Amanti, Neff, & Gonzalez, 1992; Park, Goodwin, & Lee, 2001; Tharp & Gallimore, 1988). Students perform more successfully on all levels when there is greater congruence between their cultural backgrounds and such school experiences as task interest, effort, academic achievement, and feelings of personal efficacy or social accountability.

As the challenge to better educate underachieving students intensifies and diversity among student populations expands, the need for multicultural education grows exponentially. Multicultural education may be the solution to problems that currently appear insolvable: closing the achievement gap; genuinely not leaving any children behind academically; revitalizing faith and trust in the promises of democracy, equality, and justice; building education systems that reflect the diverse cultural, ethnic, racial, and social contributions that forge society; and providing better opportunities for all students.

Multicultural education is crucial. Classroom teachers and educators must answer its clarion call to provide students from all ethnic groups with the education they deserve.

REFERENCES

Banks, J. A. (1994). *Multiethnic education: Theory and practice* (3rd ed.). Boston: Allyn and Bacon.

Banks, J. A., & Banks, C. A. M. (Eds.). (2001). *Multicultural education: Issues and perspectives* (4th ed.). Boston: Allyn and Bacon.

Banks, J. A., & Banks, C. A. M. (Eds.). (2002). *Handbook of research on multicultural education* (2nd ed.). San Francisco: Jossey-Bass.

Barber, B. R. (1992). *An aristocracy of everyone: The politics of education and the future of America.* New York: Oxford University Press.

Bennett, C. I. (2003). *Comprehensive multicultural education: Theory and practice.* Boston: Allyn and Bacon.

Boykin, A. W., & Bailey, C. T. (2000). *The role of cultural factors in school relevant cognitive functioning: Synthesis of findings on cultural context, cultural orientations, and individual differences.* (ERIC Document Reproduction Service No. ED 441 880)

Bruner, J. (1996). *The culture of education.* Cambridge, MA: Harvard University Press.

Du Bois, W. E. B. (1994). *The souls of black folk.* New York: Gramercy Books.

Grant, C. A., & Gomez, M. L. (2000). (Eds.). *Making school multicultural: Campus and classroom* (2nd ed.). Upper Saddle River, NJ: Merrill/Prentice-Hall.

Hollins, E. R. (1996). *Culture in school learning: Revealing the deep meaning.* Mahwah, NJ: Erlbaum.

Irvine, J. J., & Armento, B. J. (Eds.). (2001). *Culturally responsive teaching: Lesson planning for elementary and middle grades.* Boston: McGraw-Hill.

Lee, C. (1993). *Signifying as a scaffold to literary interpretation: The pedagogical implications of a form of African American discourse* (NCTE Research Report No. 26). Urbana, IL: National Council of Teachers of English.

Lipka, J., & Mohatt, G. V. (1998). *Transforming the culture of schools: Yup'ik eskimo examples.* Mahwah, NJ: Erlbaum.

Loewen, J. W. (1995). *Lies my teacher told me: Everything your American history textbook got wrong.* New York: New Press.

McCarty, T. L. (2002). *A place to be Navajo: Rough Rock and the struggle for self-determination in indigenous schooling.* Mahwah, NJ: Erlbaum.

Moll, L. C., Amanti, C., Neff, D., & Gonzalez, N. (1992). Funds of knowledge for teaching: Using a qualitative approach to connect homes and classrooms. *Theory into Practice, 31*(1), 132–141.

Moses, R. P., & Cobb, C. E., Jr. (2001). *Radical equations: Math literacy and civil rights.* Boston: Beacon Press.

Nieto, S. (2000). *Affirming diversity: The sociopolitical context of multicultural education* (3rd ed.). New York: Longman.

Park, C. C., Goodwin, A. L., & Lee, S. J. (Eds.). (2001). *Research on the education of Asian and Pacific Americans.* Greenwich, CT: Information Age Publishers.

Shade, B. J. (Ed.). (1989). *Culture, style, and the educative process.* Springfield, IL: Charles C. Thomas.

Tharp, R. G., & Gallimore, R. (1988). *Rousing minds to life: Teaching, learning, and schooling in social context.* Cambridge, UK: Cambridge University Press.

Wlodkowski, R. J., & Ginsberg, M. B. (1995). *Diversity & motivation: Culturally responsive teaching.* San Francisco: Jossey-Bass.

29

"In These Shoes Is the Silent Call of the Earth": Meditations on Curriculum Integration, Conceptual Violence, and the Ecologies of Community and Place

DAVID W. JARDINE, ANNETTE LAGRANGE, AND
BETH EVEREST

INTRODUCTION: "SOUNDS LIKE AN INTERESTING UNIT"
The following is a portion of a recent e-mail exchange:

> Forgive the cross posting; I'm looking for a variety of points of view. I'm looking for lesson plans (or ideas that I can make in to lessons) for teaching art in math (or math in art). Specifically, what math can I see in any work of Van Gogh? This will be a workshop for 5th/6th graders.

One response received to this request was:

> How about the spirals in Starry, Starry Night and the sunflowers in picture of same name? Both can be connected to math and/or science. Spiraling procedures can be written in Logo teaching the concept of stepping. Estimations of number of sunflowers in head as well as patterns created by seeds while still in head are other ideas. You could sprout sunflower seeds and collect data: How many days average to sprout? What percentage of seeds sprouted? Does size of seeds affect sprouting speed? etc. etc. Sounds like an interesting unit. (Lugone, 1996)

Chapter 11 in David W. Jardine, Patricia Clifford, and Sharon Friesen, *Back to the Basics of Teaching and Learning*. Lawrence Erlbaum Associates, 2002. Reprinted by permission.

The authors' interest in curriculum integration is, in part, a response to an unsettling sense of fragmentation that can be found, not only in this example, but in much of our work with teachers, student-teachers, and schools. We believe that the opening citation is typical of what counts as thinking about curriculum integration in elementary schools. It betrays an almost random surface skittering over topics which casts the oddest of things together. The brilliant sunflowers in Arles in the south of France and how they bore Van Gogh's agonized attention in his final years are linked, in the imagination of those who frequent early elementary classrooms, to rows of white Styrofoam cups with masking-taped names and dried soils and neglected, dying sunflower seedlings drooped on hot Grade 1 classroom sills. Reading this e-mail exchange produced in us a strange sense of restlessness, displacement, and homelessness, a sense of no longer knowing where we are or what is required as a proper, generous, but honest response to this well-meant pursuit of "curriculum integration."

Curriculum integration poses hard questions to those involved in the educational endeavor. What does it mean to teach with integrity? What does it mean to treat one's topic of study with integrity? How might school classroom and university teachers alike teach in a way that respects the character and integrity of the lives and experiences of children and the work undertaken with them?

We suggest that part of the answer to these far-too-large questions is ecological in character. Curriculum integration has to do with keeping things in place, nested in the deep communities of relations that make them whole, healthy, and sane. We are intrigued by Berry's (1986) reminder that an orientation toward integrity and wholeness has something to do with health, healing, and the mending of relations, and, therefore, that pursuing curriculum integration in our classrooms has something to do with "choosing to be healers" (Clifford & Friesen, 1994) in relation to ourselves, the Earth, the topics taught in our schools, and the children invited into those topographies. We are intrigued as well by how such difficult, disciplined work is much more deeply *pleasurable* (Berry, 1989) for adults and children alike than the panic of "activities" that consumes so much of educational practice.

We must be generous enough to hope that the clashing together of Van Gogh and mathematics in this e-mail exchange was done in good faith, and that real, substantial, integrated, heartening work has resulted. Even if these teachers did not find their way into such work, we cannot deny that the oddness of this example is not precisely *their* problem. School teachers and university teachers all, in their own ways, are living out a deep cultural logic of fragmentation and we (for we must include ourselves here, as the authors of this chapter) have all participated, directly or indirectly, in the strange efforts at curriculum integration that sometimes result.

This exchange still stands, however, as a sign or a warning that issues of curriculum integration still need our attention. This continuing need for attention is almost too obvious: In a living system, health and wholeness and the cultivation of good relations are never simply givens, because the young are always still arriving again, ready to call what we have taken as given to account in their own lives. The Earth, too, is beginning to have its say about our character and our conduct and our ignoring of its ways.

"ONE AFTER THE OTHER"
A teacher recently mentioned on an Internet listserve called "Kidsphere" that she was thinking of doing "shoes" as a theme or a unit in her classroom. Over the course of nearly

2 weeks, the Net was inundated with dozens of responses from all across North America—different types of shoes, different styles and preferences, different materials that shoes are made of: "There was an old woman who lived in a shoe," indoor and outdoor shoes, Hans Brinker's skates, shoes and boots, cobblers and elves, different professions and their footwear, snowshoes, skis, and such, different countries and their shoes, different ways to secure them (laces, velcro, buckles, slip-ons—leading to numbers of eye-holes and lengths of laces and the idea of "pairs"), Puss and his boots, sizes of shoes, graphs of shoe sizes, graphs of shoe colors, graphs of shoelace colors, dismissing children by shoe color as a management technique, shoeprints and footprints in paint, tracks and animals in science, and perhaps a detective game that has children tracking something by its prints.

And so on.

We can all understand the giddy rush of such exchanges, and we have all participated and taken some pleasure in them. However, despite their earnestness and good will, and the conviviality with which they occur, such exchanges seem to treat each moment, each particular, with haste and a lack of careful attention. Of course, such a "continuity of attention and devotion" (Berry, 1986, p. 13) to particulars is not what such brainstorming sessions and subsequent "webbings," "mappings," or "theme-ings" are for. They are intended to give a broad and quick picture of surface similarities, surface connections, surface relations under the name of *shoes*.

However, because none of the nodes in the web is read for its rich textures and patterns and hidden discourses, none of the connections seem especially strong or robust or well-rooted. What result are connections that sometimes seem forced and trivial, betraying a rushed, ultimately unsatisfying lack of attention and care to anything in particular. Rather than providing a picture of some integrated patterns of the world or serving as a prelude to the work of settling oneself somewhere, it is as if these themes or webs of ideas concede, aggravate, or even sometimes create the very situation of fragmentation and alienation that they are meant to remedy.

Consider these words of a sixth-grade teacher:

> When you mention an idea, it's so typical of teachers to graciously share everything they can. And they start throwing ideas at you, all meant to help out. You really don't have time to think about anything. Nothing gets a chance to soak in. You get so overwhelmed by all the bits, and, after all, you don't want to leave any out now that people have offered them, so that all you can do is just present them one after the other. (Research note, December 1996)

In their own way (and this may be especially aggravated by the existence of Internet and the possibility of hundreds of comparatively instantaneous responses), such brainstorming flurries seem to work against, or at least make more difficult, settling down *somewhere*, doing *something* well, treating *something* with the integrity it warrants.

It is as if these flurries start out as emulations of the giddy rush of life, of newness, freshness, and ebullience that we find so pleasing in our children. However, in many elementary school classrooms (and so much of the work done in Faculties of Education), we let loose rushes of thin, restless activities not one of which warrants much attention or work. We then end up producing, in turn, fading attention-spans both in our children and in ourselves. And such a loss of attention is most frequently then blamed on our children. We call their shortness or lack of attention "a characteristic of young children" and we excuse our own lack of attention to the work at hand by citing the attention each individual student needs from us.

After witnessing the activity of her cooperating teacher for a semester, one student-teacher recently said something we found quite telling regarding the tempo, attention, and activity level in elementary school classrooms: "My teacher is busy all the time but she never seems to do any work" (Research note, December 1996).

CURRICULUM INTEGRATION AND CONCEPTUAL VIOLENCE

What is lost in many efforts in curriculum integration is precisely the *topography*, the *ecos*, the place of any particular thing. Many webs or themes proceed in a "heady" fashion: Each particular gains "wholeness"/integration only through the concerted intervention of a *concept* (e.g., the *concept* of "shoes"). It is the *concept* that brings the particulars together.

Pursued in this way, curriculum integration can become a sort of *conceptual violence* that tears particulars out of their intimate, particular places and re-sorts them "away from home" under general, abstract, anonymous categories. These categories are not sensuous, bodily, indigenous, and immediate, but oddly cold, ideational, fleshless, and alien. The very act meant to heal and restore communities of real, integral relations and patterns thus becomes complicit in their unwitting destruction and replacement with conceptual structures that are cleaner, clearer, and less Earthy and alluring than those living communities. The very act meant to help us attend to the integrities of our experience in a whole and healthy way becomes a form of interpretive deafness, an inability to hear what words and worlds of implication might be *already at work* in the stubborn particulars (Wallace, 1987) that come to meet us, before our conceptualizations take hold. As one teacher put it so poignantly, "the water of chemical composition and the water in which my child has drowned *don't belong together*" (Research note, December 1996), in spite of their conceptual affinities. The *world* of hydrogen, oxygen, and their combinations is not the same world as the agonies of the loss of a child, or the mysteries of the water that washes away sins, or a tall cool glass stippled with condensation on a hot summer's day. Each of these bears *its own* memories, relations, obligations, its own tales and topographies that make it whole, healthy, and livable.

The intervention of a *concept* of "water" into these worlds in order to "integrate" them is simply tactless and unbecoming—disintegrative, in fact, of the integrities of experience that are already at work without such intervention.

NARRATIVE INTEGRATION AND THE RECOVERY OF THE PARTICULAR

Our growing concerns over this portrayal of the situation of curriculum integration as a sort of thin, conceptual surface picture and the ensuing loss of the topographies of the particular, gave way to the recollection of a passage in Martin Heidegger's (1971) *Origins of the Work of Art*, in which he meditates on a Van Gogh painting of a peasant woman's shoes. This meditation, in all its convoluted twists and turns (and despite its tone of high German Romanticism), provided us with a way to begin reconceptualizing the nature of curriculum integration:

> As long as we only imagine a pair of shoes in general, or simply look at the empty, unused shoes as they merely stand there in the picture we shall never discover [them]. A pair of peas-ant shoes and nothing more. And yet from the dark opening of the worn insides of the shoes

the toilsome tread of the worker stares forth. In the stiffly rugged heaviness of the shoes there is the accumulated tenacity of her slow trudge through the furrows of the field. Under the soles slides the loneliness of the field-path as evening falls. In the shoes is the silent call of the earth, its quiet gift of the ripening grain and its unexplained self-refusal in the fallow desolation of the wintry field. This equipment is pervaded by uncomplaining anxiety as to the certainty of bread, the wordless joy of having once more withstood want, the trembling before the impending childbed and shivering at the surrounding menace of death. (pp. 33–34)

There is a profound familiarity in these words, one that recalls all the years of early childhood. Stopping, with a sort of interpretive mindfulness, over *this* pair of shoes (and not skittering past it in a brainstorming session) might itself reveal a way that our course (*currere*/curriculum) is whole/integrated in some deep, ecologically sane and sustainable way.

We can recall moments of passing by our father's or mother's or grandfather's shoes tucked by the front door or left tumbled on balconies or verandas, seeing the deep imprint of their tracks inside, the places of shiny imprint, traces of the lives they have lived and the work they have done, and how, in slipping these on our own small feet, it was not just these particular things that we engaged but a whole world, their world and its deep familial intersection with our own. We can all recall, too, how we may have warily avoided those shoes and the life they stamped on us or others.

All of us understand, somehow, that *these* shoes are not capturable with any integrity and wholeness on a web under, say, "different types of shoes" or "shoes and types of work." Rather, *these* shoes gain an integrity and place in a world full of rich memory and familiarity and use, a world full of the intractable particularities of experience, whether for good or ill or some troubling mixture of the two.

These shoes—the black boots my neighbor Harry wore in our trudging work of installing furnaces in people's basements—are not understandable in an integrated way by simply placing them alongside others in a list of different types of shoes from around the world. They do not belong alongside others, except perhaps those of his wife when he arrives home, or mine as we rested at lunch, and then how those age-old boots fit with the Thermos and lunchpail worn thin from use, like his tools, bearing the marks of his hands and the marks of age and work and craft. The world in which one might produce a web of different types of shoes is a different world than the world evoked by dark stains and smells of oil and coal dust, or the knotted pieces of broken lace as signs of Harry's odd frugality.

Understood conceptually and in general, *shoes* bear no history, no memory, no continuity, no dependencies, no place, no communities of relations. They are not *someone's, here, in this place*, and, in this sense, they are simply an *idea* of shoes, not fleshy and warm and curved just so. Despite all its calls to integration, categorizations, or thematizations such as "different types of shoes," break apart the very small, intimate threads of familiarity, obligation, and relation that actually hold *these* shoes in a real, integrated place. Such small, intimate threads and the worlds they evoke get replaced with a concept which cannot provide any of the comforts, the common strengths, of the place the particular has left behind in such severances.

Sticking with such particularity has an interesting effect. Rather than simply bogging us down in the burden of specificity (Smith, 1999), the particular takes on a certain buoyancy and lightness. It becomes a node on a web of real sustenance and import.

What emerges from taking these particular shoes seriously in their wholeness is a sense that things have integral places. Things themselves, in their very particularity, issue a sense of belonging somehow, in intractable relations of materiality, obligation, community, history, memory, and so on. The integration or wholeness that ensues, therefore, is not just about these particular shoes. Rather, the phenomenon of integration or wholeness itself, as involving an attention to place and memory and relations and community, starts to come forward.

What starts to come forward is not a bluster of activities for the classroom, but a way of taking up the world that breaks the spell of the consumptivism, exhaustion, and the panic of activities into which so much of our lives is inscribed.

This does not leave us with a "great idea" that we can now directly address or directly "apply." We now have, in its stead, *a serious, immediate, ecological obligation*, to treat things that come to meet us with integrity, to heal the ways that things have become fragmented and displaced and unsettled and dispersed into the ethers of good-hearted but ecologically suspect Internet exchanges.

ENDBIT: PARTICULARITY AND DE-ROMANTICIZING "PLACE"

In circulating the idea of this chapter to colleagues and students and friends, an odd thing began to emerge, something typical as a response to interpretive work. What arrived were particular tales of particular shoes that were, in each case, wedged deeply in the flesh and breath of the teller. As this paper proceeded, it became clear—although still somewhat mysterious—why shoes are so frequently a topic in Early Childhood Education. It seems that they always already bear a fleshy familial intimacy that we all recognize at some deep, gutty level and that belies and resists our efforts at conceptual thematization. It may be that our initial attraction to shoes reveals some mute recognition of an integrity of children's (*our* children, and therefore our own) experiences that is then unwittingly betrayed in our subsequent conceptualizations.

It may be that our curriculum integration conceptualizations are unintentionally teaching a horrible lesson.

Consider one particular response we received as we wrote and spoke of shoes and curriculum integration. A poem that brings particular shoes to life :

> David is talking about shoes, about some paper he is writing about shoes, & I am thinking about Dad's rubbers, the black rubber oversoles/overshoes that he always wears in the rain & the snow. Old man's shoes. Things that he must wear. The stamp of him. The mark that he makes in the snow, in our lives, in my own life. His father wears them too & I think that I cannot really find the shoe that fits my mother; perhaps it could be the high heels that are in the dressup box, the things that are left over from some other life that we as children never knew, can never know. But she does not wear these now & I must imagine her long legs sliding into white silk stockings. The garter belt that she throws on her wedding day all of these scenes I must imagine, as now most often I remember her in sneakers, but this is not the right word to describe my mother's footwear. Ked's? tennis shoes? sensible flats? the glass slipper? my father wears rubbers, overshoes, like he has always done because he has always been old, but my mother I cannot define so simply. Nor can I explain her passion for shoes, stored in her closet. Winter shoes: oxfords, smooth soled, vibram soled, patent leather, navy, black, brown, dark green, khaki. Summer shoes: red, white, yellow, orange, stored in boxes I hear the water running for her bath. Imagine the dressing gown folded. Her blue nightie. The large white towel. A new bar of soap. Her legs. Still slender, she steps into the bubbles. Her feet, narrow, bumpy. Her voice is soft. I cannot hear her step on the stair.

—BETH EVEREST (1996)

We wish to end with a plea for forgiveness that we ourselves require. We are all living out a deep cultural logic of fragmentation that distracts attention, that is cynical about devotion or depth, and that mocks any talk of good work, that identifies settling and quiet and meditation with passivity, and that cannot imagine how one could want anything but business in our classrooms.

What we are alluding to here is not simply another great idea for the classroom. It is not merely an issue of *teacher knowledge* or adequate *information* about a topic or a child:

> One thing we dare not forget is that better solutions than ours have at times been made by people with much less information than we have. We know, too, from the study of agriculture, that the same information, tools and techniques that in one farmer's hands will ruin land, in another's will save and improve it. This is not a recommendation of ignorance. To know nothing, after all, is no more possible than to know enough. I am only proposing that knowledge, like everything else, has its place, and that we need urgently now to *put* it in its place. (Berry, 1983, pp. 65–66)

This place into which knowledge must find its way, Berry suggests, has to do with care, character, and love—surprisingly antiquated words in the current educational milieu. Integration and wholeness have more to do with the *way* one knows, the *way* one is, the *way* one hopes children will become and how we and they will carry ourselves, and how light and careful our footfalls will be on this Earth.

The examples we have cited are from the good-hearted work of teachers who are bearing an old logic of fragmentation and distraction on our behalf. We cannot pretend that their distraction is simply *their* problem, as if our own lives were somehow precious and exempt from questions of how to proceed with integrity, as if we might pretend to have somehow solved this problem in our own lives. Each new topic we address in our work with colleagues, with children and with student-teachers requires that we raise these questions of integration all over again. Although it might initially result in frustration, we have deliberately resisted the false promises of "yet another model" of curriculum integration sold to the highest textbook bidders.

One thing, however, is certain. We, as teachers, as parents, find ourselves at an especially difficult juncture in this cultural logic that we are all living out, facing the possibility, but not the necessity, of passing it on to our children.

REFERENCES

Berry, W. (1983). *Standing by words.* San Francisco: North Point Press.

Berry, W. (1986). *The unsettling of America: Essays in culture and agriculture.* San Francisco: Sierra Club Books.

Berry, W. (1989) *The profit in work's pleasure.* Harper's Magazine, March, 19–24.

Clifford, P., and Friesen, S. (1994, October). *Choosing to be healers.* A paper presented at the JCT Conference on Curriculum Theory and Classroom Practice. Banff, Alberta.

Everest, B. (1996). [Untitled poem]. Calgary, Alberta.

Heidegger, M. (1971). *Origin of the work of art.* New York: Harper & Row.

Lugone, K. (1996). Internet message. *Kidsphere,* March.

Smith, D. (1999). *Pedagon: Interdisciplinary essays in the human sciences, pedagogy and culture.* New York: Peter Lang.

Wallace, B. (1987). *The stubborn particulars of grace.* Toronto, Canada: McLelland and Stewart.

30

The Aims of Education

Nel Noddings

PEOPLE WANT TO BE HAPPY and, since this desire is well-nigh universal, we would expect to find happiness included as an aim of education. Its failure to appear among the aims usually stated might be a sign that Western society is still mired in a form of Puritanism or, more generously, it may be generally believed that, as Orwell said, happiness cannot be achieved by aiming at it directly. If the latter is so, what should we aim at that might promote happiness?

Until quite recently, aims-talk figured prominently in educational theory, and most education systems prefaced their curriculum documents with statements of their aims. What functions have been served by aims-talk, and what have we lost (if anything) by ceasing to engage in it? What has taken its place?

I will start this chapter by arguing that we need to talk about aims, and I will fill out that argument with a discussion of aims-talk and the purposes it served in earlier educational thought. Looking at contemporary educational policymaking, we'll see that talk of aims might be considered a missing dimension in the educational conversation. Finally, by discussing aims in some depth. I will set the stage for exploring ways in which education might actively support the pursuit of happiness.

AIMS-TALK AND ITS PURPOSES

Suppose we visit an algebra class and watch a lesson on the factoring of trinomials. The learning objective is clear. The teacher has listed several familiar types of trinomials, and the students are occupied in identifying them and performing the factorizations. If we ask Ms. A (the teacher) why she is teaching this topic, she will probably reply that the next topic is combining algebraic fractions, and one cannot easily find the appropriate common denominator without a knowledge of factoring. Now, of course, one could proceed by simply multiplying denominators, but the expressions quickly become unwieldy and, to get the required answer, one would eventually have to factor. Ms. A's response is entirely

Chapter 4 in Nel Noddings, *Happiness and Education.* Cambridge: Cambridge University Press, 2003. Reprinted by permission.

appropriate if (1) we have already found good reasons for teaching algebra to these students and (2) we have agreed that algebra consists of a certain sequence of topics. When a teacher is asked about a lesson objective, she or he almost always responds with an explanation of how this learning objective fits with others that come before and after it. Today most mathematics textbooks are organized in this way.

An observer might get a somewhat deeper response from Ms. A to the question Why are you spending so much time on this topic? To this, Ms. A might reply that her course of study (or textbook) emphasizes solving equations; many of these involve rational expressions that need simplification—factoring again—and so this topic requires much attention. This answer is unsatisfactory in its apparent circularity, but it does point at a larger goal and not just at the next skill to be mastered.

Without trying to draw a sharp line of demarcation, I will associate objectives with lessons and goals with courses or sequences of courses.[1] Most of our "why" questions are answered within the prescribed system; that is, we explain why we are doing something in terms of other objectives or, occasionally, in terms of goals.

Such answers assume, as noted previously, that we have good reasons for teaching algebra to these particular students and that the course of study we are presenting as algebra will be recognized and approved by mathematics educators. The second criterion is easily tested by submission to a group of experts who are in a position to say whether a given course of study is adequate as algebra. Experts may, of course, differ on whether the course is appropriate for gifted, average, or slow learners, but that analysis brings us back to the first question: Do we have a good reason for teaching algebra to *these* students?

Discussion of aims, in contrast to that of objectives and goals, centers on the deepest questions in education. What are we trying to accomplish by teaching algebra? Who benefits? Should our efforts be designed to enhance the society (or state) or should they be directed at benefits for the individual? If we are concerned with something like self-actualization, what does this mean? Do we have to say something about human nature? If we are concerned with the welfare of the state, must we describe the sort of state in, and for, which we will educate? Is there an inherent conflict between individuals and societies? This is just a sample of the questions that must be considered when we engage in aims-talk.

Some people object to wasting time on aims-talk. Wasn't all this settled long ago? People have been debating questions concerning the aims of education since the days of Plato and, in our times (within a century or so), talk of aims has not changed schooling dramatically. Why not avoid such useless talk and get on with the practical business of educating children? Even teachers talk this way and seem to have little patience for conversations that do not culminate with something useful for tomorrow's lessons.

In response, one might argue that aims-talk is to education what freedom is to democracy. Without freedom, democracy degenerates into a form quite different from liberal democracy. Similarly, without continual, reflective discussion of aims, education may become a poor substitute for its best vision. Moreover, just as freedom takes on newer and richer meanings as times change, so must the aims of education change. Even if they might be stated in fairly constant general terms, the meaning of those constant words will take on new coloring as conditions change. To be literate today, for example, is different from being literate in the days of Charlemagne (who could read but not write) or in colonial America, where people did not need the forms of visual literacy required by present-day media.

It has always been one function of philosophers of education to critique the aims of education in light of their contemporary cultures. It has been another of their functions to criticize the society with respect to a vision of education. In the next section, we will see that some philosophers have started with a description of ideal or actual states from which they have derived recommendations for education. Others have started with a vision for the education of individuals and asked what sort of state might support that vision. Simply accepting the state as it is and the system as it is (merely pushing it to perform its perceived function more vigorously) is a dangerous (and lazy) strategy. I will argue that this is the policy we have followed for the past two decades, and it is likely to prove ruinous.

Another objection to aims-talk is that it often culminates in asking too much of schools.[2] This was an objection raised against the aims suggested in 1918 by Clarence Kingsley in the famous Cardinal Principles Report.[3] Herbert Kliebard comments:

> By far the most prominent portion of the 32-page report was the statement of the seven aims that would guide the curriculum: "1. Health. 2. Command of fundamental processes. 3. Worthy home-membership. 4. Vocation. 5. Citizenship. 6. Worthy use of leisure. 7. Ethical character."[4]

Oddly, while more radical educators such as David Snedden thought the report was still far too academic, later critics blamed it for laying the foundation of *life adjustment* education, asking the impossible of schools, and making the academic task of the schools more difficult. People in the latter camp wanted to reduce the responsibility of the schools, to academic learning. They insisted that no institution could take on such a broad array of responsibilities.

Whether the task is possible depends on how it is understood, and it is a function of aims-talk to deliberate and come to a useful understanding on this. I have always found the Cardinal Principles quite wonderful. Indeed, I do not see how schools can operate as *educational* institutions without attending to at least these aims, and obviously I want to add another—happiness. Everything depends on the next step: How shall we employ these aims in guiding what we do in constructing a curriculum, in classroom teaching, in establishing interpersonal relationships, in designing school buildings, in management and discipline, and in community relations?

If we were to proceed in the way advocated by scientific curriculum makers (for example, Franklin Bobbitt),[5] the task might indeed be impossible, because our next step would be to derive objectives from our aims. Imagine the work required to establish learning objectives for each of these large aims! Where would each objective be placed, and who would teach it? It is not necessary, however, to proceed in this fashion. We might even argue that it is a mistake to do so; specifying the entire curriculum as objectives before teachers and students begin to interact forecloses the freedom of students to participate in the construction of their own learning objectives.

As we engage in aims-talk, we have an opportunity to question the role of objectives in general. Do our aims suggest that every lesson should have a stated objective and, if so, what form should it take? Must each lesson have a specific learning objective, or is it sometimes appropriate to describe what the teacher will do and leave open what the students might learn?[6] In the midst of our aims-talk, we would pause also to note that some objectives might well be prespecified. When should this be done? By whom?

In earlier chapters, I suggested that Orwell and others might have been right when they said that happiness cannot be attained by pursuing it directly. The same can be said of several other aims in the Cardinal Principles. This does not mean, however, that they cannot function at all as aims. It means, rather, that we must continually reflect upon, discuss, and evaluate what we are doing to see if our objectives and procedures are compatible with our aims.

A little later, I will try to show that failure to engage in vigorous discussion of educational aims has marked the movement toward standardization and high-stakes testing. In that discussion, we will ask what the movement's advocates are trying to do and whether the systems and procedures they have recommended are likely to support or undermine their tacit aims. First, however, to get a better sense of how aims-talk might assist current thinking, let's look briefly at how it has functioned in the past.

AIMS IN EARLIER EDUCATIONAL THOUGHT

Plato's discussion of education is embedded in his analysis of the just state. As Socrates and his companions in dialogue try to create the design for a just state, they inevitably encounter issues concerning education. Plato does not start with the individual; that possibility with respect to the meaning of the term *just* is discarded early in the dialogue as too difficult. Talk shifts from the just man to the just state.[7] Thus, when education becomes the topic of analysis, the needs of the state are paramount. As the discussants consider the needs of the state and its collective people, they decide that the kinds of people needed fall into three categories: rulers, guardians (auxiliaries or warriors), and artisans (tradespeople and other workers).

Plato does not ignore individuals, but he treats them as representatives of classes organized according to their *natures*. Children are to be watched and tested to identify their talents and interests, and then they are to receive an education compatible with their demonstrated natures. Positions in the just state are not inherited; they are distributed through a procedure of diagnosis and education. Poor children from the artisan class may exhibit the "golden" attributes required of rulers, and children of rulers may show the "bronze" qualities typical of artisans.

Socrates brings the needs of the state and the individual together by noting that people will care for what they love. Thus, if the state needs people who will do their jobs well, it should be sure that they are trained effectively in occupations to which they are well suited. Those who love certain forms of work will care deeply about that work and become competent at it. Further, Socrates scorns the dilettante and the jack-of-all-trades. Everyone in the just state is to perform one essential job and do so expertly.

In his comments about the Platonic scheme of education, John Dewey commends the practice of providing different forms of education for children with different interests:

> We cannot better Plato's conviction that an individual is happy and society well organized when each individual engages in those activities for which he has a natural equipment, nor his conviction that it is the primary office of education to discover this equipment to its possessor and train him for its effective use.[8]

But Dewey draws back from Plato's organization of human beings into three classes. For Dewey, "each individual constitutes his own class,"[9] and the processes of education must be dynamic and flexible. Dewey's discussion of education is embedded in that of a democratic state/community, whereas Plato's aims at a perfect (some say totalitarian) state that is unchanging and hierarchically organized.

Plato had two great aims in mind for his system of education. First, for the benefit of the state, he wanted to educate the three large classes he identified, each group trained to the highest degree. Second, for the benefit of the individual, he insisted that education should be aimed at improvement of the soul, and by *soul* Plato meant the harmonious development of three parts: appetite (impulse or desire), reason, and spirit (energy).[10] The parallel to the three classes constituting the population of the just state is striking. In the individual, the three parts are also properly organized hierarchically, and a just soul places reason in the role of ruler, spirit in the role of guardian-auxiliary, and appetite in the role of artisan—one who is necessary to the whole but must be controlled by a wise ruler (reason).

We can draw a limited parallel between Plato's educational aims and those of today's reformers in the United States. First, the standards/testing movement is driven primarily by an aim that speaks to the welfare of the nation. Here the similarity is clear. If anything, the current goal in the United States is even narrower than Plato's because it concentrates almost entirely on the economic status of the country. Second, we see in Plato's plan the elements of what we now call a *meritocracy*. Offices and occupations are to be filled by those qualified, not by inheritance or political preference. This practice is also espoused (if not always enacted) by contemporary democracies.

With respect to individuals, however, the aims diverge. Plato was clear in the way he valued the three classes of individuals, and the high value he placed on rulers came directly from his underlying philosophy. The theory of forms made reason and theory superior to action and practice. Those who work with their minds were thought to be superior to those who work with their bodies. Our own society pretends to reject this ordering on the grounds that it is repugnant to a democratic society, but our actual social ordering suggests a considerable degree of hypocrisy, if not schizophrenia on the issue. The Platonic legacy is still strong, even if kept below the surface of discussion. We say we value all honest, necessary contributions equally, but we allow people who do essential manual work to live in poverty or near-poverty, and we embrace as an educational aim to prepare all children so that they will not have to do such work. We fail to ask an essential question: If we were to succeed in this effort, who would do the work so necessary and yet so despised today?

Not only do we fail to educate children along lines congruent with their *natural equipment*, but we insist that natural differences are so minimal that all children can profit from the education once reserved for a few. Unlike Plato, we do not even ask whether that education is appropriate for anyone, much less for everyone. The use of democratic language suggests that the same education for all is a generous and properly democratic measure when, in fact, it may well be both undemocratic and ineffective. It will be ineffective if Plato was right when he said that people will care for (and do well at) work they love. Many will fail in schools because they are forced to do work they hate and are deprived of work they might love.

Plato's entire discussion of education in *The Republic* is pervaded by aims-talk. He and his companions eventually accept the broad components of a traditional curriculum—music (which then included all forms of literature) and gymnastic—but not without significant modification. They do not simply turn the details over to experts in music and gymnastic. Rather, they ask why these subjects should be taught; that is, they continually return to primary aims—improvement of the soul and benefit to the state. Socrates, Plato's spokesperson in the dialogues, does not want rulers and guardians to become muscle-bound athletes from single-minded concentration on gymnastic, nor does he want them to become *effeminate* (his unfortunate label) through overconcentration on music. Improvement of the soul requires harmony among the three aspects of self.

Referring to those aims directed at establishing and maintaining the just state, Socrates recommends certain constraints on the stories and poems to be heard by children. A discussion of Plato's plans for censorship would take us too far afield. For present purposes, what is important is his continuous attention to aims. The question What shall be taught? is never answered definitively without a thorough exploration of the companion question Why?

Plato also looked at elements of private life that contribute to happiness; he was concerned about how we should live—what virtues should be cultivated and what tastes developed. Today's reformers say little about forms of personal well-being that are aimed at neither the country's nor the individual's economic status. Plato at least argued for a form of happiness that arises in doing one's chosen work well, and Dewey also noted this aspect of happiness. But neither Plato nor Dewey said much about homemaking, parenting, or a host of other everyday occupations significant in personal life. I will argue that these must be included in our discussion of educational aims if we are concerned with the happiness of individuals.

Before leaving this brief account of aims in Plato, I want to emphasize again that I am not defending a hierarchical sorting of children according to specific academic criteria, but I will strongly defend different forms of education for children with different interests and talents. It seems entirely right for a democratic society to reject the elitist scheme offered by Plato, but the rejection must be honest and carefully argued. Have we really rejected Plato's ordering when we decide that all children will be prepared (in effect) for the category once classified as best? By our very designation of that curriculum as best, we may have aggravated the denigration of interests and capacities that do not require traditional academic preparation. At its most arrogant, this attitude says to others, "Now you will have a chance to be just like me, and then you will be worth something."

Another approach to educational aims is found in the work of Rousseau. I will limit the discussion of Rousseau's philosophy of education drastically because my main point is to contrast his approach to aims with that of Plato and to emphasize once again the centrality of aims-talk in any fully developed theory of education.

In contrast to Plato, Rousseau begins his *Emile* with the individual, not the state.[11] The aims of education are derived from the basic premise that the child is born good and will develop best (as nature intends) if education by people and education by things are well coordinated with the education provided by nature. With this basic aim—to produce the best possible (natural) "man"—Rousseau sets out to describe how education by people and things (the forms over which we have some control) should take place. Everything suggested for Emile's education is tested against this aim.

Rousseau does not ignore the needs of the state or society. Recognizing that Emile must live in association with others, he asks how best to prepare him as both a citizen and a man. The citizen Emile will become should be as little different from the natural man as possible. Making enormous assumptions about the natural man, Rousseau aims to produce men who will think for themselves, be models of civic virtue, understand and practice justice, and in general become whatever they are able and willing to become.

The concept on which Rousseau depends so heavily, Nature, is both ambiguous and no-toriously problematic as he interprets it. Men and women are "naturally" different, Rousseau declares, and therefore their education should be different. Sophie, Emile's fe-male counterpart, should be obedient, amiable, and useful. She should not think for her-self but always seek the approval of proper men and society.[12] Book V of *Emile* is a feminist nightmare. But, although Rousseau's interpretations of nature are questionable and even inconsistent, he is consistent in referring to his stated aims involving nature. We can chal-lenge him intelligently today precisely because we find his answers to the "why" questions unsatisfactory and objectionable. Even if Rousseau were to experience a sort of feminist epiphany and decide, as Socrates did, that there are no relevant intellectual differences be-tween men and women so far as citizenship is concerned, we would still be able to criticize him with respect to the basic aim he has adopted—the natural man (or woman).

When John Dewey discussed aims in education, he said that his account of education "assumed that the aim of education is to enable individuals to continue their education— or that the object and reward of learning is continued capacity for growth."[13] He then went on to claim that such a view of education makes sense and can only be implemented in a democratic society. It takes a book-length discussion to support these claims and to show what they might look like in practice. But Dewey was careful later in the discussion to insist on a multiplicity of aims that change with the needs and beliefs of a society. Not only must these aims be considered together for coherence but each must be judged, we assume, in light of the overriding aim: Is the adoption of Aim X likely to further growth or impede it? Under what conditions?

At a similar level of abstraction, Alfred North Whitehead said that the aim of education should be to produce people "who possess both culture and expert knowledge in some spe-cial direction."[14] A bit later, he wrote, "There is only one subject-matter for education, and that is Life in all its manifestations."[15] Again, such statements demand full and lengthy dis-cussion, but they give us a starting point to which we continually return.

As I try to promote happiness as an aim of education. I have to offer a convincing ac-count of happiness, how it connects to human needs, what it means in the society we in-habit, how it might transform that society into a better one, and how it fits with a host of other legitimate aims. Like Dewey with growth and Whitehead with life, I have to show how happiness can be used as a criterion by which to judge other aims and the value of our aims-talk. Indeed, an important function of aims is to encourage the aims-talk that en-riches both educational thinking and the wisdom of the race. We continually ask, If you are aiming at X, why are you doing Y? How does Y fit with X?

THE MISSING DIMENSION TODAY

At the beginning of the twenty-first century, educational discussion is dominated by talk of standards, and the reason given for this emphasis is almost always economic. The underlying aims seem to be (1) to keep the United States strong economically and (2) to give every child an opportunity to do well financially. There is something worrisome about both of these aims, if indeed they are the aims that drive the standards movement. First, the idea that schools play a role in making our economy competitive is cast in intemperate language that charges the schools with failure on this task. Why should the schools be accused of undermining the American economy during a time of unparalleled prosper-ity? The aim of keeping our economy strong seems reasonable, but the demands for accountability and standards at such a time seem oddly out of place. They make us suspect that something else is operating. Second, we should be deeply troubled by the suggestion that economic equity can be achieved by forcing the same curriculum and standards on all children. The question of what is meant by equity is answered hastily and with little justification. Finally, of course, the aims (with no debate) are far too narrow. There is more to individual life and the life of a nation than economic superiority.

The standards movement had its effective start in 1983 with the publication of *A Nation at Risk*.[16] Published toward the end of a significant recession, the report used alarmist language to rouse the American public to the great danger posed by a supposedly failing school system. It spoke of "a rising tide of mediocrity" and went so far as to say, "If an unfriendly foreign power had attempted to impose on America the mediocre educational performance that exists today, we might well have viewed it as an act of war."[17] Response to the alarm was nationwide, and by 2000 every state but one (Iowa) had established new (arguably higher) standards for the achievement of school children at all levels of K-12 education.

It is interesting to note that, without a discernible change in scores on most standardized tests of achievement, the United States moved quickly into a period of unprecedented prosperity—despite its supposedly abysmal schools. Indeed, several careful analysts have challenged the claims of *A Nation at Risk*,[18] but it is not my purpose here to argue the strength of their case. Rather, I want to show what has been missed by failing to engage in a discussion of aims.

One prominent claim of the alarmists was that achievement scores had fallen badly since the late 1960s. This might be something to worry about, and critics of the report set about finding explanations for the drop. For example, it was argued that many more students now take the SATs (one measure of academic achievement) and that, with a substantially different population, we should expect different scores and norms adjusted accordingly. This is entirely reasonable from a statistical perspective.

The debate could have been more thoughtful. Had our aims changed during the period of decline? Clearly, we were trying to prepare many more students for college. Why were we doing this? Did the society need more people with a college education? With a traditional college education? The reason most often offered was that everyone in a liberal democracy should have a chance to obtain the goods of that society. That seems right. But does such a commitment imply that access to those goods must come through successful competition in traditional schooling? What happens, then, to those who do not do well in the only form of schooling we now make available in the name of equity? Suppose instead that we created rich alternative curricula and provided guidance to those students who might welcome and succeed with them? Questions such as these go to the very roots of what we believe about democracy and democratic schooling.

When we neglect these questions, a narrow educational focus is encouraged, and we distract ourselves from the social problems that cannot be solved by schools. For example, all people need adequate medical insurance, livable and affordable housing, safe neighborhoods, and nonpoverty wages for honest work. It is shortsighted and even arrogant to suppose that all people can escape these problems through better education, particularly if that education favors those with specific academic talents or resources. The jobs that today pay only poverty wages will still have to be done and, so long as we measure success in schools competitively, there will be losers.

One can see the value of aims-talk vividly here. When advocates of uniform standards claim that everyone will benefit, we can raise reasonable doubts. As we have seen, it is one function of aims-talk to challenge the existing rules by which a society has organized itself. Can poverty be traced to a lack of good education, or is the causal relation inverted? Why should anyone who works a full week at an honest job live in poverty? If everyone gets a college education, who will do today's poverty-level work? When we ask these questions, we begin to doubt the main argument offered by advocates of uniform standards. We may even be led to ask: What are these people really aiming at?

If the aim is justice—to provide all students with an education that will meet their needs—the solution is likely to involve the provision of considerable variety in school offerings and to include material that might contribute to personal as well as public life. Offering a variety of curricula does not mean putting together a set of courses labeled *easy*, *average*, and *hard* and then equating *hard* with *best*. It means cooperatively constructing rigorous and interesting courses centered on students' interests and talents. It means that the schools should show the society that a democracy honors all of its honest workers, not just those who finish college and make a lot of money.

John Dewey, in lines often misappropriated, said, "What the best and wisest parent wants for his own child, that must the community want for all its children. Any other ideal for our schools is narrow and unlovely; acted upon, it destroys our democracy."[19] Dewey did not mean, however, that the community should give all children exactly the same program of studies. Indeed, he argued so often and so insistently against sameness in the choice of content and curricula that it is hard to understand how anyone could read him this way. The best and wisest parent, Dewey believed, would want an education that is best for each individual child. In direct contradiction to Dewey's hopes, the standards movement keeps pressing for the same education for all.

At the same time, sensitive educators have attacked the tracking system that has been in place for so long in our schools. This system, in which children are placed in *tracks* according to their perceived academic capacities, has had pernicious effects. No reasonable observer could deny this.[20] However, the problem may not be tracking itself but rather the hierarchical values we put on the tracks. There is no obvious reason why students in a commercial or industrial track cannot develop "both culture and expert knowledge in some special direction," as Whitehead advised. The soul-destroying discrimination arises when we regard one track as better than another and place the one loaded with academic information and skills at the top. A bad situation is made worse when we refer to the students in the top track as the "good kids," and teachers often do this. We add insult to injury when we assign the least competent teachers to work with students in the "lower" tracks.

So long as schools value only academic achievement (narrowly defined as success in standard school subjects), this problem will be intractable. I have considerable sympathy for those who, observing the suffering of lower-track students, recommend total abandonment of tracking, but surely this cannot be the answer if our aim is to educate each student to a standard compatible with his or her abilities and purposes. Students who seek careers that require knowledge and skills very different from the standard academic material are not given a fair chance by simply placing them in academic courses with those who actually want these courses. How fair is it to ignore students' own legitimate interests and coerce them into competing with students whose interests lie in the area of coercion? This issue goes to the very heart of democratic education, and I will devote considerable space to it in later chapters. The questions asked here are simply skipped over in the rush to standardized solutions.

Consider the way in which the National Council of Teachers of Mathematics (NCTM) begins its draft of *Standards 2000*.[21] No Socrates-like character asks "And shall we teach mathematics?" Even if the answer is a preordained "Of course, Socrates," asking the question raises a host of others: To whom shall we teach mathematics? For what ends? Mathematics of what sort? In what relation to students' expressed needs? In what relation to our primary aims? And what are these aims?

After a brief statement on "a time of extraordinary and accelerating change"[22] and the widespread use of technology, the document launches into "principles," the first of which is "The Equity Principle." It is worthwhile to examine this principle in some detail. It states as a basic assumption that "all students can learn to think mathematically."[23] It does not even try to make a convincing argument for this claim. It does not tell us what this means or why students should do so. Instead, it says:

> An emphasis on "mathematics for all" is important because of the role that school mathematics has historically played in educational inequity. A student's mathematical proficiency is often used as a basis for decisions regarding further schooling and job opportunities. Furthermore, mathematics has been one of the subjects frequently associated with "tracking," a practice in which students are sorted into different instructional sequences that often results in inequitable opportunities and outcomes for students.[24]

Therefore, everyone must become proficient in mathematics. Without further argument, this is a non sequitur. Writers of the report do not pause to consider other, more generous ways of alleviating the inequity that has historically been associated with mathematics. For example, why not abandon the requirement that all college-bound students, regardless of their interests and abilities, present academic credits in mathematics? Why not consider ways to improve non-college courses so that the mathematics actually needed is taught sensitively and practically within those courses? Why decide that the road to equity is established by coercing everyone into becoming proficient in mathematics? A thorough discussion of aims might lead in a different direction.

We need a careful analysis of what is meant by equity, and we need a discussion of educational aims that moves in two directions—toward the aims we hold as a liberal democracy and into the actual activities we will provide in classrooms. Educational aims always reflect the aims—explicit or implicit—of the political society in which they are developed. A totalitarian state will engender educational aims that primarily benefit the state. A liberal democracy should generate aims more focused on the needs of individuals. Indeed, it must do this because it depends for its legitimacy on the capacity of its citizens to freely endorse and maintain it. And how is such a capacity developed? Surely, it grows, at least in part, out of guided practice in making well-informed choices. Thus we have an important argument against coercion right from the start.

Another argument against coercion is that coercion makes people resistant and unhappy. If we are serious about promoting happiness, we will recognize that every act of coercion raises a question. There are times when, after considering the question raised, we will still have to use coercion, but there are many times when, because we have paused to think, we will be able to use persuasion or even abandon the end toward which we planned to coerce. As we consider whether or not to coerce, our deliberation will almost always involve an analysis of needs and a commitment to negotiation.

REVIVING AIMS-TALK

I have argued that we need to talk about aims because aims provide criteria by which we judge our choices of goals, objectives, and subject content. Aims-talk can also be directed at the larger society and its policies. Both functions are important.

During the twentieth century, we made considerable progress in humanizing our schools. Corporal punishment has fallen into disfavor (and is illegal in many states), more students go to high school and more graduate, girls are encouraged to take courses in mathematics and science, programs are designed for children with disabilities, and meals are provided for poor children.

American education can be rightly proud of these attainments and aspirations. Still, we could do better in securing these goals and others by analyzing the aims that gave rise to them. Why, for example, have we decided to encourage young women to study math and science? Well, because it's the fair thing to do! Equity seems to require it. If equity is the aim, however, why are we not concerned that so few young men become nurses, elementary school teachers, social workers, early childhood teachers, and full-time parents? The response to this is that equity refers to equitable financial opportunities, and the occupations traditionally available to women do not pay well. But are they important? Well, of course. Why not pay appropriately for them, then, and strive for a balanced form of equity?

As we ask deeper questions about our aims—why are we doing X?—we uncover new problems and new possibilities for the solution of our original problem. In the case under consideration here, we are also led to use caution in encouraging young women to choose careers in math and science. If they want to study in these areas, our encouragement should be backed by generous support, but very bright young women are sometimes led to believe that any other choice is beneath them. Some girls interested in elementary school teaching, for example, have been told, "You're too good for that!" Their self-worth comes to depend on their rejecting traditional female roles. Inferred needs and internal wants are then in conflict, and the joy of doing something wholeheartedly may be lost.

Consider next the goal of providing a free, appropriate education to every child in the least restrictive environment compatible with that goal.[25] Trying to meet this goal has turned out to be enormously expensive, and it has also led to a proliferation of services and demands for services. Are too many children now labeled *learning disabled*? Why did we establish such a goal? Again, the answer seems to be equity. But what is meant by equity in this area?

Unless we ask this question, we are likely to engage in foolish and harmful practices. For instance, in some states, children labeled learning disabled (even those in special classes) must now take the standardized tests required of students in regular classes. It certainly makes sense to monitor the progress of these students and to ask continually whether we are doing the best possible job with them. Are we catching errors in labeling? Are we working hard enough to move capable students out of special education—to relieve them of any possible stigma attached to the label?[26] Are all the children learning something? Granted that these questions should be answered conscientiously, forcing all children to take these tests seems counterproductive. Some probably should be encouraged to take them, with only positive stakes attached. It is outrageous, however, to force these tests on all students in special education. From all over the country, we hear stories of sick stomachs, trembling hands, and wet pants. If by *equity* we mean providing an appropriate education for every child, it is dead wrong to expect the same performance from each child. Having forgotten our aim, we act as though all children are academically equal and can be held to the same standard.

We could analyze each of the goals I listed as admirable from the perspective of underlying aims, and it would be useful to do so. Sometimes the goals themselves require such analysis (as in the two cases just discussed). In other cases, we have to look at the outcomes associated with the goals and then go back to the original aim to see where we might have gone wrong. It seems entirely right, for example, to forbid corporal punishment and sexual harassment in schools, but does that mean that a teacher should never touch a student? Are appropriate hugs ruled out? Is a firm restraining hand on an angry arm ruled out? In the widespread use of zero-tolerance rules, good judgment is often sacrificed. The original aim is forgotten.

Even in the matter of feeding hungry children, we too often lose sight of our aim. Many people claim that we feed children because "hungry children can't learn." A better answer would be this: We feed hungry children because they are hungry! That answer helps us to direct attention to social problems beyond the classroom. Should we stop feeding hungry children if, after being well fed, they still do not learn as well as we think they should?

I want to turn now to an examination of practices that should raise questions about the aims of education. It is often helpful to see a familiar scene through the eyes of an intelligent and sympathetic stranger,[27] so let's pretend that a visitor from another world has visited our schools and wants to share his or her observations with us. The visitor talks with a representative educator, Ed.

Visitor: It struck me as odd that, although your people spend much of their time in homemaking, parenting, and recreation, these topics are rarely addressed in your schools.

Ed: That's because we regard the school as a somewhat specialized institution. Its job is to teach academics—the material that cannot easily be taught at home. Homemaking, parenting, and worthwhile forms of recreation are taught at home. Indeed, most of us believe that it would be an improper intrusion into family life for schools to teach such topics.

Visitor: Ah, yes. This is part of your liberal heritage, is it not? But what is done about the children who come from homes where these matters are not taught well? From what I've seen, there are many such children.

Ed: You're right, and this does worry us. However, we believe that people who have a thorough command of the fundamental processes will be able to learn these other matters on their own. They will have the skills to do so. And they will qualify for good jobs, so they will be able to provide the material resources characteristic of good homes.

Visitor: Hmm. Well, of course, there is something to that. But if children from poor homes (not necessarily poor in the financial sense, you understand) have great difficulty learning, it would seem that a society ought to attack the problem at all levels—do something to eliminate poverty, encourage adult interest in homemaking and parenting, and teach these things in school.

Ed: But parents don't want us to do this! They don't want the schools to prescribe methods of parenting or to pronounce one way of homemaking better than another. We have a hard time teaching any sort of values in our schools.

Visitor: You would not want to indoctrinate, I understand. But these topics need not be presented dogmatically. In your English classes, high school students could read and discuss children's literature. In social studies, they could study the development of the home and forms of housing. In art, they might study the aesthetics of homemaking. In science, child development. In foreign language, patterns of hospitality might be studied. In mathematics, they might look at statistical studies that show the high correlation between socioeconomic status and school achievement. These are just examples, of course.

Ed: And very good examples! However, our schedules are already so full that I don't see how we could make room for all these things.

Visitor: Perhaps, if you will forgive my saying so, you haven't thought deeply enough about what you are trying to do.

Ed: We want to give all children the opportunity to learn what they need to succeed in our society. All children!

Visitor: That is commendable, very fine. But how do you define success? Have the schools failed a child if he wants to become an auto mechanic? Do they help a girl who wants to be a beautician?

Ed: We believe they should make those choices later. First, get a sound, basic education.

Visitor: In watching many classes and talking to many students, it seems that—because their interests and talents are ignored in school—many young people fall into these occupations instead of choosing them proudly. They feel they are not good enough for more desirable work. There is an injury inflicted on them.

Ed: We are getting off the subject. What has this to do with teaching homemaking and the like?

Visitor: It has to do with happiness, and that was my reason for bringing up those topics in the first place. If happiness is found in domains other than salaried work, shouldn't those other domains be treated in education? And since one's occupation also influences happiness, that too should be included in education. But I was just getting started . . . .

Ed: I hesitate to ask.

Visitor: It seems that your society, your government anyway, has been waging a losing war on drugs—

Ed: Now I've got you! We *do* teach about the dangers of drug abuse.

Visitor: Yes, yes. But your television commercials are filled with ads for drugs, some of them quite dangerous. Do you help students to see how they are being manipulated?

Ed: Well, we worry most about illegal drugs.

Visitor: Have you noticed that many teenagers from low socioeconomic status neighborhoods wear expensive name-brand clothing? They could clothe themselves for far less money and perhaps avoid taking part-time jobs that keep them from their studies.

Ed: So you want us to engage in consumer education as well as homemaking, parenting, and—you're not finished, are you?

Visitor: Perhaps we should let it be for now. It just seems so sad that, when everyone seeks happiness, the schools do so little to promote it.

Ed: Well, I promise to think more about it. (Shaking his head) I just don't see what we can do.

In this chapter, I have argued that aims-talk plays a vital role in sustaining a rigorous and relevant program of education, and I've tried to show how it has done this in the past. Today, with recent changes in social thought and massive changes in technology, it is more important than ever to consider why we are promoting certain goals in schooling and why we continue to neglect education for personal life and for happiness in our occupations.

NOTES

1. William Schubert argues, rightly I think, that there is no settled hierarchy of educational purposes, but he notes that aims, goals, and objectives are widely thought to represent a sequence of decreasing generality. See Schubert, *Curriculum: Perspective, Paradigm, and Possibility* (New York: Macmillan, 1986).

2. See Schubert, pp. 190-191, on this.

3. See National Education Association, *Cardinal Principles of Secondary Education* (Washington, D.C.: U.S. Government Printing Office, 1918).

4. Herbert M. Kliebard, *The Struggle for the American Curriculum* (New York: Routledge, 1995), p. 98.

5. See Franklin Bobbitt, *How to Make a Curriculum* (Boston: Houghton Mifflin, 1924).

6. For an excellent analysis of the problems involved in establishing objectives, see Elliot W. Eisner, *The Educational Imagination* (New York: Macmillan, 1979).

7. See Plato, *The Republic*, trans. B. Jowett (Roslyn, NY: Walter Black, 1942), Book II.

8. John Dewey, *Democracy and Education* (New York: Macmillan, 1944/1916), p. 90.

9. Ibid.

10. See *The Republic*, Book III.

11. For an introduction to *Emile*, see William Boyd, ed., *The Emile of Jean Jacques Rousseau: Selections* (New York: Teachers College Press, 1962).

12. For informative analyses of Rousseau's recommendations for Sophie's education, see Jane Roland Martin, *Reclaiming a Conversation* (New Haven, CT: Yale University Press, 1985); also Susan Moller Okin, *Women in Western Political Thought* (Princeton, NJ: Princeton University Press, 1979).

13. Dewey, *Democracy and Education*, p. 100.

14. Alfred North Whitehead, *The Aims of Education* (New York: Free Press, 1967/1929) p. 1.

15. Ibid., pp. 6-7.

16. See National Commission on Excellence in Education, *A Nation at Risk* (Washington, D.C.: U.S. Government Printing Office, 1983).

17. Ibid., p. 5.

18. See David Berliner and Bruce Biddle, *The Manufactured Crisis: Myths, Fraud, and the Attack on America's Public Schools* (New York: Perseus, 1996); also Gerald Bracey, *Setting the Record Straight: Responses to Misconceptions about Public Education in the United States* (Alexandria, VA: Association for Supervision and Curriculum Development, 1997).

19. Dewey, *The School and Society* (Chicago: University of Chicago Press, 1900), p. 3.

20. See Jeannie Oakes, *Multiplying Inequalities: The Effects of Race, Social Class, and Tracking on Opportunities to Learn Mathematics and Science* (Santa Monica, CA: Rand, 1990); also Oakes, *Keeping Track: How Schools Structure Inequality* (New Haven, CT: Yale University Press, 1995). But for an argument on both the positive and negative effects of tracking, see James E. Rosenbaum, "Track Misperceptions and Frustrated College Plans: An Analysis of the Effects of Tracks and Track Perceptions in the National Longitudinal Survey," *Sociology of Education* 53, 1980: 74-88.

21. See National Council of Teachers of Mathematics, *Principles and Standards for School Mathematics*, Discussion draft (Reston, VA: NCTM, 1998).

22. Ibid., p. 15.

23. Ibid., p. 23.

24. Ibid.

25. For a comprehensive review of the problems involved in meeting this goal, see James Paul, Michael Churton, Hilda Rosselli-Kostoryz, William Morse, Kofi Marfo, Carolyn Lavely, and Daphne Thomas, eds., *Foundations of Special Education* (Pacific Grove, CA: Brooks/Cole, 1997); also Paul, Churton, Morse, Albert Duchnowski, Betty Epanchin, Pamela Osnes, and R. Lee Smith, eds., *Special Education Practice* (Pacific Grove, CA: Brooks/Cole, 1997).

26. For powerful accounts of how difficult it can be for children to escape the label, see Theresa A. Thorkildsen and John G. Nicholls, *Motivation and the Struggle to Learn* (Boston: Allyn & Bacon, 2002).

27. This is a familiar technique used in describing utopias. Two well-known examples are Edward Bellamy, *Looking Backward* (New York: New American Library, 1960/1888), and Samuel Butler, *Erewhon* (London: Penguin, 1985/1872).

Index